INTERMEDIATE

The IDEA MAGAZINE FOR TEACHERS®
MAILBOX®

2012–2013 YEARBOOK

The Education Center, LLC
Greensboro, North Carolina

The Mailbox® 2012–2013 Intermediate Yearbook

Managing Editor, *The Mailbox* Magazine: Sherry McGregor

Editorial Team: Becky S. Andrews, Diane Badden, Kimberley Bruck, Karen A. Brudnak, Pam Crane, Chris Curry, David Drews, Phyllis Gaddy, Karen Brewer Grossman, Tazmen Fisher Hansen, Marsha Heim, Lori Z. Henry, Troy Lawrence, Tina Petersen, Gary Phillips (COVER ARTIST), Mark Rainey, Greg D. Rieves, Hope Rodgers-Medina, Rebecca Saunders, Donna K. Teal, Sharon M. Tresino, Zane Williard

ISBN 978-1-61276-417-7
ISSN 1088-5552

Printed in the United States of America.

The Mailbox® Yearbook
PO Box 6189
Harlan, IA 51593-1689

Look for *The Mailbox*® 2013–2014 Intermediate Yearbook in the summer of 2014. The Education Center, LLC, is the publisher of *The Mailbox*®, *Teacher's Helper*®, and *Learning*® magazines, as well as other fine products. Look for these wherever quality teacher materials are sold, call 1-866-477-4273, or visit www.themailbox.com.

HPS249268

Contents

www.themailbox.com

Common Core Skills Index

Reading and Language Arts

Reading & Language Arts TIPS & TOOLS

Walk, Talk, Tap
Reading comprehension (RI.4.1, RI.5.1)

Here's a supersimple way to find out how well your students understand a reading selection. Choose one student to begin. Guide the student to walk toward a classmate while he talks about a fact from the reading selection. When he reaches the classmate, he taps her and returns to his seat. The tapped child then gets up, walks while she talks about a different fact from the selection, and then taps another classmate. Continue in this manner until everyone has had a chance to walk, talk, and tap!

The Goliath beetle can be up to five inches long and weigh up to 3½ ounces!

Shannon Diano, Winman Junior High Warwick, RI

Fish Pond
Prefixes (RF.4.3, RF.5.3)

There's nothing fishy about this fast-paced (yet quiet) vocabulary game! Laminate a copy of page 8; then cut apart the cards and place magnetic tape on the back of each one. Divide the class into four teams and assign each team a different prefix. Put the prefix cards on the board and draw a fish pond to the side. Explain that only hand signals—no talking—are allowed during the game. Then deal six word cards to each team captain and guide students to follow the directions shown. At the game's end, have each team read aloud and define its words. Then redistribute the cards and play again. *Kenda Armstrong, Imogene Glenn Elementary, Yantis, TX*

Directions:
1. Each captain shows his team a card.
2. The team decides whether the word can be combined with its prefix to make a word. If so, a team member puts the card on the board under the team's prefix. If the word can't be used with the team's prefix, a team member puts the card in the fish pond.
3. Continue until the captain is out of cards. Then the team chooses one member to "fish" in the pond for cards that can be used with the team's prefix.
4. The game is over when all cards have been matched to their prefixes and the pond is empty.

Picture That!

Action and helping verbs, descriptive writing (L.4.3a, L.5.3a)

For an activity that highlights several language arts skills, divide the class into groups. Have each group choose a sport or outdoor activity and list at least eight vivid action verbs associated with it. Then have each student in the group write four sentences about the activity, using a different verb from the list and at least one helping verb in each sentence. Next, the group meets, chooses each group member's best sentence, and then creates a mural on bulletin board paper that illustrates the four sentences. If the students think the sentences they've chosen don't have enough details to make their mural interesting, they revise their sentences together before illustrating them. *Debbi Sgambato, Winsor Hill Elementary, Johnston, RI*

The climber has been clinging nervously to the ledge with one shaky h...

What are the characters in this panel doing?
What do you think happened in the panel before this one?
What do you think will happen in the next panel?
If you added a character to this scene, what character would you add?
What would the character do?
What would the character say?

Comic Panel Pondering

Critical thinking

To engage students in a little critical thinking, cut out several intriguing panels from comic strips or cartoons. Then glue each panel to a sheet of construction paper and add critical-thinking questions, such as those shown, and place the pages at a center. At the center, a student chooses a page and writes the answer to each question on his own paper. What a great way to engage reluctant readers in critical-thinking activities!

Verb Concentration

Subject-verb agreement

Concentrate on sharpening subject-verb agreement skills with this partner game. Have each pair of students cut apart the cards and key from a copy of page 9 and then follow the directions below to play Verb Concentration.

Directions for two players:
1. Shuffle the cards and spread them facedown.
2. When it's your turn, flip two cards. If the subject and verb on the cards agree, keep them and take another turn. If the cards don't agree, flip them back over to complete your turn.
3. The game is over when no more matches can be made.
4. Check your matches using the key. The player with more correct matches wins.

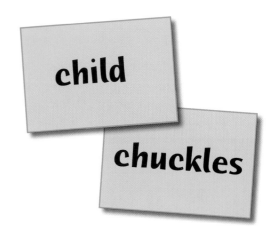

child

chuckles

Game Cards

Use with "Fish Pond" on page 6.

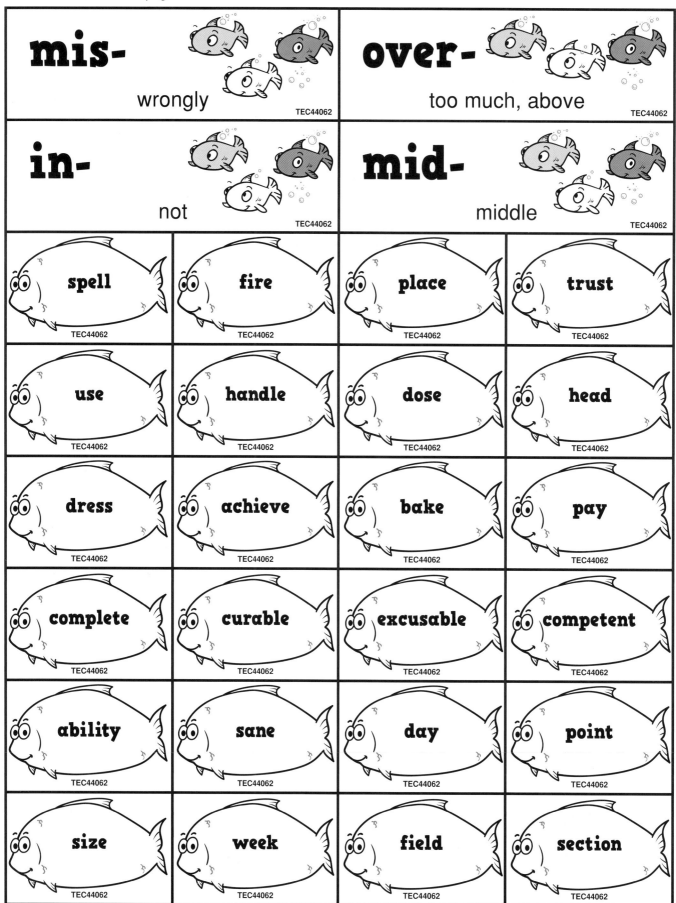

mis- wrongly
TEC44062

over- too much, above
TEC44062

in- not
TEC44062

mid- middle
TEC44062

spell	fire	place	trust
TEC44062	TEC44062	TEC44062	TEC44062
use	handle	dose	head
TEC44062	TEC44062	TEC44062	TEC44062
dress	achieve	bake	pay
TEC44062	TEC44062	TEC44062	TEC44062
complete	curable	excusable	competent
TEC44062	TEC44062	TEC44062	TEC44062
ability	sane	day	point
TEC44062	TEC44062	TEC44062	TEC44062
size	week	field	section
TEC44062	TEC44062	TEC44062	TEC44062

student	mechanic	tiger	pizza
TEC44062	TEC44062	TEC44062	TEC44062
dolphin	doctor	meerkat	football
TEC44062	TEC44062	TEC44062	TEC44062
monkeys	geese	runners	aliens
TEC44062	TEC44062	TEC44062	TEC44062
drivers	coyotes	boulders	painters
TEC44062	TEC44062	TEC44062	TEC44062
bounces	is peeking	roars	is wishing
TEC44062	TEC44062	TEC44062	TEC44062
sizzles	leaps	chuckles	mumbles
TEC44062	TEC44062	TEC44062	TEC44062
are snacking	were howling	climb	honk
TEC44062	TEC44062	TEC44062	TEC44062
hurry	have been chattering	sleep	tumble
TEC44062	TEC44062	TEC44062	TEC44062

Answer Key for "Verb Concentration"

Singular subjects match singular verbs.

doctor, dolphin, football, mechanic, meerkat, pizza, student, tiger

Singular verbs match singular subjects.

bounces, chuckles, leaps, mumbles, is peeking, is wishing, roars, sizzles

Plural subjects match plural verbs.

aliens, boulders, coyotes, drivers, geese, monkeys, painters, runners

Plural verbs match plural subjects.

are snacking, climb, have been chattering, honk, hurry, sleep, tumble, were howling

TEC44062

Reading & Language Arts TIPS & TOOLS

On Your Mark!

Explaining the function of prepositions (L.4.1e)

Need to bring students up to speed on identifying prepositions and their roles in sentences? Try this simple-to-set-up small-group center! Cut apart a copy of the directions and answer key at the top of page 12 and make a class supply of the sentences on the bottom of the page. Put the materials in a plastic resealable bag and guide each group of four students to follow the directions to practice spotting prepositions in sentences and identifying their functions. *adapted from an idea by* **Lisa Senne, West Delaware Middle School, Manchester, IA**

Themes in Bud, Not Buddy

friendship growing up family

caring for others persistence bravery

A Show of Hands

Determining a theme (RL.4.2, RL.5.2)

Here's an idea that makes describing a story's theme more approachable. Begin with a selection all students have read. Next, list on the board adjectives and phrases that describe major and minor themes in the selection. Then name each one and ask students to raise their hands to vote for themes they think are reflected in the selection. Jot each student's name under the theme or themes for which they vote. After that, use the lists to organize groups of students to discuss each theme. Then have each group create a poster about how the theme is conveyed in the story, showing supporting details from the story. **Karen Slattery, Dunrankin Drive Public School, Mississauga, Ontario, Canada**

On Second Thought

Conducting research to answer questions

Use a popular Internet quiz to inspire your students' research. Post the questions shown and then challenge each pair of students to find the answers using oldfangled resources such as encyclopedias, atlases, and informational texts! *Carol Patterson, Prairie Point Elementary, Oswego, IL*

- How long did the Hundred Years' War last? *(116 years)*
- Which of these are ground squirrels: chipmunks, marmots, or prairie dogs? *(They're all ground squirrels.)*
- When do Russians celebrate the October Revolution? *(November 7)*
- For which animal were the Canary Islands off the northwest coast of Africa named? *(dogs)*
- What was King George VI's first name? *(Albert)*
- Which of these are true berries: blackberries, blueberries, grapes, green peppers, bananas, or strawberries? *(blueberries, grapes, green peppers, and bananas)*

The facts from today's reading that are the most important are

I don't understand what

A Note Just for the Teacher

Responding to literary sources

Here's a simple tip for giving your students a little extra support as they stretch their reading skills! Have each student draw a colorful squiggly line down the right side of her paper before she responds to a reading selection. After she finishes her response, encourage the child to jot in the space to the right of the line comments and questions she didn't have time to ask during class or that she's too shy to share. Then, when you read the student's response, you have an extra opportunity for insight into her needs and to clarify any misunderstandings! *Patricia Glynn, Wayland, MA*

Creative Conversations

Using dialogue to show characters' responses to situations (W.4.3b, W.5.3b)

What could a baby and a pro basketball player possibly have to say to each other? Plenty, with this fun partner activity! Have each student look through a discarded magazine and cut out an interesting picture of a person. Then randomly partner students. Each duo looks at its two pictures and then works collaboratively to write an interesting conversation between the two people. Once the conversation has been edited for correct punctuation, students glue their pictures on construction paper and copy the conversation below the pictures. *Megan Cancerius, Orange Street Elementary, Berwick, PA*

 Short on class time? Cut out the pictures in advance of the activity.

ON YOUR MARK!

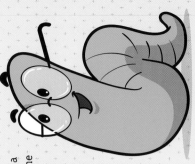

Materials for each group of four students: timer, stopwatch, or clock with a second hand and four copies of the sentences on the bottom half of this page

DIRECTIONS:

1. Each player needs a copy of the sentences. For the first round, one player takes the role of host.

2. The host takes the answer key and timing device, chooses a sentence, announces its number, and signals players to begin.

3. The players have 20 seconds to circle the sentence's preposition or prepositions and write above each one a number that describes the preposition's function in the sentence.

4. When time is up, the host uses the key to check each player's labels. The host awards one point for each correct circle and one point for each correct number. Each player keeps track of his or her score.

5. Then the next student in the group becomes the host and repeats Steps 2 through 4. After 12 rounds, the player with the highest total score wins.

TEC44063

Answer Key for "On Your Mark!"

1. He's ⓞⁿ the fifth row ⓞf the bookshelf.
2. It may look like Noah's napping, but he never sleeps ⓓurⁱⁿg the day.
3. Noah thinks there's no difference ⓑetween napping and wasting time.
4. Noah sleeps ⓕor only two hours ⓐt night.
5. Noah wakes ⓑefore 4:00 AM and eats his breakfast—a Brussels sprout ⓦith an almond.
6. He solves math puzzles ⓕrom his favorite book ⓤntil 9:00 AM.
7. Then he leaves and heads ⓣoward the library.
8. Noah strolls ⓘnto the library and reads ten books ⓞn the shelf.
9. ⓐfter three hours ⓘn the library, Noah piles six books ⓞn the table.
10. He heads ⓣo the park ⓓown the street.
11. ⓐt the park, Noah waves ⓣo a friend wandering ⓐlong the sidewalk.
12. Then he sits ⓤnder a tree and starts reading ⓦith a happy sigh.

TEC44063

Name _____

Date _____

On Your Mark!

Preposition Code

1 = Shows location.
2 = Shows direction.
3 = Shows time.
4 = Shows how two words or ideas are related to each other.

Noah Lott is ⓞver there.

1. He's on the fifth row of the bookshelf.

2. It may look like Noah's napping, but he never sleeps during the day.

3. Noah thinks there's no difference between napping and wasting time.

4. Noah sleeps for only two hours at night.

5. Noah wakes before 4:00 AM and eats his breakfast—a Brussels sprout with an almond.

6. He solves math puzzles from his favorite book until 9:00 AM.

7. Then he leaves and heads toward the library.

8. Noah strolls into the library and reads ten books on the shelf.

9. After three hours in the library, Noah piles six books on the table.

10. He heads to the park down the street.

11. At the park, Noah waves to a friend wandering along the sidewalk.

12. Then he sits under a tree and starts reading with a happy sigh.

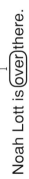

Note to the teacher: Use with "On Your Mark!" on page 10.

Reading & Language Arts TIPS & TOOLS

Pattern Practice
Building word analysis skills (RF.4.3, RF.5.3)

Remind students to pay attention to vowel and consonant patterns—and then apply the patterns to unfamiliar words—with this anytime challenge. Post a standard vowel and consonant pattern. Then challenge students to brainstorm words with the pattern and record their ideas. Leave the list posted for several days, encouraging students to add to it. Before replacing the list with a different vowel and consonant pattern, discuss the words with students and guide them to draw conclusions about spelling and pronunciation rules and exceptions to those rules. *Isobel Livingstone, Rahway, NJ*

V C C V
also
pattern
consonant
challenge
discuss

V C C C V
constant
conclusion
brainstorm
laughter
hundred

Standing Tall
Determining main ideas, explaining how they're supported (RI.4.2, RI.5.2)

After reading a selection, guide each pair of students to identify three of its main ideas. Next, have the partners follow the directions shown to describe the main ideas and supporting details. When students finish, display their work on a shelf or table along with the title "Main Ideas Stand Tall With Supporting Details." *Patricia Twohey, Smithfield, RI*

1. Draw a ¼" margin along the short edges of a sheet of legal-size paper. Then divide the paper into three 4½" x 8½" columns.
2. Draw a red line across the paper two inches from the top.
3. Describe a different main idea in each top section. Then describe the details that support each main idea in the matching lower section.
4. When you have fully supported each of your main ideas, fold the paper along the vertical margin and column lines. Then glue the margins together to create a triangle.

Mount St. Helens' activity in the months before May 18, 1980, warned that the volcano was ready to erupt.

- There was an earthquake near the peak March 20.
- Ashes shot skyward March 27.
- Large cracks opened up along the north side of the mountain.

A Note by Any Other Name

Key words, taking notes (L.4.5c, L.5.5c)

With this tip, independent reading takes on more meaning! After each student reads a selection, have him review the text and identify ten key terms. Have the child write each term and then list synonyms for five of them. For the other five terms, have the student record antonyms, drawing boxes around them to show they mean the opposite. If the student can write on the selection, have him circle each key word and then write its synonym or antonym in the margin. *Chad Donohue, Snohomish, WA*

The Riddle of the Bones

In a marshy field on a farm in New York (ancient) bones were hidden under the soil. By the time a farmer found them, some easily crumbled to dust and others had turned to stone. The bones were [huge]—monstrous! What kind of creature could have left behind such bones?

Native American legends told of huge creatures that once roamed the land. They killed the deer, elk, and bison. They destroyed homes. The Great Man who lived above hurled lightening bolts. He wiped out all of the monstrous animals except one. Could the bones belong to one of these ancient animals?

Charles Willson Peale decided to find out. Peale had founded America's first natural history museum. He heard that hip bones, a tusk, and parts of a skull had been dug up by the farmer. Maybe the huge bones belonged to a (mammoth) such as those found in Kentucky and Siberia. So far, no one had found enough mammoth bones to make a (complete) skeleton. If enough could be found, Peale could display a (skeleton) in his museum.

Leading a scientific **expedition**, Peale headed to New York State. He could not believe the number of bones the farmer had collected. Among the **fossils**, he found a five-foot-long piece of curved tusk. What a find!

Peale hired local men and boys to help dig. They dug through layer after layer of earth. They hacked through thick yellow roots, shoveled out ashy soil, and scooped up decayed

(margin words: petite, incomplete, prehistoric, huge)

Word	First Dictionary Definition	Base Word	Base Word Definition	What the Word Really Means
arrival	the act of arriving	arrive	to reach the place you started out for	having reached the place you started out for

brighten
brilliance
celebrity
consumer
defiant
fertilize
government
producer
sequential
translation

Dictionary

Table It!

Using a dictionary (L.4.4c, L.5.4c)

Do your students need help deciphering definitions that use forms of the words they're defining? Try this! Have each child create a chart like the one shown. Then have the student look up a word from the list and record the word and its first definition. *(It will include a form of the base word without actually explaining what the word means.)* Next, have the child look up the base word and record its meaning. Then guide the student to combine the definitions from the second and fourth columns and explain in the last column what the original word means. After that, have each student practice the process with the remaining words in the list. *Beth Turnpaugh, South Newton Elementary, Kentland, IN*

Term Spotting

Acquiring new vocabulary (L.4.6, L.5.6)

Keep new terms fresh in students' minds! After your class has defined a set of vocabulary terms, display an enlarged copy of page 39 and challenge students to be on the lookout for the words in their daily lives. Next, explain that each time a child hears one of the terms, says one, reads one, or uses one in her writing, she should make a note. Then, when the student comes to class, she records her observation on the display. As you check students' entries, award a point for each find. When students reach a prearranged number of points, celebrate with a class reward! For independent practice instead of group practice, challenge each student to complete a copy of page 39. *Andrea Halterman, Lincoln Elementary, Mundelein, IL*

 Check out the **analogies practice page** on page 40!

Reading & Language Arts TIPS & TOOLS

Features in a Flash!

Identifying text features and information presented visually or quantitatively (RI.4.7)

For this picture-perfect idea, give each pair of students access to a digital camera, a supply of informational books, and a copy of the checklist on page 17. Next, challenge the duo to find each feature or graphic aid on the checklist. When the partners find an item, have them snap a photo of it, record the photo number, the text feature's or graphic item's purpose, and the book title and page number. When time is up, have the twosome add its points as guided on the page and then turn in the page along with the camera for you to quickly check its work. *Jami Bicknell, Riddle Elementary, Plano, TX*

tip → Want to have more than one pair of students working at a time? Collect several old camera phones or MP3 players with cameras!

S.Q.U.I.R.T. (Sitting Quiet "Un-Interrupted" Reading Time)

Acquiring the habit of reading independently (RL.4.10, RL.5.10, RI.4.10, RI.5.10)

Want to motivate even your reluctant readers to read independently? Plan a reading auction! For each Accelerated Reader quiz, book report, or reading journal entry a student successfully completes, award her a Book Buck. Then collect items to auction, such as packages of candy, sticky notes, small denomination gift cards, or books from your book club order. Display the items that will be auctioned and set a date. On the day of the auction, assign each student a bidding number, have her make a paddle, and then auction off each item. Your students will love the auction, but finding books and authors they love to read is the real prize! *Bonnie Finke, St. Martin's Lutheran School, Winona, MN*

A Way With Words
Word analysis, prefixes, suffixes (L.4.4b, L.5.4b)

Here's an activity that reminds students to look for affixes when they're analyzing unfamiliar words. To begin, write a word on the board. Next, guide students to add prefixes and suffixes to the word and discuss the ways they change the word's meaning. Record students' ideas, making a word web. Then assign each pair of students a word from the list shown and challenge the duo to create a web of related words, jotting each new word's meaning on the web. Follow up by reminding students to use what they know about prefixes and suffixes and how they change words' meanings when they analyze unfamiliar words.

read	cheer	open	wind
happy	fix	call	joy
prove	move	like	agree

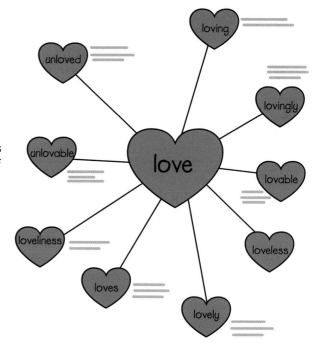

In Other Words
Identifying reasons and providing supporting points, speaking clearly (SL.4.4, SL.5.4)

Sharpen reading, thinking, and speaking skills with this lighthearted idea! Collect comic strips and cartoons, or invite students to bring in their favorite strips, so you have one for each small group of students. Next, give each group a strip and challenge the students to explain the comic's joke and identify supporting reasons for their explanation. Then set aside time for each small group of students to read and interpret the strip for the rest of the class. Not only does this activity improve interpretive reading, but it's a great opportunity to share a giggle or two with your students.

In this comic strip,

An Activity a Day
Spelling grade-appropriate words correctly (L.4.2d, L.5.2e)

To keep spelling practice fresh, start each day's spelling session by displaying a copy of the whiteboard-ready activity spinner on page 18. Then have a child spin to determine the day's spelling activity. For homework variety, have each child keep a copy of the page in her notebook and spin the spinner each night to guide her evening practice. Simple! *Rebecca Boudin, Oak Hollow Elementary, Draper, UT*

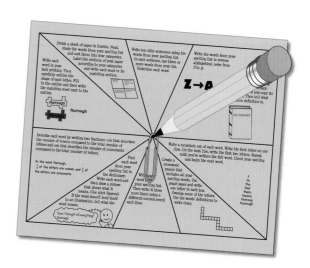

Flip to **page 42** for a practice page on **correlative conjunctions**!

The Search Is On!

Names _____

Date _____

Find an example of each item on the list. Then take a picture of it and fill out the chart.

Feature, Organizational Aid, or Graphic Aid	Picture Number	Book Title	Page Number	Purpose of Feature or Aid	Points Earned	Point Value
table of contents						5
heading						5
subheading						5
illustration with caption						10
bold or italic print						5
chart						10
graph						10
diagram						10
timeline						10
appendix						10
glossary						10
index						10
				Total Points		100

©The Mailbox® • TEC44065 • Feb./Mar. 2013 (RI.4.7)

Note to the teacher: Use with "Features in a Flash!" on page 15.

THE MAILBOX **17**

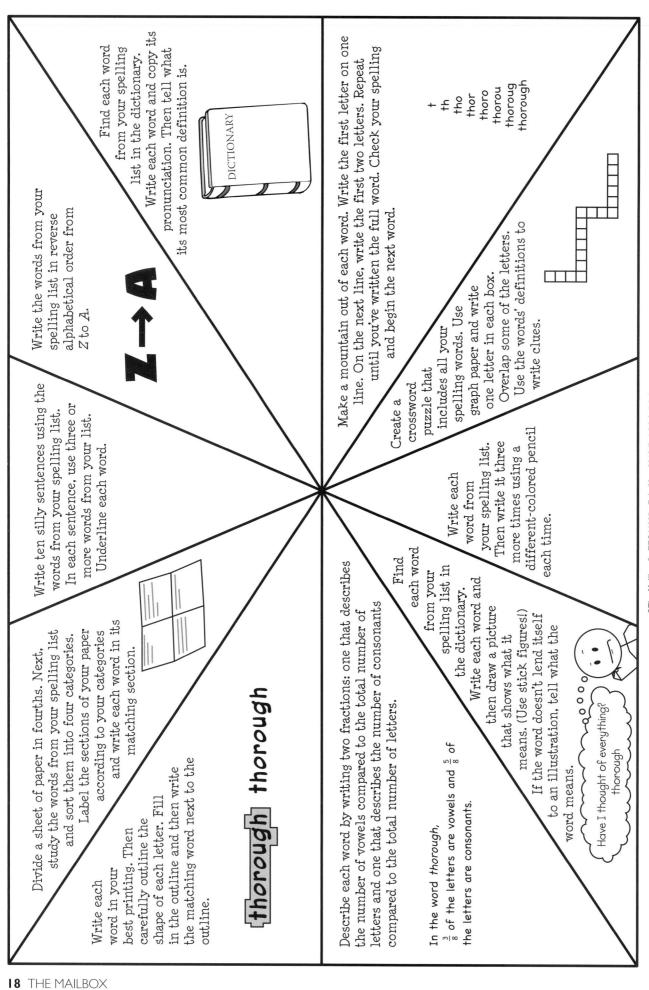

Find each word from your spelling list in the dictionary. Write each word and copy its pronunciation. Then tell what its most common definition is.

DICTIONARY

Write the words from your spelling list in reverse alphabetical order from Z to A.

Z → A

Make a mountain out of each word. Write the first letter on one line. On the next line, write the first two letters. Repeat until you've written the full word. Check your spelling and begin the next word.

t
th
tho
thor
thoro
thorou
thoroug
thorough

Create a crossword puzzle that includes all your spelling words. Use graph paper and write one letter in each box. Overlap some of the letters. Use the words' definitions to write clues.

Write ten silly sentences using the words from your spelling list. In each sentence, use three or more words from your list. Underline each word.

Divide a sheet of paper in fourths. Next, study the words from your spelling list and sort them into four categories. Label the sections of your paper according to your categories and write each word in its matching section.

Write each word in your best printing. Then carefully outline the shape of each letter. Fill in the outline and then write the matching word next to the outline.

thorough thorough

Describe each word by writing two fractions: one that describes the number of vowels compared to the total number of letters and one that describes the number of consonants compared to the total number of letters.

In the word *thorough*, $\frac{3}{8}$ of the letters are vowels and $\frac{5}{8}$ of the letters are consonants.

Find each word from your spelling list in the dictionary. Write each word and then draw a picture that shows what it means. (Use stick figures!) If the word doesn't lend itself to an illustration, tell what the word means.

Write each word from your spelling list. Then write it three more times using a different-colored pencil each time.

Have I thought of everything? thorough

©The Mailbox® • TEC44065 • Feb./Mar. 2013 (L.4.2d, L.5.2e)

Note to the teacher: Use with "An Activity a Day" on page 16.

Reading & Language Arts TIPS & TOOLS

SPECIAL ASSIGNMENT:
Search for Sentences With Compound Subjects
- If the subjects are joined by <u>and</u>, use the plural verb form.
- If the subjects are joined by <u>or</u>, use the verb form that matches the subject after <u>or</u>.

Special Assignment: Search for... Sentences With Compound Subjects

My shoes and socks are under the bed.   plural verb

Either my brothers or my sister is picking me up.   singular verb

On Assignment
Usage, language progressive skills

Help students master challenging language skills by putting extra focus on them! Start by posting the heading "Special Assignment: Search for…" on your board. Next, identify a skill with which your students need practice, such as verb agreement with compound subjects. Then title the search and write it next to the heading, conducting a quick mini lesson on the topic if necessary. After that, challenge each student to find and record ten or more examples throughout the day or week. To follow up, have each small group of students use its examples to present a mini lesson on the topic. Repeat with other progressive skills, rotating challenging skills back into the search frequently.

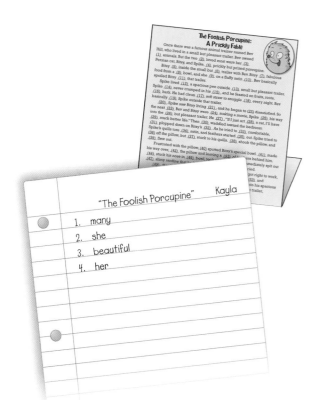

"The Foolish Porcupine"   Kayla
1. many
2. she
3. beautiful
4. her

Filling In the Pieces
Context clues (RF.4.4.c, RF.5.4.c)

For this skill-building activity, cut apart the cards on a copy of page 21 and fold the bottom of each card back to hide the answer key. Next, have a child take a card, record the title on her paper, and number it to match the selection's blanks. Then guide the student to read the passage without guessing any of the missing words. After that, have the child read it again, guessing and recording a word for each missing one. Then have the student reread the selection, substituting her guesses for the blanks and correcting words that don't make sense. Then have the child unfold the key to check her work. *idea by Ann Fisher, Toledo, OH*
selections by Carol Lawrence, Madera, CA;
and Teri Nielsen, Chesapeake Beach, MD

Stand-Up Characters

Character analysis (RL.4.3)

For this idea, have each child fold a sheet of paper in half to create two columns and then label the page as shown. Next, guide the student to think about the main character from a current reading and list important traits that describe the character, numbering each trait. Then have her skim the story to find details that show each trait. When the child finds a supporting detail, she records it on the right side of the page and adds the matching trait number in a circle. To follow up, have each student use her notes to describe the character, being sure to list supporting details from the story. *adapted from an idea by Valerie Hunter, Saddle Brook, NJ*

To introduce static and dynamic characters, have the student use one side of the page to describe the character at the beginning of the story. Then have her flip her paper and repeat the steps to describe and then compare the character's traits at the end of the story.

Traits

1. rebellious
2. smart
3. _____
4. _____

Supporting Thoughts, Words, and Actions

① Ella holds a bowl when Mandy asks her to hold it but she moves around the room so Mandy has to follow her.

② _____

③ _____

④ _____

Aw, Shucks!

Commas in direct address (L.5.2.c)

I think you are the best speller in class, Jacob.

Help students master this challenging skill with a little positive interaction. To begin, review with students that a noun in direct address is set off from the rest of a sentence with a comma or commas. Then give each child a class list and have him write a complimentary sentence to each classmate on colorful paper, setting off the classmate's name with a comma or commas. After checking students' sentences for appropriateness, have each child cut apart his strips and pass them out to his classmates. If desired, give each student a blank strip to use for a cover, a brad, and access to a hole puncher. Then have him assemble his strips into a booklet destined to become a well-punctuated keepsake!

Holding All the Cards

Comprehension (RI.4.10, RI.5.10)

Want to give your students the upper hand when it comes to reading complex text? Try this! First, choose two articles—one from a popular children's magazine and one from an encyclopedia. Next, display and read aloud the magazine piece, using a copy of the cards on page 22 as reminders to employ reading strategies as you read the engaging text. Then display and read aloud the encyclopedia article, explaining that even though the text is complex, you use the same reading strategies to understand and remember it. After reading, have each student cut out a copy of the cards and keep them handy to use when reading complex text. *adapted from an idea by Katie Hartman, Sinking Springs Elementary, York, PA*

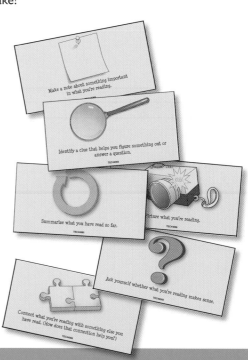

Make a note about something important in what you're reading.

Identify a clue that helps you figure something out or answer a question.

Summarize what you have read so far.

Picture what you're reading.

Ask yourself whether what you're reading makes sense.

Connect what you're reading with something else you have read. (How does that connection help you?)

The Foolish Porcupine: A Prickly Fable

Once there was a famous animal trainer named Bev Hill, who lived in a small but pleasant trailer. Bev owned __(1)__ animals. But the two __(2)__ loved most were her __(3)__ Persian cat, Bitsy, and Spike, __(4)__ prickly but prized porcupine.

Bitsy __(5)__ inside the small but __(6)__ trailer with Bev. Bitsy __(7)__ fabulous food from a __(8)__ bowl, and she __(9)__ on a fluffy satin __(10)__. Bev basically spoiled Bitsy __(11)__ that trailer.

Spike lived __(12)__ a spacious pen outside __(13)__ small but pleasant trailer. Spike __(14)__ never cramped in his __(15)__, and he feasted on fruits, roots, __(16)__ bark. He had clean __(17)__ soft straw to snuggle __(18)__ every night. Bev basically __(19)__ Spike outside that trailer.

__(20)__, Spike saw Bitsy living __(21)__, and he began to __(22)__ dissatisfied. So the next __(23)__ Bev and Bitsy were __(24)__ making a movie, Spike __(25)__ his way into the __(26)__ but pleasant trailer. He __(27)__, "If I just act __(28)__ a cat, I'll have __(29)__ much better life." Then __(30)__ waddled toward the bedroom __(31)__ plopped down on Bitsy's __(32)__. As he tried to __(33)__ comfortable, Spike's quills tore __(34)__ satin, and feathers started __(35)__ out. Spike tried to __(36)__ off the pillow, but __(37)__ stuck to his quills. __(38)__ shook the pillow, and __(39)__ flew out.

Frustrated with the pillow, __(40)__ spotted Bitsy's special bowl. __(41)__ made his way over, __(42)__ the pillow and leaving a __(43)__ of feathers behind him. __(44)__ stuck his nose in __(45)__ bowl, took a big __(46)__, and immediately spit out __(47)__ slimy sardine that had __(48)__ in the bowl. "Yuck!" he cried.

__(49)__, the door swung open. Bev and Bitsy __(50)__ in. Bev got right to work, __(51)__ the satin pillow off Spike's __(52)__. She gathered all the __(53)__ and cleaned up the __(54)__ sardine. She helped Spike __(55)__ back into his spacious pen. Then everyone inside and outside the small but pleasant trailer, satisfied to be where they were, took a nap!

TEC44066

Answer Key for "The Foolish Porcupine: A Prickly Fable"

1. many	12. in	23. time	34. the	45. Bitsy's
2. she	13. the	24. away	35. spilling	46. bite
3. beautiful	14. was	25. dug	36. get	47. a
4. her	15. pen	26. small	37. it	48. been
5. lived	16. and	27. thought	38. He	49. Suddenly
6. pleasant	17. and	28. like	39. feathers	50. walked
7. ate	18. into	29. a	40. Spike	51. pulling
8. special	19. spoiled	30. he	41. He	52. quills
9. slept	20. However	31. and	42. dragging	53. feathers
10. pillow	21. inside	32. pillow	43. trail	54. slimy
11. inside	22. feel	33. get	44. Spike	55. crawl

Deadly, Irritating, or Just Another Sea Creature?

This shape-shifting creature moves smoothly through the water, riding the ocean currents. Its soft body can be as __(1)__ as glass, or it __(2)__ be brightly colored. It might be so __(3)__ you need a microscope to __(4)__ it. Or it might __(5)__ seven feet wide. Tentacles __(6)__ from the creature's body. __(7)__ has no bones, no heart, __(8)__ blood, and no organ systems. It __(9)__ even have a brain! What __(10)__ it? It's a jellyfish!

A __(11)__, or jelly, is not __(12)__ a fish at all. It's __(13)__ invertebrate marine animal. It __(14)__ its shape from a gel- or __(15)__-like substance instead of a skeleton. A __(16)__ body, or bell, is symmetrical. __(17)__ body spreads out evenly __(18)__ its center. A jelly's __(19)__ helps it sense and react to signals that __(20)__ from any direction. Most __(21)__ are bell or umbrella shaped. __(22)__ are flatter, almost dish __(23)__, and some are round like __(24)__.

The other parts of a __(25)__ are its tentacles and oral arms. A __(26)__ uses its oral arms to __(27)__ food to its mouth. It __(28)__ its tentacles to catch the __(29)__. In some jellyfish species, __(30)__ are short, not much __(31)__ than the creatures' bodies. __(32)__ the tentacles of other __(33)__, such as the Arctic lion's mane, can __(34)__ 100 feet. And lurking __(35)__ those tentacles are poisonous __(36)__ that, when touched, are released __(37)__ tiny poison arrows. The toxin, or __(38)__, in some barbs is just __(39)__ enough to stun a small __(40)__ or give a person __(41)__ itchy rash. But there's a __(42)__ that lives off the northern Australian coast to __(43)__ out for. The poison __(44)__ a box jellyfish's, or sea wasp's, __(45)__ can kill a human in __(46)__ than five minutes. Despite their deadly __(47)__, jellyfish are a key __(48)__ of the marine food __(49)__. Sunfish, sea turtles, spadefish, and __(50)__ jellies prey on jellyfish. Some species of jellyfish are popular in human diets too.

TEC44066

Answer Key for "Deadly, Irritating, or Just Another Sea Creature?"

1. clear	11. jellyfish	21. jellyfish	31. longer	41. an
2. may	12. really	22. Some	32. Yet	42. jellyfish
3. small	13. an	23. shaped	33. jellyfish	43. watch
4. see	14. gets	24. balls	34. reach	44. in
5. be	15. jelly	25. jelly	35. inside	45. barbs
6. dangle	16. jellyfish's	26. jellyfish	36. barbs	46. fewer
7. It	17. Its	27. carry	37. like	47. poisons
8. no	18. from	28. uses	38. poison	48. part
9. doesn't	19. symmetry	29. food	39. strong	49. web
10. is	20. come	30. tentacles	40. fish	50. other

Reading Strategy Cards

Use with "Holding All the Cards" on page 20.

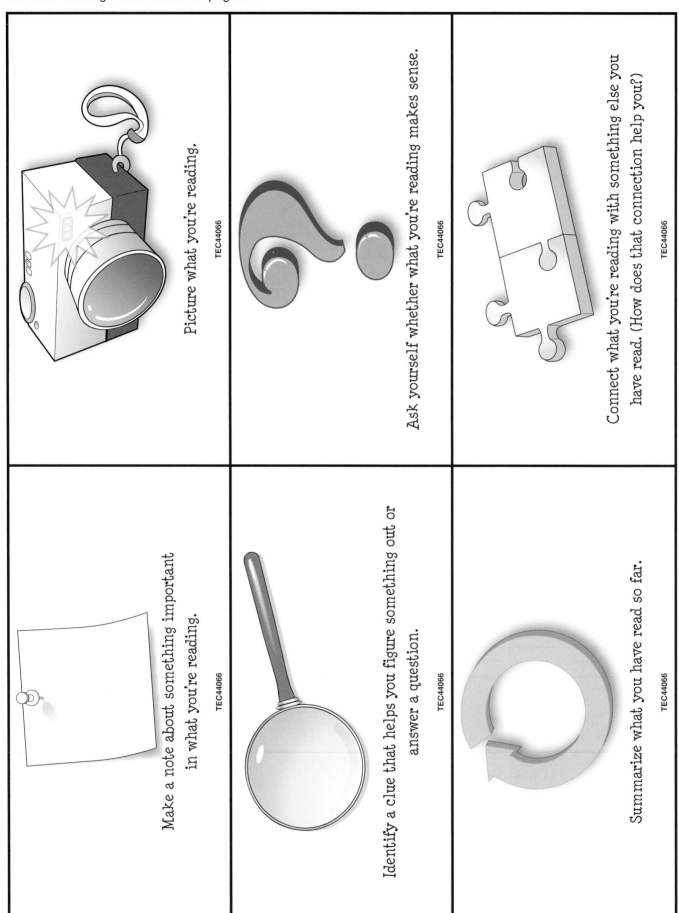

Picture what you're reading.

TEC44066

Ask yourself whether what you're reading makes sense.

TEC44066

Connect what you're reading with something else you have read. (How does that connection help you?)

TEC44066

Make a note about something important in what you're reading.

TEC44066

Identify a clue that helps you figure something out or answer a question.

TEC44066

Summarize what you have read so far.

TEC44066

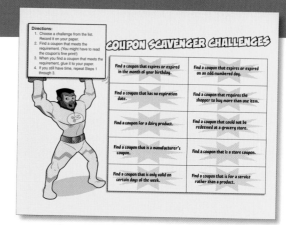

Coupon Clipping and Skill Building

Locating and interpreting information (RI.4.7; RI.5.7)

For this idea, stock a center with a variety of coupons and a copy of page 24. A student chooses a challenge from the list and sorts through the coupons to find one that meets the requirement. The child records the qualifier and glues the coupon to his paper. Then he chooses another challenge and continues as time allows.

Over There

Prepositional phrases (L.4.1e)

Build students' prepositional phrase concepts with this simple idea! Have one student hide a silly object, such as a stuffed animal, somewhere in the classroom while the rest of the students put their heads down. Once the object is hidden, have students take turns asking questions about the object's location by writing prepositional phrases on individual whiteboards. If desired, have each student circle the preposition and underline its object. Then let the student who guesses correctly hide the object next. *Angie Paisley, Millstadt, IL*

Piecing Together Theme

Determining theme (RL.4.2; RL.5.2)

Looking for help in teaching students how to find the theme of a story? Have each student make a booklet that walks her through the process! First, have the child cut out the vase from a copy of page 25. Have her trace its outline on a sheet of construction paper and six sheets of lined paper. Next, have the student cut apart the pieces of the vase along the lines and glue each piece onto a separate lined paper cutout. Have her arrange the sheets in order and staple them together with the construction paper vase on top. Then, as she reads, have the child answer each question in her booklet. Follow up with a class discussion about the story and its well-explored theme. *Chris Clemenson, Estell Manor, NJ*

COUPON SCAVENGER CHALLENGES

Directions:

1. Choose a challenge from the list. Record it on your paper.
2. Find a coupon that meets the requirement. (You might have to read the coupon's fine print!)
3. When you find a coupon that meets the requirement, glue it to your paper.
4. If you still have time, repeat Steps 1 through 3.

Find a coupon that expires or expired in the month of your birthday.	Find a coupon that expires or expired on an odd-numbered day.
Find a coupon that has no expiration date.	Find a coupon that requires the shopper to buy more than one item.
Find a coupon for a dairy product.	Find a coupon that could not be redeemed at a grocery store.
Find a coupon that is a manufacturer's coupon.	Find a coupon that is a store coupon.
Find a coupon that is only valid on certain days of the week.	Find a coupon that is for a service rather than a product.

©The Mailbox® • TEC44067 • June/July 2013 (RI.4.7; RI.5.7)

Note to the teacher: Use with "Coupon Clipping and Skill Building" on page 23.

1. Examine the title or titles.
What clues do the story title and/or chapter titles give you about what is most important about this story?

2. Examine the setting.
When and where does the story take place? How does this setting affect what is most important about this story?

3. Examine the characters.
How do the main characters' actions, statements, or goals relate to what is most important about this story? How do the characters relate to each other? How do the characters or their personalities change?

4. Examine the symbols.
Look for certain objects or words in the story that have special meaning to the main characters and/or the story's plot. What are they? What do they seem to mean?

5. Examine the author's or narrator's statements.
What does it seem like the author or narrator is really trying to say? What hints are there about what is most important in this story?

6. Make your case.
Based on the evidence you've found, what do you think the theme of this story is? Give reasons for your answer.

ON THE MOVE

Directions for two players:

1. Stack the cards facedown. Then place your marker on Start.
2. When it's your turn, have the player on your left draw a card and read it aloud. Tell whether the statement is a complete sentence, a sentence fragment, or a run-on sentence. Have your partner check the letter on the card against the code.
3. If you're correct, move your marker one space. If you're incorrect, your turn is over. Have your partner put the card at the bottom of the pile.
4. The first player to reach Finish wins.

CODE

C = complete sentence
F = sentence fragment
R = run-on sentence

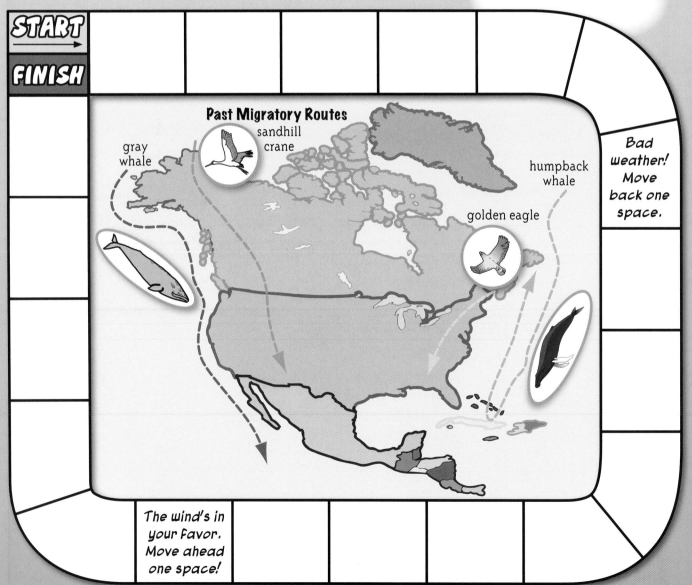

START
FINISH

Bad weather! Move back one space.

Past Migratory Routes

gray whale

sandhill crane

humpback whale

golden eagle

The wind's in your favor. Move ahead one space!

Center Cards

Use with "On the Move" on page 26. Students will need game markers.

Sandhill cranes are the most common cranes in the world. TEC44063 **C**	Every humpback whale's tail has a unique pattern. TEC44063 **C**	Gray whales sometimes go near boats and let people touch them. TEC44063 **C**	The golden eagle is North America's largest bird of prey. TEC44063 **C**
South to Mexico and Cuba, and as far west as Siberia. TEC44063 **F**	The humpback whale's body. TEC44063 **F**	Gray whales' skin is scratched up it has barnacles some has orange whale lice. TEC44063 **R**	Are dark brown, with light brown feathers on their heads and necks. TEC44063 **F**
Sandhill cranes in the northern United States, Canada, and Alaska. TEC44063 **F**	The whale's flippers up to one-third the length of its body. TEC44063 **F**	Name from gray patches and white spots on dark skin. TEC44063 **F**	A golden eagle dives to catch its prey it can dive faster than 150 miles per hour. TEC44063 **R**
Make long journeys to spend winter in Florida, Texas, Utah, Mexico, and California. TEC44063 **F**	A male humpback whale can be 35 feet long a female may be 40 feet long. TEC44063 **R**	The gray whale has no dorsal fin it has a dorsal hump. TEC44063 **R**	Today, protected golden eagles. TEC44063 **F**
Most sandhill cranes live in freshwater wetlands they nest there too. TEC44063 **R**	They feed on krill and small fish. TEC44063 **C**	The gray whale's fluke can be 12 feet across it has a deep notch in the center. TEC44063 **R**	A pair of golden eagles' territory up to 60 square miles. TEC44063 **F**
Cranes eat grains they eat mice and snakes and they eat insects and worms. TEC44063 **R**	A newborn humpback calf can weigh one ton it can be 15 feet long! TEC44063 **R**	An adult gray whale male may be 46 feet long. TEC44063 **C**	They eat rabbits and ground squirrels they also eat reptiles and fish. TEC44063 **R**
Because cranes dig up tubers. TEC44063 **F**	In summer, humpbacks go to polar water in winter, they go to tropical water. TEC44063 **R**	These whales feed during summer they eat tube worms and small crustaceans. TEC44063 **R**	Golden eagles make high nests in places such as cliffs, trees, or even telephone poles. TEC44063 **C**
Sandhills are gray with red on their heads and they can look brown. TEC44063 **R**	Can throw themselves out of the water and swim on their backs. TEC44063 **F**	The gray whale's migration 10,000 to 14,000 miles round trip. TEC44063 **F**	A female lays from one to four eggs and both parents sit on them. TEC44063 **R**
Sandhill cranes often dance, run, and leap in the air. TEC44063 **C**	Some whales sing their own songs one song can last twenty minutes. TEC44063 **R**	In October, leave their feeding grounds in the Bering Sea to migrate south. TEC44063 **F**	Range from Mexico to Alaska. TEC44063 **F**
Females often lay just two eggs, both parents incubate the eggs. TEC44063 **R**	Worldwide protection in 1966. TEC44063 **F**	The gray whales' journey south two to three months. TEC44063 **F**	Alaskan and Canadian eagles migrate south in the fall. TEC44063 **C**

Greek and Latin roots

MUMMY MAZE

Directions for two players:

1. Place your game markers on Start. Place the root cards and the "Risk It!" cards facedown in two separate stacks.
2. In turn, draw a root card. Find and name the meaning of the root on the pyramid.
3. Check the key. If correct, choose one of the following to do:
   - Move one number ahead on the path to King Tut's treasure. Then return the card to the bottom of the stack.
   - Draw a "Risk It!" card and follow its instructions. If you draw the last "Risk It!" card, shuffle the cards and stack them again.

   If incorrect, do not move or draw a card.
4. The first player to reach the treasure wins.

Meaning Bank

air
animal
change, move
death   heat
earth
judge
life
measure   light
place
one, single
skin
sound   small
star
throw
time

to break
to build
to carry
to drag, pull
to hear
to look
to say
to write
voice, to call
water

START

King Tut's Treasure!

©The Mailbox® • TEC44065 • Feb./Mar. 2013 (L.4.4b, L.5.4b)

Center Cards

Use with "Mummy Maze" on page 28. Students will need game markers.

1. aster/astr
TEC44065

2. dict
TEC44065

3. jud
TEC44065

4. therm
TEC44065

5. voc
TEC44065

6. loc
TEC44065

7. mono
TEC44065

8. spect
TEC44065

9. geo
TEC44065

10. aud
TEC44065

11. derm
TEC44065

12. struct
TEC44065

13. meter/metr
TEC44065

14. migr
TEC44065

15. aer
TEC44065

16. aqua
TEC44065

17. phon
TEC44065

18. port
TEC44065

19. scrib/script
TEC44065

20. bio
TEC44065

21. micro
TEC44065

22. fract
TEC44065

23. chron
TEC44065

24. mort
TEC44065

25. trac/tract
TEC44065

26. zoo
TEC44065

27. ject
TEC44065

28. photo/phos
TEC44065

RISK IT! Take an extra turn.
TEC44065

RISK IT! Move back one number.
TEC44065

RISK IT! Your opponent must move back one number.
TEC44065

RISK IT! Lose a turn.
TEC44065

RISK IT! Move forward one number.
TEC44065

RISK IT! Your opponent takes an extra turn.
TEC44065

Answer Key
"Mummy Maze"

1. star
2. to say
3. judge
4. heat
5. voice, to call
6. place
7. one, single
8. to look
9. earth
10. to hear
11. skin
12. to build
13. measure
14. change, move
15. air
16. water
17. sound
18. to carry
19. to write
20. life
21. small
22. to break
23. time
24. death
25. to drag, pull
26. animal
27. throw
28. light

TEC44065

MAD ABOUT THE MALL!

Nacho Mucho

I Scream Shop

N-OVATION SUPERSTORE

Greased Lightning Electronics

Directions for two players:

1. Turn the answer key facedown. Then shuffle and stack the cards.
2. Place your game marker on Entrance. In turn, roll the die and move your marker.
3. Draw a card. Read the card and find the mistakes. Then record the card number and the corrections on your own paper. Have your partner check the key. If you are right, leave your marker. If you're not right, move back one space.
4. The first player to reach Exit wins.

Exit

Entrance

Conventions, Grammar, Usage, Mechanics Cards

Use with "Mad About the Mall!" on page 30.

1 Find the misused and misspelled words.

Luis and Hanna are comeing to.

TEC44067

2 Find the missing punctuation.

Lily said Lets get pizza!

TEC44067

3 Find the misspelled words.

I thougt we were meeting tomorow.

TEC44067

4 Find the misused word and missing punctuation.

Dont you have there phone number?

TEC44067

5 Find the missing punctuation.

Lets go to the childrens museum.

TEC44067

6 Find the misused and misspelled words.

Come sit at are tabel over here.

TEC44067

7 Find the misspelled words.

Can you beleive we shoped for four hours?

TEC44067

8 Find the misused words.

Are we aloud to eat in their?

TEC44067

9 Find the missing punctuation.

Ellen said I have to leave at 2:00.

TEC44067

10 Find the missing punctuation.

What do they sell in that store Seth asked.

TEC44067

11 Find the misused words.

Lily and Ellen said their going to by coffee.

TEC44067

12 Find the misspelled words.

Woud you beleive me if I said I'm hungry again?

TEC44067

13 Find the misused and misspelled words.

Seth is worried he migt loose his phone.

TEC44067

14 Find the misused word and missing punctuation.

Weve walked passed this store five times!

TEC44067

15 Find the missing punctuation.

Hanna says Those were the best nachos ever!

TEC44067

16 Find and correct the misused words.

There in a hurry too get home.

TEC44067

17 Find the misspelled word and missing punctuation.

Luis bouht a game and Seth got new earbuds.

TEC44067

18 Find the misspelled word and missing punctuation.

Ellen Hanna and Lily walk togeter.

TEC44067

19 Find the missing punctuation.

We had tacos nachos and ice cream today Seth said.

TEC44067

20 Find the misused word and missing punctuation.

Lily told Ellen Your the best shopper.

TEC44067

21 Find the missing punctuation.

Its Saturday but the mall isnt crowded at all.

TEC44067

22 Find the misspelled words.

Wenever we go shoping, I get tired!

TEC44067

23 Find the misused word and missing punctuation.

Its time to go. Did Luis and Seth get there stuff?

TEC44067

24 Find the missing punctuation.

When are we going shopping Ellen asked

TEC44067

Answer Key for "Mad About the Mall!"

1. coming, too
2. Lily said, "Let's get pizza!"
3. thought, tomorrow.
4. Don't, their
5. Let's, children's
6. our, table
7. believe, shopped
8. allowed, there
9. Ellen said, "I have to leave at 2:00."
10. "What do they sell in that store?" Seth asked.
11. they're, buy
12. Would, believe
13. might, lose
14. We've, past
15. Hanna says, "Those were the best nachos ever!"
16. They're, to
17. Luis bought a game, and Seth got new earbuds.
18. Ellen, Hanna, and Lily walk together.
19. "We had tacos, nachos, and ice cream today," Seth said.
20. Lily told Ellen, "You're the best shopper."
21. It's Saturday, but the mall isn't crowded at all.
22. Whenever, shopping
23. It's, their
24. "When are we going shopping?" Ellen asked.

TEC44067

"Paws-ing" for Spelling

Write each of your spelling words on a bone. Then use the activities below to study your words.

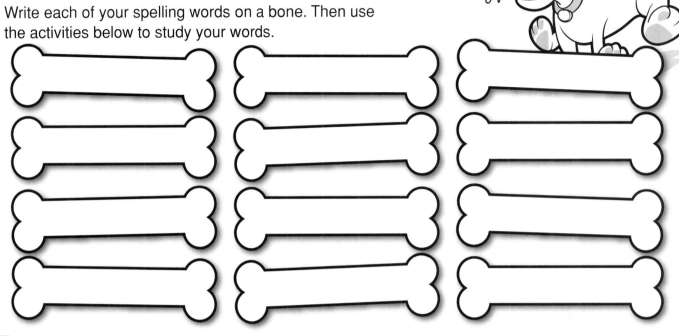

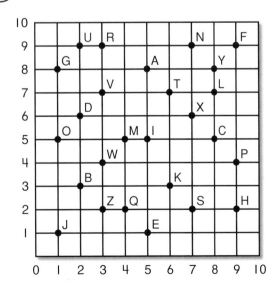

Write each spelling word and then list all the smaller words you can find within it. If one of the smaller words has something to do with what the word means, circle it. (For example: spotlight—(spot), pot, (light))

Using the grid below, write the coordinates that spell each word.

Look up each word in a dictionary and copy its pronunciation. Then practice saying each word three times in a row.

Write each word and then write a fraction that represents the number of vowels in the word. Next, write a fraction that represents the number of consonants in the word. Then add the fractions. The sum should be one. (For example: vivid—$\frac{2}{5}$ letters are vowels, $\frac{3}{5}$ letters are consonants, $\frac{2}{5} + \frac{3}{5} = 1$)

Create a jingle or catchy song in which you sing each word and its spelling.

Create a mini poster that shows each word and its syllables. Make the poster eye-catching.

Use your spelling words in a story about a real or an imaginary dog.

Write a rhyming word, synonym, antonym, or definition for each word.

©The Mailbox® • TEC44062 • Aug./Sept. 2012 (L.4.2d, L.5.2e)

How to Use Have each child write her words on a copy of the page at the beginning of the week and then use the page to guide her spelling practice for the rest of the week.

Mad About Ads

Mistake Symbols

! = misspelled word

X = incomplete sentence

↝ = run-on sentence

Part 1: Use the symbols to identify the mistake in each advertisement.

AT OUR PLACE YOUR ALWAYS NEXT IN LINE!

①

Our customers—happy—all the time!

②

No unhappy customers here.

③

THIS IS PROBLY THE BEST BURGER EVER!

④

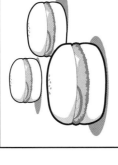

Don't delay call us today!

⑤

PIZZA AND GAMES JUST FOR KIDS!

⑥

$ $ $

Our prices will allways beat the others'!

⑦

Try our pizza you'll be back for more!

⑧

YOUR BEST FRIEND IN INTERNET SERVICE.

⑨

Haveing trouble with your Internet? **Call me!**

⑩

HAVE YOU HEARD PEOPLE ALL OVER TOWN LOVE US!

⑪

Because we make the best burgers in town!

⑫

Part 2: Write the correct spelling of each misspelled word.

⑬ ⑭

⑮ ⑯

Bonus: Rewrite each incomplete sentence so it is a complete sentence.

Name_____

Date_____

Short and Sweet

 **1** What is the selection's title? _____

2 Describe the selection's main idea in your own words.

3 List important words from the selection.

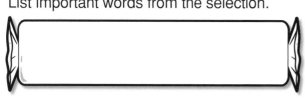

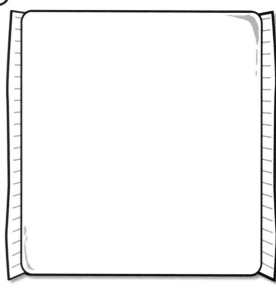 **4** List important details from the selection.

 5 Reread your description of the main idea. Underline the part that tells exactly what the main idea is.

 6 Reread your lists of words and details. Circle the most important ones.

 7 Using the parts you circled and underlined, write a paragraph that summarizes the selection.

_____

_____

_____

_____

_____

_____

_____

_____

_____

_____

_____

©The Mailbox® • TEC44062 • Aug./Sept. 2012 (RI.4.2)

How to Use Have each child use a copy of the page to plan and then write a summary of a chapter or other reading selection.

Traveling Through Time

Pretend that you can jump into a machine and travel in time and/or space to interview the subject of the biography or autobiography you read. Complete the interview form below.

Book title: _____

Author: _____

I am interviewing _____, who is best

known for _____

Tell me about your early life.

What has been the biggest challenge you ever faced?

If you could change one thing about your life, what would you change and why?

What has been a turning point in your life?

What advice would you give others?

What has been your greatest lifetime achievement?

Bonus: What might the subject of this book be doing if he or she lived in your community?

©The Mailbox® • TEC44063 • Oct./Nov. 2012 (RI.4.2, RI.5.2)

Name _____

Date _____

GABBY AND MAURICE

Write the correct plural form of the noun in parentheses at the end of each sentence.

1. Maurice grew up in a huge herd of _____ . (moose)

2. Gabby lives with a great gaggle of _____ . (goose)

3. Even though Maurice and Gabby are different _____, they are best friends. (species)

4. While they hang out, Gabby feasts on _____ of bread left behind on the shore. (loaf)

5. Maurice wades along the lake's edge, nibbling on pondweed _____. (leaf)

6. He uses his strong _____ to grab each floating leaf. (tooth)

7. Thankfully, _____ don't often bring their boats to this lake. (person)

8. Tasty insects hover over the surface drawing _____ from all over the lake. (fish)

9. A group of rowdy _____ on the opposite shore tries to reel in a big fish. (fisherman)

10. Maurice and Gabby decide to rid the lake of those pesky fish _____. (thief)

11. First, they sneak around the lake, hiding _____ in the bushes. (himself and herself)

12. Then they pop out and make as much noise as a couple of _____. (hippopotamus)

13. The anglers drop their fishing poles and run away liked frightened little _____. (mouse)

14. A trio of _____ peek out and howl as the humans skedaddle. (wolf)

15. Soon, all the animals at the lake, even a family of _____, are adding noises to chase away their pests. (deer)

BONUS: Copy the words shown. Then list each word's plural form. Use a dictionary if necessary.

basis, crisis, diagnosis, emphasis, hypothesis

©The Mailbox® • TEC44063 • Oct./Nov. 2012 • Key p. 306

A Dream Destination

Choose a book about a city or country you would like to visit one day. As you read, take notes about the location and four of the main topics from the list. When you finish reading, write each topic on the outline next to a roman numeral. Then organize your notes onto the outline.

_____
book's title

Main Topics

population	culture	climate
history	economy	natural resources
transportation	tourist attractions	

Subject: _____

I. The location of _____

    A. _____

    B. _____

    C. _____

II. _____

    A. _____

    B. _____

    C. _____

III. _____

    A. _____

    B. _____

    C. _____

IV. _____

    A. _____

    B. _____

    C. _____

V. _____

    A. _____

    B. _____

    C. _____

Bonus: Use your outline to summarize your book.

A Wintry Research Scavenger Hunt

How Many Answers Can You Roll Out? (Be Sure to Cite Your Sources!)

Hint:

To cite an encyclopedia, record the encyclopedia title, encyclopedia edition, encyclopedia publication date, the article's author (if available), and the article's title.

To cite a website, record the article's author and article's title, the site's title, the sponsor of the site, the date the site was created, and the date you accessed the site.

To cite a book, record the book's title, author, publication date, and city of publication.

1. This author has a winter birthday and wrote *The Call of the Wild* and *White Fang*, stories set in Canada's wintry Yukon territory. Who is the author, and when was he born?

2. What are the birthstones that should bring those born in December and January good luck?

3. January is named after the Roman god Janus. Why was this god unusual?

4. The word *December* comes from a Latin word for a number. What is the Latin word and what does it mean?

5. Three famous Revolutionary War personalities were born in January. Their initials are B. F., E. A., and B. A. One was a famous statesman, one led the Green Mountain Boys, and one was a traitor. What are their names, and when was each person born?

6. This state became the 28th state on December 29, 1845. Which state is it? What are the state flower and the state bird?

7. Franklin Delano Roosevelt was the 32nd president of the United States. When was he born, and what presidential record does he hold that cannot be broken?

8. When was the United States Constitution ratified, or formally approved? Which state was the first to ratify it?

9. National Handwriting Day is observed on January 23. It's observed in honor of the first man who signed the Declaration of Independence. Who was he, and when was he born?

10. Born on Christmas Day in 1821, Clara Barton was called the Angel of the Battlefield during the Civil War. How did she earn this nickname?

11. Orville and Wilbur Wright made the first controlled airplane flight on December 17, 1903. Where were they, and how long did the flight last?

12. The Montgomery bus boycott ended December 21, 1956. When did it begin? How long did it last?

©The Mailbox® • TEC44064 • Dec./Jan. 2012–13 • Key p. 306 (W.4.8, W.5.8)

How to Use Display and challenge each student or pair of students to answer each question, citing the source of each answer. Use as a research center, a free-time activity, or as a whole-class contest.

Vocabulary S-s-s-potting

I heard it!

Term	Sentence in which it was used

I wrote it!

Term	Sentence in which it was used

I saw it!

Term	Sentence in which it was used

I said it!

Term	Sentence in which it was used

©The Mailbox® • TEC44064 • Dec./Jan. 2012–13 (L.4.4a)

Note to the teacher: Use with "Term Spotting" on page 14.

Name

Date

Penguin Puzzlers

Read each analogy and circle the letter next to the word that best completes each one.

1. hive : bee :: nest : _____

   A. kitten
   B. fish
   C. penguin
   D. dog

2. nursery : rookery :: marsh : _____

   B. plant
   C. desert
   D. swamp
   E. Antarctica

3. chick : baby :: victim : _____

   C. predator
   D. animal
   E. prey
   F. hunt

4. chick : fluffy :: adult penguin : _____

   D. square
   E. swim
   F. food
   G. sleek

5. Antarctica : continent :: penguin : _____

   E. mammal
   F. seal
   G. bird
   H. reptile

6. ice : cold :: cookie : _____

   F. jar
   G. much
   H. sweet
   I. wafer

7. flipper : wing :: beak : _____

   G. head
   H. eye
   I. mouth
   J. tooth

8. swimming : penguin :: floating : _____

   H. rock
   I. iceberg
   J. kitten
   K. marble

9. school : fish :: rookery : _____

   L. crooks
   M. seals
   N. names
   O. penguins

10. trip : stumble :: walk : _____

   O. waddle
   P. swim
   Q. run
   R. fly

11. emperor : name :: New Zealand : _____

   R. penguin
   S. place
   T. food
   U. leaf

12. brooding : sitting :: gather : _____

   T. flock
   U. hatch
   V. swim
   W. escape

What does a penguin need in order to spot a glacier from far away?

To solve the riddle, write each circled letter on the matching numbered line.

It needs "___ ___ ___ ___ ___ ___ ___ ___ ___ ___ ___ ___ ___!"
            5 10 9 2 8 1 3 11 7 4 6 12

Bonus: Write two analogies of your own. Use synonyms in one analogy and antonyms in the other.

©The Mailbox® • TEC44064 • Dec./Jan. 2012–13 • Key p. 306

The Final Shot

Read the story.

① The basketball tournament was coming to an end. ② Only two teams, the Bank-Shot Bears and the Slam-Dunk Storks, were left in the competition. ③ The gym was packed with fans from both teams. ④ The place was so crowded that not everyone could find a seat.

⑤ The game began as soon as the referee tossed the ball into the air for tip-off. ⑥ By halftime, the Storks were ahead with a score of 35 to 34. ⑦ The fans filed out of the gym to the snack bar. ⑧ Each team supporter spoke with conviction that her team would win.

⑨ The referees and teams returned to court at the start of the second half. ⑩ The ball was tossed, and the game continued. ⑪ Fans cheered back and forth as the teams took turns scoring points. ⑫ The Bears took the lead, and then the Storks made a comeback.

⑬ The score was tied with only ten seconds left on the clock. ⑭ Both teams had scored 72 points. ⑮ The Bears stole the ball from the Storks and scored. ⑯ The Bears were in the lead by two points. ⑰ With only three seconds left on the clock, the Storks had to act quickly. ⑱ A player took one final shot as the buzzer sounded. ⑲ The Slam-Dunk Storks' fans moaned and groaned as they dragged themselves out of the gym.

Write **accurate** or **inaccurate** after each statement. Then write the sentence number or numbers that helped you draw a conclusion.

1. More than two teams played in the tournament.

_____   _____

2. There were plenty of seats in the gym for the fans.

_____   _____

3. The Storks played better than the Bears in the first half.

_____   _____

4. Fans could get snacks at the game.

_____   _____

5. The fans did not try to predict the winner of the game.

_____   _____

6. There were at least two referees at the game.

_____   _____

7. The fans did not pay close attention to the game.

_____   _____

8. The Storks kept the lead for most of the second half.

_____   _____

9. Both teams had an equal chance of winning the game.

_____   _____

10. The Storks couldn't keep control of the ball.

_____   _____

11. A Storks player made the last-second basket to win the game.

_____   _____

12. The Bank-Shot Bears won the game with 74 points.

_____   _____

Bonus: Draw two conclusions about what the Bank-Shot Bears' fans do at the end of the story. Write about it.

Name _____

Date _____

Lights Out!

Write the correct pair of conjunctions in each sentence.

> **Correlative Conjunctions**
> both…and   either…or
> neither…nor   whether…or
> not only…but also

1. _____ Max _____ Jamal were looking forward to watching their favorite movie together.

2. _____ _____ did Jamal make popcorn, _____ he _____ stored soft drinks in a cooler.

3. The boys were _____ surprised _____ disappointed when the power went out.

4. Max wondered _____ a power line was blown down by wind _____ a power line was struck by lightning.

5. To see, the boys had to use _____ flashlights _____ candles.

6. Unfortunately, they had _____ a candle _____ a match.

7. Max said, "We can _____ play flashlight tag _____ a board game."

8. Jamal said, "It doesn't matter _____ we play tag _____ a game. I am just glad we are together!"

Read the question. Use the conjunction pairs to write each answer in a complete sentence.

What are your weekend plans?

9. (either…or) meet my friends at the mall/play soccer

_____

_____

10. (both…and) finish my science project/my history report

_____

_____

11. (not only…but also) take my dog for a walk/build a tree house

_____

_____

12. (whether…or) go skateboarding/visit my cousins _____

> **Bonus:** Use one pair of conjunctions in a sentence about the book you are currently reading.

©The Mailbox® • TEC44065 • Feb./Mar. 2013 • Key p. 306 (L.5.1e)

Name _____

Date _____

Race to the Food

Read the poem below. Circle the correct word that completes each line.
Then write each circled word on the crossword puzzle.

1. Follow the (rode/road) to a tasty meal.
2. Hold (real/really) tight to the steering wheel.
3. Each correct word will keep you on (course/coarse).
4. You'll move quicker (than/then) a fast racehorse!

• 5. Along the way, you (can/may) find a plate of spaghetti.
6. Then (chose/choose) to eat it when you feel you're ready
7. And (pore/pour) yourself a giant glass of tea.
8. Take all you want, since the (whole/hole) meal is free!

• 9. Be sure to save room for a delicious (desert/dessert).
10. Having one is (alright/all right), but seconds might hurt.
11. (Our/Are) pies are fantastic;
12. (Their/They're) thick and sweet.
13. A (piece/peace) of chocolate cake is quite the treat!

• 14. Don't slow down now; (your/you're) near the end of the maze!
15. (It's/Its) when you cross the finish line that you'll get some praise.
16. To complete this race is truly a great (feat/feet).
17. Look! You (past/passed) the finish line!
18. You've done (good/well)—now EAT!

©The Mailbox® • TEC44065 • Feb./Mar. 2013 • Key p. 306 (L.4.1g)

Name

Date

Turn Up the Base!

Write the base word for each group of words.

Remember, a base word is the simplest form of a word before prefixes and suffixes are added to it.

Bonus: Which of these words does not have the same base word as the other three words? How do you know?

discount   uncountable

countertop   miscounted

1. bicycle   recyclable   cyclone

2. appearance   disappear   appearing

3. disbelieve   believer   believable

4. historian   historical   prehistoric

5. loveless   lovable   unloved

6. discomfort   uncomfortable   comforter

7. encircled   semicircle   recirculate

8. ungovernable   government   governor

9. dedication   rededicate   dedicating

10. unkindly   kindliness   kindly

11. distasteful   tasty   tasteless

12. hopelessness   hopefully   unhopeful

13. addition   additive   addend

14. preexist   nonexistent   existence

15. movement   removable   immovable

16. musician   musical   musically

Name _____

Date _____

Too Many Moose!

Read each sentence. If the plural nouns are correct, check the box at the end of the sentence. If the sentence has an incorrect plural noun, cross out the box. Then write the correct plural noun on a numbered line.

Find eight plural noun mistakes!

Wanda Wilson's Wildlife Blog
Posted April 2:

This morning, a family of Canada gooses waddled around our pond. ☐ I grabbed my binoculars from the shelfs to get a better look. ☐ A few yards away, there were several deer drinking silently from the pond. ☐ Sadly, the animals scattered when three noisy childs raced by on their way to school. ☐

Wanda Wilson's Wildlife Blog
Posted April 20:

My father flew to Alaska with men and women on his research team last night. ☐ When they stopped for breakfast this morning, they spotted three moose right outside the restaurant window! ☐ While they were working that afternoon, they heard several wolfs howling nearby. ☐ The howling must not have bothered my dad because he stayed to go fishing and caught six large troutes. ☐

Wanda Wilson's Wildlife Blog
Posted May 25:

After this week's rain, the mosquitoes have come out in full force! ☐ Six of them attacked me while I was out checking the tomatos in my garden. ☐ The bunnies have had a field day in there; every plant's leafs have been nibbled on! ☐ I wonder where those little leaf-loving thiefs are hiding. ☐

1. _____
2. _____
3. _____
4. _____
5. _____
6. _____
7. _____
8. _____

Write the plural form of each noun.

9. scarf _____

10. hero _____

11. fish _____

12. elf _____

13. piano _____

14. ox _____

15. roof _____

16. tooth _____

Bonus: The plural form of *brother-in-law* is *brothers-in-law*. Why do you think *brother* is the word that becomes plural? Use this pattern to write the plural forms of *father-in-law*, *mother-in-law*, and *sister-in-law*.

Classified Clues

Answer each question. Using the color in parentheses, circle the detail or details in each ad that help you.

Appliance sale! This Saturday only! Dishwashers starting at $250. All ovens 20% off. Buy a washer and get the dryer half-price. 415 North Highland Ave.

1. Which of the homes for rent will cost less per month? (red) _____

2. If you have a cat, should you try to rent the condo? Why or why not? (yellow) _____

3. If you offered to buy the sports car for $6,500, would the person selling it consider your offer? Why or why not? (green) _____

4. Alyssa wants to apply for the job at Nick's Jewelry Store, but she has never worked at a jewelry store before. Should she apply? Why or why not? (blue) _____

5. What do you have to do to get free feather pillows at the mattress sale? (orange) _____

6. Tom's dryer works great, but his washing machine just quit. Should he look for a deal at the appliance sale? Why or why not? (purple) _____

7. Where should you look if you want to find the lost cat? (brown) _____

8. Can you tell whether the appliance sale is at a store? Why or why not? (pink) _____

9. You have $45 and want to buy hockey equipment. What could you buy? (black) _____

10. Would the handyman be a good person to call if you need someone to patch holes in your roof? Why or why not? (gray) _____

For Rent

3-bedroom apartment. $650/month. Balcony and air-conditioned. Quiet location. Available Oct. 1. Call 555-0185 after 6 PM.

2-bedroom condo. $795/month. Unfurnished but comes with refrigerator, stove, washer, and dryer. No pets allowed. Available immediately. Call 555-0123. Leave message.

Help Wanted

Friendly salesperson needed at Nick's Jewelry Store. Starting rate, $15/hour. Part-time. No experience needed. Must be available to work weekends. Apply in person.

For Sale

1976 classic muscle car. Excellent condition! No rust. 90,000 miles. Needs new tires. Asking price $6,800 or best offer. Call 555-0111 anytime.

Junior hockey equipment. Never used. Goalie pads $75; helmet, $40; pants, $35; glove and stick, $90; or $200 for the whole set. Call 555-0188.

Lost and Found

Lost family cat. Orange tabby, 1 year old, named Ginger. Last seen on Main and 5th streets. $100 reward! Call 555-0122.

Work Wanted

Handyman looking for work. 25 years of experience as a painter, roofer, and carpenter. No job is too big or small. Call 555-0144.

Merchandise

Mattress sale! 25% off all sizes: twin, double, queen, and king. Free home delivery and setup. Mention this ad and get two feather pillows FREE! 396 Main St.

Bonus: Write and answer your own question about the classified ads.

©The Mailbox® • TEC44066 • April/May 2013 • Key p. 306 • (RI.4.1; RI.5.2)

Name

Date

Same Difference

Write the missing word that completes each analogy in the puzzle.

Across

2. Baseball is to throw as soccer ball is to _____.

5. Canada is to the United States as the United States is to _____.

8. Lawyer is to courtroom as teacher is to _____.

11. Waddle is to duck as _____ is to frog.

12. Perfume is to nose as music is to _____.

13. Sour is to pickle as _____ is to candy.

14. Wheat is to flour as _____ is to sawdust.

16. Noise is to loud as whisper is to _____.

19. Grass is to green as sky is to _____.

Down

1. Boat is to water as airplane is to _____.

3. Shower is to bathroom as refrigerator is to _____.

4. Skin is to humans as scales are to _____.

6. Windows are to curtains as _____ are to sunglasses.

7. Water is to wet as desert is to _____.

9. Skin is to apple as _____ is to nut.

10. Bark is to dog as _____ is to cat.

13. Smell is to nose as touch is to _____.

15. Eat is to apple as _____ is to milk.

17. Big toe is to foot as _____ to hand.

18. Broccoli is to vegetable as apple is to _____.

Bonus: Write an analogy of your own.

©The Mailbox® • TEC44066 • April/May 2013 • Key p. 306

Name _____

Date _____

Please Release Me!

Circle the letter in the column to tell whether each clause is dependent or independent.

If a clause is independent, use editing marks to make the clause a sentence.

If a clause is dependent, draw a box around the relative pronoun (*who, whom, whose, that,* or *which*) that introduces the clause.

≡ = Capitalize a letter.
⊙ = Add a period.

#	Clause	Independent	Dependent
1.	each spring, we welcome flutters of monarch butterflies	I	O
2.	that they spent the winter in Mexico	E	U
3.	which fly from Mexico to the United States	L	R
4.	my brother and I met an entomologist	O	A
5.	whom we invited to speak to our nature club	W	Y
6.	she wants to help save monarch butterfly populations	E	O
7.	she explained one way we could help	A	I
8.	that monarch larvae eat milkweed leaves	G	L
9.	then the entomologist taught us how to spot a monarch egg	H	F
10.	so we planted milkweed in our yard	M	P
11.	that we found under the leaf of a milkweed plant	R	S
12.	we checked on the egg every day	F	D
13.	that it hatched and ate its shell	J	C
14.	which grew quickly, shedding its skin five times	Q	T
15.	that it became a hard, green chrysalis	K	B
16.	it finally emerged as a beautiful orange-and-black butterfly	N	M

What would you get if you ate caterpillars?
To find out, write each circled letter on its matching numbered line or lines.

___ ___ ___ ___ ___ ___ -
15   2   14 14   6   3

___ ___ ___ ___ ___
12   8   1   6   11

___ ___
1   16

___ ___ ___ ___
5   4   2   3

___ ___ ___ ___ ___ ___ ___ !
11 14   4   10   7   13   9

Bonus: Choose four dependent clauses. Add an independent clause to each one to make a complete sentence.

©The Mailbox® • TEC44067 • June/July 2013 • Key p. 306 (L.4.1a)

Name _____

Date _____

Tricky Trios

Rearrange the letters in each set of three-letter words to spell the word from the word bank that matches the definition. Use a dictionary to help.

1. list of items a company has in stock

ivy, ten, nor

i n v e n t (o) r y

2. feeling unwilling or not eager

let, car, nut

3. to block off with a barrier, or something that blocks the way

air, arc, bed

4. working parts of a machine or instrument

cry, aim, hen

5. person who receives something

per, ice, tin

6. every other

are, let, tan

7. serious infection of the lungs

one, aim, pun

8. most important of all, or supreme

map, our, tan

9. to handle something badly

man, lid, she

10. print of an architect's plan, or a detailed plan of action

lit, rub, pen

11. plan that promises protection

arc, inn, use

12. playful or imaginative

law, sic, him

Word Bank

alternate	mishandle
barricade	paramount
blueprint	pneumonia
insurance	recipient
inventory	reluctant
machinery	whimsical

What's the best way to clean the instruments in the marching band?

To find out, write each circled letter on its matching numbered line or lines.

With a __ __ __ __ __ __
6 1 7 2 9

"__ __ __ __ __ __ __ __ __ __ __ __ __ "
8 11 3 4 10 4 12 8 5

!

Bonus: Rearrange the letters of *tea*, *bit*, and *rut* to spell a nine-letter word that means a quality belonging to a person or thing.

Shop Talk

In each statement, look for misused or misspelled words and punctuation errors. Then use editing marks to correct each mistake you find.

Editing Mark	Symbol
Insert.	∧
Delete.	℺
Add quotation mark.	∨∨
Add apostrophe.	∨
Add comma.	∧
Add period.	⊙

1 Ellen asked Luis if he was reddy to go shoping with her.

2 Its to early. We just went yesterday groaned Luis.

5 Excelent I wonder if Lily can come to, said Ellen.

4 I'll go becase there getting a new game today said Luis.

3 Ellen said I promise well go to the electronics store.

6 If your calling Lily said Luis then Im calling Seth.

7 Lily said They have to check with they're mom but they can probably come with us.

8 Wen are we leaveing asked Seth?

11 Lily told me there not aloud to go too the mall two days inn a row.

10 I better hurry up and get ready then Luis siad.

9 Ellen said I think we shoud try to get their by 11:00.

12 Rats! said Seth Oh well, lets go shopping anyway.

13 Ill ask Mom if she can drive us Ellen said.

14 The mall's just too blocks away so lets walk Seth said.

BONUS: Rewrite sentences 1 and 11 so they are direct quotes.

©The Mailbox® • TEC44067 • June/July 2013 • Key p. 306 • (L.4.1, 2; L.5.1, 2)

Name _____

Date _____

Pick and Practice!

VERBS!

Pick _____ activities to do.

When you finish an activity, shade its number.

1 Think about your favorite thing to do outside of school. Write five action verbs related to this activity, writing each verb on a separate index card. Next, illustrate each verb. Then write four or more tenses of each verb.

explore
explored, was exploring, am exploring, will be exploring, will explore, had explored, have explored, will have explored

2 Cut out an article from a newspaper or magazine about a recent event. Use three different-colored highlighters to mark the verbs and verb phrases in the article that show past, present, and future tenses.

3 List ten words that can be used as either a noun or a verb, such as *watch* or *import*. For each word, draw a picture that shows both its noun and verb forms.

4 Each of the verbs shown has an irregular past tense form. Make a two-column chart to show the verbs and their irregular past tense forms. Find and add five more verbs that have irregular past tense forms.

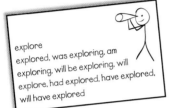

begin	rise
bring	shake
do	swim
drink	tear
Fly	weave

Present Tense Form	Irregular Past Tense Form

5 A *portmanteau* is a word that blends two or more words. For example, *squirm + wiggle = squiggle* and *smack + mash = smash*. Invent eight of your own action-word portmanteaus. Write an equation to show how you made each one.

squirm + wiggle = squiggle

6 For each of the verbs listed, write three sentences, using the verb in each of the progressive tenses.

Example: run
I was running.
I am running.
I will be running.

talk   paint
hike   gather

7 Cut out 20 or more verbs from old magazines. Arrange the verbs so that when you read them, they have a poetic rhythm. Then glue them in that order to a page, creating a poem, and add a title.

8 Create a poster that will help classmates know when to use the helping verbs *can*, *may*, and *must*.

CAN
MAY
MUST

9 For each of the verbs listed, write three sentences, using the verb in each of the perfect tenses.

Example: speak
I had spoken.
I have spoken.
I will have spoken.

dig   hide
catch   know

Independent practice grid: Program the student directions on a copy of this page with the number of activities to be completed. Then copy the page for each student.

Name _____

Date _____

Pick and Practice!

COMMAS!

Pick _____ activities to do.
When you finish an activity, color its number.

1 For each prompt, write a sentence that includes the date. Use a calendar to help.

A. yesterday's date
B. your birthday's date three years ago
C. the date of Independence Day in five years
D. your birthday's date next year
E. the date two weeks from today

2 Write five compound sentences. Each compound sentence should include two simple sentences that have been combined using a comma and a conjunction (*and*, *or*, or *but*).

> It would be a perfect day to go skiing. It hasn't started snowing yet.
>
> It would be a perfect day to go skiing, but it hasn't started snowing yet.

3 Copy each sentence starter. Add three items to complete each sentence.

A. My favorite places to visit are…
B. On the weekends, I like to…
C. At the grocery store, we shop for…
D. My favorite things to eat are…

4 Finish this conversation between a bird and a tree. Write the dialogue, using commas and quotation marks to set apart the bird's and the tree's words.

"Hey there," the bird chirps. "Would you mind if I rested on your branches for a while?"

5 Create a poster that will help classmates remember when to use commas.

6 Rewrite each sentence, adding a person's name. Use a comma or commas to set off the person's name.

- Would you please take out the trash?
- It's your turn to set the table.
- I need your help in the kitchen.
- Will you please mop the floor?
- Don't leave your bag on the chair.

> Nancy, will you please mop the floor?

7 Write a different sentence using each interjection. Separate the interjection from the rest of the sentence with a comma.

ouch   **yikes**

awesome   **hooray**

oh well   **yippee**

8 Write five sentences about five adults in your school. Include an **appositive** about each one. Use commas to set off each appositive.

> Ms. Jones, **the school nurse,** checked my temperature before she called my mother.

9 Find ten famous places in the United States. Write a sentence about each place that includes the city and state where it's located.

> You can visit the Wright Brothers National Memorial in Kitty Hawk, North Carolina.

©The Mailbox® • TEC44064 • Dec./Jan. 2012–13 (L.4.2b–c, L.5.2b–c)

Independent practice grid: Program the student directions on a copy of this page with the number of activities to be completed. Then copy the page for each student.

Comprehension-Building Prompts to Use With ANY Book

Prompts for nonfiction:

Create a highway billboard that makes others want to read this book. Include detailed facts from the text.

Would you recommend this book to your teacher? Why or why not?

Do you think the author is an expert on this topic? Why or why not? How could you find out?

Which five facts from today's reading would be the most interesting to a racecar driver?

How could this book be changed to make its information clearer? Explain.

Sometimes there are so many facts in nonfiction text it gets hard to read. Rate this text on a scale of 1 (hard to read) to 5 (easy to read). Explain your rating.
1 2 3 4 5

Choose one sentence from the text that shows the best example of the author's writing style. Explain your choice.

Based on this book, would you like to meet the author? Why or why not?

Prompts for fiction:

How is this story like the last story you read?

Think about the writer's style. What do you like about the way he or she writes?

Which character needs to be cheered on? What would you say to cheer him or her on?

I would like to tell the author...

On New Year's Day, people think about habits they want to change. If you could make a change in the story, what would you change? Explain!

Pretend you are the main character. Do you like the way you are portrayed in the story? Why or why not?

How would you describe the conflict in this story? Explain.

If you were the main character, how would your life be different? Explain.

©The Mailbox® • TEC44064 • Dec./Jan. 2012–13 • (W.4.10, W.5.10)

How to Use Display the prompts after each independent reading session. Then have each child choose a prompt and write a thoughtful response.

Comprehension-Building Prompts to Use With ANY Book

Prompts for Nonfiction

Complete the sentence. This text would be easier to read if...

Imagine you will make your reading from today into a one-minute video. What will you show?

How do you know this is not fiction? Use features from the text to support your answer.

Make a table of contents that lists the most important facts you have read so far.

For whom do you think the author wrote this book? Why did the author write the book for these readers?

Study the book's graphic aids, such as diagrams, sketches, maps, charts, or timelines. Which ones have been the most helpful so far in helping you understand what you read? How do they help you?

What are three ways this book is different from the last nonfiction, or informational, book you read?

1.2.3

Which sentence from your reading explains the main idea? Explain your choice.

Prompts for Fiction

If you went on a field trip to this story's setting, how would you get there? Describe it.

Describe something a character from this story does that is a lot like something you do.

If the author wanted to change one thing about this story, what should he or she change? Why?

Which statement do you think would most apply to this story? Explain.
- Growing up is hard to do.
- You should always be nice to others.
- Best friends last forever.
- Good triumphs over evil.

Choose a story event that seems very real. Describe it. Why does it seem so real?

Name three or more important events that happened before this story began.

Describe the story's setting. Would the main problem be the same in a different setting? Why?

What do you think would be the main character's favorite thing to do after school? Why?

©The Mailbox® • TEC44065 • Feb./Mar. 2013 • (W.4.10, W.5.10)

How to Use Display the prompts after each independent reading session. Then have each child choose a prompt and write a thoughtful response.

BRAIN BOOSTERS

Brain Booster 1

Start with *foot*. Change one letter at a time to form a new word without rearranging the letters until you spell *ball*. Repeat with *fall* until you spell *back*.

Foot   Fall

_ _ _ _   _ _ _ _

_ _ _ _   _ _ _ _ back

_ _ _ _ ball

TEC44062

Brain Booster 2

List five homonym pairs in which one of the words begins with *kn*.

Example: **kn**ow, no

TEC44062

Brain Booster 3

Find a hink-pink, or a pair of rhyming words, that matches each description.

Example: A quick explosion is a *fast blast*.

A. cart for hauling fire-breathing monsters

B. greatest visitor

C. footwear adhesive

D. goofy flower

E. intelligent body organ

TEC44062

Brain Booster 4

The answer is *cucumber* and *zucchini*. Write five questions that would have this answer.

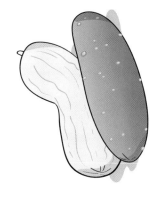

TEC44062

Brain Booster 5

What mystery word completes the sentence below? It has nine letters and three syllables. Words that can be used in its place are *crowd*, *swarm*, and *mass*.

A _____ of stars winked at us from the night sky.

TEC44062

Brain Booster 6

Change one letter in each word to complete a familiar phrase.
Example: Lime well sell. → Time will tell.

A. Sigh hive!

B. Met sore pang far tour back.

C. Is food am dew!

D. Teach fur thy stirs!

TEC44062

Brain Booster 7

Find the names of at least eight birds in the puzzle. Connect the letters up, down, left, right, or diagonally to make a word. Use each letter only once in each word. However, a letter may be used more than once to make other words.

O	D	E	S	R	I
N	V	A	O	B	N
R	E	U	G	O	W
W	A	L	C	K	A
O	L	F	D	U	H

owl

TEC44062

Brain Booster 8

Make five or more other words by adding a letter or letters to the end of this word. How many can you make?

tick

TEC44062

Brain Booster 1

It's time to vote! Write the last name of a United States president that begins with each letter in the words *vote*. Then write a slogan telling people why they should vote.

★ VOTE! ★

TEC44063

Brain Booster 2

List three or more words that tell what each term is. Then list three different words that tell what it is not.

A. plateau

B. resource

C. wetland

D. landform

TEC44063

Brain Booster 3

Find ten or more four-letter words that begin with *a* in the puzzle.

A	D	A	O	O	A	Y
O	T	U	A	S	B	M
A	Y	W	L	R	L	R
Q	C	A	L	I	E	A
U	M	R	Y	A	W	A
A	X	L	E	U	A	R

TEC44063

Brain Booster 4

Spell the names of four kinds of fruit by replacing one letter in each word and then rearranging the letters.

Example: MAPLE, APPLE

A. PATCH

B. PAGES

C. MICE

D. GROANS

E. TAPIOCA

TEC44063

Brain Booster 5

Suppose a pumpkin had a say about whether it became a jack-o'-lantern or a pumpkin pie. Write a dialogue between the pumpkin and the farmer who planted it.

TEC44063

Brain Booster 6

What do the words in each pair have in common? Explain.

A. fuchsia, magenta

B. kale, chard

C. chinook, sirocco

D. duvet, comforter

E. skink, anole

TEC44063

Brain Booster 7

For each phrase below, write an antonym for the adjective and a synonym for the noun that rhymes with the new adjective.

Example: *a thin feline* becomes *a fat cat.*

A. unsuccessful twirling

B. first eruption

C. warm fungus

D. dry dog

E. shallow nap

TEC44063

Brain Booster 8

Unscramble the letters to spell five common road signs.

eon ywa

on isnpsga enzo

od tno treen

od otn spsa

apss twhi erca

TEC44063

©The Mailbox® • TEC44063 • Oct./Nov. 2012 • Key p. 307

LANGUAGE ARTS

Brain Booster 1

Change one letter in each word to spell three words that are related.

A. band, aim, peg

B. poke, track, middle

C. soda, chain, beg

TEC44064

Brain Booster 2

Write four-word sentences to complete this chart.

A. Band			
B.	band		
C.		band	
D.			band.

TEC44064

Brain Booster 3

What happened before and after this event?

The tree crashed to the ground, and ornaments clattered across the floor.

TEC44064

Brain Booster 4

Write a synonym for *part* to complete each word. Hint: Five words are nouns. Four words are verbs. One word is an adverb.

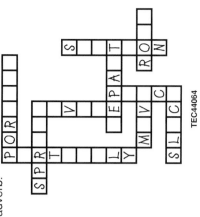

TEC44064

Brain Booster 5

Can you make more three-letter words using the letters in *Thursday* or the letters in *Friday*?

THURSDAY

FRIDAY

TEC44064

Brain Booster 6

The answer is *a penguin*. What are all the questions you can think of that could have this answer?

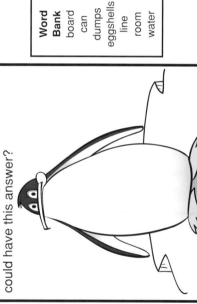

TEC44064

Brain Booster 7

Write a different noun from the word bank to complete each idiom.

A. elephant in the ___

B. walking on ___

C. fish out of ___

D. opened up a ___ of worms

E. down in the ___

F. back to the drawing ___

G. hook, ___, and sinker

Word Bank
board
can
dumps
eggshells
line
room
water

TEC44064

Brain Booster 8

Rewrite each sentence so it makes sense. Use antonyms for the adjectives that are incorrect.

A. Mr. Punny's jokes are so sensible, you have to laugh.

B. The crowd was silent; hearing the speaker was nearly possible.

C. I was so hungry; I was too active to watch the game.

D. Because there were countless options, it was easy to choose.

TEC44064

Brain Booster 1

Write the familiar phrase, saying, or word represented by each arrangement of letters and/or symbols.

1. ban ana

2. wear
   ―――
   long

3. | M | E |
   |---|---|
   | A | L |

4. LEAST

5. sign . . . .

TEC44065

Brain Booster 2

What two missing letters complete each word?

m __ ll

t __ le

h __ ll

t __ r

TEC44065

Brain Booster 3

Write the geometric term that each item illustrates. The first letter of the word is given.

1. 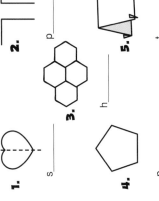 s ___

2. ___

3. h ___

4. p ___

5. v ___
   t ___   p ___

TEC44065

Brain Booster 4

For each set of words, tell what they have in common.

1. puree, whisk, sauté

2. smorgasbord, jambalaya, medley

3. braising, searing, poaching

4. sourdough, pumpernickel, whole wheat

5. baked Alaska, chocolate mousse, cheesecake

TEC44065

Brain Booster 5

Find two words in each boldfaced word.

A. **redouble**—color words

B. **chapter**—fruit

C. **spinach**—countries

D. **flattery**—US presidents' last names

E. **examinations**—US states

TEC44065

Brain Booster 6

Write the state capitals that share names with famous people.

1. Abraham _____, NE

2. Sir Walter _____, NC

3. Christopher _____, OH

4. James _____, WI

5. Andrew _____, MS

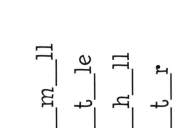

TEC44065

Brain Booster 7

Write the name of an eating utensil to complete each word below.

1. _____ bill   2. pitch _____

3. _____ lift   4. pocket _____

5. jack _____   6. _____ feed

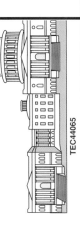

TEC44065

Brain Booster 8

Add together both the row number and column number to find the value of each letter. Some of the letters have equal values. Decode the winter words.

	1	2	3	4	5
6	E	R	A	T	N
7	Y	O	L	M	Z
8	C	D	I	W	L
9	S	F	K	B	H

1. I C E - S K A T E
   11 9 7   10 12 11 9 10 7

2. __ W __ __ __ __ __
   10 11 9 12 11 9 11

3. __ O __ __ __
   11 8 9 10 10

4. __ I __ __ __ __ __
   13 10 11 12 9 8 10

5. __ I __ __ __
   11 10 7 11 10

TEC44065

How to Use Display this page or give each student a copy of the page (or one card at a time) to work on during free time.

BRAIN BOOSTERS

LANGUAGE ARTS

Brain Booster 1

Find the name of a famous American in each phrase. To find the name, replace each word or syllable with a rhyming name.

Example: *con madams* becomes *John Adams.*

A. commas heifer ton (president)

B. shark lane (author)

C. tarry human (president)

D. spartan truth-or swing (civil rights leader)

E. pal soar (vice president)

TEC44066

Brain Booster 2

Which words mean something important and which mean something is unimportant?

A. **urgent**

B. **paramount**

C. **minor**

D. **trivial**

E. **frivolous**

F. **critical**

TEC44066

Brain Booster 3

Use the letters in each bold word to make other words as guided.

Hint: The number or numbers in parentheses tell how many letters each new word has.

multiplication
two flowers (5, 5)

boisterous
state capital (5)

celebrated
two pieces of furniture (3, 5)

bulletin
three action verbs (4, 4, 3, 3, 3)

TEC44066

Brain Booster 4

Marla dropped these cards. Help her sort them into two groups—math and reading.

intersect	moral
selection	theme
probability	range
surface	metaphor
equation	summarize
integer	simile

TEC44066

Brain Booster 5

Write a homophone for each word.

through
allowed
ate
chili
raise
whole
wood
sore
hall
great

TEC44066

Brain Booster 6

Remove one letter from each word. Then rearrange the remaining letters to form a new word. Each set of new words belongs to the same category. The first category is color words. What is the second category?

ruble →
dear →
gnat → blue

horse →
shreds →
stove →

TEC44066

Brain Booster 7

What kind of day would you have had if you had a *red-letter day?*

Why would you want to *cut through the red tape?*

What kind of mood would you be in if you were *seeing red?*

What is something worth if it's *not worth a red cent?*

TEC44066

Brain Booster 8

Write the word for each clue.

e		a		r			t			h	

to use again
garbage
Recycling paper saves these.
Cans made from this are 100% recyclable.
soil formed from organic plant or animal matter

TEC44066

©The Mailbox® • TEC44066 • April/May 2013 • Key p. 307

How to Use Display this page or give each student a copy of the page (or one card at a time) to work on during free time.

BRAIN BOOSTERS

Brain Booster 1

Complete each book's title. Then explain how the words you added are related.

The Cat _____ the Hat

The Miraculous Journey _____ Edward Tulane

A Wrinkle _____ Time

Hop _____ Pop

_____ the Sidewalk Ends

Cloudy _____ a Chance _____ Meatballs

_____ the Mixed-Up Files _____ Mrs. Basil E. Frankweiler

TEC44067

Brain Booster 2

Use the letters shown to write six rhyming words. (Hint: Four of the words are four-letter words. Two of the words are five-letter words.)

a   c   e   h

i   n   r   s

cane

TEC44067

Brain Booster 3

Write the familiar saying that is represented in each item.

another one thing
It's just one thing after another.

A.
E
L
K
C
U
B

B.
you just me

C.
reading

D.
p   a   y

TEC44067

Brain Booster 4

Tell whether the words in each pair are synonyms or antonyms.

A. sure—dubious
B. mistakes—blunders
C. native—indigenous
D. docile—unruly
E. wealth—affluence
F. frugal—thrifty
G. rash—reckless
H. short—extensive

TEC44067

Brain Booster 5

For each clue, write a word that, when spelled in reverse, makes a new word. Then write the new word and a clue to its meaning.

to cease: stop, pots (pans)

A. makes by looping yarn with special needles
B. fruit, pie, and cakes
C. outdoor game played on a course
D. hearty meat and vegetable dish

TEC44067

Brain Booster 6

Finish spelling the names of these important rivers.

R _ _ _ _ (Europe's most important inland waterway)

_ I _ _ (longest river in the world)

V _ _ _ _ (longest river in Europe)

_ _ _ _ _ E _ _ _ _ (longest river in Canada)

_ _ _ R _ (longest river in the United States)

_ _ _ _ _ S (longest waterway within England)

TEC44067

Brain Booster 7

Answer. Use diagrams and words to explain your answers.

Would you rather be **bamboozled** or told you are **astute**? Why?

If you were told you are **susceptible** to being **hoodwinked**, would this be a compliment? Why or why not?

Would you rather have a **lackadaisical** worker in your group or one who is **diligent**? Why?

Which would you rather call home: an **edifice** or a **vestibule**? Explain.

TEC44067

Brain Booster 8

Design a method for peeling a banana. There's only one rule: your hands cannot touch the banana peel. Write about and illustrate your method.

TEC44067

WAKE-UP CALL

Word choice

For each general noun, list three specific nouns. For each common verb, list three vivid verbs. Then use at least 12 of your specific nouns and vivid verbs in a story about a time you slept late and had to scramble to get ready for school.

book

eat

student

clothes

go

food

make

look

TEC44062 (W.4.3, W.5.3)

Building morphology skills

Prefixes	Word Roots	Suffixes
in-	rupt (to break)	-able, -ible
pre-	scrib, script (to write)	-or, -ar, -er
dis-	cred (to believe, to trust)	-ly
con-	ject (throw)	-ful
re-	port (to carry)	-tion
inter-	struct (to build)	-less

TEC44063 (L.4.4, L.5.4)

TACKLING WORD ANALYSIS

Use the prefixes, word roots, and suffixes shown to make 15 or more words. Then use the word parts' meanings to tell what each word means.

TIME FOR A TUNE-UP

Greek and Latin roots

Copy each set of words and underline the Greek or Latin root the words have in common. Next, look up each word in a dictionary. Then use your own words to explain how the word's root is part of its definition.

chronological • chronic • synchronize • chronicle

hydrant • dehydrated • hydraulics • hydroplane

dictator • contradict • dictate • predict

spectator • inspection • prospect • spectacular

TEC44062 (L.4.4b, L.5.4b)

A BURST OF COLOR

Using synonyms and antonyms to understand words

For the different-colored word in each sentence, list two synonyms and one antonym.

1. Anita was sure she was too **mature** to have a piñata at her party.
2. However, this piñata was **spectacular**.
3. It was the most **vibrant** one she had ever seen.
4. Anita said it was a shame to **fracture** the piñata; she wanted to save it.
5. Anita's uncle swung the piñata, **enticing** her to take up the bat and swing it.
6. After **observing** several passes of the piñata, Anita gave in.
7. Anita's mom spun her around under the **shifting** piñata.
8. Then Anita started swinging **uncontrollably**, missing the piñata.
9. Anita's uncle swung the piñata back and forth so **rapidly** no one could hit it.
10. Then, on Anita's second turn, she took a **colossal** backswing, outsmarted her uncle, and connected with the piñata.

TEC44063 (L.4.5c, L.5.5c)

Language Arts Activity Cards

Cut out a copy of the cards to use as center or free-time activities.

ON TRACK

Editing, revising sentences

Find six incomplete sentences. Then rewrite the paragraph, making sure each sentence is complete.

Snowshoeing is one of our favorite winter activities. At least, my dad's favorite activity! He likes to snowshoe across golf courses. Walking trails and state parks too. This year we took a trail that was 12 miles long. Snowshoe 12 miles? I wasn't thrilled. The trail was beautiful though. It followed an icy stream through the woods. Stopping often to look, rest, and have snacks. I was actually having a pretty good time. We'd gone about two miles when my dad saw tracks that made him freeze. Not a bear's tracks or a mountain lion's. The tracks of a cross-country skier. For some reason, Dad hates sharing a trail with cross-country skiers. So instead of slogging along 12 miles. We turned around, headed home, and had a lovely four-mile hike!

TEC44064 (L.4.1f)

Framing the Story

Narrative writing

Choose a story beginning and ending and then brainstorm the problem, its solution, and details that will make the story believable. Write the story.

Rhonda strapped on her helmet, buckled her seatbelt, settled into her seat, and turned the key to start the racecar's roaring engine.

Ronnie shook his head and chuckled; that was a first—fixing a car, a limousine no less, that belonged to someone that important.

Grandpa repeated himself, "Now that was a great trip!"

Rhonda had never driven a racecar before, but she loved everything about racing.

As a mechanic, Ronnie was used to working on all sorts of cars for all sorts of customers.

Grandpa Bill invited his favorite grandchild to ride to Alaska with him.

TEC44067 (W.4.3, W.5.3)

ON THE PLUS SIDE

Vocabulary, connotation

Copy each word pair. Circle the word in each pair that seems positive and underline the word that seems negative. Then write four more word pairs that show positive and negative connotations.

speedy   hasty

1. scent, odor
2. skinny, slim
3. curious, nosy
4. cheap, inexpensive
5. young, childish
6. easygoing, lazy
7. sloppy, casual
8. challenging, difficult
9. debate, argue
10. impatient, eager

TEC44064

By George!

Compound sentences

Choose two sentences. Then combine them using a comma and a coordinating conjunction to write a compound sentence. Write six sentences in all.

- Margaret plants roses in her garden.
- She plants pansies and snapdragons.
- Frederick may ride his pony this afternoon.
- He may go fishing.
- Phillip loves to play cricket.
- He watches every cricket match he can.
- Gertrude got up at 4:00 AM.
- She wanted to watch the sunrise.
- Elizabeth missed her friends.
- She invited them to a tea party.
- For dinner, Reggie wants fish and chips.
- Margaret prefers vegetable soup.

Conjunctions
and   but
for   or
nor   so
       yet

TEC44067 (L.4.2c)

A Messy Room!

Using prepositional phrases

Write the letter(s) of the prepositional phrase that best completes each sentence.

1. Mom walked _____ and saw my messy bedroom.
2. There were clothes _____ and dishes _____.
3. _____, I heard her scream.
4. "Shoes go _____!" Mom shouted.
5. She found an overdue library book _____.
6. I started the cleanup by grabbing the socks hanging _____.
7. _____, Mom returned to my room.
8. I made a promise to take my dirty dishes _____ and keep my room neat.

A. to the kitchen
B. down the hall
C. on the floor
D. under the bed
E. After two hours
F. in the closet
G. From the basement
H. behind my pillow
I. over the lamp shade

TEC44065 (L.4.1e)

From the Heart

Capitalization and punctuation

Rewrite each sentence. Add capital letters and the correct punctuation where needed.

1. madison and alex wanted to help the animals at the local shelter
2. the students would raise money by having a yard sale
3. thank you very much madison told each person who bought an item
4. when one man heard what the students were doing he gave them a hundred dollar bill
5. alex said the money will help the dogs cats and birds at the shelter
6. a story about the students was printed in the springfield newspaper
7. a news reporter asked why did you decide to do this project
8. we want to help the animals find good homes alex answered
9. the students picture was put on the front page of the springfield times
10. the article was titled from the heart

TEC44065 (L.4.2a, L.5.2)

FAR OUT

Synonyms

Use a thesaurus to sort these words into five groups of three related words.

extend
succession
base

decrease
enlarge
survey

sequence
assess
continuation

support
reduce
increase

measure
foundation
descend

TEC44065 (L.4.5c, L.5.5c)

Make No Mistake

Multiple meanings

Aim for the nail, not the thumb.

Identify each underlined word as a noun or a verb. Then use the underlined word in another way to write your own sentence.

1. The carpenter pounds the nail into the board with a hammer.
2. She chose yellow paint for the kitchen wall.
3. My sister dresses our cat in doll clothing.
4. Each time I pet my cat, it purrs.
5. My favorite singer sang her number-one hit at the concert.
6. We will light the candles on the birthday cake.
7. The train whistle blew loudly for all the passengers to hear.
8. The queen's diamond collection was on display at the art museum.
9. Our dog guards the backyard from any intruders.
10. He sat in the hotel lounge and read the newspaper.

TEC44065 (L.4.4, L.5.4)

WORDS ON THE MENU

Choose an activity and follow the directions using your vocabulary list.

A The Long and the "Sort" of It

1. Fold a sheet of paper into fourths and label each section as shown.
2. Say each vocabulary word to yourself and decide how many syllables it has.
3. Write the word in the matching section on your paper.
4. Use a dictionary to check your syllable counts.
5. Repeat for each word on your list.

One or Two Syllables	Three Syllables
Four Syllables	Five or More Syllables

B At the Root

1. Write your vocabulary words, skipping a line between each one.
2. Draw a star over every prefix, draw a dot over every suffix, and circle every root or base word.
3. Using the word parts, tell what you think each word means. If there aren't any word parts, take a guess at the word's meaning.
4. Check each word's meaning in a dictionary.

*in·spec·tor

C Puzzled

1. Using a dictionary and/or a thesaurus, write a clue for each word on separate strips of paper.
2. Create a word search that includes all the vocabulary words.
3. Scramble the clues. Then number them and write them next to your puzzle.
4. Challenge a classmate to solve your puzzle.

D Outside the Box

1. Draw a two-inch square and make it into a 3-D cube. Write a vocabulary word below the cube.
2. Write the word's main definition on one of the cube's faces.
3. On another of the cube's faces, draw a picture that shows what the word means or use the word in a sentence.
4. On the third face, show the word's pronunciation.
5. Repeat for each word on your list.

shrut·n·īz
to study something very closely

E "Skim-Deep"

1. Skim the reading selection from which the vocabulary words came.
2. When you find a word, list the page and copy the sentence containing the word. Use quotation marks to show that you are quoting the textbook.
3. Circle the vocabulary word or words in the sentence. If you find a word more than one time, circle it every time you find it.
4. Continue until you have found every word from the list at least once.

F On the Bubble

1. Make a bubble map like the one shown.
2. Write a vocabulary word in the center bubble.
3. In each of the other bubbles, write a synonym of the word. If there aren't enough synonyms, write a word or words that will help you remember what the vocabulary word means.
4. Repeat for each word on your list.

©The Mailbox® · TEC44062 · Aug./Sept. 2012 · (RF.4.3, L.4.4c, L.4.4c, L.4.5c, L.4.4b, L.5.5b, L.5.4c, L.5.5c)

How to Use Post the menu of activities to use as center or free-time activities.

AN ADJECTIVE Safari

Post the chart below and teach students how to **order adjectives** with any of these ferociously fun activities! (L.4.1d)

IN A SNAP!
Ordering adjectives within a sentence

ADJECTIVE ORDER

1 articles (a, an, the)
2 opinions (silly, cute, wonderful)
3 size (tall, taller, widest, long, deep)
4 shape (round, triangular, irregular)
5 age (old, teenage, young)
6 color (blue, yellow, reddish brown)
7 origin (American, Canadian, Latin)
8 material (plastic, paper, metal)
9 noun being described

Struggling with teaching students how to arrange adjectives? Try this! Sit in a circle with the class and practice the following sequence:

Slap, slap (on knee).
Clap, clap.
Snap, snap (with fingers).
Clap, clap.

Next, name a noun and have the class start the sequence. At the last clap, turn to the child on your left and challenge her to add an adjective following the order to modify the noun. Then lead students to clap again; turn to the next student; and have him repeat the noun phrase, adding another adjective and following the order. If students name six adjectives for the noun, celebrate with several rounds of the clapping sequence and then name a new noun. If a student fails to come up with an adjective, announce a new noun, and have the next child start the order over. Before long, ordering adjectives will be second nature!

> An ugly, long, bumpy, old, green pickle!

SAVAGELY SILLY
Ordering adjectives

For this idea, have each student write a short adventure story. Before the child edits his story, have him add three to five adjective blanks in front of five nouns in the story. Then have him label each blank with the type of adjective he'd use to describe the noun, making sure the order matches the chart. Next, have each student tell a partner the number and type of adjectives needed to complete his story. Each partner makes a list. Then students take turns reading their stories out loud, filling in the blanks with adjectives from their partners' lists. Students will roar with laughter!

I picked the wacky, little, orange sock.
The object is yucky, fat and round.

"SOCK" IT TO ME
Ordering adjectives

To set up this hands-on center, collect five or more clean socks of different colors, patterns, and sizes. Put a different object inside each sock and stock the center with index cards. At the center, a student chooses a sock and describes it, following the order on the chart, on an index card. Then she reaches into the sock, feels the object and writes a sentence describing it, using adjectives, in order. When she's finished, she flips her card and jots a guess about what the object is. As time allows, the child repeats with other socks. After all students rotate through the center, reveal each sock's contents!

Leigh Newsom, Cedar Road Elementary
Chesapeake, VA

Poetry—Getting to the Core

Standards-based ideas for reading and understanding poems!

So the Story Goes

Summarizing poetry (RL.4.2)

Reading narrative poems aloud to students is a great way to interest them in a style of poetry with which they aren't familiar. The following list includes poems that tell great stories, can be found quickly on the Internet, and can be read aloud in one sitting. After reading a poem, lead each student to write a paragraph that summarizes the poem's story.

 tip After you read a narrative poem, put a copy of it in your class library or post several narrative poems where students line up. You might be surprised by how many kids find this narrative form fascinating!

Narrative Poems

"Adventures of Isabel" by Ogden Nash
"Casey at the Bat" by Ernest Thayer
"Casey's Revenge" by James Wilson
"Casey—Twenty Years Later" by Anonymous
"The Duel" by Eugene Field
"An Elegy on the Death of a Mad Dog" by Oliver Goldsmith
"Paul Revere's Ride" by Henry Wadsworth Longfellow
"The Raven" by Edgar Allen Poe
"A Visit From St. Nicholas" by Clement Clarke Moore

> Water on the beach,
> Washing over grains of sand,
> Flowing back to sea.

Loud and Clear

Reading poetry orally (RF.4.4b, RF.5.4b)

The brief format of haiku is the perfect platform for building poetry-reading skills. Tell students that the manner in which a haiku is recited helps communicate its mood. Have each pair of students read a haiku, discuss its mood, and create a mini poster that illustrates the haiku. Next, have each student, in turn, practice reciting the haiku to his partner. Then have each duo share its poster and recite its haiku in unison.

Take Note!

Structural elements of poems (RL.4.5)

Make identifying poetic elements less overwhelming by having each student bring in a copy of the lyrics of her favorite song, emphasizing that it must be appropriate for school. After providing your approval, have each small group of students use its lyrics to compare and discuss the verses, rhyme schemes, and meter. Students will quickly see that poetry has been part of their lives all along and that it isn't so difficult to understand!

More Than the Once-Over

Theme of a poem (RL.4.2, RL.5.2)

To help students find a poem's theme, encourage them to read and reread! First, have each child draw a chart labeled like the one shown. Then have the student read a poem and describe its topic. Next, have the child read the poem a second time and describe the poem's elements. Then have him read the poem a third time and explain what the poem means. Finally, have each student read his poem again before using his notes and ideas to describe the poem's theme.

"Casey at the Bat"		
First Reading What It's About	Second Reading Poetic Elements	Third Reading What It Means

7 SUPER TIPS

for using Grade-Level Texts with Students on Different Levels

by LaVone Novotny, Liberty Elementary, Caledonia, OH

1 To help students with the vocabulary in class reading assignments, post each selection's important vocabulary. Then have each child record the terms along the margin of her paper. Have the student put a check next to a term each time she hears or reads it. Have the child draw a star next to the word when she figures out its meaning or draw a question mark next to it at the end of the reading if she's still not sure what it means. With a quick peek at students' notes, you can see whether the vocabulary is holding them back.

2 Make buddy reading an organized task! Pair each struggling reader with a proficient one and give the duo a specific number of pages to read. Next, explain the assignment's purpose, such as answering comprehension questions, completing an activity, or preparing for a discussion. Finally, establish a time limit, and let the pair get to work!

3 Prior to a class reading assignment, identify and post the text's main points. Then have each student jot the points on a sheet of paper, leaving space between each point for writing notes—such as facts, ideas, and questions about the point—while he reads.

tip →

Don't have a document camera or interactive whiteboard that makes it easy to print and copy your notes? Take a picture of them with a smartphone and email them to yourself. Then just click on the attachment and print it!

4 Read short sections from the text aloud. After each passage, guide students to name the main idea and record it on the board. Then have students look for supporting details and add them to the board. Depending on each student's needs, have the child take notes during the discussion, have her copy the notes from the board, or give the child a copy of the notes from the board to study.

5 Find volunteers to read and record the pages you will be reading in class. Struggling and disengaged students can use headphones to listen to and repeat passages as they read. Plus listening to different voices—male and female, from young adults to retirees—can motivate all your students! (Just take a couple of minutes to give each volunteer a quick lesson in pacing so his or her reading will be helpful!)

6 Set aside 15–20 minutes at the end of each class period for work on independent projects and then meet with small groups of students for additional help, mini lessons, or quick formative assessments.

7 Supplement grade-level textbooks with lower-level, engaging books on the same topic. Choose books that include glossaries and full-color illustrations and place the supplementary books at a center so they're available for all students. If desired, make a quick scavenger hunt for facts in the books to engage everyone in your class and help your struggling readers glean concepts they may be missing in the grade-level text.

PICTURE BOOKS

It Takes All Sorts
**Author's purpose, organization, and style
(RL.4.10, RL.5.10, RI.4.10, RI.5.10)**

Stock a center with a variety of fiction and information picture books. At the center, have each student sort the books according to their authors' purposes. Next, have the child make a chart like the one shown and list each book's title in the appropriate column. Then guide the student to study each book and record notes about the book's organization and author's style. Once a small group of students has rotated through the center, discuss with the group its notes and observations, leading students to draw conclusions about an author's purpose and how it affects her techniques. **Patricia Twohey, Smithfield, RI, and Michele Anszelowicz, Forest Lake Elementary, Wantagh, NY**

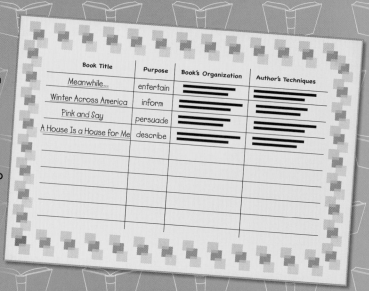

Book Title	Purpose	Book's Organization	Author's Techniques
Meanwhile...	entertain		
Winter Across America	inform		
Pink and Say	persuade		
A House Is a House for Me	describe		

Make 'em Personal
Problem solving

Read *Math Curse* by Jon Scieszka aloud to students. Then challenge each child to write a math adventure that includes ten to 15 problems based on his own life. List skills you expect students to include in their problems; then remind them to make their problems as interesting as those in the book. Once a child finishes writing his problems, have him put them together in a book, complete with illustrations and an answer key in the back. Then keep students' books on display and challenge students to solve each others' problems and check their work. **Heather Finn, Grant Line Elementary, New Albany, IN**

I was born on August 26, 2000. I'm 12 years old now; when will I be as old as my dad?
Suddenly it's a problem.
- In what year will I be 35?
- What will I be doing?
- Where will I be?

A Meaningful Search
**Understanding figurative language
(L.4.5, L.5.5)**

To build students' word skills, collect a supply of picture books. Then give each child a copy of the figurative language recording sheet from page 69. Challenge the student to find an example of each type of figurative language in the picture books. When a child finds an example, she figures out what it means and records it as guided on the page.

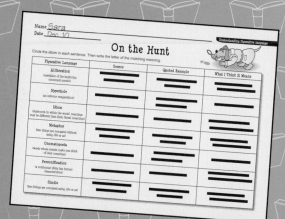

Name _____

Date _____

On the Hunt

Figurative Language	Source	Quoted Example	What I Think It Means
Alliteration (repetition of the beginning consonant sounds)			
Hyperbole (an extreme exaggeration)			
Idiom (statement in which the words' meanings may be different than their literal meanings)			
Metaphor (two things are compared without using *like* or *as*)			
Onomatopoeia (words whose sounds make you think of their meanings)			
Personification (a nonhuman thing has human characteristics)			
Simile (two things are compared using *like* or *as*)			

©The Mailbox® · TEC44064 · Dec./Jan. 2012–13 · (L.4.5, L.5.5)

Note to the teacher: Use with "A Meaningful Search" on page 68.

Gotta Read!

4 Simple Ways to Encourage Independent Reading

1 With this simple tip, your students will literally rip into reading! Use painter's tape to mark off a section of a classroom wall. Add the title "Rip Into Reading" within the space. Each time a student reads a book independently, he meets briefly with you to discuss the book's topic or plot. Then he records the title, the author, the genre, and his name on a piece of paper from your scrap box. After ripping around the edges of the paper, the student tapes it onto the wall. When the entire section is wallpapered with the evidence of your students' reading, reward the class with a special treat or activity.

The Best Book of Sharks by Claire Llewellyn
Nonfiction
Nia

The Upstairs Room by Johanna Reiss
Historical Fiction
Miles

2 Every month, help each student set an independent reading goal in terms of the number of pages read. When a student finishes a book, he writes the number of pages read on a slip of paper and has a parent sign it. Once he has met his monthly goal, any additional pages read count as "prize points" (one point per page). Keep a class tally of prize points earned on a chart displayed near the class bookshelves. If the entire class reaches 1,000 points (or another total of your choice), reward students with a special activity or treat.

3 Whenever a student shows extra effort or improvement in her independent reading, place a sticky note on her desktop. Label the note with a point value from +1 to +4. Then allow the student to place the note on any quiz or test and add these points to her score.

4 Let America's national pastime encourage reading with this home run of an idea! Near your classroom bookshelf, stack a supply of paper baseball patterns. Each time a student reads a book independently, she writes a brief summary of the book on a paper baseball. When she has turned in four baseballs, reward her with a no-homework coupon or another special privilege.

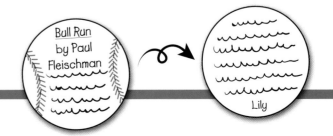

Bull Run by Paul Fleischman

Lily

KEEP 'EM READING THIS SUMMER!

Ideas for helping students keep their hard-earned reading skills fresh!

LITERARY ADVENTURES

Narrative writing (W.4.3; W.5.3)

Here's a book sure to be on your students' top ten summer reading list—it's one full of stories they write! To begin, copy and cut apart a class supply of the prompts from the top of page 72. Have students draw prompts and have those with the same prompt work together to write an adventure story response. After the students in each group write and edit their story, have them enter it in a word-processing document and create a cover illustration. Finally, combine the groups' stories and illustrations in a class anthology, add a special dedication, and make a copy for each student. Then, on the last day of school, give each child a book with a reminder that reading is an adventure!

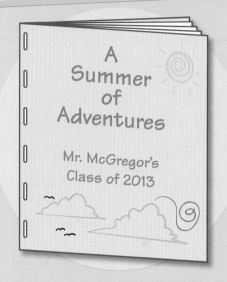

A
Summer
of
Adventures

Mr. McGregor's
Class of 2013

Places to Read
in the bathtub
sitting in or under a tree
in or under my bed
at the pool
at the lake
in a boat
in the yard
behind the couch

Things to Read
list of ingredients on food packages
pamphlets
comics in the newspaper
magazine article
newspaper headlines and then choose one article to read
letters to the editor
closed captioning text on television
directions for playing a new game
directions for putting something together

READING REMINDERS

Reading literary and informational texts (RL.4.10; RI.4.10; RL.5.10; RI.5.10)

To inspire a wide range of reading, post a copy of the poem from the bottom of page 72 and lead students to choral read it with you. Then remind students that keeping their reading skills strong this summer doesn't just mean reading a book on the couch. Next, lead students to brainstorm lists of places to read and kinds of reading material available during the summer. Follow up by having each student create a mini poster of the lists. Then have him take it home for a summerlong reading reminder.

BOOK ORDER INSPIRATION

Identifying genre (RL.4.5)

Got a pile of extra book club order forms? Use them to review genres and stimulate students' reading interests! Give each small group of students a stack of forms, a large sheet of construction paper, scissors, glue, and markers. Next, have the group divide its paper so there's a space for each genre you've studied. Then challenge the students in each group to find books on their forms that fit in each genre. When a student finds a qualifying book, she cuts out the cover illustration and book description and then glues them in the appropriate section. When students finish, post their work in the hall for a display of reading ideas from multiple genres. **Sharon Moder, North Dearborn Elementary, Guilford, IN**

Realistic Fiction	Historical Fiction	Fantasy
Informational	Biography	Poetry

You are an explorer charting an island that has never been explored. TEC44067	You find an old map that seems to lead to a buried treasure. TEC44067
You spot and track an animal everyone thought was extinct. TEC44067	You encounter a group of sneaky but harmless aliens. TEC44067
You won a free ride in a hot-air balloon, but the pilot gets sick and needs you to steer! TEC44067	You wake up to find that you are the size of an ant. TEC44067
You discover that your bike is really a time machine. TEC44067	You're at the zoo, and a squirrel monkey hops on your shoulder. TEC44067

THE BEAR AND I

The other day
I met a bear,
Up in the woods
Way up there.
He looked at me; I looked at him.
He sized me up; I sized up him.
And then I ran away from there,
But right behind me was that bear!
And so I jumped into a tree
But missed the branch—what misery!
Now don't you fret, and don't you frown!
I caught that branch on the way back down!
Then I turned around—oh glory be!
I'd dropped my book beneath the tree!
Would you believe? (And this is true!)
That bear—he read my book straight through!
After that he left, so I climbed down.
A bookish bear I'd somehow found.
As you can see, my book saved me.
A lucky choice—won't you agree?
And now, I guess, this story's done
Until I write another one!

©The Mailbox® • TEC44067 • June/July 2013

Note to the teacher: Use the prompt strips with "Literary Adventures" on page 71. Use "The Bear and I" with "Reading Reminders" on page 71.

WRITING

WRITE NOW!

I bet you didn't know that ancient Egyptians believed there was a Nile River in heaven too.

"Ancient Egyptian Beliefs" by Dusty Pages History Online, Web accessed October 8, 2012

Betcha Didn't Know
Conducting short research projects (W.4.7, W.5.7)

For this idea, have each student choose a topic and research it to find ten fantastic facts. Next, have the child paraphrase or quote each fact on an index card, beginning with the clause "I bet you didn't know…." Then have the student cite her source on the card's flip side. Next, have the student punch a hole in each card and tie her cards together with a length of yarn. For an informative follow-up, point to a student and say, "I bet you didn't know." Then have her read one of her facts. When the child finishes, she points to another student, who reads one of his facts, and so on as time allows.

Donna Jeffress, Linden Avenue Middle School, Red Hook, NY

The Soccer Game

The afternoon bell rang. Mark closed his math book and went to the playground. It was time for the soccer game, but Mark's team needed one more player.

He looked around and pointed to Jake, who was standing alone near the swings. Some of the boys weren't very nice about letting Jake play on their team. Mark ignored their groans and ran over to Jake. He asked Jake to play on the team.

I'd add the sound of the bell ringing. "Rrrring!"

Author's Circle
Revising with support from peers (W.4.5, W.5.5)

Want your students to learn to trust their own and their classmates' revising skills? Try this! Start by writing a simple short story. Then have each student grab his writing journal and a pencil and sit with you in a circle. Next, read your story aloud and guide students to jot notes about ways you might improve it, such as elaborate on its plot, improve word choice and sentence variety, or make the characters more believable. After that, have each student share his idea as you model accepting it. To extend the activity, display your story and have each student rewrite it. Then post the original story along with students' versions on a board titled "From One Author to Another."

Tracey Shuckhart, Rock Hill, SC

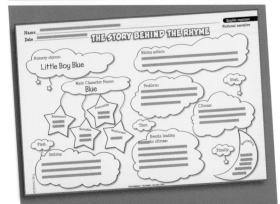

A Whimsical Start
Developing imagined experiences (W.4.3, W.5.3)

Get students' creative juices flowing with nursery rhyme prompts! Have each child choose a nursery rhyme and plan a full-length story based on it using a copy of the organizer on page 75. Next, guide the student to write the story she's planned. Then have her write the final version of her story on paper cut into cloud shapes. Finally, have each child read her story along with the original nursery rhyme to a younger student.

Name

Date

THE STORY BEHIND THE RHYME

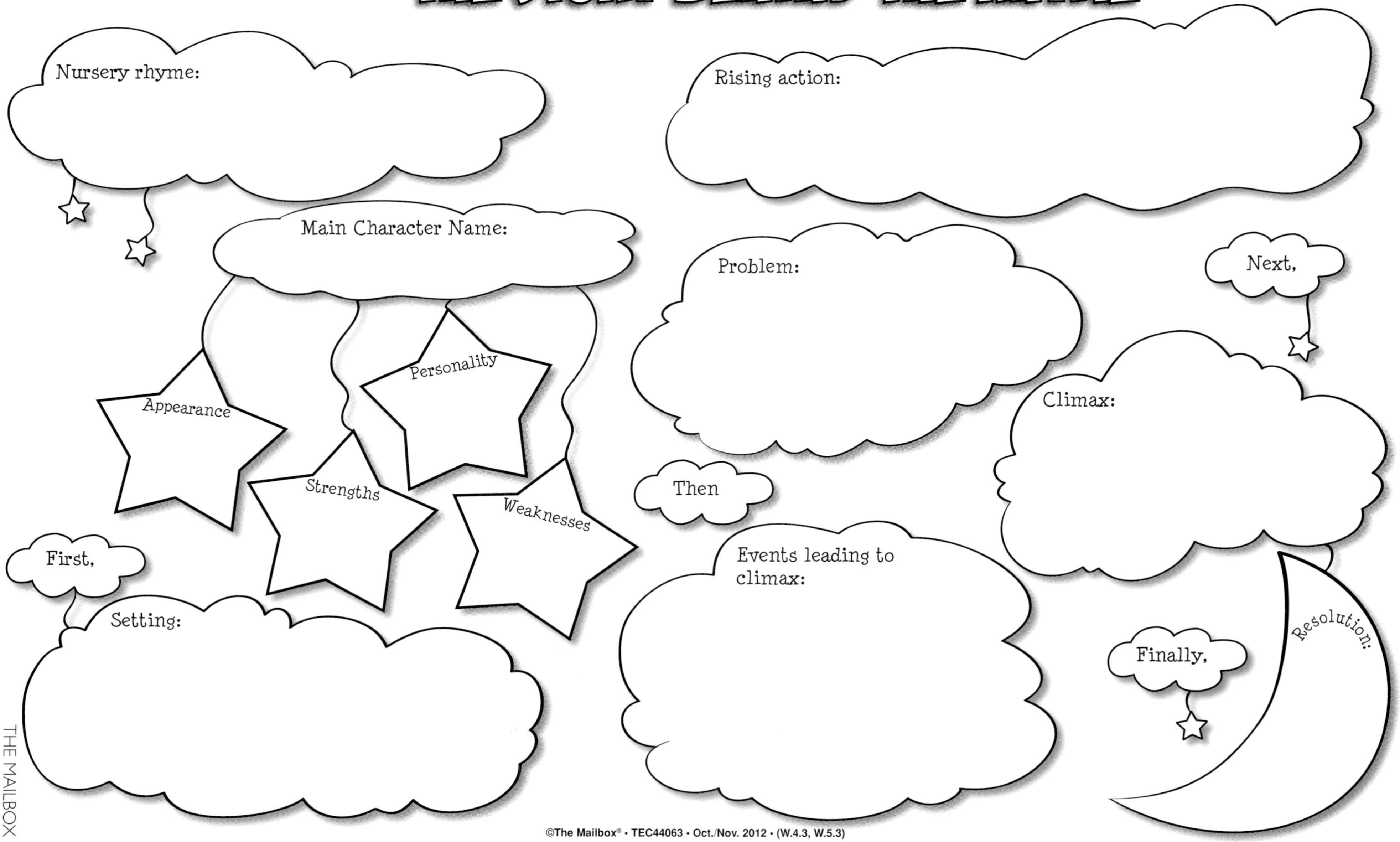

Nursery rhyme:

Main Character Name:

Personality

Weaknesses

Strengths

Appearance

Setting:

First,

Rising action:

Problem:

Next,

Climax:

Then

Events leading to climax:

Finally,

Resolution:

©The Mailbox® • TEC44063 • Oct./Nov. 2012 • (W.4.3, W.5.3)

Note to the teacher: Use with "A Whimsical Start" on page 74.

WRITE NOW!

Rolling With Writer's Block
Narrative writing (W.4.3, W.5.3)

Cool Characters

1. Ms. Johansson
2. old sea captain
3. Joey's little brother
4. Amelia Earhart

Surprising Situations

1. _____
2. _____
3. _____
4. _____

Help your young authors jumpstart their writing with this simple-to-use tool. Give each pair of students a card stock copy of the cube pattern from page 77. Have the partners brainstorm and record topics for each category on the pattern. Next, have the pair glue the cube together and put it in a basket at your writing center. Then, anytime a student is struggling with a narrative writing assignment, she can come to the writing center, take a cube, roll it for an idea or two, and get back to work!

adapted from an idea by Amy Barsanti, Pines Elementary, Plymouth, NC

Action!
Narrative writing, using sensory details (W.4.3, W.5.3)

produce section of a grocery store

dentist's office

school bus on the first day of school

school's media center

Friday night at a skating rink

Want your students to give settings more elaborate descriptions? Try this! Divide your class into four small groups and assign each group a different setting, such as one of those shown. Then give each group five minutes to plan a short pantomime that will reveal the setting. Next, have a group perform its skit and challenge the class to name the setting (not the action). Then direct each student to write a paragraph that describes the setting of the pantomime, including things she might see, hear, smell, and feel. Remind her to use words, phrases, and figurative language that create sensory images in a reader's mind. Repeat with the other three groups and then have students share their paragraphs with their groups.

Diana Boykin, DeZavala Elementary, Midland, TX

It All Adds Up!
Sentence variety

1. article + adjective + plural noun + present tense verb + prepositional phrase
2. compound subject + past tense verb + prepositional phrase
3. proper noun + present progressive verb + adverb
4. prepositional phrase + pronoun + helping verb + action verb + noun (direct object)
5. pronoun + past tense form of *to be* + article + adjective + noun; + pronoun + form of *to be* + article + adjective + noun

Encourage students to write sentences with different structures by posting sentence formulas such as those shown. Before a writing assignment, challenge each student to write sentences using one or more of the formulas in his writing. If a child uses a formula, he writes the formula's number and circles it in his paper's margin. If the student's sentence is correct, add a bonus point to his paper or award a point toward a small reward. Before you know it, writing sentences with different structures will be automatic!

Isobel Livingstone, Rahway, NJ

Cube Pattern

Use with "Rolling With Writer's Block" on page 76.

Glue.

Surefire Solutions

1. ______

2. ______

3. ______

4. ______

Glue.

Splendid Places

1. ______

2. ______

3. ______

4. ______

Glue.

Cool Characters

1. ______

2. ______

3. ______

4. ______

Glue.

Surprising Situations

1. ______

2. ______

3. ______

4. ______

Glue.

PUZZLING PROBLEMS

1. ______

2. ______

3. ______

4. ______

Themes That Make the World Go Round

1. ______

2. ______

3. ______

4. ______

TEC44064

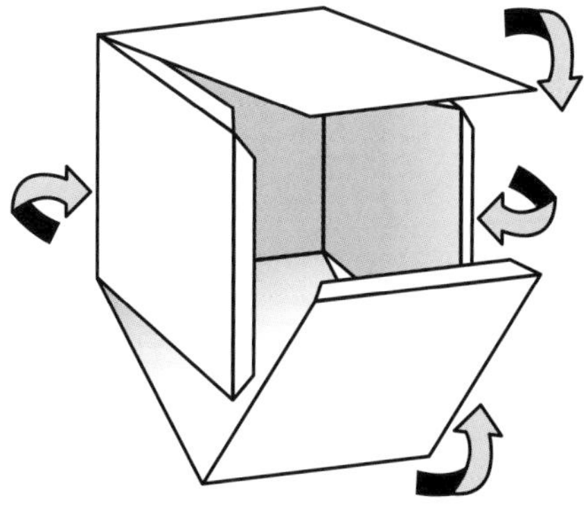

WRITE NOW!

Power of Persuasion
Opinion writing (W.4.1, W.5.1)

Here's a fun way to challenge your students' persuasive writing skills. Cut apart a copy of the consumer cards from page 79. Then place them with sales advertisements from various newspaper circulars at a center. A student selects an ad and a consumer card. Then he writes a radio commercial script for the product that targets the consumer listed on the card, carefully choosing words and phrases that will persuade the consumer to buy the item. At a later time, have the students revisit the center to read the commercial scripts and guess which consumer each ad is directed toward.

Cynthia Holcomb, San Angelo, TX

Keeping It Real
Using concrete details to develop a topic (W.4.1, W.5.1)

For this idea, present the class with a topic, such as qualities of a good friend. Have each student make a three-dimensional prop (such as a mobile or clay figure) that illustrates the student's ideas on the topic. Then have her present the prop to the class while she responds to the topic. After all the props are presented, direct each child to write about the topic. Guide students to use some of the ideas that were shared to write a clearer and more focused response with specific examples.

Kimberli Carrier, Nashua, NH

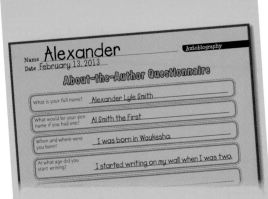

Get to Know the Author
Biographical sketch (W.4.2, W.5.2)

Want to help your young writers connect with their readers? Have them create about-the-author profiles! Give each student a copy of the questionnaire on page 80. Direct the child to have fun answering the questions but to be truthful with his responses. When the questionnaire is complete, instruct the student to make a cover sheet that includes his photo or self-portrait. Then staple together the cover sheet, questionnaire, and any previously published work. Place the author profiles in your classroom library for other students to read.

Elizabeth Jorgensen, Waukesha, WI

A successful
student

TEC44065

An elderly
woman

TEC44065

An enthusiastic
coach

TEC44065

A creative
teacher

TEC44065

A spoiled
teenager

TEC44065

A mother of
triplets

TEC44065

A man who loves
the outdoors

TEC44065

A discouraged
athlete

TEC44065

About-the-Author Questionnaire

What is your full name? _____

What would be your pen name if you had one? _____

When and where were you born? _____

At what age did you start writing? _____

What or who inspires you to write? _____

What are your favorite writing materials? _____
_____

Where is your favorite place to write? _____

What do you like to write about? _____
_____

What do you do to get ready to write? _____
_____

What advice would you give to other writers? _____
_____
_____
_____

WRITE NOW!

One Sentence Wonder

Revising (W.4.5; W.5.5)

Get your students pumped up about revising! First, have each child copy a boring sentence from a current piece of writing on an index card. Next, have students bring their cards and pencils and sit in a circle. Then turn on a lively musical selection and have students pass their cards around the circle. After several seconds, stop the music. Have each child read the card she's holding and add a vivid adjective that improves the sentence. Next, restart the music and have students pass the cards again. Stop and start the music four or five more times, guiding students to revise the sentences each time. Finally, let the music play until each child gets her own card and keeps it to use as revising inspiration!

Jami Bicknell, Riddle Elementary, Plano, TX

It's All in the Attitude!

Opinion writing (W.4.1; W.5.1)

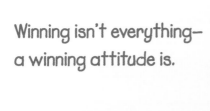

For this idea, post the Vince Lombardi quote "Winning isn't everything; it's the only thing." Then discuss with students how winning can become too important and what it means to be a good sport. Next, guide students to give examples of good sportsmanship they have seen exhibited and erase the quote. Replace it with the sentence shown and guide each child to use the sentence to introduce an essay on good sportsmanship. Remind the student to link his opinions with supporting details and then paraphrase the sentence in his concluding statement.

The Heart of the Matter

Letter writing, writing purpose (W.4.4; W.5.4)

To start this real-world activity, display a copy of page 82 to review the form and rules for writing a business letter. Then brainstorm with students a list of local businesses and divide the class into pairs. Next, have each partner choose a business and write a letter to the business as a customer requesting information, lodging a complaint, praising good service, or placing an order. Then have each student read her partner's letter and write a response as the business owner or manager.

64 Sea Drive
Wood, PA 09904

April 10, 2013

Manager, Rainbow Fish Farm
168 Barracuda Boulevard
Wood, PA 09995

To Whom It May Concern:

Start the first paragraph with a friendly but brief opening. (You want your reader to want to read your letter and give you what you want or do what you want.) Then write two or three sentences that clearly state your purpose for writing.

In the second paragraph, give the details or reasons that support your purpose. The details may include a brief summary of your experience or facts or details that will persuade your reader to do what you want.

You may write another paragraph that gives details or reasons that support your purpose. Be concise but clear.

In your last paragraph, briefly restate the purpose of your letter and tell why it is important to you. This is a good place to thank your reader for his or her time. If you want him or her to write back or contact you, it can help to let him or her know you are looking forward to that response.

Sincerely,

Gil Gibson

Gil Gibson

©The Mailbox® • TEC44066 • April/May 2013

Note to the teacher: Use with "The Heart of the Matter" on page 81.

WRITE NOW!

The Moral of the Story Could Be...

The early bird catches the worm.
Don't cry over spilled milk.
If the shoe fits, wear it.
Don't make a mountain out of a molehill.
Look before you leap.
Every cloud has a silver lining.
A stitch in time saves nine.
A fool and his money are soon parted.

The Rest of the Story
Fictional narrative, proverbs (W.4.3a, L.4.5b; W.5.3a, L.5.5b)

For this idea, post proverbs that could be morals of stories, such as those shown. Next, discuss the lesson behind each proverb. Then give each student a copy of page 89. Have the child choose a proverb, record it on the organizer, and create a story about a character who learns that lesson. When students finish, have them read their work to partners for editing feedback. Then have students sit in a circle and read their final versions as if they were teaching lessons through stories like oral history traditions of old!

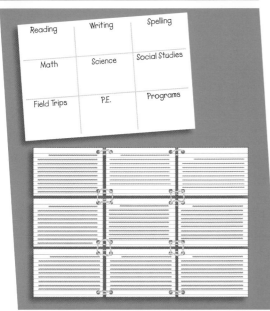

Reading	Writing	Spelling
Math	Science	Social Studies
Field Trips	P.E.	Programs

Make Mine Memorable!
Narrative writing (W.4.3; W.5.3)

This activity's just right for the end of the year! Begin by having each student divide a sheet of paper into nine sections and label the sections with topics such as those shown. Next, have the child think about lessons or events from each topic. Then name a topic, set a timer for two minutes, and have each student jot notes in that section about his memories of the topic. Repeat for each of the topics. After that, have the child describe a memorable event from each topic on an index card and illustrate the event on the card's back. Finally, have the student punch holes in each card's corners and tie the cards together with yarn as shown for an easy-to-fold memento of the year.

Teri Nielsen, Chesapeake Beach, MD

The Bigger Picture
Opinion writing (W.4.1; W.5.1)

To give students practice expressing and supporting a point of view, have each student choose a person she admires. Next, have the child draw a picture of the person. Then have her write an essay about the person by introducing him or her, giving three or more reasons the person should be admired, supporting those reasons with facts or details, and concluding the essay by summarizing the person's admirable qualities. After the student edits her work, have her glue her final copy to the back of her illustration, punch a hole at the top, and tie a ribbon loop through the hole. Hang students' work in your classroom for a meaningful mobile or have each student present her work to her admirable subject!

"Mysteri-ology"

1 Prompt

Your best friend has just announced that he or she is going to be an entomologist, a herpetologist, an ichthyologist, a mammalogist, an ornithologist, or a paleontologist and wants you to be one too! What are you going to tell him or her?

Circle the topic you think your BFF might pick and then research it.

My best friend would probably want to be…

- an entomologist
- an ichthyologist
- an ornithologist
- a herpetologist
- a mammalogist
- a paleontologist

2 Research

What is it?

What kind of education and training is required?

What are tasks someone in this field does?

What are some interesting facts about this field?

Why is this an important field?

What are some drawbacks of this work?

Sources (Record every source you use.)

©The Mailbox® • TEC44063 • Oct./Nov. 2012 • (W.4.8, W.5.8)

84 THE MAILBOX   **Note to the teacher:** Use with page 85.

Which job are you researching: entomologist, herpetologist, ichthyologist, mammalogist, ornithologist, or paleontologist? Circle it.

3 Plan

Would you like to join your best friend in this field of science? Why or why not?

Write three important facts (from your notes) about this field of science that support this reason. Then rank the facts by numbering them 1–3.

What do you think is the most interesting fact (from your notes) about this field?

Which fact (from your notes) about this field bothers you most? Why?

4 Write

Now that you know all about this field of science, write a letter that is five paragraphs long or longer to your best friend. In your letter, tell whether you are interested in becoming a specialist. Include details and facts that support your decision. In the last paragraph, summarize your main points.

Note to the teacher: Use with " 'Mysteri-ology' " on page 84.

THE MAILBOX **85**

Name _____

Date _____

WRAPPING THINGS UP

Each sentence below is a topic sentence. Write a concluding statement for each topic sentence by restating it.

Wrapping a present can be challenging. It may look easy, but I'd rather make a gift than wrap it!

Your conclusion leaves a lasting impression on your reader.

1. Hank Miller loves being a dairy farmer even though he has to get up very early every morning. _____

2. Tales about pirates go back for over 2,000 years, but the most famous pirates roamed the seas from the 1500s through the 1700s. _____

3. There is nothing worse than jumping out of bed early on a Saturday morning because you think it's a school day. _____

4. Crossword puzzles are popular all over the world. _____

5. Matthew Henson and Admiral Robert Peary began trying to reach the North Pole in 1891. _____

6. Most times, I think it is better to give than to receive. _____

7. When someone tells me that I am doing a good job, it makes me feel proud. _____

8. Washing your hands is an easy way to keep from spreading germs. _____

9. A monster truck is a four-wheel drive pickup truck with giant tires. _____

10. When the United States was formed, its leaders wanted a national symbol. _____

BONUS: Choose a topic sentence above and write three or more paragraphs on the topic. Then use your concluding statement in your conclusion.

©The Mailbox® • TEC44064 • Dec./Jan. 2012–13 • (W.4.1d, 2e, 3e; W.5.1d, 2e, 3e)

Name _____

Date _____

Beast or Bust?

1 Prompt

Stories about legendary creatures are told around the world. Some people believe the creatures are real. Many people don't. Research three legendary creatures, such as those listed below. Then form your own opinion about these animals and whether any of them are or might be real.

Yeti, or Abominable Snowman
Bigfoot, or Sasquatch
Boggy Creek Monster, or Fouke Monster

Loch Ness Monster
Champ (sea monster of Lake Champlain)

Ogopogo (sea monster of Lake Okanagan)
Thunderbird, or Birdzilla

2 Research

Legendary Animal	Details	Origin of Legend	Sightings	My Opinion

Sources (Record every source you use.)

©The Mailbox® • TEC44066 • April/May 2013 (W.4.1; W.5.1; SL.5.4)

Note to the teacher: Use with page 88.

3 Plan

This is how I feel about legendary animals.

These are facts that support the way I feel.

These are a fact and a reason why I disagree with the opposite viewpoint.

Here is an opposite viewpoint on legendary animals.

4 Write

Write a speech that will persuade others to think about legendary animals from your perspective. Start with an attention-getting introduction, give your opinion and supporting reasons, and restate your opinion in your closing.

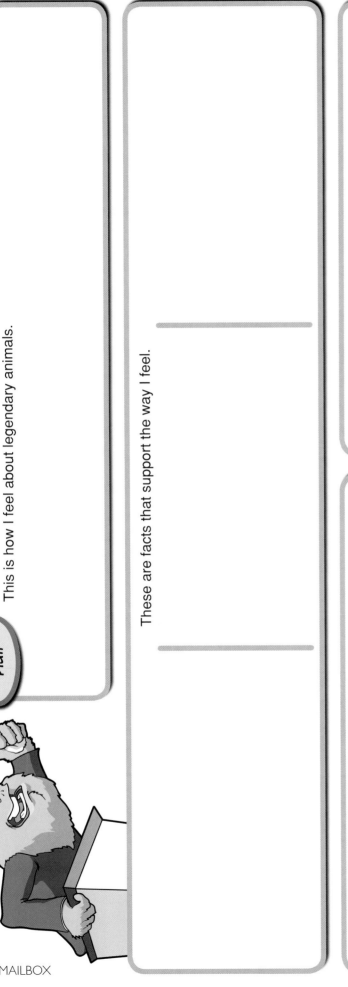

©The Mailbox® • TEC44066 • April/May 2013

Note to the teacher: Use with "Beast or Bust?" on page 87.

Graphic organizer

Fictional narrative

The Rest of the Story

Proverb:

Main Character

Name:

Appearance:

Personality:

Strengths:

Weaknesses:

Sensory and Other Details that Make the Story Interesting

Problem that will teach the character the lesson:

Setting:

Rising action:

Events leading to the climax (when the character learns the lesson):

Climax:

Resolution (including the moral of the story):

September Writing Prompts

If Patriot Day, September 11, were a day off from work and school, what do you think we should do to observe the day? Explain.

Yarrrr! September 19 is International Talk Like a Pirate Day. Write a letter to your best friend using pirate lingo, such as *matey, ahoy, avast,* and *arrr!* In the letter, describe the book you are currently reading.

Imagine you are the first leaf that falls off a tree in autumn. What do you think, say, feel, and do? Write your story.

Shoo fly! A fly keeps pestering you while you study. Write a letter to the fly convincing it to leave you alone while you work.

Write a three-paragraph summary of school so far this year. Include the good and the bad.

Write a song or a poem to introduce yourself to your new teacher and classmates.

Make a list of your favorite things to eat for breakfast, with your most favorite at the top. Then create a mini poster that reminds fellow students that breakfast is the most important meal of the day.

September is Library Card Sign-Up Month. Imagine that an alien has suddenly appeared in your library. What does it do? What does your librarian do? Write a story about the alien in your library.

If you could change one thing about your bedroom, what would it be? Describe the change and tell why you would change it.

When he became president, John F. Kennedy said, "...Ask not what your country can do for you—ask what you can do for your country." What do you think President Kennedy meant? Explain.

©The Mailbox® • TEC44062 • Aug./Sept. 2012 • (W.4.10, W.5.10)

August Writing Prompts

Make a list of six cool things you did this summer. Then make a list of six cool things you plan to do next summer.

How do you get to school? Do you ride in a car, on a bus, or on a bike or do you walk? Write six or more steps that explain how you get to school.

The principal has asked the students in your class to design the school's new uniforms. Describe the uniform you would design or draw a quick sketch of it. Then write a letter that will persuade the principal to choose your plan.

Would you rather watch a movie or play a video game? Give three reasons that explain your choice.

Imagine on the very first day of school, you notice something sticking out from under a bush. You dig it out and discover it's a sack with $2,500,000 inside. What happens?

Write a fascinating tale in which you save the life of a talking catfish.

Imagine you go to the county fair and end up competing in a watermelon-eating contest. What is the best part of the contest? What is the worst part? How do you do?

In honor of Children's Vision and Learning Month, describe the most beautiful thing you have ever seen and where you were the first time you saw it.

If you designed a school bus, what would it be like? Compare a regular school bus with the bus you would design.

What goals do you have for the new school year? Write a letter to yourself about what you think you should achieve this year.

©The Mailbox® • TEC44062 • Aug./Sept. 2012 • (W.4.10, W.5.10)

November Writing Prompts

Think about the main characters from your favorite book. Then imagine another adventure, challenge, or problem that would be perfect for the characters. Write the story.

Should humans be the only ones to enjoy a Thanksgiving Day feast? Write a letter to your parents that will convince them to cook a fancy feast for your pet or pets (or your neighbors').

It's Lung Cancer Awareness Month. Design a poster that will persuade kids they should never start smoking.

Write four or more steps that explain how to make your bed.

Albert Einstein? Harriet Beecher Stowe? Your mom or uncle? Think about someone who inspires you to reach your goals. Then explain why this person is a great role model for you.

Which would you rather have—a furry, feathered, or scaly classroom pet? Why?

Don't wait! Start writing your autobiography now. Start by writing the story of your earliest memory.

How do you feel about eating Thanksgiving Day leftovers? Explain your feelings in an email to your best friend.

You are in charge of planning the Thanksgiving Day feast, and you can put anything you want on the menu. What would you plan for the best Thanksgiving Day meal ever? Describe it.

Does today feel more like a fall day or a winter day? Describe the weather using all your senses.

©The Mailbox® • TEC44063 • Oct./Nov. 2012 • (W.4.10, W.5.10)

October Writing Prompts

Grilled cheese, macaroni and cheese, string cheese—it's American Cheese Month! In honor of this gooey, creamy food, write a couplet (two lines of rhyming verse with a complete thought) about your favorite or least favorite way to eat cheese.

Pretend you are a dentist who's writing an article for your newspaper. In your piece, convince kids to trade their Halloween candy for toothbrushes, dental floss, and toothpaste.

Legend has it that during the 1932 World Series, baseball great Babe Ruth pointed to the bleachers and then hit a home run over that very spot. Call your shot like the Babe. Describe one of your goals and make a plan for reaching it.

Which fall sport—volleyball, football, soccer, or cross-country—do you think is best? Why?

What do squirrels really think about fall? Write a journal entry from the outlook of a squirrel that has been busily getting ready for winter.

If you created a new magazine for kids, would it be about an animal, a sport, music, or something else? Why would kids want to read it? List eight or more kinds of articles you would feature. Then design the magazine's first cover.

The Model T was introduced in 1908. (It cost $850.) Imagine that cars had never been invented. What would your life be like? Write a story about a day in a world without cars.

Do you think children 13 years and older should be allowed to trick-or-treat? Write a letter to the editor of your newspaper that will convince local citizens to agree with you.

The cafeteria staff is looking for some fresh menu ideas. Make a list of six or more different lunch menus.

Describe the best Halloween costume you have ever seen.

©The Mailbox® • TEC44063 • Oct./Nov. 2012 • (W.4.10, W.5.10)

January Writing Prompts

Celebrate National Soup Month! Write a note to your parents that describes your favorite soup and persuades them to serve it for dinner tonight.

At the start of a new year, many people set goals about what they want to accomplish in the next 12 months. Instead of doing that, list actions you took this past year that you plan *not* to repeat this year.

Imagine that your favorite sports team is playing for a national championship. The team is giving away two tickets to its number one fan. Write a letter convincing the team that you are its top fan.

Martin Luther King Jr.'s birthday is celebrated in January. Design a birthday cake for Dr. King. Add decorations that represent his life. Then write a paragraph explaining your cake's decorations.

National Puzzle Day is January 29. There are many different types of puzzles: jigsaw, crossword, logic, and others. Write an essay that compares your favorite type of puzzle to your least favorite.

The company that makes your favorite brand of markers has decided to use cheaper materials. Though the markers will cost less, they won't last as long. Write a paragraph that explains your opinion of this idea.

Imagine that the power has gone out due to a large winter storm. How are you going to keep yourself entertained without power? List at least ten activities you will do.

In honor of National Popcorn Day on January 19, write an essay that explains how to make popcorn with your favorite topping.

January 31 is Backward Day. One way you could celebrate this day is by watching the end of a movie first. Pretend that you just celebrated Backward Day. Write a diary entry that explains how you spent your day.

January 25 is National Opposite Day. Some people say opposites attract. Is it good to be friends with someone who is the total opposite from you? Why or why not?

©The Mailbox® • TEC44064 • Dec./Jan. 2012–13 • (W.4.10, W.5.10)

December Writing Prompts

December is Write to a Friend Month. Write a letter to a friend about your favorite television show. Explain why you just can't miss a single episode!

Write an email to your school principal. In it, convince him or her to cover the hallway floors with ice so students can ice-skate from one class to another.

The company that produces this year's most popular game for kids your age just asked you to create a TV ad for it. Write a description of your commercial.

December can be one of the busiest months of the year. Which day do you enjoy more: a day when there is a whole lot to do or a day when there's nothing on your schedule? Why?

You just won a day of being driven around in a sports car worth $80,000! Write a journal entry about the day you spend riding around in this super set of wheels.

On December 17, 1903, the Wright Brothers—after several attempts—made their first successful flight at Kitty Hawk, North Carolina. Write about a time when you were successful at doing something after a long time of trying.

Traditional songs like "Rudolph the Red-Nosed Reindeer" and "Frosty the Snowman" are popular in December. Write a new set of lyrics to use with a holiday tune like one of these.

There are only a few days left in this year. List five things you are really glad you did this year. Then list five things you still want to accomplish before the year is over.

Pretend that you wake to discover that everyone—including you—has turned into living snow people. List ten rules you must now live by in order to avoid melting away.

Imagine that 20 close family members and friends will be staying at your home during winter break. Create a plan of where everyone is going to sleep, eat, and play in your home.

©The Mailbox® • TEC44064 • Dec./Jan. 2012–13 • (W.4.10, W.5.10)

March Writing Prompts

March 20 is the International Day of Happiness. Finish this sentence ten different ways: I am really happy when....

Pretend a wind storm has caused a power blackout in your area. No television, computers, or cell phones can be used. Write about what you would do to calm your teenage brother (or sister), who is totally freaking out right now.

Alexander Graham Bell, inventor of the telephone, was born on March 3, 1847. Describe how an average day for you would be different if cell phones did not exist.

March is Youth Art Month. What would be a fun but inexpensive way for your school to observe this special month? Describe your plan in a letter to your principal.

There are just a few months left in the school year. List all the things you hope to accomplish before the school year is over.

March 2 is Dr. Seuss Day and Read Across America Day. List different ways your class can celebrate this day. Then choose your favorite idea and write a persuasive paragraph convincing your teachers to do it.

Birds chirping, the smell of freshly cut grass—spring is in the air! Describe your favorite spring sounds, smells, and sights.

Imagine that on St. Patrick's Day (March 17), you arrive at school only to find out that everything in your classroom has turned bright green! Write about what happens next.

In honor of Save Your Vision Month, design the coolest pair of sunglasses ever. Then write a television commercial convincing people to buy the new shades.

Easter Bunny comes to town this month and needs a song for the kids to sing. Use the tune of "Jingle Bells" to write a song about Easter Bunny.

©The Mailbox® • TEC44065 • Feb./Mar. 2013 • (W.4.10, W.5.10)

February Writing Prompts

American Heart Month is celebrated in February. Describe something that you recently put your heart into (did with a lot of effort). Tell why this task was so important to you.

The penny was the first regular US coin to honor an actual person, Abraham Lincoln. If a special coin were to be issued to honor someone at your school, who would you choose? Explain why this person deserves such special recognition.

By the time February rolls around, most students have been in school for almost 100 days. List ten things you would love to do every day for 100 days. Then list ten things you'd never want to do for that long.

Imagine that it is freezing outside and you long for warmer weather. Describe what you would be doing today if the temperature were more summerlike.

The US president is one of the most famous people in the world. Consider the following: It would be awesome to be famous like the president. Do you agree? Why or why not?

In honor of Groundhog Day, design an underground mansion that a groundhog would never want to leave. Draw and label your diagram. Then write a letter inviting the groundhog to move in.

February is Black History Month, a time to celebrate the achievements and culture of African Americans. Do you think it's easier to honor people's achievements with a special holiday or a month-long observance? Explain.

February 12 is National Lost Penny Day. Write a conversation between two pennies that are on the sidewalk waiting and hoping to be picked up.

Valentine's Day is only one day a year. What other jobs could Cupid do for the remaining 364 days? List ten job opportunities for Cupid. Explain why he is perfectly suited for each job.

George Washington's birthday is celebrated on the third Monday in February. Plan a fabulous bash to celebrate. Write a schedule of events for the party and a shopping list. Then create an invitation.

©The Mailbox® • TEC44065 • Feb./Mar. 2013 • (W.4.10, W.5.10)

May Writing Prompts

If you were to spend a perfect summer day outside, what would you be doing? Describe it.

Imagine you are lying outside watching clouds in the sky. What happens while you are watching the clouds? Write a creative story about it.

If you were the governor of a state that bordered an ocean, what would you do to protect the ocean from pollution?

A major food company wants to create the perfect snack food for kids. It must be nutritious, delicious, safe for your teeth, and a hit with kids! Invent a snack and write a speech that will convince the company to buy your creation.

The English language grows each year as new words are created. Be a "wordologist" and create five new words. Tell how each word is spelled, pronounced, and what it means. Then write each word in a sentence to show how it's used.

What do you think is the most difficult thing about being a principal? Explain.

In honor of May Day (May 1), write the word *FLOWERS* vertically. Then write seven sentences about spring that each begin with one of the letters in the word.

Who is the most loyal person you know? Write a short story about a time this person was loyal.

During National Police Week (the week of May 15), we recognize the hard work of police officers. Think of a way you and fellow students might honor your local police. Then write an email to convince your teacher you should do it.

Summer is nearly here. Make a list of eight things you plan to do this summer. Then choose the number one thing you want to do and explain why.

April Writing Prompts

If your teacher won an extreme classroom makeover, what do you think your new classroom would look like? Describe it.

What do you think is the most important quality a friend should have? Explain.

Imagine you've just accidentally hit a baseball through your neighbor's front window. Write a friendly letter to apologize for the large hole that is now decorating her front window.

Thomas Jefferson, who was born April 13, 1743, once said, "When angry, count ten, before you speak; if very angry, an hundred." Describe a time when you should have followed this advice.

Imagine you are attending an unidentified flying object (UFO) convention and you are the keynote speaker. Your topic is "UFOs—Fact or Fiction?" Write this speech.

April Fools' Day is a time for playing tricks on others. Write five statements about today's weather. Make one a tricky false statement and the other four true.

Write a story about the craziest spring day ever. Your story can be true, or you can make it up.

Imagine you are on a nature walk with your class. As you're walking, you see an insect you've never seen before. In fact, no one has ever seen it before. Describe the insect and its surroundings.

You've learned a lot so far this year. Which of the skills you've learned was the most challenging? How did you feel when you realized you had learned it? Explain.

For Earth Day (April 22), make a list of 12 things you can do to help take care of our planet.

Summer Writing Prompts

In honor of the Fourth of July, make a list of ten or more adjectives that describe fireworks. Write each adjective in a burst.

What is something you hope will never end? Explain.

You've been invited to camp out in your friend's backyard. Write a scary story to tell while you hold a flashlight under your chin. (Make sure your story's not too gory!)

In the fable "The Boy Who Cried Wolf," no one believed the boy when he finally told the truth. Write about a time when you learned that honesty is the best policy.

Describe your favorite place to be in summer without naming the place. Then write the name of the place on the back of your page.

Write a critical review of your favorite television show, movie, or play. (In a critical review, you give a short summary and tell what you think is good and bad about something.)

Describe the sights, smells, and sounds from a summer cookout from a puppy's point of view.

Plan a picnic for you and your best friend. Where will you go? How will you get there? What will you eat and drink? What will you do?

A magic genie appears out of a dusty old vase in your attic. He grants you three wishes. What would you wish for? Explain.

Does summer feel like the longest season of the year, the shortest season of the year, or the same length as all the others? Explain.

©The Mailbox® • TEC44067 • June/July 2013 (W.4.1–3; W.5.1–3)

June Writing Prompts

June is National Dairy Month. Pretend you are a dairy cow. Create a poster that will convince kids who don't like milk to give it a chance.

June is National Adopt-a-Cat Month. Are you a cat person, a dog person, or neither one? Explain.

Describe the personalities of two members of your family.

Make a list of words that rhyme with June. Then use as many of the words as you can to write a silly poem about summer.

What are the three most important things you learned this year? Why do you think these things are so important?

If your classmates were asked to describe you, what do you hope they would say?

Make a list of ten or more locations in your town that fly the US flag.

Imagine you have been invited to spend the night at the nearest zoo or aquarium. What would you do? Where would you sleep? Describe your plans for the night.

The first day of summer is June 21. Make a list of everything you hope you can do this summer. Then write a plan of how you can accomplish the first three items on your list.

When our country was being settled, people used tall tales to amuse one another in the face of many hardships. What do you do to amuse yourself or your family when you face hardships?

©The Mailbox® • TEC44067 • June/July 2013 (W.4.1–3; W.5.1–3)

CHEW ON THIS!

Build critical-thinking skills with prompts all about a topic kids love—bubble gum!

1 List 15 adjectives that describe bubble gum.

2 Invent your own brand of bubble gum. What would be unique about it? How would it be made? How would you advertise it?

3 The first bubble gum was produced in 1906. However, it did not hit the market for 22 years. What do you think kept bubble gum off the market and out of stores for so long? Explain.

4 People used to believe that if you swallowed your gum, it would sit in your stomach for seven years. (That's not true. Gum moves right through your digestive system, but it doesn't have any nutrients.) Write a letter to Mrs. Murple, who still believes the myth. In your letter, convince Mrs. Murple that gum will not stay in her stomach for seven years.

5 Create an original bubble gum wrapper that will keep gum fantastically fresh.

6 Create a word search puzzle with 15 or more terms that are bubble gum related.

7 If you entered a contest to blow the biggest bubble gum bubble, what would your strategy be? Describe it in detail.

8 Write five questions to ask a store manager about his bubble gum sales. Make sure your questions will require the manager to give thoughtful answers, not just "yes" or "no."

9 Survey 20 or more people to find the most popular bubble gum brand. Make a line plot to show your results.

10 Why do you think it's so much easier to blow bubbles with bubble gum than with regular gum? Explain.

11 Make predictions about how bubble gum might change in the next ten years. Describe the bubble gum of the future using all your senses.

12 Draw a Venn diagram and compare the ingredients of a sugarless bubble gum with those of bubble gum that has sugar.

How to Use Display this page to guide independent or small-group work or give each student a copy of this page to work on during free time.

PEARLS OF WATERY WISDOM

Recognizing and explaining the meaning of figures of speech

Directions:
1. Choose a figure of speech.
2. Fold a sheet of paper into three sections. Unfold the paper and write the phrase across the top of your paper.
3. In the first section, illustrate the literal meaning of the phrase.
4. In the second section, illustrate the nonliteral (true) meaning of the phrase.
5. In the third section, write a short story that explains the phrase or uses it as the moral of a story.

It's raining cats and dogs.

- Love comforteth like sunshine after rain.
- Someone is in hot water.
- Blood is thicker than water.
- Don't throw out the baby with the bathwater.
- I feel like a fish out of water.
- A mill cannot grind with water that is past.
- That's just the tip of the iceberg.

- You can lead a horse to water, but you can't make it drink.
- That's water under the bridge.
- She's wet behind the ears.
- The rain does not fall on one roof alone.
- Go with the flow.
- Beware of a silent dog and still water.
- Keep your head above water.

- Still waters run deep.
- April showers bring May flowers.
- Into each life some rain must fall.
- Don't make waves.
- Cast thy bread upon the waters.
- When it rains, it pours.
- Although it may rain, cast not away the watering pot.
- Oil and water don't mix.

©The Mailbox® · TEC44065 · Feb./Mar. 2013 · (L.4.5b, L.5.5b)

Note to the teacher: Display this page on your whiteboard or place it in a plastic page protector and set it at a center. Each child needs a sheet of construction paper to complete the activity.

Art in Action

What You Need
- used holiday cards
- white construction paper
- drawing materials
- scissors
- glue

1 Choose a card and cut out a scene or picture from it.

2 Glue the cutout to a sheet of white construction paper.

3 Draw to extend the picture all the way across the paper.

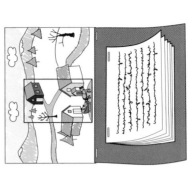

4 Copy and complete the organizer shown to plan a story set in this scene.

main characters

problem

solution

5 Write the story that takes place in this scene. Then edit and revise your story.

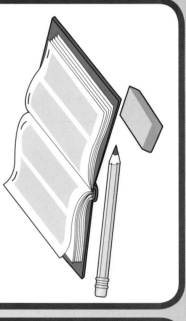

6 Write the final draft of your story. Mount it on construction paper and staple it to the bottom of your art project.

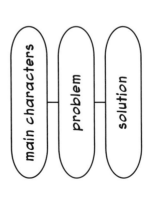

©The Mailbox® • TEC44064 • Dec./Jan. 2012–13 • (W.4.3, W.5.3)

Step-by-step craft: Slide a copy of this page in a plastic page protector. Then put the materials listed above and this page at a center.

BUILDING BETTER PARAGRAPHS

Ideas for helping students write structurally sound, informative paragraphs! (W.4.1–2, W.5.1–2)

NOW PRESENTING!

Topic sentence

Writing topic sentences can be intimidating. Teach your young authors these three simple steps! Then, once students are confident topic-sentence writers, show them that good conclusions are simply paraphrased versions of their topic sentences.

1. Name your topic.
2. Answer this question: What do you want to say about your topic? (In other words, how do you feel about it? What do you want people to know about it? What do you want to prove about it?)
3. Write your answer as an interesting sentence.

IN THE BAG

Supporting details

Use this simple demonstration to remind students that each paragraph should contain strong details that support the topic. In advance, fill a grocery bag with several kitchen items and one nonkitchen item. Next, empty the bag and ask students to identify the items' topic. *(They are items used in the kitchen.)* Then ask students to point out any items that do not match the topic and explain why. *(The nonkitchen item is not used in the kitchen.)* Conclude by reminding students that in a good paragraph, the supporting details are directly related to the topic—just as the items in the bag should all have been related to the kitchen.

 tip To extend the idea, place in the bag several items for each of three different rooms in a house. Then have students sort the items by room and compare the exercise to grouping related information in paragraphs.

PARAGRAPH STARTERS

- The coach of a sports team has to be organized.
- Being president of the United States would be a true challenge.
- There is a lot I can do to help keep the environment clean.
- There are several interesting places to visit in our town.
- Playing football can be dangerous.
- It would be fascinating to have a twin.
- Smoking is bad for your health.
- People read books for different reasons.
- Having a pet can be a lot of work.
- The hippopotamus is an unusual animal.
- A [dog] makes a great pet.
- You can't always believe TV commercials.

DETAIL ORIENTED

Supporting details

Help students organize their details with this partner activity. Have each student write his supporting detail or fact sentences on separate index cards. Next, have the child clip each card to a length of yarn. Then pair students and have one student hold his line up while the other reads the sentences. After she reads the sentences, the partner removes the cards that don't clearly support the topic and arranges the cards in logical order. Then the partners switch and repeat the procedure.

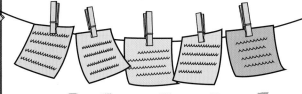

See page 100 for a reproducible graphic organizer!

PARAGRAPH UNDER CONSTRUCTION

 1 What is your topic?

_____

 2 What do you want your reader to know about your topic?

_____

Rewrite your answer as an interesting introductory/topic sentence.

_____

_____

 3 For each hardhat, write a detail or fact sentence that supports, explains, or proves what you want your reader to know about your topic.

 _____

 _____

 _____

 _____

_____

 4 Read each of your details or facts.

- If a detail tells something important about the topic, shade its hardhat.
- If a detail explains something about the topic, shade its hardhat.

- If a detail proves something about the topic, shade its hardhat.
- If a detail does not truly support your topic, draw an X in its hardhat.

 5 Decide how to arrange the details by the shaded hardhats. Number them.

6 Write your conclusion by paraphrasing your topic sentence.

_____

_____

7 On another sheet of paper, write your paragraph. Start with the topic sentence, add the detail sentences, and end with your conclusion.

©The Mailbox® • TEC44062 • Aug./Sept. 2012 • (W.4.2, W.5.2)

MATH

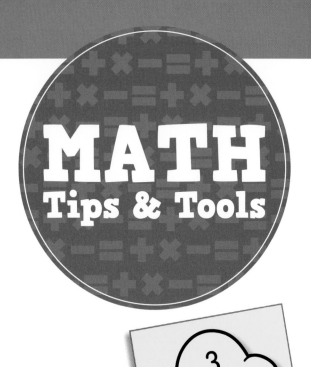

MATH
Tips & Tools

Pop On Over!
Equivalent fractions (4.NF.A.1)

For this anytime review, have each pair of students cut apart the cards and key from a copy of page 104 and spread the cards facedown. Then have each partner take a turn flipping two cards and deciding whether the fractions are equivalent. If they are, the student keeps the cards. If the fractions are not equivalent, the child turns the cards back over and her partner takes a turn. Once all the matches have been made, the student with more cards wins.

Jennifer Otter
Oak Ridge, NC

Building Blocks of Understanding
Multiplication as a comparison (4.OA.A.1)

Need to help students understand multiplication as a comparison? Try this! Write "4 x 3 = 12" on the board. Next, read the equation aloud; then rewrite it as "12 = 4 x 3" and explain that it can also be read as "12 is four times as many as three." As you explain, display three blocks and then arrange four groups of three blocks nearby. Next, rearrange the blocks to show that 12 is three times as many as four. Then give each pair of students a supply of blocks and have them practice modeling and rewriting multiplication equations as comparisons.

Jennifer Otter

12 is four times as many as three.

Putting It in Perspective
Place value to 1,000,000 (4.NBT.A.1)

For this idea, make 12 construction paper cards—two labeled with commas and ten numbered 0–9 on one side and labeled "0" in a different color on the other side. Then have up to seven students each take a card and stand in front of the room, guiding volunteers to separate the numerical periods with comma cards. Next, ask the class to name the value of the digit in the thousands place. Have students who are holding cards in the other places flip their cards to show zero. Once students name the value of the digit, have the students in line flip their cards back and ask the class to identify the values of other digits. Then have students return their cards and bring a new group of students to the front.

Annette Bright, Frances Willard Elementary, Kansas City, KS

tip Give students practice with decimal place value by adding a decimal point card and asking a volunteer to hold the decimal point so there are digits in the tenths and hundredths places.

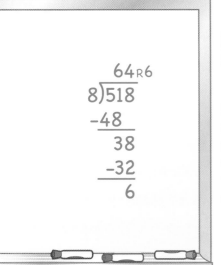

Step-by-Step Review
Division (4.NBT.B.6, 5.NBT.B.6, 6.NS.B.2)

Are your students' division skills a bit rusty? Try this confidence-building review! To begin, give each student a small dry-erase board and a wipe-off marker. Next, write on the board the division problem shown and guide students to calculate each step mentally and write the step's answer on his board. After students show their responses, add the answer to the board and move to the next step. When you finish, erase the problem and write another one on the board. After just a few practice sessions, students will be confident and ready for independent practice.

Living Factor Trees
Finding prime factors (4.OA.B.4)

Here's an idea students are sure to get into! Begin by assigning each small group of students a different number. Provide access to scrap paper and have the students make a factor tree for the number. Next, have the students in each group write the factors on separate pieces of paper, tape one factor to each of their shirts, and arrange themselves as a human factor tree. When the students are ready, have the student at the top of the tree announce her number and then have the students call out their factor pairs in order. After each group shares its tree, assign different numbers and repeat as time allows.

Stephanie Johnson, Bear Branch Elementary, Magnolia, TX

 Flip to **page 147** for an independent practice page on **factors!**

Fraction Cards

Use with "Pop On Over!" on page 102.

$\frac{2}{3}$	$\frac{3}{4}$	$\frac{2}{5}$	$\frac{3}{5}$	$\frac{4}{5}$	$\frac{5}{6}$
TEC44062	TEC44062	TEC44062	TEC44062	TEC44062	TEC44062
$\frac{3}{8}$	$\frac{5}{8}$	$\frac{7}{8}$	$\frac{3}{10}$	$\frac{7}{10}$	$\frac{5}{12}$
TEC44062	TEC44062	TEC44062	TEC44062	TEC44062	TEC44062
$\frac{4}{6}$	$\frac{9}{12}$	$\frac{4}{10}$	$\frac{9}{15}$	$\frac{8}{10}$	$\frac{15}{18}$
TEC44062	TEC44062	TEC44062	TEC44062	TEC44062	TEC44062
$\frac{9}{24}$	$\frac{10}{16}$	$\frac{21}{24}$	$\frac{6}{20}$	$\frac{14}{20}$	$\frac{15}{36}$
TEC44062	TEC44062	TEC44062	TEC44062	TEC44062	TEC44062
$\frac{10}{15}$	$\frac{18}{24}$	$\frac{12}{30}$	$\frac{15}{25}$	$\frac{36}{45}$	$\frac{30}{36}$
TEC44062	TEC44062	TEC44062	TEC44062	TEC44062	TEC44062
$\frac{12}{32}$	$\frac{25}{40}$	$\frac{14}{16}$	$\frac{21}{70}$	$\frac{21}{30}$	$\frac{10}{24}$
TEC44062	TEC44062	TEC44062	TEC44062	TEC44062	TEC44062

$\frac{12}{18}$	$\frac{27}{36}$
TEC44062	TEC44062
$\frac{18}{48}$	$\frac{20}{32}$
TEC44062	TEC44062

Answer Key for "Pop On Over!"

$$\frac{2}{3} = \frac{4}{6}, \frac{10}{15}, \frac{12}{18}$$

$$\frac{3}{4} = \frac{9}{12}, \frac{18}{24}, \frac{27}{36}$$

$$\frac{2}{5} = \frac{4}{10}, \frac{12}{30}$$

$$\frac{3}{5} = \frac{9}{15}, \frac{15}{25}$$

$$\frac{4}{5} = \frac{8}{10}, \frac{36}{45}$$

$$\frac{5}{6} = \frac{15}{18}, \frac{30}{36}$$

$$\frac{3}{8} = \frac{9}{24}, \frac{12}{32}, \frac{18}{48}$$

$$\frac{5}{8} = \frac{10}{16}, \frac{20}{32}, \frac{25}{40}$$

$$\frac{7}{8} = \frac{14}{16}, \frac{21}{24}$$

$$\frac{3}{10} = \frac{6}{20}, \frac{21}{70}$$

$$\frac{7}{10} = \frac{14}{20}, \frac{21}{30}$$

$$\frac{5}{12} = \frac{10}{24}, \frac{15}{36}$$

TEC44062

Smart Journals
Writing mathematic explanations

We've all heard of smartphones and smart technology, but here's an idea for smart journals that's truly sweet! Give each student a roll of Smarties candies and then set high expectations for elaborate math journal responses with any or all of the activities shown. Follow up by picking a homework problem each morning and having students explain their solutions in their smart journals.

Jennifer Otter
Oak Ridge, NC

1. Using your candies, solve the equations. Then explain in your smart journal the differences between the equations. Use diagrams of your candies to make your explanations clear.
   $15 \div 5 = x$
   $15 \div 3 = x$
   $15 \div 2 = x$
   $15 \div 1 = x$
2. Explain how you would divide one roll of 15 candies fairly among four people. Use diagrams to make your explanation clear.
3. Write the rest of a problem that begins "Zander had 15 rolls of 15 candies." Next, solve the problem and explain how you solved it. Then explain how another student might solve the problem.

A Different Race to the Top
Extending fraction concepts (4.NF.A.1–2)

For this partner game, have each pair of students cut apart the totem poles mat, questions grid, and answer key from a copy of page 107. Next, each partner chooses a totem pole and names each fraction model. Then the players read a question from the grid, figure out the answer together, circle it, and check the answer key. If they are correct, they look for the matching fraction model on their totem poles. The player who finds the fraction on his or her totem pole shades that section. If the students are incorrect, they erase their circle and choose another question. The first student to shade her entire totem pole wins.

Jennifer Otter

In Step With the Order of Operations
Using parentheses in numerical expressions (5.OA.A.1)

Help students remember to solve an equation in order with this simple reminder! Draw three steps labeled as shown. Then post a problem and guide students to walk down the steps as they solve it.

Amy Stokes
Lebanon Road Elementary
Charlotte, NC

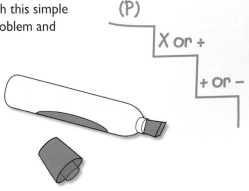

(P)

X or ÷

+ or –

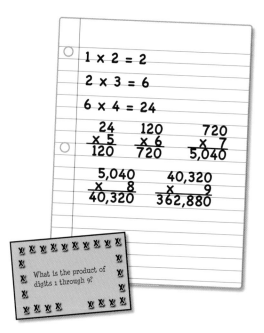

1 x 2 = 2

2 x 3 = 6

6 x 4 = 24

$$\begin{array}{r} 24 \\ \times\ 5 \\ \hline 120 \end{array}$$ $$\begin{array}{r} 120 \\ \times\ 6 \\ \hline 720 \end{array}$$ $$\begin{array}{r} 720 \\ \times\ 7 \\ \hline 5{,}040 \end{array}$$

$$\begin{array}{r} 5{,}040 \\ \times\ 8 \\ \hline 40{,}320 \end{array}$$ $$\begin{array}{r} 40{,}320 \\ \times\ 9 \\ \hline 362{,}880 \end{array}$$

What is the product of digits 1 through 9?

Time to Practice
Multiplying a whole number of up to four digits by a one-digit whole number (4.NBT.B.5)

For this anytime practice, cut apart the cards from a copy of the top of page 108. Then, when students have a minute or two between classes, draw a card. Challenge each student to find the product and check her work before time is up!

tip → Because addresses, birthdates, and zip codes may contain zeroes, this activity is a natural springboard for a discussion about the zero property of multiplication too!

Thinking Outside the Boxes
Understanding volume (5.MD.C.5b)

Here's an idea that has students extend what they know about volume. Display the directions from the bottom of page 108. Then have each pair of students draw and label a box that matches each description. If a twosome finishes early, challenge the duo to flip its paper and draw a box with different dimensions that matches each description.

Jennifer Otter
Oak Ridge, NC

 Flip to page 134 for a practice page on **estimating products.**

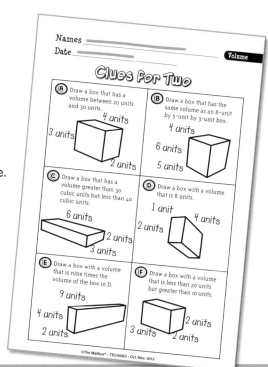

Names _____
Date _____   Volume

Clues for Two

(A) Draw a box that has a volume between 20 units and 30 units.
4 units
3 units
2 units

(B) Draw a box that has the same volume as an 8-unit by 5-unit by 3-unit box.
4 units
6 units
5 units

(C) Draw a box that has a volume greater than 30 cubic units but less than 40 cubic units.
6 units
2 units
3 units

(D) Draw a box with a volume that is 8 units.
1 unit
4 units
2 units

(E) Draw a box with a volume that is nine times the volume of the box in D.
9 units
4 units
2 units

(F) Draw a box with a volume that is less than 20 units but greater than 10 units.
2 units
3 units 2 units

©The Mailbox® • TEC44063 • Oct./Nov. 2012

Totem Poles Mat, Questions Grid, and Answer Key

Use with "A Different Race to the Top" on page 105.

① Which fraction is not equivalent to $\frac{1}{4}$? $\frac{3}{12}$ $\frac{1}{6}$ $\frac{2}{8}$	**②** Which fraction is greater than the bar? $\frac{7}{10}$ $\frac{8}{10}$ $\frac{9}{10}$	**③** Which fraction describes the bar? $\frac{3}{10}$ $\frac{3}{8}$ $\frac{1}{3}$	**④** Which fraction is not in lowest terms? $\frac{5}{6}$ $\frac{3}{8}$ $\frac{8}{10}$
⑤ What fraction of the boxes is striped? $\frac{3}{10}$ $\frac{3}{8}$ $\frac{1}{3}$	**⑥** What fraction of the bar is not shaded? $\frac{2}{3}$ $\frac{3}{4}$ $\frac{1}{3}$	**⑦** Which of the fractions is in lowest terms? $\frac{5}{12}$ $\frac{5}{10}$ $\frac{4}{12}$	**⑧** Which fraction is nearest one? $\frac{7}{8}$ $\frac{3}{4}$ $\frac{5}{6}$
⑨ Which fraction is not equivalent to $\frac{1}{3}$? $\frac{2}{6}$ $\frac{4}{12}$ $\frac{3}{5}$	**⑩** Which fraction describes the shaded shapes? $\frac{1}{3}$ $\frac{1}{6}$ $\frac{1}{2}$	**⑪** Which fraction is greater than $\frac{1}{2}$? $\frac{3}{8}$ $\frac{4}{5}$ $\frac{5}{12}$	**⑫** Which fraction is in lowest terms? $\frac{2}{3}$ $\frac{8}{12}$ $\frac{3}{9}$
⑬ Which fraction is equivalent to $\frac{5}{6}$? $\frac{15}{12}$ $\frac{10}{12}$ $\frac{25}{24}$	**⑭** Which fraction is $\frac{3}{12}$ in lowest terms? $\frac{1}{3}$ $\frac{3}{8}$ $\frac{1}{4}$	**⑮** Which fraction is equivalent to $\frac{2}{5}$? $\frac{4}{5}$ $\frac{4}{10}$ $\frac{2}{10}$	**⑯** Which fraction is equivalent to $\frac{1}{5}$? $\frac{2}{10}$ $\frac{3}{20}$ $\frac{2}{15}$
⑰ Which fraction is closest to 0? $\frac{1}{5}$ $\frac{1}{8}$ $\frac{1}{6}$	**⑱** Which fraction is $\frac{15}{20}$ in lowest terms? $\frac{3}{5}$ $\frac{1}{3}$ $\frac{3}{4}$	**⑲** Which fraction is less than $\frac{1}{8}$? $\frac{1}{4}$ $\frac{1}{6}$ $\frac{1}{10}$	**⑳** Which fraction is $\frac{35}{56}$ in lowest terms? $\frac{5}{7}$ $\frac{7}{8}$ $\frac{5}{8}$

Answer Key for "A Different Race to the Top"

1. $\frac{1}{6}$
2. $\frac{9}{10}$
3. $\frac{3}{8}$
4. $\frac{8}{10}$
5. $\frac{3}{10}$
6. $\frac{1}{3}$
7. $\frac{5}{12}$
8. $\frac{7}{8}$
9. $\frac{3}{5}$
10. $\frac{1}{2}$
11. $\frac{4}{5}$
12. $\frac{2}{3}$
13. $\frac{10}{12}$
14. $\frac{1}{4}$
15. $\frac{4}{10}$
16. $\frac{2}{10}$
17. $\frac{1}{8}$
18. $\frac{3}{4}$
19. $\frac{1}{10}$
20. $\frac{5}{8}$

TEC44063

A Different Race to the Top

Multiplication Challenge Cards

Use with "Time to Practice" on page 106.

What is the product of the five digits in your zip code? TEC44063	What is the product of the digits in your telephone number? TEC44063	What is the product of digits 1 through 9? TEC44063
What is the product of the digits in your school's street address? TEC44063	What is the product of the digits in your home street address? TEC44063	What is the product of the digits in your birthdate? TEC44063
What is the product of the digits in your school's phone number? TEC44063	What is the product of the digits in the number of students in your school? TEC44063	What is the product of the digits in your best friend's phone number? TEC44063

Names _____
Date _____

Volume

Clues For Two

A Draw a box that has a volume between 20 units and 30 units.

B Draw a box that has the same volume as an 8-unit by 5-unit by 3-unit box.

C Draw a box that has a volume greater than 30 cubic units but less than 40 cubic units.

D Draw a box with a volume that is 8 units.

E Draw a box with a volume that is nine times the volume of the box in D.

F Draw a box with a volume that is less than 20 units but greater than 10 units.

Note to the teacher: Use with "Thinking Outside the Boxes" on page 106.

MATH
Tips & Tools

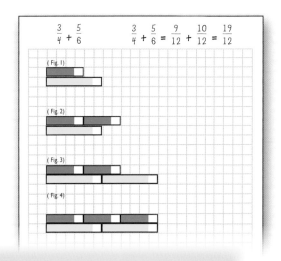

A Shuffleboard Challenge
Finding factor pairs, greatest common factor (4.OA.B.4, 6.NS.B.4)

Here's a simple version of shuffleboard that gives students practice finding factors! To play, give each pair of students a copy of page 111, a penny, and access to scrap paper. Then have each player choose a side of the gameboard. On scrap paper, each player lists the factor pairs for the number on his Round 1 lane. Then he writes the factors in order in his lane's circles. Next, the partners compare their factors and identify the greatest common factor (GCF). Each partner draws a box around the GCF in his lane. Then each player, in turn, puts the penny on Start, flicks it toward the GCF in his partner's lane, and traces the penny where it stops. The player whose penny stops closer to his partner's GCF wins the round. The player who wins the most rounds is the GCF shuffleboard champ.

Amy Payne, Clara J. Peck Elementary, Greensboro, NC

I See!
Finding common denominators, adding fractions with unlike denominators (5.NF.A.1)

Do you have students who don't understand how or why to find common denominators? Here's an awesome idea sure to help them! Begin by introducing a problem such as the one shown. Then follow the steps below.

Lori Carrigan, Wallace Middle School, Bristol, VA

$$\frac{3}{4} + \frac{5}{6} \qquad \frac{3}{4} + \frac{5}{6} = \frac{9}{12} + \frac{10}{12} = \frac{19}{12}$$

(Fig. 1)

(Fig. 2)

(Fig. 3)

(Fig. 4)

Directions:
1. On a sheet of graph paper, draw a rectangle with a box for each denominator. Then shade boxes within each rectangle to equal the numerator. (Figure 1)
2. Guide students to compare the fraction bars and recognize that their lengths (denominators) are not equal, so the fractions cannot be added.
3. To find the fractions' equal length or common denominator, draw another fraction bar equal to the small fraction, pointing out that the bars still aren't equal. (Figure 2) Next, add a fraction bar equal to the large fraction, noting that the fraction bars are not yet equal. (Figure 3) Continue until the fraction bars are equal. (Figure 4)
4. Have students count the number of boxes in each row. That is the fractions' common denominator. Next, have students count the number of shaded boxes in each row. That is each fraction's numerator. Rewrite the problem with the equivalent fractions and solve!

Chipping Away
Decomposing fractions (4.NF.B.3b)

To introduce this skill, give each student a handful of base ten blocks. Next, guide each child to form a unit of four blocks, draw a diagram that represents them, and record an equation that describes them. Then have the child make two groups of two blocks each, diagram them, and record their equation. After that, have the student make two groups—one with three blocks and one with one block—diagram the blocks, and record their equation. Repeat the process, using other whole numbers and fractions.

LaVone Novotny, Liberty Elementary, Caledonia, OH

$\frac{1}{4} + \frac{1}{4} + \frac{1}{4} + \frac{1}{4} = \frac{4}{4} = 1$

$\frac{2}{4} + \frac{2}{4} = 1$

$\frac{3}{4} + \frac{1}{4} = 1$

$\frac{1}{8} + \frac{1}{8} + \frac{1}{8} + \frac{1}{8} + \frac{1}{8} + \frac{1}{8} + \frac{1}{8} + \frac{1}{8} = \frac{8}{8} = 1$

$\frac{2}{8} + \frac{1}{8} + \frac{1}{8} + \frac{1}{8} + \frac{1}{8} + \frac{1}{8} + \frac{1}{8} = \frac{8}{8}$

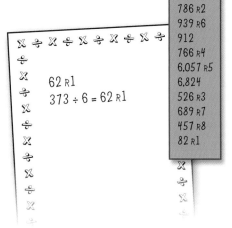

62 R1

373 ÷ 6 = 62 R1

786 R2
939 R6
912
766 R4
6,057 R5
6,824
526 R3
689 R7
457 R8
82 R1

The Great Divide
Multiplication, division (4.NBT.B.6, 5.NBT.B.6, 6.NS.B.2)

Here's a different approach to computation practice! Post quotients to several division problems, such as those shown. Next, challenge each student to create a problem with one or two divisors for each quotient. Then have each child trade his paper with a partner and solve each other's problems to check his work.

adapted from an idea by Jennifer Otter, Oak Ridge, NC

Build Your Own
Understanding angle concepts (4.G.A.1)

For this hands-on idea, give each student a bit of clay and two coffee stirrers. Then guide the child to use the materials to build different angles. Once students can reliably create acute, obtuse, and right angles, have each child create an angle on her desktop. Next, have students rotate to each other's desks and then record each student's name and the type of angle she made. When students finish, have them return to their desks. Then walk around the room, calling out students' names, naming their angles, and having students check their work.

Susanna Joubret, Grady A. Brown Elementary, Hillsborough, NC

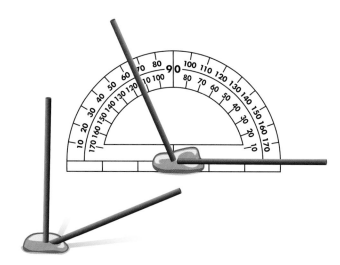

 tip

When it's time to teach students how to measure angles, have each child create an angle using clay and stirrers and then place the protractor's center on the clay vertex. The clay helps hold the protractor still, making it easier for students to learn how to line up the rays and measure the angle. (4.MD.C.6)

 Flip to **page 135** for a practice page on **decomposing mixed numbers**!

Greatest Common Factor Shuffleboard Player B

		Round 6	Round 6			
Start	105	⬭⬭⬭⬭⬭⬭⬭			70	Start
Start	56	⬭⬭⬭⬭⬭⬭⬭	Round 5	Round 5	⬭⬭⬭⬭⬭⬭⬭	24	Start
Start	42	⬭⬭⬭⬭⬭⬭	Round 4	Round 4	⬭⬭⬭⬭⬭⬭	64	Start
Start	30	⬭⬭⬭⬭⬭⬭	Round 3	Round 3	⬭⬭⬭⬭⬭⬭	40	Start
Start	20	⬭⬭⬭⬭⬭	Round 2	Round 2	⬭⬭⬭⬭⬭	18	Start
Start	16	⬭⬭⬭⬭	Round 1	Round 1	⬭⬭⬭⬭⬭	12	Start

Greatest Common Factor Shuffleboard Player A

MATH
Tips & Tools

Out and About
**Multiplying, adding decimals
(5.NBT.B.7)**

For a real-world center that's easy to update, collect the weekly grocery ads from your local paper. Next, make a grocery list of multiple items that are common to the ads and post it along with the ads. Then have each student choose a store's flyer, jot its name on her recording sheet, find each listed item, and multiply to get the total cost. When the child finishes, have her add the items and circle the total cost. For an extra challenge, have each student study the ads and find each item's best price before calculating the total cost. Once all students have rotated through the center, just post new ads and a new list!

3 dozen eggs
2 pounds of carrots
3 packages of
    paper towels
5 bananas

Rifky Schlesinger, Bais Rochel School, Brooklyn, NY

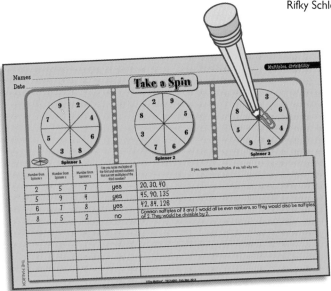

Take a Spin
**Gaining familiarity with multiples, divisibility
(4.OA.B.4)**

For this idea, display a copy of page 114. Spin each spinner and record each number in the columns as guided. If you spin the same number, spin again. Next, lead students to decide whether you can name a number that is a multiple of the first two numbers but not of the third number, recording students' thoughts as guided. Repeat for several trials and then have each student complete a copy of the page. Follow up with a class discussion of multiples and divisibility.

Amy Alferman, Hermann Middle School, Hermann, MO

Expression Go Fish
Writing and interpreting numerical expressions (5.OA.A.1–2)

To give students practice with this important skill, have a small group of students remove the face cards from, shuffle, and deal a deck of cards to play a game of Go Fish! Instead of asking each other for cards, students must write numerical expressions that describe the cards' numbers. Depending on students' skills, direct them to include parentheses, brackets, braces, and different operations in each expression. When it's a student's turn, she writes an expression that results in the number matching a card she needs. Then the child passes the note to the player she chooses, who evaluates the expression and hands over the matching cards or tells the player to "go fish."

Cynthia Poast, Hamilton Intermediate School, Columbus, OH

Hidden Numbers
Building precision

Differentiation is the name of this computation game! To begin, have each pair of students make a 6 x 6 grid on a sheet of paper. Next, guide the twosome to fill in the grid with randomly placed numbers, fractions, mixed numbers, or decimals, depending on what the students need practice with. Then have the pair cover each number with a checker. To play, direct the students to add, subtract, multiply, or divide, depending on their area of need and guide them to follow the steps shown.

Isobel Livingstone, Rahway, NJ

Directions for two players:
1. Player 1 lifts two checkers. Both players add, subtract, multiply, or divide (as you have been directed) the numbers that Player 1 reveals.
2. Compare your answers. If they are different, check your work to determine which one is correct.
3. If Player 1 is correct, he or she keeps both checkers and Player 2 takes a turn. If Player 1 is incorrect, he or she returns the checkers to the grid. Then Player 2 takes a turn.
4. Keep playing until all the numbers are revealed or time is up. The player with more checkers wins the game.

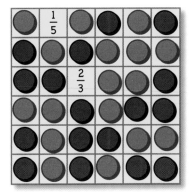

One-fifth times two-thirds.

Merry Old Tales of Measurement
Customary measurements of liquid volume (4.MD.A.1, W.4.3, W.5.3)

Help students remember capacity equivalencies with this creative take on the gallon man idea! First, have each student imagine an island named Gadzooks (gallon) that is ruled by four queens (quarts). Each queen has two princes or princesses (pints), and each prince or princess has two cats (cups). Next, have each student write a story set on the island that includes all the characters and cats. Follow up by having students share their stories in small groups, and they're sure to remember that there are four quarts in a gallon, two pints in a quart, and two cups in a pint!

Deb Gribben, Crestview Elementary, Henrico, VA

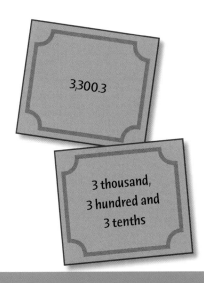

3,300.3

3 thousand, 3 hundred and 3 tenths

Mix and Match
Decimal number forms, place value (5.NBT.A.3a)

For this thought-provoking game, have each pair of students cut out a copy of the cards from page 115 and then spread them facedown. Next, have each student, in turn, flip two cards and check to see if they describe the same number. If the cards match, have the child keep them. If the cards don't match, have her flip them back over. Allow students to play until all the matches are made and declare the player with more matches the winner. Then have each student arrange her cards in order from least to greatest and record the numbers on a separate paper using <, >, and = signs to compare the values.

Name _____

Date _____

Take a Spin

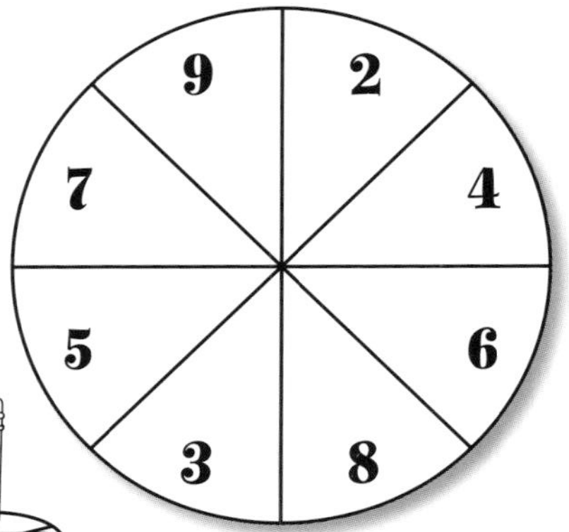

Spinner 1

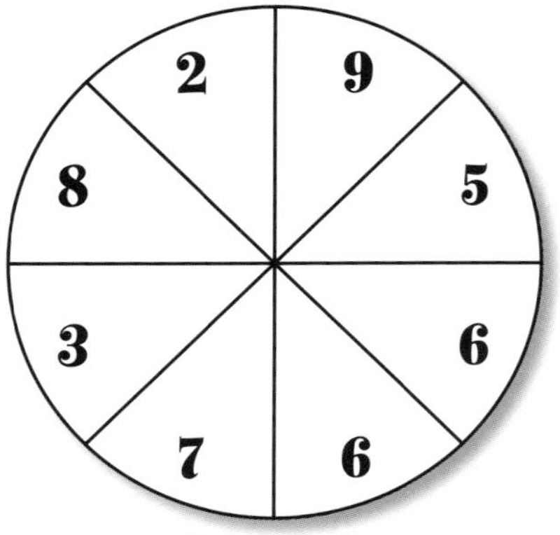

9	2	4
7		6
5	3	8

Spinner 2

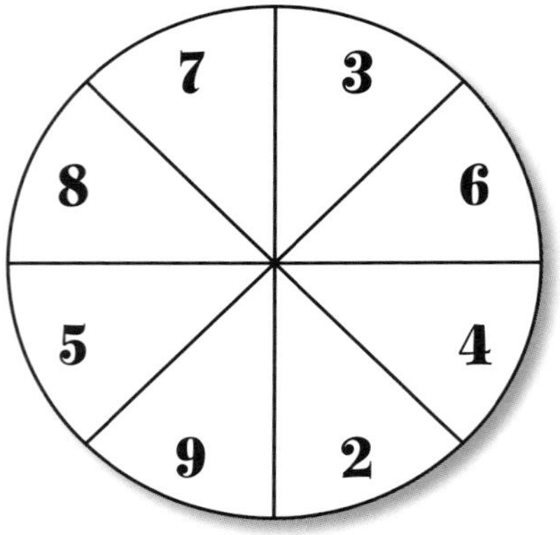

9	5
2		6
8	7	6
	3	

Spinner 3

3	6
7		4
8		2
5	9	

Number from Spinner 1	Number from Spinner 2	Number from Spinner 3	Can you name multiples of the first and second numbers that are not multiples of the third number?	If yes, name three multiples. If no, tell why not.

©The Mailbox® • TEC44065 • Feb./Mar. 2013 • (4.OA.B.4)

Note to the teacher: Use with "Take a Spin" on page 112.

3,300.3 TEC44065	30 thousand, 3 hundred and 3 hundredths TEC44065	thirty thousand, three hundred and three thousandths TEC44065	3,000 + 300 + 0.3 TEC44065
30 thousand, 3 hundred and 3 thousandths TEC44065	3 thousand, 3 hundred and 3 tenths TEC44065	30,300.003 TEC44065	thirty thousand, three hundred and three tenths TEC44065
30,300.3 TEC44065	thirty thousand, three hundred and three hundredths TEC44065	3,000 + 300 + 0.003 TEC44065	3 thousand, 3 hundred and 3 hundredths TEC44065
30,000 + 300 + 0.03 TEC44065	3 thousand, 300 and 3 thousandths TEC44065	3,300.03 TEC44065	30,000 + 300 + 0.003 TEC44065
three thousand, three hundred and three tenths TEC44065	3,000 + 300 + 0.03 TEC44065	three thousand, three hundred and three hundredths TEC44065	3,300.003 TEC44065
30,000 + 300 + 0.3 TEC44065	three thousand, three hundred and three thousandths TEC44065	30,300.03 TEC44065	30 thousand, 3 hundred and 3 tenths TEC44065

MATH Tips & Tools

Signed, Sealed, and Delivered
Problem solving (4.OA.A.2, 3; 5.NF.A.2)

Help students make real-world math connections by having them write their own problems. As students master each grade-level operation, review its real-world applications. Then guide each child to write and solve a problem based on the skill. After you review the student's work, have her write the problem on the back of an envelope. Next, have her write on an index card an equation that represents the problem along with its solution. Then have her slip the index card inside the envelope. Finally, collect students' envelopes, wet the adhesive on each one, and stick it to the front of another envelope as shown, making an accordion book that's perfect for problem-solving practice!

Christine Hooper, Weston Elementary, Manchester, NH

Day 1 = 3

Day 2 = 3 x 3 = 9

Day 3 = 3 x 3 x 3 = 27

Day 4 =

During the last week of school, the principal handed out awards to students with stellar behavior. On the first day, she gave out a total of three awards for stellar behavior. Then, for each day after the first day, she gave three times as many awards as the previous day. How many awards did the principal give out on the third and fourth days?

A Dreamy Backyard
Perimeter, area (4.MD.A.3) with fractional side lengths (5.NF.B.4b)

Here's a fun idea that has students using formulas to find perimeter and area measurements. To begin, have each child imagine five or more features he would want in his ideal backyard. Next, have the student draw his dream backyard, using an overhead view of the yard. Guide each child to clearly show his yard's perimeter and draw the features so they have straight lines. (If desired, have students use graph paper.) Then have the child label his yard's and each feature's length and width. Finally, guide each student to calculate the area and perimeter of each shape and record the measurements on a chart similar to the one shown. **For a more challenging version**, have students use fractional side lengths.

Katie Hartman, Sinking Springs Elementary, York, PA

My Dream Yard				
Yard or Feature	Length	Width	Perimeter (2l + 2w or s + s + s + s)	Area (l x w)
yard	250 ft	165 ft	830 ft	41,250 ft²
swimming pool	70 ft	60 ft	260 ft	4,200 ft²
basketball court	94 ft	50 ft	288 ft	4,700 ft²
dog mansion	45 ft	40 ft	170 ft	1,800 ft².
mini golf course	130 ft	70 ft	400 ft	9,100 ft²
fresh fruit orchard	130 ft	15 ft	290 ft	1,905 ft²

My Dream Yard

The Envelope Please...
Values of variables

For this idea, cut apart the equation cards and owl pattern on page 118. Glue the owl pattern on a manila envelope and store the cards in a resealable bag inside the envelope. For the activity, clip an equation card to the owl as shown. Then pass the envelope to a student, who evaluates the equation and writes the variable's value on a strip of scrap paper along with her name. Next, she puts the strip inside the envelope and passes it to the next student. Once the envelope has been routed to everyone in the class, review the equation's solution and draw one or two strips from the envelope. If the responses are correct, award those students with a small treat or bonus points on a future assignment.

Colleen Dabney, Williamsburg, VA

① $x - 9 = 1$
What does x equal?

Compare and Contrast
- a standard ruler and a metric ruler
- any two different place value periods, such as thousands and ten millions
- any two sets of multiples
- an acute angle and an obtuse angle
- a bar graph and a line graph
- two operations, such as multiplication and division
- using mental math and using a calculator
- a rhombus and an equilateral triangle

In the Balance
Mathematical practices: communication

Build students' analytical and communication skills with this simple idea. Start one math lesson each week by having students draw a Venn diagram. Next, announce a pair of topics, such as one of those shown, and challenge students to fill out the diagram to compare and contrast the topics. Then display a Venn diagram and have students share their work.

Spin a Winner!
Multiplication, division review (4.NBT.B.5; 5.NBT.B.5, 6)

This game works with two or four students. To play, students need a copy of page 119, a calculator, and a paper clip. The students take turns using the paper clip to spin each spinner. Each child records the numbers and operation spun and then solves the problem. When all the players have solved the problem, the one who spun the spinners checks the problem on the calculator. Each player who solved the problem correctly earns a point, and then the next player spins the spinners. The student with the most points when time is up wins the game!

Marie E. Cecchini, West Dundee, IL

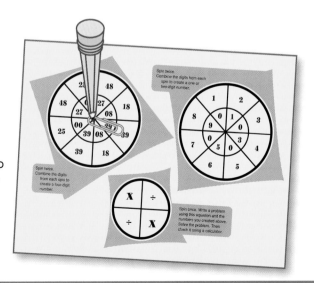

Owl Pattern and Equation Cards

Use with "The Envelope Please…" on page 117.

TEC44066

①
$$x - 9 = 1$$
What does x equal?

TEC44066

②
$$4x + 1 = 49$$
What does x equal?

TEC44066

③
$$x + 7 = 18$$
What does x equal?

TEC44066

④
$$2x - 5 = 25$$
What does x equal?

TEC44066

⑤
$$8x - 6 = 58$$
What does x equal?

TEC44066

⑥
$$(40 + x) \div 7 = 8$$
What does x equal?

TEC44066

⑦
$$3(x + 8) = 36$$
What does x equal?

TEC44066

⑧
$$84 \div (x - 2) = 21$$
What does x equal?

TEC44066

Spin twice.
Combine the digits from each spin to create a one or two-digit number.

Spin once.
Write a problem using this operation and the numbers you created above. Solve the problem. Then check it using a calculator.

Spin twice.
Combine the digits from each spin to create a four-digit number.

Note to the teacher: Use with "Spin a Winner!" on page 117.

MATH Tips & Tools

Math With Fairy-Tale Roots
Problem solving (4.OA.A.3; 5.NF.B.6)

Challenge students to write word problems with fairy-tale characters as the subjects. Then have each student trade her problem with a partner to proofread and solve each other's work. After that, have each child record her problem on a large index card, illustrate it, and write the answer on the card's flip side. Store students' cards in an envelope for a great problem-solving center that's ready to use when school starts next year!

Isobel Livingstone, Rahway, NJ

If Goldilocks spends $5.79, $12.38, and $4.25 on hair products, how much of her $25 allowance will she have left to buy oatmeal cookie bars?

$2.58

For Good Measure
Relative sizes of metric units (4.MD.A.1; 5.MD.A.1)

To keep students' measurement skills sharp, copy and cut apart the cards on page 122. Then keep them handy. When students are standing in line or transitioning between classes, have a student draw a card and read the question aloud, keeping the answer to herself. For every question students answer correctly, award the class a bonus point. When the class earns a predetermined number of bonus points, celebrate with a few minutes of extra recess or other small treat!

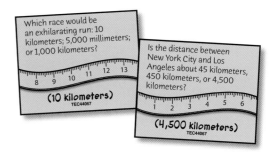

Which race would be an exhilarating run: 10 kilometers; 5,000 millimeters; or 1,000 kilometers?

(10 kilometers)
TEC44067

Is the distance between New York City and Los Angeles about 45 kilometers, 450 kilometers, or 4,500 kilometers?

(4,500 kilometers)
TEC44067

Factor Toss
Factors, multiples (4.OA.B.4)

To make this simplified version of a classic carnival ring-toss game, just glue several small eight-ounce plastic containers (from softened cream cheese or sour cream) to a sturdy piece of cardboard. Then tape the cups' edges together with clear packing tape. Using a wipe-off marker, write a different number in the base of each cup. Next, have a student stand back from the gameboard and toss a small beanbag or Koosh ball into a cup. Then have the child read the cup's number and announce its factors and two or more of its multiples.

Robin Cubbage, Luray Elementary, Luray, VA

tip → To address different skills using the gameboard, simply wipe off the numbers and write vocabulary terms, decimals, fractions, or operation symbols inside the cups. Then use the game to practice vocabulary, create equations, or practice math facts.

What's the Pattern, Partner?
Number, shape patterns (4.OA.C.5)

For this partner game, each pair of students needs a copy of the chart from below, different-colored pencils, and a die.

Colleen Dabney, Williamsburg, VA

Directions:
1. In turn, roll the die and find the matching column on the grid.
2. Choose a row and circle the space along that row that is in the matching column. Identify the pattern in the row and then write the number or symbol that will continue the pattern in the circled space. Use a different-colored pencil than your partner.
3. If there are no open spaces in the column that matches your roll, your turn is over.
4. When all the spaces are filled, check the key. The player with more correct numbers and symbols wins the game.

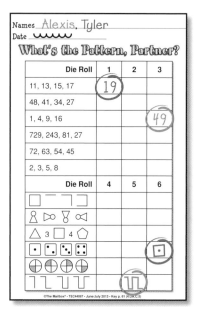

Names _____
Date _____

What's the Pattern, Partner?

Die Roll	1	2	3
11, 13, 15, 17			
48, 41, 34, 27			
1, 4, 9, 16			
729, 243, 81, 27			
72, 63, 54, 45			
2, 3, 5, 8			

Die Roll	4	5	6

©The Mailbox® • TEC44067 • June/July 2013 • Key p. 308 • (4.OA.C.5)

Note to the teacher: Use with "What's the Pattern, Partner?" on this page.

Measurement Cards

Use with "For Good Measure" on page 120.

Is the circumference of a pencil about 25 millimeters, 25 centimeters, or 250 millimeters?	When you take one step, do you cover a distance of about 2.5 meters, 0.5 meters, or 25 millimeters?	Is the distance around the bases of a softball field about 500 centimeters, 2,000 meters, or 75 meters?
(25 millimeters) TEC44067	**(0.5 meters)** TEC44067	**(75 meters)** TEC44067
Is the distance between New York City and Los Angeles about 45 kilometers, 450 kilometers, or 4,500 kilometers?	Is the height of a basketball rim about 3,000 centimeters, 3 meters, or 30 millimeters?	Is the diameter of a car's tire about 60 centimeters, 6.0 meters, or 60 millimeters?
(4,500 kilometers) TEC44067	**(3 meters)** TEC44067	**(60 centimeters)** TEC44067
Would your hat size be about 50 centimeters, 5.5 centimeters, or 500 centimeters?	Which race would be an exhilarating run: 10 kilometers; 5,000 millimeters; or 1,000 kilometers?	Is a sheet of paper about 200 millimeters, 2 meters, or 2.2 centimeters wide?
(50 centimeters) TEC44067	**(10 kilometers)** TEC44067	**(200 millimeters)** TEC44067
Would a stack of ten pennies be about 15 millimeters, 15 centimeters, or 1.5 meters high?	Are the writing lines on a sheet of notebook paper about 10 centimeters, 10 millimeters, or 0.1 meters apart?	Does a stop sign measure about 1 meter, 10 meters, or 0.1 meter across?
(15 millimeters) TEC44067	**(10 millimeters)** TEC44067	**(1 meter)** TEC44067
Does the distance across a watch face measure about 200 millimeters, 2 centimeters, or 20 centimeters?	Is a baseball bat about 1 meter, 1 centimeter, or 1 millimeter long?	Is a box for a large pizza about 50 meters, 50 centimeters, or 50 millimeters square?
(2 centimeters) TEC44067	**(1 meter)** TEC44067	**(50 centimeters)** TEC44067

Names

Date

BURROWING INTO DIVISION!

A Game for Two Players

Directions:

1. Choose a burrow.
2. Next, solve a problem on your path. Show your work on another sheet of paper and record the quotient on the space. Then solve another problem.
3. When both players have solved all their problems, check each other's work by multiplying each quotient by the divisor and adding any remainder. The player with more correct quotients wins!

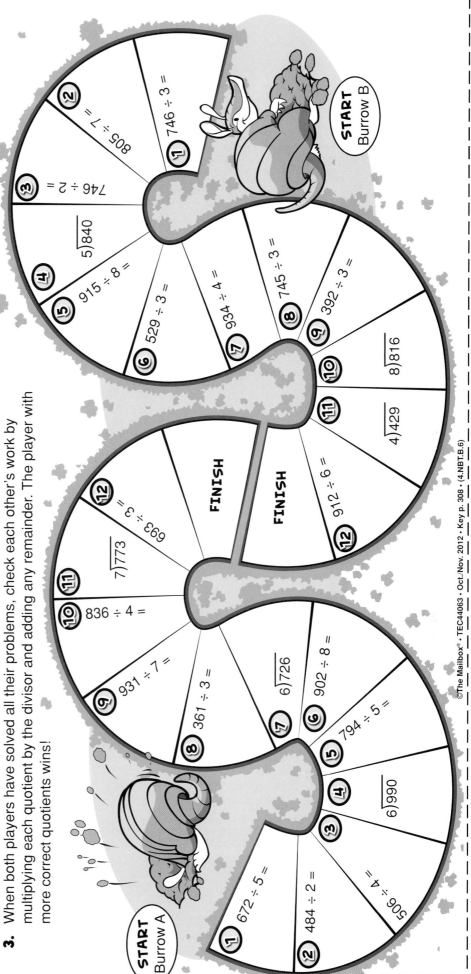

START Burrow B

1. $746 \div 3 =$
2. $805 \div 7 =$
3. $746 \div 2 =$
4. $5\overline{)840}$
5. $915 \div 8 =$
6. $529 \div 3 =$
7. $934 \div 4 =$
8. $745 \div 3 =$
9. $392 \div 3 =$
10. $8\overline{)816}$
11. $4\overline{)429}$
12. $912 \div 6 =$

FINISH

FINISH

12. $693 \div 3 =$
11. $7\overline{)773}$
10. $836 \div 4 =$
9. $931 \div 7 =$
8. $361 \div 3 =$
7. $6\overline{)726}$
6. $902 \div 8 =$
5. $794 \div 5 =$
4. $6\overline{)990}$
3. $506 \div 4 =$
2. $484 \div 2 =$
1. $672 \div 5 =$

START Burrow A

How to use: Each pair of students needs a copy of this page and paper.

Names _____

Date _____

THE FRONT RUNNER

A Game for Two Players

Directions:

1. When it's your turn, spin the paper clip.
2. Follow the directions on the spinner.
3. If you're correct, leave your marker. If you're incorrect, move back one space.
4. The first player to reach Finish wins.

Spinner:
- Move 1 space. Round the decimal to the nearest whole number.
- Move 2 spaces. Round the decimal to the nearest tenth.
- Move 3 spaces. Round the decimal to the nearest hundredth.

Start

1.353 _____

8.508 _____

4.912 _____

0.763 _____

3.467 _____

0.409 _____

13.085 _____

6.469 _____   7.123 _____

5.063 _____   12.057 _____

9.072 _____   7.238 _____

0.026 _____   0.884 _____

8.218 _____   9.513 _____

68.461 _____   57.042 _____   18.321 _____   **Finish**

21.465 _____

8.006 _____   3.145 _____   1.352 _____   0.876 _____   0.305 _____

1.501 _____   3.579 _____   4.683 _____   3.095 _____   2.316 _____   8.652 _____

Side to Side

Directions:

1. Choose a side.
2. In turn, spin the spinner five times. Write each number in any of the Round 1 boxes on your side.
3. You and your partner solve your problems on separate sheets of paper and record the quotients on this page.
4. Check each other's quotient. (Multiply the quotient by the divisor and then add the remainder if there is one. This should equal the dividend.) If your quotient is correct, shade the oval.
5. Repeat Steps 2–4 for the remaining rounds. The player with more shaded ovals wins the game.

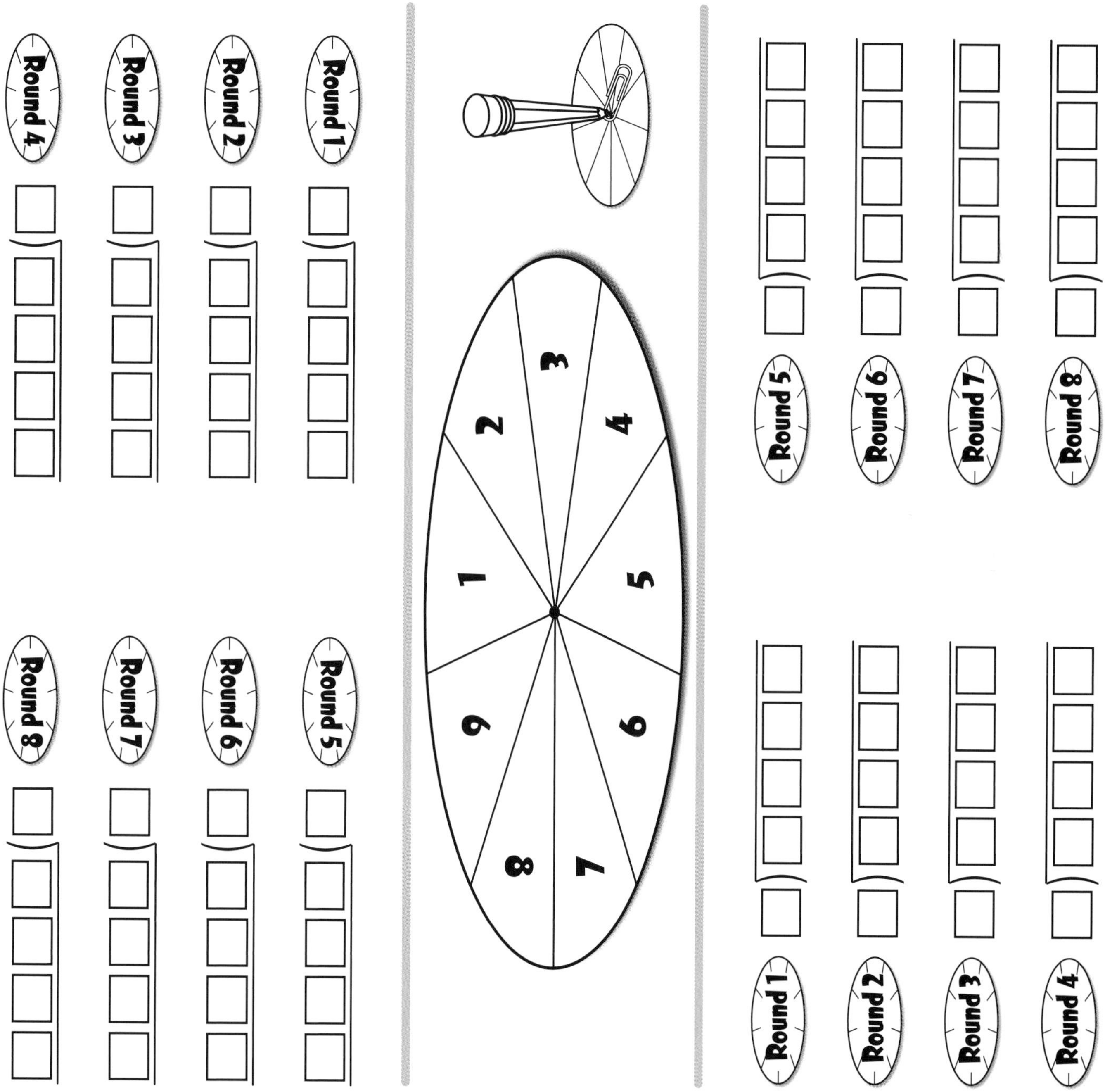

Round 4 Round 3 Round 2 Round 1

Round 5 Round 6 Round 7 Round 8

3 2 4 1 5 6 9 8 7

Round 8 Round 7 Round 6 Round 5

Round 1 Round 2 Round 3 Round 4

Names _____

Date _____

"DECIMAL-OMINOES"

Directions for two players:

1. Fold the answer key behind the page. Then choose a path.

2. When it's your turn, choose a decimal from the dominoes below. Jot the decimal in an open space on your path. Then round the decimal to the nearest whole number, tenth, or hundredth as guided on the space and record the rounded number on your paper.

3. Continue until you and your partner have filled in all the spaces on your paths. Then check the key. Circle each space that you rounded correctly. The partner with more circled spaces wins!

Left path:

| nearest tenth |
| nearest hundredth |
| nearest whole number |
| nearest hundredth |
| nearest hundredth |
| nearest hundredth |
| nearest whole number |
| nearest tenth |

Middle-left path:

| nearest whole number |
| nearest tenth |
| nearest tenth |
| nearest tenth |
| nearest whole number |
| nearest hundredth |
| nearest whole number |

Right paths:

| nearest tenth |
| nearest hundredth |
| nearest tenth |
| nearest tenth |
| nearest tenth |

| nearest hundredth |
| nearest whole number |
| nearest hundredth |
| nearest whole number |
| nearest hundredth |
| nearest whole number |

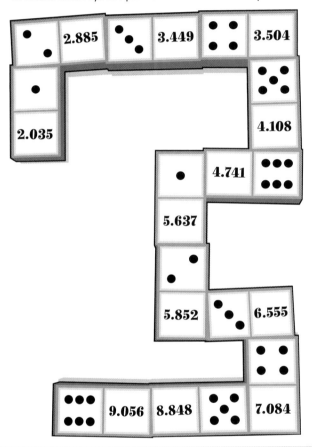

Dominoes: 2.885, 3.449, 3.504, 2.035, 4.108, 4.741, 5.637, 5.852, 6.555, 9.056, 8.848, 7.084

Answer Key for "Decimal-ominoes"

Decimal	Nearest Whole Number	Nearest Tenth	Nearest Hundredth
2.035	2	2.0	2.04
2.885	3	2.9	2.89
3.449	3	3.4	3.45
3.504	4	3.5	3.50
4.108	4	4.1	4.11
4.741	5	4.7	4.74
5.637	6	5.6	5.64
5.852	6	5.9	5.85
6.555	7	6.6	6.56
7.084	7	7.1	7.08
8.848	9	8.8	8.85
9.056	9	9.1	9.06

©The Mailbox® • TEC44067 • June/July 2013 • (5.NBT.A.4)

How to Use Each pair of students needs a copy of the page.

What a Deal!

3 Different Games Using the Same Set of Cards

Materials for each game:

copies of the cards from page 128
scissors
paper

Choose a game and follow the directions.

Game 1

1. Cut apart the cards and answer key. Spread the cards facedown.
2. When it's your turn, flip two cards.
3. If the cards are equivalent, keep them.* Have your partner check the key. If the cards aren't equivalent, turn them back over.
4. Continue until all the matches have been made. The player with more matches wins.

To show your work, record each equivalent pair.

Game 2

1. Cut apart the cards and answer key. Separate the fraction and decimal cards.
2. Stack the fraction and decimal cards in separate facedown piles.
3. In turn, flip the top decimal and fraction cards. Compare the decimal and fraction. Decide whether the fraction is equal to or greater than the decimal.* Then have your partner check the key. If you are correct, keep both cards. If you're not correct, return the cards to the bottom of each stack.
4. Play until all the cards have been played. The player with more cards wins.

To show your work, record each fraction and decimal comparison using <, >, or =.

Game 3

1. Cut apart the cards and answer key. Turn the key facedown and shuffle the cards.
2. Deal five cards to your partner and to yourself; stack the rest of the cards facedown. Then turn the top card of the stack faceup to create a discard pile.
3. In turn, discard one of your cards that is equal to or greater than the card on the discard pile. Cards equivalent to one-half or one-fourth are wild and can be played on any card.* Have your partner check the key.
4. If you can't play a card, you may draw up to three cards from the stack. If you cannot play any of those cards, your turn is over.
5. The first player to discard all his or her cards wins the game.

To show your work, record each comparison using <, >, or =.

Game Cards and Answer Key

Use with "What a Deal!" on page 127.

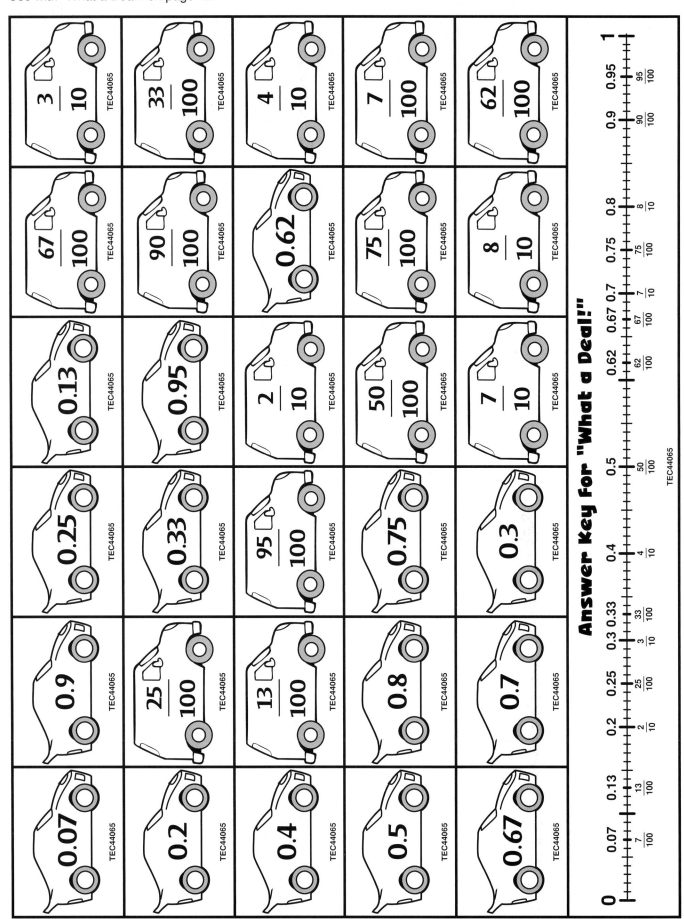

Answer Key for "What a Deal!"

TIME OUT TO SHOP!

Is everything here really on the list?

FINISH

THE CHECKOUT LINE NEVER SEEMS TO END! MOVE BACK ONE SPACE.

SUPER-DUPER BINDERS ARE BUY 2 GET 3 FREE! MOVE AHEAD ONE SPACE.

Directions for two players:
1. Stack the cards facedown. Then place each marker on Start.
2. Each player draws a card and solves the problem.
3. When you are both finished, check each other's product on a calculator. If your products are correct, move the game markers according to the code. If a product is incorrect, that player does not move the game marker.
4. Repeat Steps 2 and 3 until a player reaches Finish and wins the game.

START

Code

= Move ahead one space.

= Move ahead two spaces.

Multiplication Problem Cards

Use with "Time Out to Shop!" on page 129. Students will need paper, game markers, and calculators.

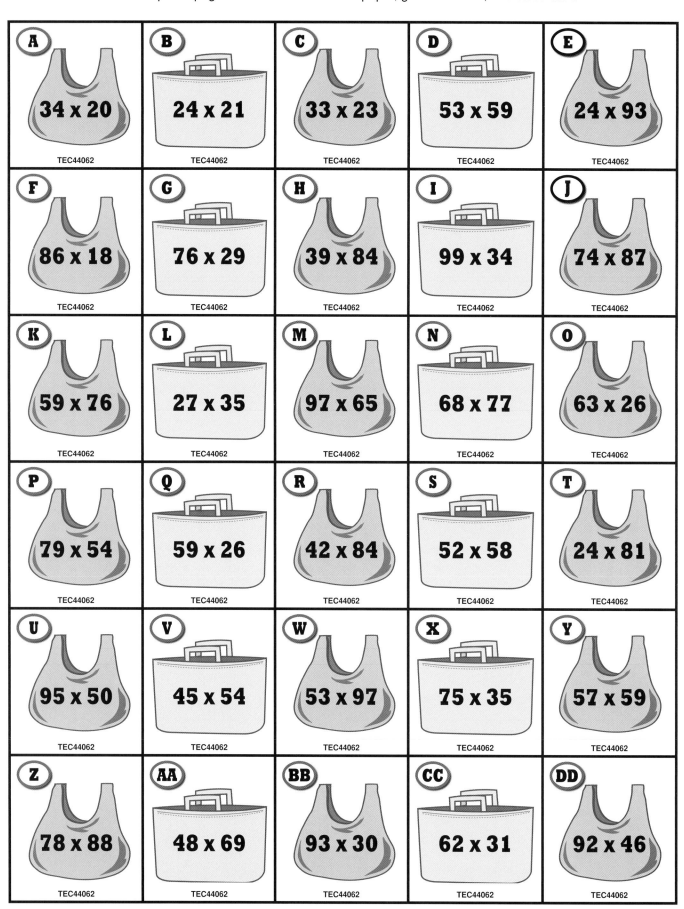

A 34 x 20	**B** 24 x 21	**C** 33 x 23	**D** 53 x 59	**E** 24 x 93
TEC44062	TEC44062	TEC44062	TEC44062	TEC44062
F 86 x 18	**G** 76 x 29	**H** 39 x 84	**I** 99 x 34	**J** 74 x 87
TEC44062	TEC44062	TEC44062	TEC44062	TEC44062
K 59 x 76	**L** 27 x 35	**M** 97 x 65	**N** 68 x 77	**O** 63 x 26
TEC44062	TEC44062	TEC44062	TEC44062	TEC44062
P 79 x 54	**Q** 59 x 26	**R** 42 x 84	**S** 52 x 58	**T** 24 x 81
TEC44062	TEC44062	TEC44062	TEC44062	TEC44062
U 95 x 50	**V** 45 x 54	**W** 53 x 97	**X** 75 x 35	**Y** 57 x 59
TEC44062	TEC44062	TEC44062	TEC44062	TEC44062
Z 78 x 88	**AA** 48 x 69	**BB** 93 x 30	**CC** 62 x 31	**DD** 92 x 46
TEC44062	TEC44062	TEC44062	TEC44062	TEC44062

Name _____

Date _____

Identify and draw lines of symmetry

A SPLIT DECISION

Use a straight edge to draw a line of symmetry between two points on each figure.

1.

2.

3.

4.

5.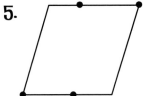

6.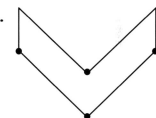

7.

8.

9.

10.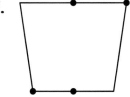

11.

12.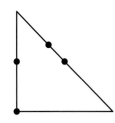

13.

14.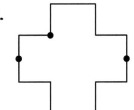

15.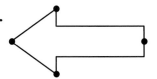

BONUS: Which of the figures above have only one line of symmetry? Color each one yellow.

Name

Date

The Right Fit

Find the volume of each shoebox.

A.
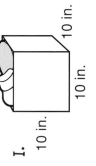
4 in. 9 in. 5 in.
v = _____ in.³

E.
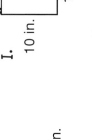
12 cm 30 cm 15 cm
v = _____ cm³

H.
6 in. 3 in. 12 in.
v = _____ in.³

I.
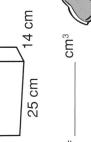
10 in. 10 in. 10 in.
v = _____ in.³

J.
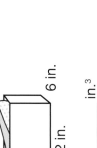
5 in. 10 in. 8 in.
v = _____ in.³

K.
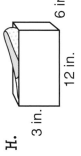
11 cm 28 cm 18 cm
v = _____ cm³

N.
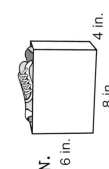
6 in. 8 in. 4 in.
v = _____ in.³

O.
24 cm 10 cm 13 cm
v = _____ cm³

R.
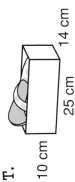
5 in. 7 in. 6 in.
v = _____ in.³

T.
10 cm 25 cm 14 cm
v = _____ cm³

Knock-knock.

Who's there?

Wooden shoe.

Wooden shoe, who?

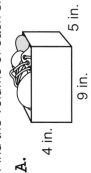

To solve the riddle, write each letter on its matching numbered line or lines.

"Wooden shoe" I

180   192   3,120   3,500   216   5,400   1,000   5,544   5,400   3,500   3,120   216   5,544   5,400   400   3,120   5,400   210   180   210
?

Bonus: What is the length of a shoebox with a 4-inch height, a 3-inch width, and a 144-inch³ volume? Explain how you found your answer.

©The Mailbox® • TEC44063 • Oct./Nov. 2012 • Key p. 308 • (5.MD.C.5b)

Name _____

Date _____

Line plot

Pulling a Few Strings

Use the information from the paragraph to complete the line plot.
Use your line plot to answer the questions. The first strand that
Mr. Knotts yanked from the ball has been plotted.

> The art teacher, Ty Din Knotts, is untangling a giant ball of string. In
> his first try, Mr. Knotts yanks out one $\frac{1}{8}$-yard, three $\frac{1}{4}$-yard, two $\frac{1}{2}$-yard,
> and one $\frac{3}{4}$-yard strands. Next, Mr. Knotts wrenches loose three $\frac{1}{8}$-yard,
> three $\frac{1}{2}$-yard, and one $\frac{3}{4}$-yard lengths. Finally, with one mighty tug,
> Mr. Knotts drags one full yard of string from the ball.

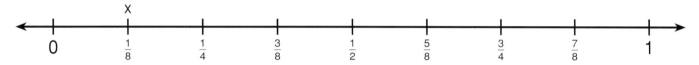

Lengths of String
(in yards)

1. Which length of string is the most common? Which length is the least common?	**2.** If Mr. Knotts put all the $\frac{1}{4}$-yard lengths of string together end to end, how long would they be?
3. Which group of strings put together end to end would be closest to three yards? How long are they?	**4.** If Mr. Knotts puts the $\frac{1}{4}$-yard strings and the $\frac{3}{4}$-yard strings together end to end, how many yards of string will he have?
5. How many more $\frac{1}{8}$-yard lengths of string would Mr. Knotts need to make one yard?	**6.** What is the difference between the total length of $\frac{1}{4}$-yard strings and the total length of $\frac{1}{8}$-yard strings?
7. How much longer is the total of $\frac{1}{2}$-yard string lengths than $\frac{1}{8}$-yard string lengths?	**8.** Mr. Knotts needs eight yards of string for his next art project. How much more string does he need to drag out of the giant ball of string?

Bonus: If Mr. Knotts pulls out six strands of $\frac{1}{4}$-yard string and three strands of $\frac{1}{2}$-yard string, how much string will he have? How did you find your answer?

Name _____

Date _____

"Orange" You Glad You Checked?

Estimate each product. Color the orange with the matching number.
Then solve the problem and use your estimate to check your work.

A   39   Estimate
     x 28
	B 46 Estimate
	     x 22
		C 39 Estimate
		     x 41

D   81   Estimate
     x 61
	E 11 Estimate
	     x 67
		F 55 Estimate
		     x 12

G   78   Estimate
     x 49
	H 86 Estimate
	     x 22
		I 68 Estimate
		     x 75

J   93   Estimate
     x 41
	K 22 Estimate
	     x 36
		L 53 Estimate
		     x 86

M   72   Estimate
     x 38
		N 85 Estimate
		     x 32

Why did the orange go to the doctor?

5,600   1,000

1,800   4,800   600

1,600   4,500   2,700   4,000

1,200   700   3,600   800   2,800

It wasn't "peeling" very well.

Bonus: How can you tell the number of places that will be in the product of this problem without solving it? Explain.

73 x 27

©The Mailbox® • TEC44063 • Oct./Nov. 2012 • Key p. 308 • (4.NBT.A.3, 4.NBT.B.5)

Name

Date

Double Trouble

What fraction or mixed number must be added to the fractions or mixed numbers in the loops to equal the mixed number at the left? Write it on the ball of yarn.

A. $3\frac{5}{8} =$ $\frac{3}{8}$ $1\frac{5}{8}$ $1\frac{5}{8}$

$\frac{3}{8} + 1\frac{5}{8} + 1\frac{5}{8}$

B. $2\frac{2}{3} =$ $\frac{1}{3}$ $1\frac{1}{3}$

C. $1\frac{3}{4} =$ $\frac{1}{4}$ $\frac{3}{4}$

D. $3\frac{5}{6} =$ $\frac{1}{6}$ $2\frac{3}{6}$

E. $4\frac{7}{12} =$ $\frac{5}{12}$ $1\frac{3}{12}$

F. $2\frac{9}{10} =$ $\frac{3}{10}$ $1\frac{1}{10}$

G. $1\frac{3}{5} =$ $\frac{2}{5}$ $\frac{4}{5}$

H. $6\frac{1}{4} =$ $\frac{3}{4}$ $3\frac{1}{4}$

I. $5\frac{7}{8} =$ $\frac{5}{8}$ $2\frac{7}{8}$

J. $4\frac{1}{6} =$ $\frac{2}{6}$ $3\frac{2}{6}$

K. $3\frac{7}{10} =$ $\frac{7}{10}$ $2\frac{1}{10}$

L. $2\frac{3}{12} =$ $\frac{7}{12}$ $1\frac{1}{12}$

Bonus: Fill in the loops and yarn ball with fractions or mixed numbers that equal $4\frac{3}{5}$.

$4\frac{3}{5} =$

Name _____

Date _____

"Sew" Many Rectangles

Find the perimeter of each rectangle below.
Reduce fractions to lowest terms.

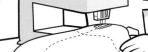

"Sew" far "sew" good!

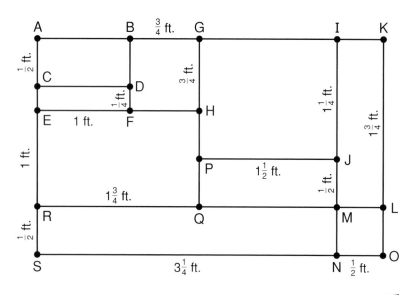

Workspace

1. perimeter of ABDC = __3 feet__

2. perimeter of BGHF = _____

3. perimeter of GIJP = _____

4. perimeter of IKLM = _____

5. perimeter of CDFE = _____

6. perimeter of EHQR = _____

7. perimeter of PJMQ = _____

8. perimeter of RMNS = _____

9. perimeter of MLON = _____

10. perimeter of ABFE = _____

11. perimeter of IKON = _____

12. perimeter of GIMQ = _____

Bonus: Name three different rectangles from the quilt above. Find the perimeter of each one.

©The Mailbox® • TEC44064 • Dec./Jan. 2012–13 • Key p. 308 • (4.MD.A.3, 5.NF.A.1)

Name _____

Date _____

Hole in One!

Solve. Shade the flag with the matching answer.

A. $\frac{1}{8} \div 4 = \frac{1}{32}$

B. $4 \div \frac{1}{8} =$

C. $\frac{1}{3} \div 6 =$

D. $\frac{1}{10} \div 9 =$

E. $12 \div \frac{1}{4} =$

F. $18 \div \frac{1}{3} =$

G. $\frac{1}{3} \div 7 =$

H. $7 \div \frac{1}{3} =$

I. $10 \div \frac{1}{10} =$

J. $\frac{1}{2} \div 5 =$

K. $11 \div \frac{1}{5} =$

L. $\frac{1}{9} \div 3 =$

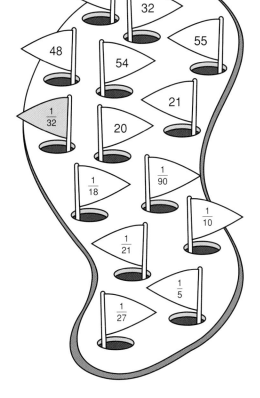

Use the numbers on the unshaded flags to write and solve the following problems:

1. a whole number divided by a fraction

2. a fraction divided by a whole number

Circle the term that completes each sentence.

3. When you divide a unit fraction by a whole number other than 1,

the answer is always a _____.   whole number   unit fraction

4. When you divide a whole number by a unit fraction, the answer

is always a _____.   whole number   unit fraction

Bonus: Which whole number can be divided by $\frac{1}{6}$ to equal 30?
Which unit fraction can be divided by 4 to equal $\frac{1}{20}$? Explain.

On the Trail

Solve. Show your work on another piece of paper.

To convert a small unit to a large unit, divide. To convert a large unit to a small unit, multiply.

1,000 milligrams	= 1 gram
1,000 grams	= 1 kilogram
1,000 milliliters	= 1 liter
1,000 meters	= 1 kilometer
100 centimeters	= 1 meter
10 millimeters	= 1 centimeter

1. Mia measures 1.5 liters of water for a science experiment. She adds 150 milliliters of oil and 150 milliliters of alcohol to the water. Does the liquid completely fill a 2-liter container? Why or why not?

2. Kelly places one 10-kilogram weight on the left side of a scale. On the right side of the scale, she places ten 100-gram weights. To balance the scale, how much weight must Kelly add? To which side must the weight be added?

3. Charlotte trains for a 5-kilometer race. On Monday, she starts with a 400-meter run. Then, on Tuesday and Wednesday, Charlotte runs 800 meters each day. On Saturday, she runs 1 kilometer. How many kilometers did Charlotte run in one week?

4. Gummy Gators cost $20.00 per kilogram. Alex buys 250 grams of Gummy Gators. How much does Alex spend on Gummy Gators?

5. Jasmine needs 8 meters of ribbon. She finds 5 lengths of ribbon in a scrap box. Each ribbon length is 250 centimeters. How many lengths of ribbon will Jasmine use?

6. Cameron's mother has 2 kilograms of ground beef to make hamburger patties with. Each patty has 120 grams of beef. How many patties can Cameron's mother make? How much ground beef is left?

7. Riley has 3 beetles in her insect collection. One beetle weighs 250 milligrams, and another beetle weighs 500 milligrams. The combined weight of the beetles is 2.8 grams. How many grams does the third beetle weigh?

8. Lila's kitten weighed 600 grams at birth. The kitten gained 500 grams in the first month. During the next 3 months, the kitten gained 550 grams, 600 grams, and 650 grams. If this pattern continues, how many kilograms will the kitten weigh when it is 6 months old?

9. Seth's cat chases a squirrel 10 meters up a tree and back down 300 centimeters. Then the cat climbs 1 meter higher and back down 600 centimeters. How many meters high is Seth's cat from the ground?

10. Logan's quartz rocks vary in length: 50 millimeters, 52 millimeters, 30 millimeters, 35 millimeters, and 44 millimeters. He divides a box lid into 6 rectangles. The length of each rectangle is 5 centimeters. Can Logan fit each quartz rock in one of the spaces? Explain.

Bonus: Write and solve a multiplication word problem that includes 30 meters and 1 kilometer.

©The Mailbox® · TEC44065 · Feb./Mar. 2013 · Key p. 308 · (5.MD.A.1)

Name _____

Date _____

A Babysitting Venture

Use the poster to answer each question.
Show your work.

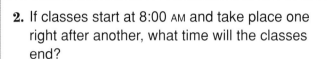

Be the Best Babysitter on the Block!

Sign up now for these great classes and get ready to start earning your own money!

- How to Find Babysitting Jobs (15 minutes)
- Recognizing Safety Hazards (30 minutes)
- Emergencies! (1 hour)
- How to Handle a Tantrum (45 minutes)
- How to Change a Diaper (1 hour)
- All About Bottles (30 minutes)
- How to Feed a Toddler (30 minutes)
- Naptime (15 minutes)
- Babysitting Review (1 hour 15 minutes)

1. Della signs up to take every class. How long will she spend in babysitting classes?

2. If classes start at 8:00 AM and take place one right after another, what time will the classes end?

3. If classes start at 8:00 AM and take place one right after another, what time will "All About Bottles" start?

6. Ian can only attend classes for $1\frac{1}{2}$ hours during the morning. To attend the most classes in that time, which classes should he take? Use the schedule in question 5.

4. If classes start at 8:00 AM and take place one right after another, but there is a one-hour break for lunch at 11:30, what time will the babysitting classes end?

7. Jade is attending the following classes: "Recognizing Safety Hazards," "How to Handle a Tantrum," and "All About Bottles." How long will she be in class?

5. If classes start at 8:00 AM and take place one right after another, but there is a one-hour break for lunch at 11:30, what time will the "Babysitting Review" start?

8. Ernie takes "All About Bottles," "How to Change a Diaper," and five other classes. He takes three hours and 45 minutes of classes in all. Which other classes does he take?

Bonus: Choose four classes you might take. How long would you be in class if you took those classes?

Name _____

Date _____

TAKING SHAPE

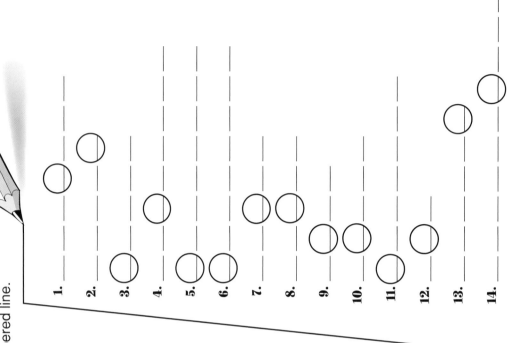

To complete each statement, write the missing word on the matching numbered line.

1. A _____ is a closed figure with straight sides.

2. On an isosceles triangle, two _____ are the same length.

3. An _____ angle measures less than 90°.

4. Squares, rectangles, and rhombuses are parallelograms because their opposite sides are _____.

5. All three sides of an equilateral _____ are the same length.

6. A _____ has five sides and angles.

7. A rhombus has four sides that are _____ in length.

8. Each _____ in a square measures 90°.

9. All quadrilaterals have _____ sides.

10. Rectangles and squares have four _____ angles.

11. A polygon with six sides and angles is a _____.

12. A trapezoid has _____ pair of parallel sides.

13. An _____ angle measures greater than 90°.

14. When _____ lines meet, they form four 90° angles.

What do a joke and a pencil have in common?
To answer the riddle, write each circled letter on its matching numbered line or lines.

12	13	10	5	11	13	4	9	7	5	3	10	2	3	12	13	10	5
		W															

8	9	14		10			3	6	2	9	10	12	5	1

1. _____ ○
2. _____ ○
3. _____ ○
4. _____ ○
5. _____ ○○
6. _____ ○
7. _____
8. _____
9. _____ ○
10. _____ ○
11. _____ ○
12. _____ ○
13. _____ ○
14. _____ ○

BONUS: Draw and then name three polygons that always have perpendicular lines.

©The Mailbox® • TEC44066 • April/May 2013 • Key p. 308 (4.G.A.2; 5.G.B.3)

Name_____

Date_____

CHECKING IN

Find each sum or difference. Write each one in simplest form.

O $\dfrac{1}{4} + \dfrac{1}{3} =$

N $\dfrac{3}{8} - \dfrac{1}{3} =$

M $\dfrac{2}{5} + \dfrac{1}{4} =$

E $\dfrac{1}{3} + \dfrac{4}{5} =$

S $\dfrac{3}{5} - \dfrac{1}{8} =$

H $\dfrac{1}{3} - \dfrac{3}{10} =$

R $\dfrac{3}{4} + \dfrac{2}{5} =$

I $\dfrac{1}{6} + \dfrac{4}{5} =$

F $\dfrac{5}{8} + \dfrac{5}{6} =$

A $\dfrac{5}{8} - \dfrac{1}{3} =$

Y $\dfrac{3}{4} - \dfrac{7}{12} =$

D $\dfrac{7}{10} + \dfrac{1}{2} =$

Cowboy Cal rode into town on Friday, checked into a hotel, stayed two days, and then rode out of town on Friday. How did he do it?

To answer the riddle, write each letter on the matching numbered line or lines.

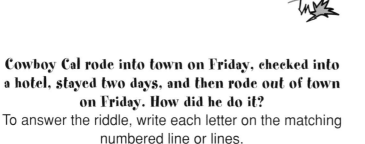

$\dfrac{1}{30}$ $\dfrac{29}{30}$ $\dfrac{19}{40}$ $\dfrac{1}{30}$ $\dfrac{7}{12}$ $1\dfrac{3}{20}$ $\dfrac{19}{40}$ $1\dfrac{2}{15}$ $\dfrac{29}{30}$ $\dfrac{19}{40}$

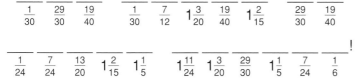

$\dfrac{1}{24}$ $\dfrac{7}{24}$ $\dfrac{13}{20}$ $1\dfrac{2}{15}$ $1\dfrac{1}{5}$ $1\dfrac{11}{24}$ $1\dfrac{3}{20}$ $\dfrac{29}{30}$ $1\dfrac{1}{5}$ $\dfrac{7}{24}$ $\dfrac{1}{6}$

BONUS: Which of the problems was the most challenging to solve? Explain.

SKILL AND DRILL

Write the factor pairs for each number. Then, in each table, shade the spaces you don't need.

 1 | **18**

1	18
2	9
3	6

2 | **72**

3 | **56**

4 | **35**

5 | **27**

6 | **48**

WORK SPACE

7 | **12**

BONUS: How do you know when you've found all the factor pairs for a number? Explain.

8 | **81**

9 | **24**

10 | **60**

11 | **32**

12 | **96**

©The Mailbox® • TEC44066 • April/May 2013 • Key p. 309 • (4.OA.B.4)

Name _____

Date _____

AND THE CROWD GOES WILD!

Find each pattern's rule and write the rule's letter next to the pattern. Then write the next two numbers in the pattern.

1 1, 3, 5, 7, 9, _____, _____ _____

2 7, 2, 9, 4, 11, 6, 13, _____, _____ _____

3 6, 18, 19, 57, 58, _____, _____ _____

4 98, 96, 94, 92, _____, _____ _____

5 30, 15, 18, 9, 12, _____, _____ _____

6 5, 50, 42, 420, 412, _____, _____ _____

7 90, 30, 36, 12, 18, _____, _____ _____

8 4, 2, 6, 3, 7, $3\frac{1}{2}$, $7\frac{1}{2}$, _____, _____ _____

9 8, 16, 24, 32, _____, _____ _____

10 3, 6, $5\frac{1}{2}$, 11, $10\frac{1}{2}$, 21, _____, _____ _____

11 4, 8, 12, 24, 28, 56, _____, _____ _____

12 40, 34, 41, 35, 42, _____, _____ _____

This is *not* going to hurt!

A. Subtract 2.
E. Multiply by 2; subtract $\frac{1}{2}$.
F. Multiply by 3; add 1.
H. Add 8.
I. Subtract 6; add 7.
N. Add 2.
O. Multiply by $\frac{1}{2}$; add 4.
R. Subtract 5; add 7.
S. Divide by 3, add 6.
T. Multiply by 10; subtract 8.
X. Divide by $\frac{1}{2}$; add 4.
Y. Divide by 2; add 3.

How do baseball players stay cool on a hot summer day?

To find out, write each letter on its matching numbered line or lines.

$\dfrac{}{6}\ \dfrac{}{9}\ \dfrac{}{10}\ \dfrac{}{5}\quad\dfrac{}{7}\ \dfrac{}{12}\ \dfrac{}{6}\quad\dfrac{}{1}\ \dfrac{}{10}\ \dfrac{}{11}\ \dfrac{}{6}$

$\dfrac{}{6}\ \dfrac{}{8}\quad\dfrac{}{6}\ \dfrac{}{9}\ \dfrac{}{10}\ \dfrac{}{12}\ \dfrac{}{2}\quad\dfrac{}{3}\ \dfrac{}{4}\ \dfrac{}{1}\ \dfrac{}{7}\ !$

BONUS: Which of the rules shown will create a pattern in which each number will be larger than the number before it? How do you know?

A. Multiply by $\frac{1}{4}$; add 1.　　B. Add 2; multiply by 3.　　C. Add 10; divide by 2.

©The Mailbox® • TEC44067 • June/July 2013 • Key p. 309 • (5.OA.A.3)

Name _____

Date _____

Eye to Eye

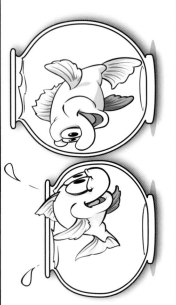

Write a story for each problem. Use the model to find the quotient.
Then draw a model that illustrates the problem.

1 $\frac{1}{5} \div 5 =$ _____

Sarah wants to make the last $\frac{1}{5}$ of the fish food last five more days. How
much food should she feed her fish each day to make the food last?

2 $5 \div \frac{1}{4} =$ _____

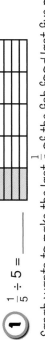

Sarah is filling the fishbowls and needs to add five cups of water. Her
measuring cup holds $\frac{1}{4}$ cup. How many times will she have to fill the measuring
cup to add five cups of water?

3 $\frac{1}{2} \div 8 =$ _____

4 $5 \div \frac{1}{5} =$ _____

5 $\frac{1}{6} \div 3 =$ _____

6 $\frac{1}{3} \div 4 =$ _____

7 $7 \div \frac{1}{3} =$ _____

8 $6 \div \frac{1}{4} =$ _____

Bonus: What part of this page was hardest for you? What was easiest? Explain.

©The Mailbox® • TEC44067 • June/July 2013 • Key p. 309 • (5.NF.B.7a, b)

In and Out of the Doghouse

Solve each problem. Then cross off the matching number on the doghouse.

1. The doghouse floor is 21 inches wide. The floor's perimeter is 90 inches.

    a. How long is the floor? _____

    b. What is the floor's area? _____

2. The dimensions of the doghouse's front wall are 21 inches by 15 inches.

    a. What is the wall's area? _____

    b. What is the wall's perimeter? _____

    c. What is the wall's area once an 80-inch^2 doorway is cut out for Sparky? _____

    d. What is the combined area of the front wall (with the doorway cut out) and the back wall, which is the same size as the front wall but without the doorway? _____

3. The area of each side wall is 360 inches^2.

    a. If each wall is 15 inches wide, how long is it? _____

    b. What is the perimeter of each side wall? _____

    c. What is the combined area of both side walls? _____

4. The perimeter of each half of the doghouse roof is 64 inches. Each half of the roof is 8 inches wide.

    a. What is the length of each half of the doghouse roof? _____

    b. What is the area of each half of the doghouse roof? _____

    c. What is the combined area of the entire roof? _____

Sparky

24   504
24   720
235 192
315 72
78   550
24   384

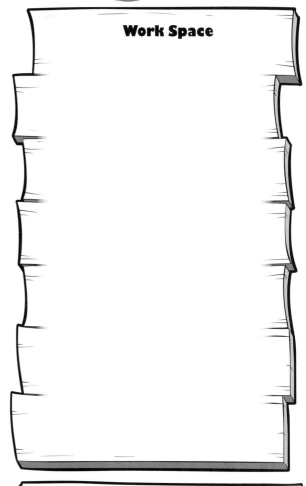

Work Space

Bonus: If roofing tiles are 2-inch by 2-inch squares, how many tiles would it take to cover the doghouse roof? How did you find your answer?

In Other Words

On the lines, write the term from the word bank that best matches each definition.

1. number that contains a decimal point __ __ __ __ __ __ __

2. any of the numbers, fractions, or decimals that are multiplied to get a product __ __ __ __ __ __

3. to divide __ __ __ __ __ __ __ __ __

4. one part of ten equal parts of a whole __ __ __ __ __

5. fractions such as $\frac{1}{4}$, $\frac{1}{3}$, $\frac{1}{2}$, $\frac{2}{3}$, and $\frac{3}{4}$ that can be easily compared with other fractions to estimate size __ __ __ __ __ __ __ __ __

__ __ __ __ __ __ __ __

6. with the same value __ __ __ __ __ __ __ __ __ __

7. number that stands for part of a whole or part of a group

__ __ __ __ __ __ __ __

8. number with a whole number part and a fractional part

__ __ __ __ __   __ __ __ __ __ __

9. number below the line in a fraction that tells how many equal parts a whole has been divided into __ __ __ __ __ __ __ __ __ __ __

10. one part of 1,000 equal parts of a whole __ __ __ __ __ __ __ __ __ __

11. to analyze fraction or decimal values in relation to each other

__ __ __ __ __ __ __

12. addition, subtraction, multiplication, or division

__ __ __ __ __ __ __ __ __

13. product of a whole number and any other whole number

__ __ __ __ __ __ __ __

The grass is always so much greener over there!

14. one part of one hundred equal parts of a whole

__ __ __ __ __ __ __ __ __

15. fractions that have equal values or name the same part of a whole

__ __ __ __ __ __ __ __ __ __   __ __ __ __ __ __ __ __ __

16. to separate a number or fraction into its simpler parts

__ __ __ __ __ __ __ __ __

17. number above the line in a fraction that tells how many equal parts are described by the fraction __ __ __ __ __ __ __ __ __

18. fraction with a numerator of 1 __ __ __ __   __ __ __ __ __ __ __ __

Word Bank
benchmark fractions
compare
decimal
decompose
denominator
equivalent
equivalent fractions
factor
fraction
hundredth
mixed number
multiple
numerator
operation
partition
tenth
thousandth
unit fraction

What happened when the clumsy ox forgot to watch where it was going?

To find out, write each circled letter on its matching numbered line below.

Bonus: Choose five terms from the word bank. Illustrate each one.

__ __   __ __ __   " __ __ - __ __ __ __ __ __ "
5 7   14 12 1   2 3   11 8   18 16 17 9 13

©The Mailbox® • TEC44067 • June/July 2013 • Key p. 309 • (L.4.6;L.5.6)

Name_____

Date_____

Pick and Practice!

Pick _____ activities to do.
When you finish an activity, color its number.

The greatest common factor between two or more numbers is the largest number in a list of common factors.

1 Find a factor that can be multiplied by 3 to match each description below. Then write each complete equation.

_____ x 3 = _____

A. odd product between 10 and 20

B. even product between 20 and 30

C. even product greater than 30 but less than 40

D. product less than 40 with two identical digits

2 Match each number pair with its greatest common factor (GCF).

GCF	Number Pair
10 •	• 35 and 63
8 •	• 16 and 28
4 •	• 20 and 30
7 •	• 36 and 54
9 •	• 32 and 72

3 For which three sets of numbers is 6 the greatest common factor?

12, 24, 36   18, 54, 72

24, 48, 72   36, 60, 66

30, 42, 60   24, 42, 72

4 List the factors for each number.

A. 16

B. 27

C. 30

D. 14

5 Make a factor tree for each number.

Example: 20
          2   10
             2   5

36   48   18

12   60

6 Draw and label a three-column chart as shown. In the second column, write each number in the appropriate row. Then list the number's factors.

17   18   25   27   81

Number of Factors	Number	Factors
2		
3		
4		
5		
6		

7 Roll a pair of dice and make a two-digit number. List all the factors of the number rolled. Repeat seven more times.

8 Cross out the word or words that make each statement incorrect. Then write the word or words that will make each statement correct.

A. The number 10 has six factors.

B. Two is the greatest common factor of 12 and 30.

C. The number 25 has more factors than the number 18.

D. The numbers 24 and 30 have six of the same factors.

9 Replace one digit in each pair of numbers so the greatest common factor is 9.

Example: 2$\cancel{5}$, 36 (7)

A. 9, 84

B. 18, 46

C. 54, 69

D. 72, 100

Independent practice grid: Program the student directions on a copy of this page with the number of activities to be completed. Then copy the page for each student. Each student will need a pair of dice.

Name _____

Date _____

Pick and Practice!

MULTIPLES!

Pick _____ activities to do.
When you finish an activity, color its number.

---

1 Find the mystery factor for each set of multiples. Then add two more of its multiples.

Mystery Factor	Multiples
	12, 21, 45
	15, 30, 55
	14, 49, 63
	22, 77, 99

---

2 Place the numbers shown in the Venn diagram. Then find another multiple you can write in each region. Use a different color to write in your new multiples.

4, 6, 9, 10, 15, 25, 30

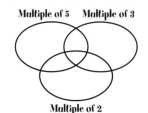

Multiple of 5   Multiple of 3

Multiple of 2

---

3 For each task, choose a number from List 1 and List 2. Then follow the directions

List 1	List 2
11	81
13	92
9	75

A. List all the multiples of six between the numbers you chose.
B. List all the multiples of 11 between the numbers you picked.
C. List all the multiples of eight between the numbers you selected.

---

4 Use the clues to name each mystery number. Then choose four mystery numbers and write clues for them.

A. [ ] is a multiple of both 5 and 2 that is between 31 and 46.
B. [ ] is a multiple of both 4 and 3 that is between 9 and 19.
C. [ ] is a multiple of both 7 and 3 that is less than 50 but greater than 30.
D. [ ] is a multiple of both 6 and 8 that is less than 40.

---

5 Create a poster that explains how to find the least common multiple of 6 and 9.

6   9
LCM

---

6 Make a chart of numbers from 1 to 100. Next, circle the multiples of 3. Draw boxes around the multiples of 4, and draw triangles around the multiples of 5. Then use the chart to find the least common multiple of 3, 4, and 5.

1 2 ③ ④ △5 ⑥ 7 □8 ⑨ △⑩
11 ⑫ 13 14 △⑮ □16 17 ⑱ 19 △⑳

---

7 Circle the multiple that does not belong in each set.

A. 32, 64, 70, 40, 16
B. 48, 54, 66, 18, 28
C. 32, 54, 40, 48, 28
D. 21, 49, 63, 41, 56

---

8 Complete the chart by naming the factor pair for each least common multiple (LCM) shown.

Factor Pair	LCM
3, 4	12
	24
	18
	30
	56
	72

---

9 Find the least common multiple for the factor trios below.

A. 3, 5, 7
B. 4, 6, 9
C. 2, 5, 8
D. 4, 5, 7

Independent practice grid: Program the student directions on a copy of this page with the number of activities to be completed. Then copy the page for each student.

Name _____

Date _____

Pick and Practice!

Pick _____ activities to do.
When you finish an activity, shade its number.

1 For each box, tell how many one-centimeter cubes would cover one layer. Next, tell how many layers of cubes would fill the box. Then tell how many cubes would fill the box.

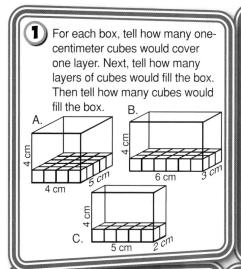

A.
4 cm
4 cm
5 cm

B.
4 cm
6 cm
3 cm

C.
4 cm
5 cm
2 cm

2 How many one-inch cubes would you need to fill each of these boxes?

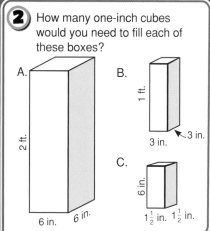

A.
2 ft.
6 in. 6 in.

B.
1 ft.
3 in. 3 in.

C.
6 in.
$1\frac{1}{2}$ in. $1\frac{1}{2}$ in.

3 If you have 100 one-centimeter cubes and you build a tower that is five cubes wide and six cubes long, how tall can the tower be? How tall can your tower be if its base is three cubes wide and four cubes long?

4 Make a mini poster that shows how to find the volume of the box shown without using a formula.

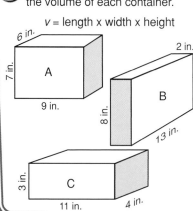

5 cm
20 cm
4 cm

5 Create a poem or song that will help classmates remember to write volume measurements in cubic units. In your work, let your classmates know why they use cubic units.

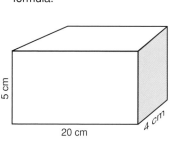

one cubic unit

6 Use the formula shown to find the volume of each container.

Volume = base* x height
*base = the area of the bottom layer, or length x width

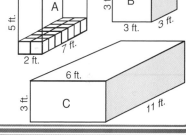

A
5 ft.
2 ft.
7 ft.

B
3 ft.
3 ft.
3 ft.

C
3 ft.
6 ft.
11 ft.

7 Use the formula shown to find the volume of each container.

v = length x width x height

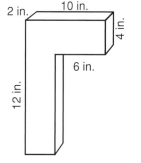

A
6 in.
7 in.
9 in.

B
2 in.
8 in.
13 in.

C
3 in.
11 in.
4 in.

8 Find the volume of each container.

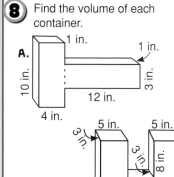

A.
1 in.
1 in.
10 in.
12 in.
3 in.
4 in.

B.
5 in. 5 in.
3 in.
3 in.
8 in.
5 in.
16 in.
15 in.

9 Explain how to find the volume of the box shown.

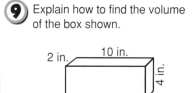

2 in.
10 in.
4 in.
6 in.
12 in.

©The Mailbox® • TEC44066 • April/May 2013 • Key p. 309 (5.MD.C.3–5)

Independent practice grid: Program the student directions on a copy of this page with the number of activities to be completed. Then copy the page for each student.

Name _____

Date _____

Pick and Practice!

Pick ___ activities to do.
When you finish an activity, shade its number.

1 Fold a sheet of paper in half and write your name underneath the fold. Then open the paper, turn it around, and copy your writing as closely as possible. If you consider your work as a whole, is it symmetrical? Why or why not?

Theo

2 How many lines of symmetry does a square have? Use a ruler to draw a square. Then draw all its lines of symmetry.

3 Which figure or figures have no lines of symmetry? How do you know?

A.   B.

C.   D.

4 Create a mini poster that explains how to decide if a two-dimensional figure is symmetrical.

5 Look around. Find four or more real-world items that are symmetrical, such as the shape of a water bottle or the pattern in some cloth. Draw each example and label it. Then draw and label its line or lines of symmetry.

6 How many lines of symmetry does each figure below have?

A.   B.

C.   D.

7 Look in old magazines for eight or more pictures that show symmetry. Cut out each picture and draw its line or lines of symmetry. Then glue the pictures on a sheet of construction paper and title your work "A Symmetry Montage."

8 Copy the statement shown. Next, choose from the words shown to complete the statement. Then draw two or more examples that support the statement.

A regular polygon, or a polygon with equal sides and angles, has the same number of ___ as ___ of ___.

lines   symmetry   sides

congruency   shapes   data

9 Draw four different figures that have two or more lines of symmetry.

Math in Minutes Ⓐ

7 **NUMBER & OPERATIONS**

A leap year occurs every four years. This year, 2012, is a leap year. Find the next ten leap years. How old will you be ten leap years from now? How do you know?

4 **MEASUREMENT**

Ms. Brady makes an $8\frac{1}{2}$-foot-long banner that says WELCOME BACK TO SCHOOL. Each letter is four inches wide. She leaves one inch between each letter and two inches between each word. Is there enough room for two five-inch-wide football cutouts? Why or why not?

2 **NUMBER & OPERATIONS**

Find four different pairs of numbers that have a difference of 187. How did you find your answers?

5 **PROBABILITY**

Miquel has read five out of every twenty books in the school library. If he randomly selects a book from the library without looking at its title, what is the probability that he will get a book he has already read? Explain.

3 **MEASUREMENT**

Kendra's two favorite towns measure $12\frac{1}{2}$ inches apart on a map. According to the map scale, one inch equals 50 miles. How far apart are the two towns?

50 MILES

0

6 **GEOMETRY**

Floor tiles will be laid in the school's new cafeteria. The cafeteria is 40 feet long and 60 feet wide. Each square tile is 12 inches long and 12 inches wide. How many tiles are needed to cover the entire floor? Draw a picture and explain.

Math in Minutes Ⓑ

4 **MEASUREMENT**

Mara finished cleaning the classroom fish tank 2 hours and 50 minutes ago. It is now 1:25 PM. What time did she finish the job? How did you find your answer?

1 **NUMBER & OPERATIONS**

At Elmwood Elementary School, 145 students walk to school. That is one-fifth of the students who attend the school. Is the total number of students at Elmwood Elementary School greater than or less than 750? How do you know?

5 **GEOMETRY**

Lena draws a polygon. The measurement of its angles totals 360°. Lena asks Ricky to guess what shape she drew. He guesses a triangle. Is he correct? Why or why not?

2 **NUMBER & OPERATIONS**

Emily opens her book and tells Ty that the product of the two page numbers on her open book is 600. Ty guesses that Emily opened her book to page 24. Is he correct? Why or why not?

6 **NUMBER & OPERATIONS**

Grace checks her work to make sure she rounded each number to the nearest tenth. Correct Grace's work and then explain what she did wrong.

A. 457.35 rounded to <u>457.3</u>
B. 18.99 rounded to <u>18.0</u>
C. 4.436 rounded to <u>4.54</u>
D. 10.831 rounded to <u>10.9</u>

3 **ALGEBRA**

In which problem does x have the greatest value? Explain.

$$\frac{405}{x} = 81 \qquad 10x = 2$$

Math in Minutes Ⓑ

4 | GEOMETRY

Use a different letter of the alphabet to make a diagram for each of the following terms:

acute angle   right angle

intersecting lines   parallel lines

obtuse angle   perpendicular lines

 intersecting lines

5 | MEASUREMENT

Hank makes punch with 900 milliliters (mL) of juice, 700 mL of soda, and 400 mL of water. How many liters of punch does Hank make? Explain how you know.

6 | NUMBER & OPERATIONS

When it was time for practice to start, $\frac{1}{4}$ of Grace's teammates were late; $\frac{1}{8}$ were sick; and $\frac{1}{16}$ were injured. What fraction of Grace's teammates showed up on time and ready for practice? How did you find your answer?

7 | NUMBER & OPERATIONS

Mia had 30 minutes of free time. She spent two-thirds of her time reading. How much did that leave her to draw? How did you find your answer?

2 | NUMBER & OPERATIONS

To pay for the field trip group's admission to the Mammoth Museum, Ms. Ella Phant wrote a check for $328.50. Each adult ticket was $5.50, but five of the ten chaperones were admitted free. How much did each of the 86 student tickets cost? How do you know?

3 | ALGEBRAIC THINKING

Insert parentheses to make each equation true. Then explain how you figured out where to put the parentheses.

$4 + 6 \times 8 = 80$

$96 \div 4 \times 8 = 128$

©The Mailbox® • TEC44063 • Oct./Nov. 2012 • Key p. 309

Math in Minutes Ⓐ

4 | PROBABILITY

Emma, Kyle, and Mason are the only three students who have not given their pilgrim reports. How many different ways could the teacher arrange the order in which they will present their reports? Make a list and explain how you made it.

5 | NUMBER & OPERATIONS

Micah says there are more prime numbers between ten and 20 than there are between 20 and 30. Is he correct? Explain.

6 | ALGEBRAIC THINKING

Add the next four numbers in the pattern below. What do you notice about the numbers in the pattern? Describe it.

3, 6, 12, 24, 48, ___, ___, ___, ___

7 | NUMBER & OPERATIONS

Micah wants to try solving 47 × 28 in a different way. He multiplies 40 × 20 first, and then he adds the product of 7 × 8. Will this give Micah a correct answer to the original problem? Why or why not?

2 | NUMBER & OPERATIONS

Ms. Schultz is making caramel apples for the 27 students in her class. She buys two bags of apples, and she needs to buy one bag of caramels for every six apples. How much will Ms. Schultz spend altogether? How did you find your answer?

$2.99	$3.50
bag of caramels	bag 18 apples

3 | MEASUREMENT

Ashley is setting up a cornhole station for the fall festival. She wants to set the platform 25 feet away from the starting line. How many times will Ashley place a yardstick on the floor to measure the distance? Draw a diagram to explain your answer.

©The Mailbox® • TEC44063 • Oct./Nov. 2012 • Key p. 309

Math in Minutes Ⓑ

4 GEOMETRY

How many quadrilaterals can you name that have both parallel and perpendicular lines? How many quadrilaterals can you name whose sides are all congruent? How can you check your lists?

1 NUMBER & OPERATIONS

Coach Kay recorded the time it took each student to run two miles around the track. The students' times are in random order. Arrange the times in order from fastest to slowest. How did you find your answer?

19.28   19.5   19.35   19.05   18.94

5 ALGEBRAIC THINKING

A pair of parentheses is missing in this problem. Write the equation and add the parentheses. How did you figure out where they belonged?

8 + 12 ÷ 4 × 2 = 14

2 NUMBER & OPERATIONS

At 10:15 AM, Kiki announces, "Tomorrow afternoon at 2:30, we will be leaving school for winter break!" "That's in 12 $\frac{1}{2}$ hours!" Declan says. Is Declan correct? Why or why not?

6 ALGEBRAIC THINKING

Write an expression for the statement and then solve it. What was harder: writing the expression or solving it? Explain.

nine times as many as 48 shared by eight

3 MEASUREMENT AND DATA

Jen and Jake were debating whose lunchbox can hold more. Whose will hold more? How do you know?

	Jen's lunchbox	Jake's lunchbox
length	6 $\frac{1}{2}$"	6"
width	6 $\frac{1}{2}$"	4 $\frac{1}{2}$"
height	3"	4 $\frac{1}{2}$"

©The Mailbox® • TEC44064 • Dec./Jan. 2012–13 • Key p. 309

Math in Minutes Ⓐ

4 GEOMETRY

What is the shape of a stop sign called? How many lines of symmetry does it have? Describe a line of symmetry.

1 NUMBER & OPERATIONS

Ian missed three out of ten problems on his math test. Cassie missed 40 out of 100 problems on her test. Which student has the higher score? Explain.

5 ALGEBRAIC THINKING

Lyle solved this problem incorrectly. What is the correct answer? How do you think Lyle found his answer? Explain.

4 + 6 × 3 − 4 = 26

2 NUMBER & OPERATIONS

A hot cocoa recipe calls for 14 ounces of condensed milk. The recipe makes 8 servings. If 12 guests will be at the party, how many ounces of milk are needed to make hot cocoa for all 12 guests? How do you know?

6 ALGEBRAIC THINKING

List both numbers' factors. Which number has more factors? How do you know you found all the factors?

24   48

3 MEASUREMENT AND DATA

The class made a chart of the daily precipitation for one week. Use the chart to find the week's total feet of precipitation. How did you find your answer?

Mon.	Tues.	Wed.	Thurs.	Fri.
4 $\frac{4}{10}$"	3 $\frac{2}{10}$"	3 $\frac{4}{10}$"	2 $\frac{7}{10}$"	4"

©The Mailbox® • TEC44064 • Dec./Jan. 2012–13 • Key p. 309

Math in Minutes Ⓑ

4 MEASUREMENT

Matt planned to meet his best friend, James, at the park at 1:45 PM. Matt arrived 15 minutes early. James arrived 35 minutes later. What time did James arrive? How do you know?

5 MEASUREMENT

A 12-meter-long stick is standing in a pond. If $\frac{1}{5}$ of the stick is buried in mud, and 0.3 of it is between the mud and the surface, how much of the stick is above the surface of the pond? Explain.

6 NUMBER & OPERATIONS

While Kelsey's mom was checking them into a hotel, Kelsey took the elevator from the ground floor to the 18th floor, down six floors, up eight floors, down ten floors, and then up two floors. Which floor is Kelsey on now? How did you find your answer?

1 NUMBER & OPERATIONS

Half of the 480 students at Round Robin Elementary donated books to the community library. One-third of the students donated books to a local charity. The rest of the students gave books to children in other communities. How many students were in each group? How did you find your answers?

2 MEASUREMENT AND DATA

Ms. Reddy's office measures 12 feet x 15 feet. The teachers' lounge measures twice as long and twice as wide. How do the areas of the two rooms compare? Explain.

3 ALGEBRAIC THINKING

Add parentheses to correct each equation. How did you decide where to put them? Explain.

A. $5 + 10 \times 9 - 6 = 89$

B. $12 \div 6 \times 11 + 9 = 40$

©The Mailbox® • TEC44065 • Feb./Mar. 2013 • Key p. 309

Math in Minutes Ⓐ

4 MEASUREMENT AND DATA

Mr. Green has five yards of fencing. Is this enough to enclose a square garden that measures 4 feet on each side? Why or why not?

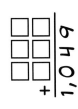

5 ALGEBRAIC THINKING

Jade is helping her dad hang lights on their deck. The deck is 72 feet wide. There is one bulb every eight feet on the string of lights. How many bulbs are in 72 feet of lights? How did you find your answer?

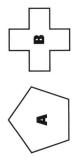

6 GEOMETRY

Colby used a protractor to draw a triangle. He measured one 14 degree angle and noticed that he had two congruent angles. What do each of the angles of his triangle measure? Explain.

7 NUMBER & OPERATIONS

Use the digits 2, 3, 5, 6, 7, and 9 to complete this problem. Then explain how you figured out where to place the digits.

$$\begin{array}{r} \square\square \\ + \square\square \\ \hline 1{,}049 \end{array}$$

2 NUMBER & OPERATIONS

Which mixed number in each row is not equivalent to the other two? How do you know?

A. $3\frac{1}{2}$ $3\frac{2}{4}$ $3\frac{5}{8}$

B. $5\frac{9}{12}$ $5\frac{10}{16}$ $5\frac{6}{8}$

C. $7\frac{2}{8}$ $7\frac{4}{12}$ $7\frac{3}{9}$

3 GEOMETRY

Which shape has more lines of symmetry? How did you find your answer?

A   B

©The Mailbox® • TEC44065 • Feb./Mar. 2013 • Key p. 309

Math in Minutes Ⓑ

4 | ALGEBRAIC THINKING

Complete the table. If you formed ordered pairs for each number pair and then graphed the ordered pairs, what would the graph look like? Explain.

$y = x + 3$	
x	y
6	
4	
3	
2	

5 | GEOMETRY

Is the statement shown correct? Why or why not?

All rectangles have four right angles, and rectangles are parallelograms, so all parallelograms have four right angles.

6 | NUMBER & OPERATIONS

Melvin has $2.31 left from his birthday money. He bought his favorite movie's sound track for $14.95 and three new video games for $22.58 each. How much birthday money did Melvin have to begin with?

1 | NUMBER & OPERATIONS

Games R Us workers are shipping 1,440 of their latest video games. They've put 56 games each in 12 boxes, and they have 16 more boxes. How many games will they have to put in each box? How do you know?

2 | NUMBER & OPERATIONS

Mike ate $\frac{1}{4}$ of a 12-ounce box of raisins. Michaela ate $\frac{2}{3}$ of a 9-ounce box. Who ate more raisins? How much more? Explain.

3 | MEASUREMENT

Find the volume of the box. Then draw a box with different measurements but the same volume. How did you figure out the measurements of your box?

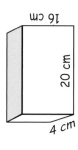

16 cm
20 cm
4 cm

Math in Minutes Ⓐ

1 | NUMBER & OPERATIONS

Marbles galore! Sammy shares 324 marbles with 3 friends. Tammy shares 1,542 marbles with 6 friends. Kami shares 2,151 marbles with 9 friends. Whose friends get the most marbles? How do you know?

4 | GEOMETRY

Of the angles in each figure, how many are right, acute, and obtuse? How might you check your answers without using a protractor? Explain.

A

B

2 | NUMBER & OPERATIONS

Which fractions are greater than one-half? Explain your process.

$$\frac{3}{4} \quad \frac{4}{9} \quad \frac{7}{10} \quad \frac{6}{14}$$

$$\frac{4}{7} \quad \frac{8}{15} \quad \frac{5}{12}$$

5 | ALGEBRAIC THINKING

Find the number that is seven times the greatest common factor of 12 and 60. How do you know your answer is correct?

GCF

3 | MEASUREMENT

Edna left home at 6:15 AM and drove 50 minutes to the airport. She waited one hour to board the plane which took off 15 minutes later and then touched down 3 hours and 20 minutes after that. What time did the plane land? How do you know?

6 | NUMBER & OPERATIONS

Round each number to the nearest hundred. Then explain your strategy.

A. 3,807
B. 491
C. 203,611
D. 90,999

Math in Minutes Ⓑ

4 | GEOMETRY

Which of these statements are true? How do you know?

A. All quadrilaterals have right angles.

B. All rhombuses are quadrilaterals, but not all quadrilaterals are rhombuses.

C. All trapezoids have two parallel sides.

5 | NUMBER & OPERATIONS

Use the same one-digit number in both boxes. Which one-digit numbers can be used so that the quotient will always be greater than 50? How do you know?

6 | NUMBER & OPERATIONS

A farmer bought a horse for $2,379 and sold it for $2,265. He later bought the horse again for $2,175, but then he sold it for $1,960. How much money did the farmer lose on this horse? How did you find your answer?

1 | NUMBER & OPERATIONS

A car's odometer reads 34,678 miles. How many more miles must the car travel before all five digits of the odometer are the same? How did you find your answer?

2 | NUMBER & OPERATIONS

If you multiply 100 by 0.99, 0.98, 0.97, or 0.96, will any of the products have a value that is greater than 100? Explain.

3 | MEASUREMENT

Sara is making a curtain for the class play that must be 22 yards wide. She has sewn a piece of cloth that is $31\frac{1}{2}$ feet wide to a piece that is $33\frac{1}{4}$ feet wide. How much more fabric does Sara need to add? How did you find the answer?

©The Mailbox • TEC44067 • June/July 2013 • Key p. 310 • (CCSS)

Math in Minutes Ⓐ

4 | GEOMETRY

If the sum of angle ABE is 170°, and angle EBC is a right angle, what do angles DBE and ABC measure? How did you find your answers?

5 | ALGEBRAIC THINKING

If the pattern shown is continued, will the fifth, sixth, and seventh numbers be even or odd? How do you know?

13, 26, 39, 52...

6 | MEASUREMENT

About how many years would it take you to spend $1,000,000 if you spent $50 a day? Explain.

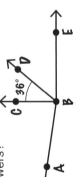

1 | NUMBER & OPERATIONS

Choose the item in each row that is not equivalent to the others. Explain your choice.

A. 0.7 $\frac{7}{10}$ $\frac{7}{100}$

B. 0.25 $\frac{25}{1,000}$ $\frac{25}{100}$

C. 0.09 $\frac{9}{10}$ $\frac{9}{100}$

2 | NUMBER & OPERATIONS

Which problem or problems could have a remainder greater than 5? How can you decide without solving each problem?

419 ÷ 7

4,017 ÷ 4

2,212 ÷ 9

3 | MEASUREMENT

The area of a room is 108 square feet. Which of the following measurements could not describe the room? How do you know?

A. 9 ft. x 12 ft.

B. 4 ft. x 27 ft.

C. 4 ft. x 16 ft.

©The Mailbox • TEC44067 • June/July 2013 • Key p. 310 • (CCSS)

MIND BUILDERS + × ÷ − % = × + %

MATH

MIND BUILDER 1

Find the number that is three less than half the difference between 1,420 and 986. Then write and solve two more problems like this.

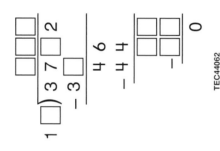

TEC44062

MIND BUILDER 2

To which set does each of these numbers belong: 5, 9, 18, 27, 41? How do you know?

Set A: 23, 50, 14, 32

Set B: 30, 21, 63, 42

TEC44062

MIND BUILDER 3

Find the missing digits in this division problem.

```
          □ □
   1 □ ) 3 7 □ 2
       - 3 □
         ─────
           4 6
         - 4 4
         ─────
           □ □
         - □ □
         ─────
             0
```

TEC44062

MIND BUILDER 4

The distance around the outside of a stop sign is 15 feet. What is the length of each side in inches?

TEC44062

MIND BUILDER 5

A square plus a circle always equals a square. A square plus a square always equals a circle. A circle plus a circle always equals a circle. Which shape represents odd numbers: squares or circles?

TEC44062

MIND BUILDER 6

Labor Day is always the first Monday in September. Rewrite each statement so that it is correct.

A. The earliest date for Labor Day is September 7.

B. The latest possible Labor Day date is September 8.

C. Since Labor Day is September 3 this year, it will be September 4 next year.

D. Labor Day will be on September 8 in 2015.

TEC44062

MIND BUILDER 7

How many letters on this T-shirt will look exactly the same in the mirror? (Hint: Count a letter each time it is used.)

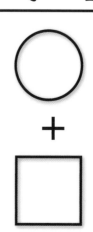

LANSING, MICHIGAN
The Capitol City

TEC44062

MIND BUILDER 8

Suppose you have four coins of three different types. None of the coins are dollars or half-dollars. What is the largest total value the coins could have? What is the smallest value?

TEC44062

©The Mailbox® • TEC44062 • Aug./Sept. 2012 • Key p. 310

How to Use Display this page or give each student a copy of the page (or one card at a time) to work on during free time. Have the student solve the problems on a separate sheet of paper.

MIND BUILDERS

MIND BUILDER 1

Between which two holidays are there usually more days: Halloween and Thanksgiving Day or Thanksgiving Day and Christmas? Explain.

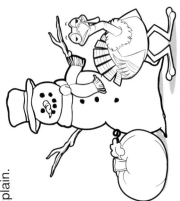

TEC44063

MIND BUILDER 2

If you drew a pair of horizontal parallel lines and then drew another pair of parallel lines that intersected the first pair, name and describe all the different figures that might be created.

TEC44063

MIND BUILDER 3

Multiply any whole number by 6. Divide the product by 3. Add 12 to the sum. Divide the sum by 2. Do you have a remainder? Will you ever have a remainder? Why or why not?

TEC44063

MIND BUILDER 4

Ed runs every Monday, Wednesday, and Friday from 5:00 to 6:00. Luke runs every weekday but Wednesday between 5:00 and 6:00. Jan runs Tuesday, Thursday, and Friday from 6:00 to 7:00, but only if it rains. Who's running Tuesday at 5:30?

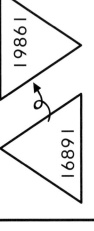

TEC44063

MIND BUILDER 5

Which problems' answers will be greater than 1,000? Use mental math to solve each problem and find out.

A. 5 × 22 × 10

B. 8,265 − 7,301

C. (98,600 ÷ 20) ÷ 5

D. 24 + 67 + 548 + 410

TEC44063

MIND BUILDER 6

Solve the problem shown. Then find two factors whose product is the same as the problem's sum.

$$
\begin{array}{r}
560 \\
389 \\
706 \\
+\ 1,369 \\
\hline
\end{array}
$$

TEC44063

MIND BUILDER 7

The digits 0, 1, 6, 8, 9 are unusual numbers. When turned upside down, each digit either looks the same or like another number. Use the digits to write ten or more four-digit numbers that read the same when turned upside down.

Example:

16891   19861

TEC44063

MIND BUILDER 8

What is the largest number that can be represented by t?

$$1{,}000 + t < 143 \times t < 2{,}000 - t$$

TEC44063

©The Mailbox® • TEC44063 • Oct./Nov. 2012 • Key p. 310

How to Use Display this page or give each student a copy of the page (or one card at a time) to work on during free time. Have the student solve the problems on a separate sheet of paper.

MIND BUILDERS ×∵ +

MATH

MIND BUILDER 1

Harold is selling his 100-book comic book collection. Which store is offering Harold the better deal?

Bert's Books
We sell each book for $4.50.
You keep $\frac{7}{10}$ (or 70%) of the sales.
No extra fees!

CAROL'S COMICS
We sell each book for $4.50.
You keep $\frac{9}{10}$ (or 90%) of the sales.
Pay a onetime $30 fee.

TEC44064

MIND BUILDER 2

What is the sum of all the letters in the alphabet according to the pattern shown? Try to find the answer in two different ways.

$$A = 1, B = 2, C = 3... Z = 26$$

TEC44064

MIND BUILDER 3

Finish each analogy.

A.

B.

C.

D.

TEC44064

MIND BUILDER 4

True or false?

A. All squares are rectangles, but not all rectangles are squares.

B. All rectangles are quadrilaterals, and all quadrilaterals are rectangles.

C. All quadrilaterals have four sides, and all pentagons have four sides.

D. Some quadrilaterals are rectangles, and some quadrilaterals are squares; but all quadrilaterals are polygons.

TEC44064

MIND BUILDER 5

Use all the numbers shown and only the numbers shown to write an equation that equals 6. You may use addition, subtraction, multiplication, and/or division.

Hint: Use parentheses and brackets in your equation.

5   5   5

5   5

TEC44064

MIND BUILDER 6

How many factors of 96 are divisible by 3? What are they?

96

TEC44064

MIND BUILDER 7

The clues below describe a number between 1 and 3. What is the number?

• The number is odd.

• The digit in the hundredths place is four times the digit in the ones place.

• The digit in the ones place is one less than the digit in the thousandths place.

• The sum of the number's four digits is 14.

TEC44064

MIND BUILDER 8

If these figures were dipped into a bucket of green paint, how many block faces on each figure would be green? How many would be green in all?

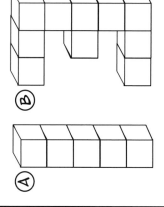

Ⓐ

Ⓑ

TEC44064

©The Mailbox® • TEC44064 • Dec./Jan. 2012–13 • Key p. 310

How to Use Display this page or give each student a copy of the page (or one card at a time) to work on during free time. Have the student solve the problems on a separate sheet of paper.

MIND BUILDERS × ÷ % + =

MIND BUILDER 1

Mr. Sullivan receives $13.05 in change from a $20 bill. He purchased three items from the menu. What did Mr. Sullivan buy?

Menu

hamburger ... $2.95
fries $1.75
hot dog $2.50
milk shake ... $2.25
cola $1.50

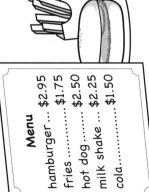

TEC44065

MIND BUILDER 2

For his birthday, Bobby received money from his grandmother. He used it to buy a DVD for $8.99, three candy bars for $0.89 each, a $4.00 movie ticket, a pair of sneakers for $45.99, and lunch for $5.55. After making his purchases, Bobby had $17.80 left. How much money did he get from his grandmother?

TEC44065

MIND BUILDER 3

Copy the equation(s) that can be used to solve this word problem. Then solve it.

Cherie took 35 fruit pies to the bake sale. She sold all but 8 pies. How many pies did Cherie sell?

A. $35 = n - 8$
B. $35 + n = 8$
C. $8 + 35 = n$
D. $8 + n = 35$

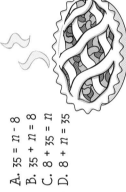

TEC44065

MIND BUILDER 4

Write an equation to find the area of the unshaded region using only the variables shown.

w

a

b

l

TEC44065

MIND BUILDER 5

Explain the difference between these two statements. Tell whether either statement is true.

Every square is a rectangle.
Every rectangle is a square.

TEC44065

MIND BUILDER 6

Solve each problem. Then sort the problems from least to greatest.

A. $3,402 - 1,385$
B. $5,982 + 2,080$
C. $900 - 472$
D. $3,853 - 2,619$
E. $600 - 285$
F. $4,782 + 896$

TEC44065

MIND BUILDER 7

Match the angle measurements to the types of angles. Then draw each angle.

$90°$ obtuse

$27°$ right

$180°$ acute

$149°$ straight

TEC44065

MIND BUILDER 8

Chinese Numbers

1 一	6 六
2 二	7 七
3 三	8 八
4 四	9 九
5 五	10 十

The ancient Chinese wrote 76 as
七 十 六
$(7 × 10) + 6$
What would these numbers be?
A. 八 + 四
B. 三 + 九
C. 五 + 二

TEC44065

©The Mailbox® · TEC44065 · Feb./Mar. 2013 · Key p. 310

How to Use Display this page or give each student a copy of the page (or one card at a time) to work on during free time. Have the student solve the problems on a separate sheet of paper.

MIND BUILDERS

MIND BUILDER 1

Find the number in each box that does not belong. What's the pattern?

A.
28	7
5	14

B.
12	3
15	25

C.
8	56
40	14

D.
36	24
42	46

TEC44066

MIND BUILDER 2

Solve each equation. What's the pattern?

$9 \times 1 + 2 =$

$9 \times 12 + 3 =$

$9 \times 123 + 4 =$

$9 \times 1,234 + 5 =$

$9 \times 12,345,678 + 9 =$

TEC44066

MIND BUILDER 3

Which fraction matches each set of clues?

$\frac{2}{3}$ $\frac{3}{5}$ $\frac{1}{3}$ $\frac{2}{6}$ $\frac{1}{5}$ $\frac{5}{15}$

A. My numerator and denominator are odd numbers. I am less than $\frac{1}{2}$ but greater than $\frac{1}{4}$. I cannot be reduced.

B. My numerator and denominator are odd numbers. I am less than $\frac{1}{3}$ but greater than $\frac{1}{6}$. I cannot be reduced.

C. My numerator and denominator are odd numbers. I am less than $\frac{1}{2}$ but greater than $\frac{1}{4}$. I can be reduced.

TEC44066

MIND BUILDER 4

Name each figure.

A.

B.

C.

TEC44066

MIND BUILDER 5

Imagine that you built this cube using centimeter cubes and then painted it orange.

6 cm 6 cm 6 cm

A. How many centimeter cubes would you use?
B. How many centimeter cubes would have only one orange face?
C. How many centimeter cubes would have four orange faces?

TEC44066

MIND BUILDER 6

Continue this pattern.

$7 \times 8 = 56$
$7 \times 80 = 560$
$70 \times 80 = 5,600$

A. $70 \times 800 =$
B. $700 \times 800 =$
C. $700 \times 8,000 =$
D. $7,000 \times 8,000 =$

TEC44066

MIND BUILDER 7

Decide how the letters and numbers relate. Then find the missing values.

$Y = 25$
$D = 4$
$J = 10$
$P = ?$
$F = ?$
$N = ?$

TEC44066

MIND BUILDER 8

Rewrite each statement by writing the matching word for each capital letter.

Example: 4 = S on a Q
(sides on a quadrilateral)

A. 3 = A in a T
B. 4 = R A in a S
C. 90 = D in a R A
D. 5 = S in a P

TEC44066

How to Use Display this page or give each student a copy of the page (or one card at a time) to work on during free time. Have the student solve the problems on a separate sheet of paper.

MIND BUILDERS ×·%·−·+

MATH

MIND BUILDER 1

Leroy has two equivalent squares. He wants to create a new square that is twice the size of just one square. He can only use the two squares, and the new shape must still be a square. How can he do it? Hint: He can divide one square into four equal pieces.

TEC44067

MIND BUILDER 2

Find the item in each box that does not belong. Then explain your choice.

1,245
1,020
2,005
1,002

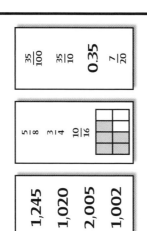

| $\frac{5}{8}$ |
| $\frac{3}{4}$ |
| $\frac{10}{16}$ |

| $\frac{35}{100}$ |
| $\frac{35}{10}$ |
| 0.35 |
| $\frac{7}{20}$ |

TEC44067

MIND BUILDER 3

Write the letter for each ordered pair shown. (6, 5) (1, 1) (3, 1) (3, 1) (1, 8) (7, 3) (7, 7) (3, 5) (3, 5) (4, 8) (6, 1)!

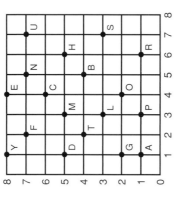

TEC44067

MIND BUILDER 4

The first number in each pair is related to the second one. Decide how they are related and complete each pair in the set. Then describe the pattern the number pairs create.

52,328 ; 20

3,675 ; _____

769 ; 22

46,058 ; _____

13,398 ; _____

203,596 ; 25

TEC44067

MIND BUILDER 5

Solve. Then find and describe three attributes the answers share.

A. 9,027 ÷ 17 = n

B. 10,949 × 9 = n

C. $229.59 ÷ 3 = n

D. 799.09 + 855.7 + 3,854.41 + 3,145.1 = n

MIND BUILDER 6

On what date is the 90th day of 2014?
On what date is the 150th day of 2014?
On what date is the 220th day of 2014?

TEC44067

MIND BUILDER 7

Suppose there is a math operation called ✵. Figure out what ✵ means in the following math sentences. (Hint: It may stand for a combination of two operations.)

4 ✵ = 17

5 ✵ = 26

8 ✵ = 65

10 ✵ = 101

12 ✵ = 145

TEC44067

MIND BUILDER 8

How many triangles are in this picture?

TEC44067

©The Mailbox® · TEC44067 · June/July 2013 · Key p. 310

How to Use Display this page or give each student a copy of the page (or one card at a time) to work on during free time. Have the student solve the problems on a separate sheet of paper.

Math Activity Cards

Cut out a copy of the cards to use as center or free-time activities.

Problem solving

"Grid-Pid-Pid"

Copy the grid. Then fill in the grid with the numbers 2, 4, 6, and 8 so that no number is in any row twice. This includes vertical, horizontal, and diagonal rows. There are many possibilities.

TEC44062

Comparing decimals to hundredths

Apple Pie Order

Choose 18 decimals and then arrange them from least to greatest. How did you choose the numbers to arrange? Explain

5.45   2.03   5.36   3.17   1.02   4.76

2.31   3.12   5.19   3.34   2.13   5.72

3.22

1.07   5.21   4.29   3.28   1.69   2.90   2.21

5.61   4.39   4.21   3.21   2.99   1.09

4.04   2.92   2.72   4.23   1.28   3.39

5.92   1.93   4.07

TEC44063 • (4.NF.C.7, 5.NBT.A.3b)

Division and multiplication

Going for a Spin

Spin each wheel and record the numbers to write a division problem. Then multiply to check your work. Repeat.

DIVIDEND

514 468 237
359 175 286

DIVISOR

3 5 8 2
6 7 4 9

TEC44062 • (4.NBT.B.6)

Multiplying whole numbers and fractions

A Work in Progress

Copy the web. Then multiply the number in the center by each group of fractions and numbers going out from the center. Write your products in the outside section of the web. Then add the products. They should equal ten.

4   4 $\frac{1}{2}$

$\frac{1}{10}$ $\frac{1}{3}$

$\frac{1}{4}$ 3 $\frac{1}{5}$ 3

$\frac{1}{8}$ $\frac{1}{6}$

8   1

For example, multiply 3 by $\frac{1}{4}$ by 4.

TEC44063 • (4.NF.B.4)

Math Activity Cards

Cut out a copy of the cards to use as center or free-time activities.

Problem solving, place value

Happy New Numbers!

Use the digits on the balloon to write numbers that match the descriptions below.

1. Write a five-digit number in which the product of the thousands, tens, and ones digit is 15.

2. Write a five-digit number in which the sum of the hundreds, tens, and ones digit is equal to the value of the digit in the ten thousands place.

3. Write a five-digit number in which no consecutive odd numbers are next to each other. (The 9 is not next to the 7, the 7 is not next to the 9 or the 5, and so on.)

4. Write a five-digit number that is divisible by five. Then name the quotient.

5. Write a five-digit number in which the product of the digits in the ten thousands and the ones places is 24 more than the product of the digits in the thousands, hundreds, and tens places.

TEC44064

Numerical patterns

Missing Links

Find the missing numbers in this chain.
Then describe the rule and the pattern created by the rule.

1, 3, 6, 10, ___, ___,

21, ___, ___, 45, ___,

66, 78, ___, ___, 120,

___, ___, 171, ___, ___

TEC44067 • (4.OA.C.5, 5.OA.A.3)

Problem solving, making an organized list

Too Many Snacks

If Santa takes one cookie, one drink, and one piece of candy at each house, how many possible snack combinations can Santa take? Make a list of all the combinations.

Cookies
chocolate chip
sugar
gingerbread

Drinks
milk
hot chocolate
eggnog

Candy
candy cane
lollipop

TEC44064

Comparing decimals

AT THE MEET

The 100 meter results are in! Using the table, arrange the runners' times from each heat in order.
Then name the runner in each race with the fastest time. Which runner had the best time overall?

Racer's Name	Heat 1	Heat 2	Heat 3
Jacob	12.53	12.48	12.51
Hailey	13.36	13.26	13.17
Anna	12.58	13.01	13.04
Ryan	13.45	13.36	13.27
Grace	12.51	12.49	12.53
James	12.56	12.98	12.50

TEC44067 • (4.NF.C.7, 5.NBT.A.3b)

Polly Want a Cracker?
Attributes of polygons

Answer the questions about the shapes of Polly's crackers.

1. Which crackers are regular polygons?
2. Which crackers are quadrilaterals?
3. How many crackers are irregular polygons?
4. How many crackers are triangles?
5. Which crackers have right angles?

TEC44066 • (4.G.A.2, 5.G.B.4)

May Flowers
Multiply one-digit by multidigit numbers

Use the digits on each flower to make a four-digit number. Then multiply that number by the number in the center.

TEC44066 • (4.NBT.B.5, 5.NBT.B.5)

SOMETHING'S FISHY
Estimating quotients

Round each number on a fish to the nearest ten. Then use the number on the can with the rounded numbers to write and solve eight division problems.

TEC44066

That's "Sum" Difference!
Add and subtract mixed numbers

Write an equation with two mixed numbers that fit each clue.

1. a difference of 1
2. a sum greater than 9
3. a difference between 1 and 2
4. a sum greater than 5 but less than 6
5. a difference less than 1
6. a sum between 6 and 7

$4\frac{1}{2}$ $3\frac{4}{8}$ $2\frac{5}{6}$ $3\frac{1}{9}$ $1\frac{2}{5}$ $5\frac{3}{4}$

TEC44066 • (5.NF.A.1)

Is There an App for That?

There's no app for this.

Read, Solve, Explain!

1. Forrest's phone cost $234. He promises his mom he will pay her back in equal payments over six weeks. He hasn't made his first payment yet. **How much should Forrest pay his mom each week?**

2. Forrest's mom pays him $8 an hour to rake the leaves in their yard. Forrest earns $53 Saturday and $51 Sunday. **How many hours does he work on Saturday and Sunday combined?**

3. To keep from getting bored, Forrest counts leaves as he rakes. He counts 3,675 leaves and piles them in three equal piles. All of a sudden, a cat pounces in the middle pile and scatters its leaves. **How many leaves does the cat scatter?**

4. When Forrest checks his phone, he sees that he missed 139 calls. The only calls he missed were from his best friend and someone who had the wrong number. Forrest's best friend called once more than the person who had the wrong number. **How many times did Forrest's best friend call?**

5. By the time Forrest finishes raking, he has equally filled seven bags with leaves. The seven bags weigh 378 pounds altogether. **How much does each bag of leaves weigh?**

6. There are 1,000 leaves left on the tree after Forrest finishes raking. If four leaves fall off the tree every hour, **how long will it be before the tree is completely bare?**

7. Forrest's mom is so pleased with his work that she gives him a gift card to buy more apps for his phone. The gift card is worth $63. **If each app costs $5, how many apps can Forrest buy?**

8. Forrest has 126 apps on his phone. He could display 16 apps on each screen, but he likes to have just nine on each screen. **If there are nine apps on each screen of Forrest's phone, how many screens are there?**

How to Use For a quick problem-solving center, place a copy of this page in a plastic page protector. Also stock the center with a copy of page 167 for each student.

Name _____

Date _____

Read, Solve, Explain!

1 Choose a problem and write its number in the box. ☐

What I noticed in the problem that might help solve it:

2 Read the problem again and complete the organizer below.

This is the problem in my words.

Something in the problem I wonder about:

3 Solve the problem.

4 Explain how you solved the problem.

The first thing I did to solve this problem _____

To check my answer, _____

Note to the teacher: Use with "Is There an App for That?" on page 166.

Make "Weigh" for a Winner!

Read, Solve, Explain!

1. Four months ago, Iona Field planted eight giant pumpkin seeds. She nurtured each seed as it grew from a tiny stalk of green into a winding vine. Now, each vine is at least 327 centimeters long. **About how long are the pumpkin vines altogether so far?**

2. Iona already had three seeds, but she bought five of the seeds she planted. The seeds were from a champion pumpkin, and each seed cost $1,678. **Did Iona spend more or less than $8,000 on the seeds? How much more or how much less?**

3. The champion pumpkin only contained nine seeds, and the pumpkin grower sold each seed for $1,678. **How much did the grower earn by selling all the pumpkin's seeds?**

4. When Iona's pumpkins start growing, she weighs each one. Most weigh from four to nine pounds. Then Iona finds a pumpkin that weighs five times the weight of the heaviest pumpkin. She predicts that this pumpkin will grow to be 25 times as heavy as it is. **How much does the pumpkin Iona finds weigh? How much does she predict that it will weigh?**

5. Every other day, Iona fills a 425-gallon water tank that waters her pumpkins. **How much water does Iona use to water her pumpkins in four weeks?**

6. Iona's heaviest pumpkin grows at an amazing rate. During the five weeks before Iona harvests her pumpkin, it gains from 26 to 32 pounds each day. **What is the most Iona's pumpkin will have gained at the end of the five weeks? What is the least the pumpkin will have gained?**

7. When Iona gets to the Cotton County Colossal Pumpkin Contest, there are nine pumpkins that weigh at least 1,117 pounds. **At least, how much do the nine pumpkins weigh altogether?**

8. The winning pumpkin weighs 1,304 pounds. Iona's pumpkin weighs 1,203 pounds. The winning pumpkin only has seven seeds, but each seed sells for $1,543. Iona's pumpkin has 829 seeds, and each seed sells for $25. **Which pumpkin grower earns more money selling the seeds from her pumpkin? How much does that pumpkin grower earn?**

©The Mailbox® • TEC44063 • Oct./Nov. 2012 • Key p. 310 • (4.OA.A.3)

How to Use For a quick problem-solving center, place a copy of this page in a plastic sleeve. Also stock the center with a copy of page 169 for each student.

Name

Date

Read, Solve, Explain!

1 Choose a problem and write its number in the pumpkin.

What I noticed in the problem that I probably don't need:

2 Think through the problem using the organizer below.

What I noticed in the problem that I think is important:

☐ I think there is one step in this problem.
☐ I think there are two steps in this problem.

An equation or equations I will use to solve the problem:

3 Solve the problem.

4 Explain your solution. What did you do first? How did you feel about your answer when you finished?

©The Mailbox® • TEC44063 • Oct./Nov. 2012

Note to the teacher: Use with "Make 'Weigh' for a Winner!" on page 168.

Going for a Spin!

Read, Solve, Explain!

1. On the B-Ready basketball team, $\frac{1}{3}$ of the players can spin the ball for 15 to 30 seconds, and $\frac{1}{4}$ of the players can spin the ball for 30 seconds or longer. **What fraction of the team's players can spin the ball for at least 15 seconds?**

2. Sasha spends $\frac{1}{4}$ of Monday's practice shooting layups, $\frac{1}{5}$ of practice shooting free throws, and $\frac{3}{8}$ of practice learning plays. She spent the rest of practice trying to spin a basketball on one finger. **What fraction of Monday's practice did Sasha spend trying to spin a basketball?**

3. During practice, $\frac{2}{3}$ of the team practices shooting free throws, and $\frac{1}{5}$ of the players practice shooting layups. **What fraction of the team is not shooting free throws or layups?**

4. Rupert's pretty good at spinning a basketball on his finger. When he shows off, however, he tends to drop the ball $\frac{3}{10}$ of the time. When he isn't showing off, he drops the ball only about $\frac{1}{12}$ of the time. **What fraction of the time Rupert spends spinning the ball does he tend to drop it?**

5. After practice, $\frac{2}{5}$ of the players walk home and $\frac{1}{3}$ of the players get car rides home. The rest of the players take the bus home. **What fraction of the players take the bus home?**

6. Before the first game starts, Coach Candu gives $\frac{1}{2}$ of her speech. During halftime, Coach Candu gives $\frac{2}{5}$ more of her speech. **How much of her speech does Coach Candu save for the end of the game?**

7. During the first game, $\frac{3}{8}$ of the players scored baskets. During the second game, $\frac{1}{3}$ of the players scored. **What fraction of the players scored in the first or the second game?**

8. The B-Ready basketball team won $\frac{3}{5}$ of its games and tied $\frac{1}{10}$ of them. **What fraction of the games did the B-Ready basketball team lose?**

How to Use For a quick problem-solving center, place a copy of this page in a plastic page protector. Also stock the center with a copy of page 171 for each student.

Name _____

Date _____

Read, Solve, Explain!

(1) Choose a problem and write its number in the box. ☐

The fractions in this problem that will help me solve it:

These fractions stand for parts of....

(2) Think through the problem using the boxes below.

This is the problem in my words.

To solve this problem, I will

☐ need to find a common denominator.

☐ not need to find a common denominator.

An equation or equations I will use to solve the problem:

(3) Solve the problem.

(4) Explain your solution. What did you do first? What was the hardest part of solving this problem?

_____
_____
_____
_____
_____
_____
_____
_____
_____

©The Mailbox® • TEC44064 • Dec./Jan. 2012–13

Note to the teacher: Use with "Going for a Spin!" on page 170.

THE MAILBOX 171

Let 'em Fly!

Read, Solve, Explain!

1. Wendy is making a traditional diamond-shaped kite. Her kite is 1.2 meters tall and 800 millimeters wide. **How many centimeters tall and wide is Wendy's kite?**

2. Dusty made a hexagonal kite that is 260 centimeters tall. Wendy's kite is 1.2 meters tall. **How much taller than Wendy's kite is Dusty's kite?**

3. Dusty's kite has two sticks, called spars, that stretch from side to side. Each spar is 125 centimeters long. His kite's spine, the stick that stretches from top to bottom, is 260 centimeters long. **How many meters long altogether are the sticks in Dusty's kite?**

4. The tail on Wendy's kite was 1.63 meters long. Then she tied four knots in the tail that shortened it by 27 centimeters. **How many meters long is the tail on Wendy's kite now?**

5. Wendy buys a spool of kite string that is 60.96 meters long. To fly her kite, Wendy unwinds 23 meters of string. **How many centimeters of string are left on Wendy's spool?**

6. Dusty thinks his kite will fly much higher than Wendy's, so he buys a spool of kite string that is 355.4 meters longer than Wendy's 60.96-meter-long spool. Dusty thinks he needs over a kilometer of kite string. **How much more string would Dusty need to have a kilometer of string?**

7. Wendy's kite takes to the air quickly, and she lets it go until only 15.3 centimeters of the 60.96-meter string are left on the spool. **How many centimeters of string had Wendy let unwind?**

8. Before Dusty can get his kite in the air, he gets tangled in its string. By the time he gets untangled and cuts out the knotted sections, he has cut away 78.35 meters and 134.28 centimeters of kite string. **How many meters of kite string did Dusty lose to the tangles?**

How to Use For a quick problem-solving center, place a copy of this page in a plastic page protector. Also stock the center with a copy of page 173 for each student.

Read, Solve, Explain!

1 Choose a problem and write its number in the box. ☐

Hints
10 millimeters = 1 centimeter
100 centimeters = 1 meter
1000 meters = 1 kilometer

2 Think through the problem using the boxes below.

To solve this problem, I will need to convert _____ from _____ to _____.

An equation or equations I will use to make the conversion:

An equation or equations I will use to find the answer:

3 Solve the problem.

4 How did you check to make sure you did not get confused?

Note to the teacher: Use with "Let 'em Fly!" on page 172.

Go Figure...

Read, Solve, Explain!

1. Ms. Beck, five parent volunteers, and all 27 of her students are headed to the museum's Egypt exhibit. To pay for the bus, Ms. Beck and the parents each pay $1.35. Each student pays $0.85. **How much do Ms. Beck, the parents, and the students pay for the bus altogether?**

2. Before the bus driver filled up the bus's gas tank, it had only 13.26 gallons of gas. Now the bus has 49.3 gallons of gas. **How much gas did the driver add?**

3. For a pre–field trip treat, Ms. Beck brings in mini bagels and 201.6 ounces of juice. **If Ms. Beck does not drink any juice, how much will each of her 27 students and the five parents get?**

4. The class's first stop is at a farm 26.3 miles from the school. The next stop is 18.05 miles away at a state park. Then the class rides 13.48 miles farther to the museum. **How many miles will the class travel round-trip?**

5. At the museum, Ms. Beck gives the tour guide $144.45 for 27 student admissions. **How much does one student admission cost?**

6. The tour guide spends an average of 8.365 minutes talking about each of the museum's 12 exhibits. **How long does the tour guide talk about the exhibits?**

7. Ms. Beck lets her students spend 15 minutes in the gift shop. Altogether, 23 students spend a total of $296.47 on souvenirs. **If each student spends the same amount, how much does each one spend?**

8. After school, Ms. Beck adds up her costs for the day—bus trip for $1.35, four bottles of juice at $3.79 each, three dozen mini bagels at $3.85 per dozen, one pack of gum for $1.83, and a souvenir mummy for $12.89. **How much does Ms. Beck spend in all?**

©The Mailbox® · TEC44066 · April/May 2013 · Key p. 311 · (5.NBT.B.7)

How to Use For a quick problem-solving center, place a copy of this page in a plastic page protector.

What an Appetite!

Read, Solve, Explain!

1. Bingo bango bugs have gobbled all the leaves of 13 rare bingo bango trees. Each tree was worth $1,695. **How much total damage did the bugs cause?**

2. There were 1,105 bingo bango fruits on the 13 bingo bango trees. If **each tree had the same amount of fruit, how many bingo bango fruits were on each tree?**

3. A bingo bango bug can fly 38 miles per hour for 15 minutes. The rest of the time, it flies about five miles per hour. **If a bingo bango bug flew for one hour and thirty minutes without stopping, how many miles would it fly?**

4. A bingo bango bug takes an average of 1,442 bites when it eats one leaf. **How many bites would a dozen bingo bango bugs take to each eat a dozen leaves?**

5. A bingo bango bug can live up to a year. All the bugs are alive for 77 days. After 135 more days, most of the bingo bango bugs are still alive. Then 149 days later, just a few bugs are still alive and munching. **How long (in weeks and days) have the longest-living bingo bango bugs been alive?**

6. Each bingo bango bug has 32 supersensitive hairs on each leg. Since each bug is an insect, it has six legs. **How many supersensitive hairs would 17 bingo bango bugs have altogether?**

7. Brook counts 678 bingo bango bugs on one bingo bango tree. Bret finds five times as many bugs on another tree. **How many bingo bango bugs do Brook and Bret count on both trees?**

8. The bingo bango bug's only natural enemy is the fancy feeler fly. Each fancy feeler fly can eat seven bingo bango bugs a day. **How long would it take 9 fancy feeler flies to gobble up 22,995 bingo bango bugs?**

©The Mailbox® • TEC44067 • June/July 2013 • Key p. 311 • (4.OA.A.3)

How to Use   For a quick problem-solving center, place a copy of this page in a plastic page protector.

THE MAILBOX **175**

Tips for Tuning Up Students' Mental Math Skills

1 Jumpin' Jack Facts
Division

When it's time to practice division facts, have your students stand up. Then state a problem and have students show the answer by doing that number of jumping jacks. While jumping, the students count aloud until they reach the answer.

Christina Stelzl, Brinker Elementary, Plano, TX

> $54 \div 9$.

> 1, 2, 3, 4, 5, 6!

> Good morning, Taylor! What does seven times eight equal?

> Good morning, Anthony! What's the product of six times eight?

> Good morning, Olivia! What does nine times eight equal?

2 The Morning Five
Multiplication

Identify the five multiplication facts your students tend to miss most often. Then greet each student on her way into the classroom each morning by asking her to answer one of the five problems. Repeat again after lunch if possible. It won't be long before those facts are the ones your students never miss!

Carla Husband, Latta Elementary, Ada, OK

3 Practice, Practice, Practice!
Math facts

Want to get a quick idea of your students' progress without taking home a stack of papers to grade? Have each student clear a space on his desk and give him a dry-erase marker and a tissue or eraser. Then announce a math problem and have the child write the sum, difference, product, or quotient on his desk. With a quick glance, evaluate students' responses. Then have them wipe away their answers and get ready for the next fact. Your students get permission to draw on their desks for a few minutes, and you get valuable information!

Mel Fox, Isaac Fox Elementary, Lake Zurich, IL

> Seven times four.

28

4 Take Advantage of Transitions
Mental computation

Keep a copy of the checklist from page 177 handy to use during transitions. Just read a question aloud and challenge each student to work the problem in her head. If students are standing in line, have them share their answers. If students are at their desks, have them jot their answers on scrap paper for bonus points. Check off each question after you read it and then read another question as time allows.

Take Advantage of Transitions!

Keep a copy of this page handy during transitions. Check each question as you read it.

How many minutes are there in three hours? 180 minutes	What is 80,000 divided by 80? 1,000	What is $\frac{1}{2}$ of 240? 120	How many centimeters are there in four meters? 400 cm	How many angles are there in three triangles? 9 angles
What would 6,260 rounded to the nearest hundred be? 6,300	How many days are there in three weeks? 21 days	How many pints are there in four quarts? 8 pints	What is the sum of 200 + 30 + 6 + 2? 238	How many hours are there between 8:00 AM and 3:00 PM? 7 hours
What is the perimeter of a 5-inch by 9-inch rectangle? 28 inches	How many seconds are there in one half hour? 1,800 seconds	What is the value of three quarters, three dimes, and two nickels? $1.15	How many sides are there on three pentagons? 15 sides	What is the solution to this problem? (3 x 8) ÷ (2 + 4) 4
How many feet are there in six yards? 18 feet	What is the solution to this problem? 4 x 8 + 4 – 3 33	How much time is there between 5:35 PM and 7:45 PM? 2 hours, 10 minutes	What would 462 rounded to the nearest ten be? 460	What is the product of 7,000 x 400? 2,800,000
How many days are there in the months of September, October, and November? 91 days	How much change would you receive from a $10.00 bill if you spent $5.55? $4.45	What is the solution to this problem? 88 – 8 + 15 95	What is the product of 12 x 11? 132	How many ounces are there in seven pounds? 112 ounces
The temperature is –8°F. What would the temperature be if it rose 20 degrees F? 12°F	If today is Wednesday, what day was it 10 days ago? Sunday	How many inches are there in $1\frac{3}{4}$ feet? 21 inches	How many eggs are there in five dozen? 60 eggs	What is $\frac{1}{3}$ of 24? 8

©The Mailbox® • TEC44062 • Aug./Sept. 2012

Note to the teacher: Use with "Take Advantage of Transitions" on page 176.

Spring Fever MATH!

5 Challenges Sure to Help Fight Those Winter Blahs!

1 Take a neighborhood walk and have each student record housing and transportation data such as in the boxes below. Then have each child find the range, mean, median, and mode of the housing data and arrange the car color data in a bar graph. Then guide students to discuss their results.

- Count the number of houses on each street.
- Count the number of apartments in each building.
- Count the number and colors of cars in the parking lot or neighborhood.

2 You don't need to head outside for this activity, but it's fascinating, nonetheless! Pair students and have one student stand with her arms stretching out toward her sides. Then have the child's partner use a tape measure to measure her arms from the tip of her left hand to the tip of her right hand. Next, the partner measures the student's height and writes a ratio of the measurements (outstretched arms and height). Then the partners switch roles and discuss the ratios.

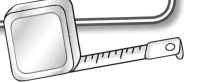

3 For this idea, have each student draw a large chalk square on the sidewalk. Then ask how many different ways each student can divide a square using only two straight lines. The lines may cross each other and go in any direction. Allow students to share their results before they dust off the drawings and repeat the challenge with three lines.

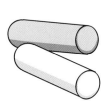

4 Ask students whether the length of a tree's shadow is always the same. Then, on a sunny day, choose a tree in the playground or nearby. Have students measure the lengths of the shadow at four different times during the day and then discuss the results.

5 Ask students to predict how many steps it will take to get from the classroom doorway to the bus stop. Have each child record his prediction. Then have students walk the distance three times in a normal manner, counting the number of steps each time, being sure to start and stop at the same point. Have students find the mean and median number of steps, compare them with their predictions, and discuss the results.

Getting a Grip on GEOMETRY

A Different Angle
Angle measurement (4.MD.C.5)

Combine geometry and technology with this idea! Teach students how to use the line-drawing tool of your word-processing program. Then have each student use the drawing tool to draw several different-size angles on a new document. Next, have the student type an estimate of each angle's measurement, inserting the degree symbol. Then print a copy of each student's page. Guide the child to measure each angle using a protractor and to record the correct measurement.

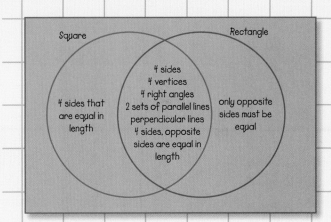

88° 85°   9° 82°

2° 5°   1° 3°

170° 150°   110° 135°

80° 60°   50° 45°

Same or Different?
Polygon attributes (4.G.A.1, 2; 5.G.B.3)

To help students focus on polygons' attributes, draw a Venn diagram on the board. Label the left circle with one polygon's name and the right circle with another. Then lead students to compare and contrast the two polygons as you record their comments in the appropriate spaces of the diagram. Follow up by having each student describe the similarities of the polygons in one paragraph and their differences in another.

Square | Rectangle

4 sides that are equal in length

4 sides
4 vertices
4 right angles
2 sets of parallel lines
perpendicular lines
4 sides, opposite sides are equal in length

only opposite sides must be equal

Around the House
Symmetry (4.G.A.3)

Lead students to identify examples of symmetry in everyday items, such as a leaf on a plant, a flower's petal, a patterned rug, or the front of a file cabinet drawer. Remind students that to be symmetrical, the example will have at least one line of symmetry. Where possible, fold each example to check its symmetry. For other examples, use a yardstick to show the line of symmetry, or draw the line or lines of symmetry with a wipe-off marker. Then, for homework, have each student draw examples of five or more objects he finds at home that have symmetry.

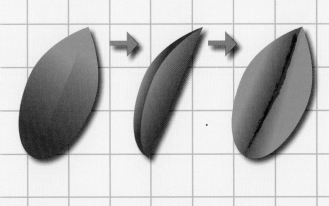

In this Corner...
Geometry vocabulary (4.G.A.1, 2; 5.G.B.3, 4) (L.4.6, L.5.6)

For this activity, draw a simple geometric picture such as the one shown without revealing the picture to your students. Next, have students draw the picture on their own papers as you give the directions, using geometric vocabulary, one step at a time. After students finish, display your drawing so they can compare their pictures to yours. To extend the activity, have each student create an original geometric drawing that includes each term and write directions for re-creating it. Then have each pair of students take turns describing and drawing each other's designs.

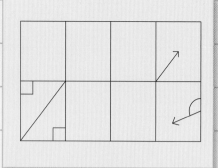

1. Draw a rectangle.
2. Draw a vertical line of symmetry through the rectangle.
3. Draw a horizontal line of symmetry through the rectangle.
4. In the right half of the rectangle, draw a line segment that is parallel to the vertical line of symmetry.
5. In the left half of the rectangle, draw a line segment that is perpendicular to the horizontal line of symmetry.
6. In the bottom left rectangle, draw a line segment that creates two right triangles.
7. In the top right rectangle, draw a ray that creates an acute angle.
8. In the bottom right rectangle, draw a ray that creates an obtuse angle.

Name _____

Date _____

All for One!

Name the attribute that the shapes in each set share.

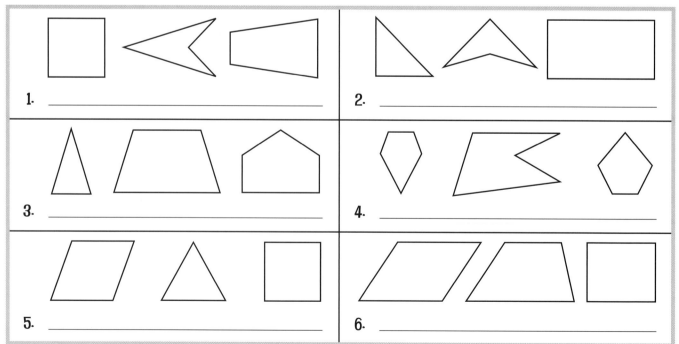

1. _____

2. _____

3. _____

4. _____

5. _____

6. _____

Bonus: Complete this statement: All quadrilaterals have four sides and four vertices. Rhombuses are quadrilaterals, so rhombuses have…

The Name of the Game

Whole-group games for reviewing computation skills!

When Lightning Strikes

Before students see it, cover each space on a copy of the grid from the top of page 182 with a marker. Then divide the class into groups, display the covered grid, and announce a problem. The first group to correctly solve the problem chooses a space on the grid by stating its coordinate pair. Remove the marker on that space. If you reveal a number, the group earns that number of points. If you reveal a lightning bolt, the group doesn't earn any points. Keep playing as time allows or until the grid is cleared. Then lead students to give the group with the most points a "charge" of furious clapping for a job well done! **Juli Engel, Flint, TX**

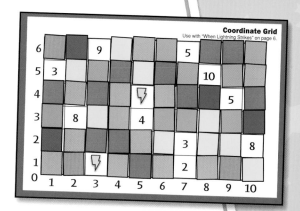

Next...

For this game, copy and cut apart the cards from the bottom of page 182 for each group of six students. Have each group of students sit in a row as a relay team. Then pass out the cards so the students in matching positions in each row have matching cards. For example, give the first student in each row a "x 7" card and the second student in each row a " ÷ 2" card.

To play, write a number on the board. The first student in each row uses the number and her card's direction to write and solve the first problem. She passes her answer to the second student on her team, who uses the answer and his card's direction to solve a new problem. Then he passes his answer to the next teammate. When the last student in the row solves her problem, she holds up her answer. The first team with the correct answer wins a point for the round. When time's up, declare the team with the most points the winner!

Order Up!

Give computation review a twist with this order of operations variation! Begin by dividing the class into groups. Next, roll two dice, add the numbers rolled, and record the sum on the board. Next, roll one die five separate times and write each of the five numbers on the board. Then challenge each group to use parentheses, brackets, any operations, and the five numbers to create a problem that equals the sum on the board. Have each group write its equation on the board. For each correct equation, award two points per operation, three points per set of parentheses, and five points per set of brackets. Repeat as time allows. **(5.OA.A.1)**

Answer 3
Equation Numbers
6, 4, 1, 2, 3

$6 \times 4 \div 3 \div 2 - 1 = 3$

8 points

Coordinate Grid

Use with "When Lightning Strikes" on page 181.

6	3	5	9	5	2	⚡	5	8	⚡	3
5	3	⚡	3	4	5	5	7	10	9	2
4	8	2	10	⚡	⚡	6	9	8	5	10
3	⚡	8	3	7	4	9	⚡	6	10	4
2	5	2	10	9	6	7	3	4	⚡	8
1	8	3	⚡	7	5	⚡	2	9	4	3
0	1	2	3	4	5	6	7	8	9	10

Math Operation Cards

Use with "Next…" on page 181.

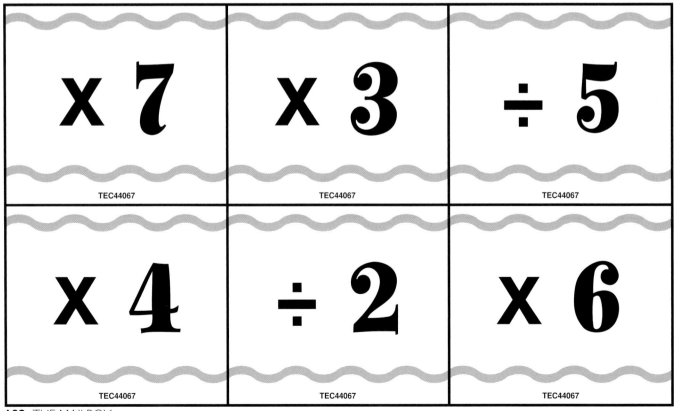

x 7	x 3	÷ 5
TEC44067	TEC44067	TEC44067
x 4	÷ 2	x 6
TEC44067	TEC44067	TEC44067

SCIENCE

simply science

rocks and minerals

A Stony Scavenger Hunt

For this activity, challenge each pair of students to find a rock that matches each of the descriptors shown. Then have the partners classify each rock according to its properties. **Emily Clark, Vernal, UT**

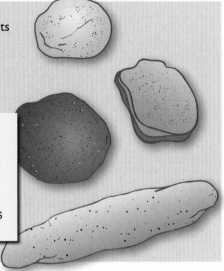

Find a Rock That Is...

as big as a dime	round
as big as a quarter	striped
flat	angular
lumpy	long and skinny
just one color	two or more colors

periodic table

"Element-ary" Exploration

Want to demystify the periodic table of the elements for your students? Try this! Display the periodic table. Then have each small group of children create words using the chemical symbols from the table. For each word it makes, have the group list the names of the elements whose symbols they used. To make the exercise a game, have students add the atomic numbers of their words' elements. Then declare the group with the highest score the periodic table title holder. **Jory Snyder, Sand Springs, OK**

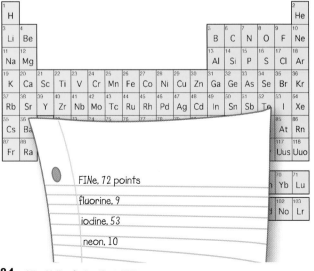

FINe, 72 points

fluorine, 9

iodine, 53

neon, 10

weather (L.4.5a, L.5.5a)

The Tempest Poetic

Help students share what they learn about severe weather with these fun-to-write poems. To begin, have each student choose a type of storm and research its destructive powers. Next, guide the child to imagine that she is the storm and write four vivid verb phrases that describe herself—the storm—in action. Then have the child write three phrases that include similes or metaphors describing sensory images of her wake or path as the storm. Finally, have the child write an alliterative statement that names her storm. As time allows, have each student illustrate her poem. Then post students' work on a display titled "Stormy Poems." **Belinda Rippon, Kiptopeke Elementary, Cape Charles, VA**

Tunneling through the fields;

Tearing down the streets;

Grabbing cars, trees, and even cows;

Swirling at up to 300 miles an hour.

As loud as a freight train,

As dangerous as a lion tracking its prey,

A beast you cannot capture,

I am a terrible tornado twisting toward town!

simply science

solar system, making a model

An Edible Solar System

For this activity, have students bring in a variety of snacks that might represent the sun, the earth and other planets, moons, dwarf planets, and objects in the solar system such as asteroids, comets, meteors, and dust. Next, have each child study the snacks available and plan how to use some of them to create a solar system model. After you approve each student's plan, give her a paper plate, provide canned frosting to use as glue, and have each child create and label her solar system model. When each student finishes, have her write a step-by-step explanation of her process. Then have students share their work before letting everyone enjoy the fruits of their efforts!
April Layfield, Millbrook Elementary, Aiken, South Carolina

human systems, skeletal system

Solid Support

To help students understand the strength of long bones, first explain that they include the femur, radius, ulna, tibia, and fibula. Next, have each pair of students roll a sheet of scrap paper into a tube, so the long sides are on the top and bottom, and then tape the tube closed. Then have each student imagine the tube is a femur. Like a femur, the tube has a compact outer layer. Guide the twosome to decide how strong the model femur is by predicting the number of books that can be stacked on the tube without crushing it. Then have the partners test their prediction by carefully stacking one book at a time on the center of their tube. To follow up, challenge students to find reasons our long bones are not solid. **Jennifer Otter, Oak Ridge, NC**

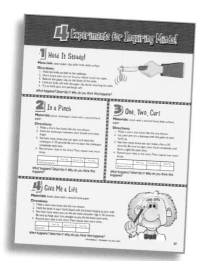

musculoskeletal system

Inquiring Minds

Engage your students' curiosity with the simple-to-set-up experiments on page 197. Simply tear out the page, slide it in a plastic sleeve, and set it at a center along with the materials listed. Then have each child, pair of students, or small group of students choose an experiment, follow the directions, and then write up the results. After students finish, they flip the page and read the experiment's explanation.

simply science

investigating mass (4.MD.A.1–2)

"Mass-ive" Milk Cartons

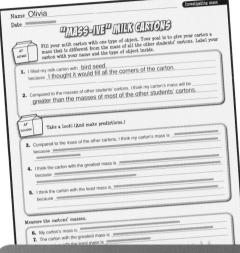

Here's an investigation students take home and then bring back to school to finish. To begin, have each child obtain a clean lunch-size milk carton. Next, challenge each student to take home her carton and fill it with one type of object so that the carton will have a different mass than other students' cartons. Have the child fill out the top of a copy of page 187 at home. Then set up a scale at a center and have students work in small groups to order the cartons according to their masses and finish filling out their pages. If desired, award small prizes for the least and greatest masses. **Amy Alferman, Hermann Middle School, Hermann, MO**

respiratory system, drawing conclusions

A Breath of Fresh Air

For this investigation, have paired students count the number of breaths their partners take in one minute while breathing normally and record their statistics. Then have one partner hold his or her breath for up to 30 seconds. When the first partner starts to breathe, the second partner should again count the number of breaths in one minute. Have students switch roles and repeat. *(The students' breathing rates will be more than before. The brain, knowing that the body has too much carbon dioxide built up, tells the lungs to breathe more.)* Then guide each pair to discuss its results and draw a conclusion. Follow up with a class discussion.

potential, kinetic energy

Energy Tag

Tag! Your energy is changing from kinetic back to potential!

Help students distinguish between the basic kinds of energy with a game of tag! To begin, head outside or to the gym. Then have each student squat into a ball full of *potential energy*. Next, tag a squatted student so she can run, changing her potential energy to *kinetic energy*. Explain that a student with kinetic energy can tag a squatted student, changing his potential energy to kinetic energy. A student can also tag another student with kinetic energy, changing his energy back to potential energy. When you return to the classroom, have students diagram the difference between potential and kinetic energy. **Becky Fuentes, Highland Elementary, Lake Stevens, WA**

Name _____

Date _____

"MASS-IVE" MILK CARTONS

AT HOME

Fill your milk carton with one type of object. Your goal is to give your carton a mass that is different from the mass of all the other students' cartons. Label your carton with your name and the type of object inside.

1. I filled my milk carton with _____

because _____

_____

2. Compared to the masses of other students' cartons, I think my carton's mass will be _____

_____

_____

AT SCHOOL

Take a look! (And make predictions.)

3. Compared to the mass of the other cartons, I think my carton's mass is _____

because _____

_____

4. I think the carton with the greatest mass is _____

because _____

_____

5. I think the carton with the least mass is _____

because _____

_____

Measure the cartons' masses.

6. My carton's mass is _____

7. The carton with the greatest mass is _____

8. The carton with the least mass is _____

9. Compared to the other cartons, my carton's mass _____

10. What surprised me most about this investigation: _____

_____

_____

_____

©The Mailbox® • TEC44064 • Dec./Jan. 2012–13 (4.MD.A.1-2)

Note to the teacher: Use with "'Mass-ive' Milk Cartons" on page 186.

THE MAILBOX **187**

simply science

scientific method

A+ Investigation

Remembering the steps of the scientific method just got a whole lot easier! Share with students the acronym "A PLUS," which stands for the following five-step scientific method process:

1. **A**: Ask the question that your investigation will try to answer.
2. **P**: Plan the steps of your investigation.
3. **L**: List the materials or tools you'll need to complete the investigation, as well as safety procedures to follow.
4. **U**: Understand your findings by writing down your data, results, and conclusions.
5. **S**: Share your results through a report, presentation, graph, or other means. Decide whether further investigation is needed.

Use this easy-to-remember process with any experiment by having students complete copies of the reproducible lab sheet on page 189. Jerri Fike, Eisenhower Elementary, Wellington, KS

---

solar system, writing an opinion (W.4.1, W.5.1)

Outer Space Journal Topics

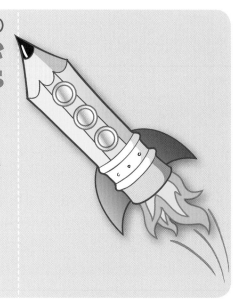

You've got to love an activity that covers two curriculum areas at once! During a study of the solar system, stars, or other outer space topics, have students practice opinion writing using the following space-related writing topics.

- On July 20, 1969, Neil Armstrong became the first person to set foot on the moon. He said, "That's one small step for [a] man, one giant leap for mankind." If you were the first human being to set foot on Mars, what would you say? Why?
- You have the opportunity to live in a space station during your senior year of high school. Explain why you would or would not go to live in the space station.
- On some of the first space flights, animals—not people—occupied the spacecrafts. What do you think about sending animals into space? Explain.

---

digestive system

A Long Trek

Distance Traveled by Food	Body Part
3 inches	mouth
10 inches	esophagus
8 inches	stomach
22 feet	small intestine
5 feet	large intestine

Here's an easy hands-on way to show students the long journey their pizza lunch will take through the digestive system. Give each small group a ball of yarn, a yardstick, masking tape, and a permanent marker. Students begin at one end of the yarn and measure each distance listed in the chart. They wrap a piece of tape around the end of each measurement and label the tape with the name of the corresponding body part. Finally, students cut the yarn after the last measurement and then stretch it out around your classroom to see how far a bite of food travels from the mouth to the large intestine.

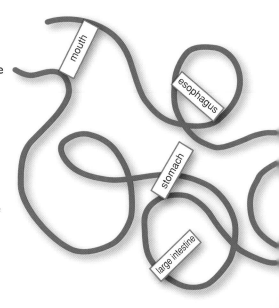

Name _____

Date _____

A+ INVESTIGATION

Complete the sections below.

1. ASK: What question will your investigation answer?

2. PLAN: What steps will you follow?

3. LIST: What materials or tools will you use?

4. UNDERSTAND: Record your data.
- What were your results?
- What were your conclusions?

Write your answers on paper you've stapled to the back of this page.

5. SHARE: Circle the method you will use to share your results with others.

graph	*chart*
presentation	*report*
poster	*other*

- -

Note to the teacher: Use with "A+ Investigation" on page 188. Have each student complete a copy of the page each time he completes an experiment.

parts of plants

Plant Parts Data Disc

An understanding of plant parts is bound to take root when students make this nifty study tool! Share the article shown to review the roles of plant parts with students. Then give each student a copy of page 191, scissors, crayons or colored pencils, a brad fastener, and another sheet of paper. Guide each child to follow the steps on page 191 to create a data disc she can use to review important plant parts and their functions. **Becky Charlton, Berry Intermediate, Lebanon, OH**

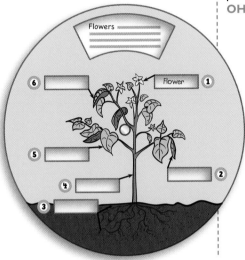

Green plants have three main parts: a stem, leaves, and roots. Besides holding a plant in place, roots absorb minerals and water from the soil. A plant uses these minerals and the water to grow. Another important function of roots is to store extra food. A stem holds up a plant's leaves and flowers. It carries water and minerals from the roots to the leaves and also carries food made in the leaves down to the roots. A plant's leaves take in sunlight, which the plant uses to make food in a process called photosynthesis. A plant's leaves also store waste. What happens to the waste? When the leaves fall off the plant, the waste goes with them!

Flowering plants grow flowers that help with pollination and with making seeds. Inside a plant's flowers, seeds grow. As the seeds grow, a fruit or pod also grows around the seeds. Eventually, the fruit or pod ripens and breaks open. The seeds are released.

plant adaptations

That's Wild!

This content- and vocabulary-rich game has students analyzing plant adaptations! Guide each small group of two to four students to follow the directions below to play.
Jennifer Otter, Oak Ridge, NC

Materials: copy of page 192; a die; and yellow, blue, red, and green markers, crayons, or colored pencils

Directions for two to four players:
1. Cut apart the cards and game pieces. Stack the cards facedown. Each player gets a game piece.
2. In turn, roll the die and follow the instructions according to your roll.

    1—That's wild! Pick a card. If you answer correctly, color any space on your game piece.
    2, 3, or 4—Pick a card.
    5—Skip a turn.
    6—Pick a card. If you answer correctly, roll again.

3. When you pick a card, have a teammate read it aloud. Then name the adaptation's category: **wet/dry environment, light, protection,** or **nutrients**.
4. If you answer correctly, color the matching space on your game piece. If the space is already colored or you answer incorrectly, your turn is over.
5. If all the cards are used before the game ends, shuffle and restack the cards.
6. The first player to color all four adaptations on his or her game piece wins.

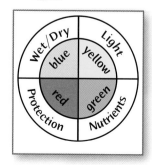

Some plants, like the rafflesia, steal their food by attaching themselves to the roots of jungle vines.
nutrients

The melastoma plant provides a home for ants. The ants keep hungry insects from eating the plant.
protection

Data Disc

Use with "Plant Parts Data Disc" on page 190.

Steps:

1. Cut out the disc and color the picture. Then cut out each box on the disc.*
2. Trace the disc on white paper. Cut out the tracing.
3. Stack the blank disc behind the plant disc. Poke a small hole through the dot in the center. Then insert a brad through this hole to connect the two discs.
4. Use the word bank to write the name of the correct plant part in Box 1. In the large box, write the main functions of that plant part, using the text your teacher provides.
5. Turn the top disc clockwise until the large box is empty. Then label Box 2 and write that plant part's functions in the large box.
6. Continue until all six parts are labeled.

Word Bank	
fruit or pod	roots
seeds	leaf
stem	flower

*For easier cutting, use the brad to poke a hole in the center of each box. Then gently push the tip of your scissors through the hole to start cutting.

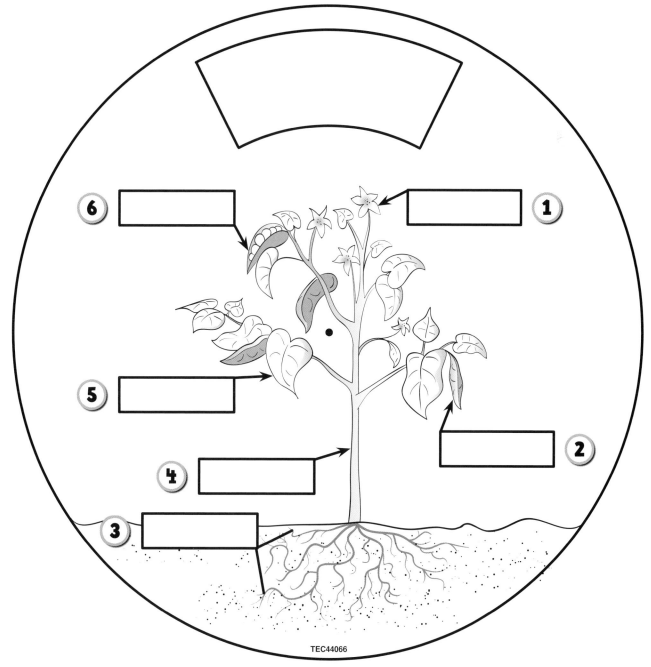

TEC44066

Game Cards and Game Pieces

Use with "That's Wild!" on page 190.

Pleats on the cereus cactus can unfold to store extra water. *(wet/dry environment)*	When an insect lands on a Venus flytrap, the leaf snaps shut. It stays closed while the plant digests the insect. *(nutrients)*	Special prop roots grow from the trunk of the mangrove tree to support the tree in its swampy environment. *(wet/dry environment)*	The baobab tree's trunk swells in the rainy season. The tree uses this stored water during the dry season. *(wet/dry environment)*
The pitcher plant has a slippery rim. Insects slide into a pool of liquid, drown, and are digested. *(nutrient)*	Plants like sedum have waxy leaves that keep water from evaporating. *(wet/dry environment)*	Many rain forest plants have spiky drip tips on their leaves that help drain off extra water. *(wet/dry environment)*	The leaves on the mint plant grow in crossed pairs so they don't shade the leaves below. *(light)*
A ginger plant's leaves grow in a spiral so they don't shade each other. *(light)*	Silver-backed leaves on the silver linden tree reflect sunlight so the plant won't get too warm. *(light)*	The aroid plant, which grows on the forest floor, has huge leaves that absorb more sunlight. *(light)*	Rather than make its own food, the Indian pipe plant feeds on dead plants and tree roots. *(nutrients)*
Some plants, like the rafflesia, steal their food by attaching themselves to the roots of jungle vines. *(nutrients)*	When the terminalia tree sheds its bark, it gets rid of unwanted vines and other pests that live in the bark. *(protection)*	The stinging nettle plant injects painful chemicals into animals that brush against its stingers. *(protection)*	An insect boring into the bark of the rubber tree is coated in liquid latex, stopping the insect in its tracks! *(protection)*
A sundew plant's sticky hairs act as a glue to trap insects. The plant then uses the insects for food. *(nutrients)*	New leaves on the clove plant contain toxins to prevent animals from eating the new growth. *(protection)*	The flower of the arctic poppy tracks the sun. Its stem rotates to follow the light. *(light)*	A cactus's sharp spines keep thirsty animals from taking its stored water. *(protection)*
The melastoma plant provides a home for ants. The ants keep hungry insects from eating the plant. *(protection)*	Spines on the golden barrel cactus collect dew. The dew falls to the ground and is absorbed by the plant's roots. *(wet/dry environment)*	The strangler fig grows around a host tree, preventing the tree from growing. The fig tree steals nutrients, killing the host tree. *(nutrients)*	The angel-leaf begonia's leaves have red undersides that catch light passing through each leaf. They reflect the light back into the leaves. *(light)*

TEC44066

Game spinners (x4): Wet/Dry – blue, Light – yellow, Protection – red, Nutrients – green

TEC44066

Domain-specific vocabulary

A Look at Light Years

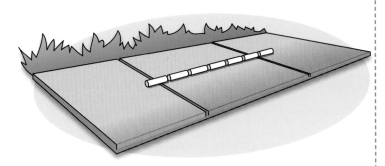

Help students understand why scientists use the unit of a *light year* (the distance that light can travel in one year). Challenge each pair of students to use a one-inch piece of a plastic straw to measure the length of the hall, a basketball court, or a sidewalk. After ten minutes, gather students and discuss whether inches were the best unit of measurement and what might have been better. Next, ask students how long they think it would take to run 63,360 inches. When students have difficulty visualizing the distance, explain that 63,360 inches is one mile. Then explain that scientists use light years instead of miles to measure the vast distances in space because light years are easier to work with—just as yards or meters would have been easier to work with in this activity.

Investigating mixtures

Mix It!

Highlight two types of mixtures with this tasty activity. Explain that a *mixture* is a combination of two or more substances. In a *homogenous mixture*, the different parts can't be seen. Have each small group mix a packet of instant lemonade mix in a pitcher of water and stir well. *(The mix dissolves, so the powder can't be seen separately from the water.)* The substances in a *heterogeneous mixture* can be seen. Have each small group mix two cups of dry cereal with a cup of M&M's candies and then add one-half cup of one or more of the following: raisins, dried cranberries, pretzels, or bagel chips. *(The parts can all be seen. The mixture is not uniform.)* Have students compare the trail mix mixture and its parts with the lemonade mixture and its parts. Then wrap up the activity by having students enjoy a snack of the lemonade and trail mix. **adapted from an idea by Regenna Biermann, Marion, IL**

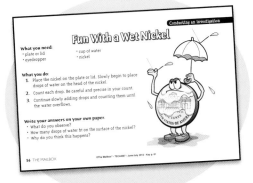

Conducting an investigation

Science in a Snap!

Looking for an easy science activity when you only have a short block of time? Try one of the simple experiments on page 194. Give each of several small groups a copy of an experiment and the materials listed for it.

Which Is Heavier: Saltwater or Freshwater?

What you need:
- 2 identical clear containers, such as pint-size canning jars
- bowl or tub large enough to set one of the containers inside
- stiff card that is large enough to cover the clear containers' openings
- water
- 10 tsp. salt
- 1 tsp. blue food coloring
- measuring spoons

What you do:
1. Fill both containers with regular tap water.
2. Set one jar in the bowl or tub. Add the salt and blue food coloring to the other container. Stir until the salt dissolves.
3. Place the card over the mouth of the saltwater container.
4. While firmly holding the card over the container of saltwater, invert it and place it on top of the container of regular tap water as shown.
5. Remove the card very slowly and carefully.

Write your answers on your own paper.
- What do you observe?
- Why do you think this happens?

Fun With a Wet Nickel

What you need:
- plate or lid
- eyedropper
- cup of water
- nickel

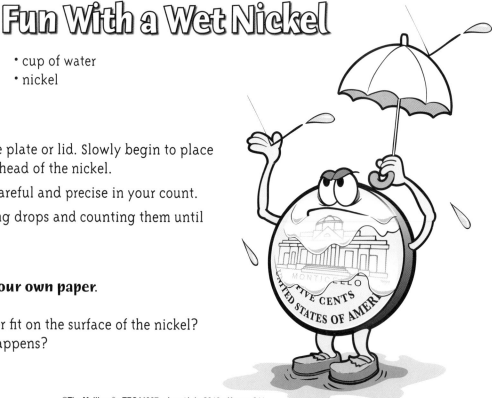

What you do:
1. Place the nickel on the plate or lid. Slowly begin to place drops of water on the head of the nickel.
2. Count each drop. Be careful and precise in your count.
3. Continue slowly adding drops and counting them until the water overflows.

Write your answers on your own paper.
- What do you observe?
- How many drops of water fit on the surface of the nickel?
- Why do you think this happens?

In a Flash
A Nervous System Investigation

1ST Grab a stopwatch. Then have students sit in a circle with their eyes closed, their arms crossed, and elbows lightly touching. Next, explain to each student that as soon as the person on her left gently nudges her elbow, she should nudge the elbow of the person on her right. Then join the circle and instruct the child on your left to say "Stop!" when he or she feels the nudge. Begin the round by gently bumping the elbow of the first student to your right. Use a stopwatch to measure the time between your nudge and the "stop" signal and record the time on the board.

2ND Discuss with students components of the nervous system and what has to happen for the message to be passed from student to student. Next, guide students to predict whether the process will get faster or slower as it is repeated. Then repeat the procedure ten more times. Don't count a trial if you observe a student bumping another student prematurely. (*The time will decrease dramatically at first. Then it will level off and cease to drop.*)

What's happening: *Receptors (neurons) in the skin of each student's left arm feel the bump. The receptors send the message through nerves up the child's arm to his spinal cord and then to his brain. The sensory part of his brain processes the message and decides what response is needed. Then it sends signals with specific instructions through neurons back down his spinal cord, shoulder, and arm to the nerve that tells his muscle what to do (nudge the next student's elbow).*

> How would our time be affected if we waited a week and tried the elbow-nudge investigation again?

3RD Have each student describe the experiment, its results, and her reactions. Then challenge each student to write a question about a similar nervous system investigation. As time allows, have students conduct their experiments.

> What would happen to our time if we went the opposite direction?

4TH Have each pair of students follow the directions on a copy of page 196 to investigate the speeds of their nerve impulses. The students will also need a ruler with metric markings.

Name _____

Date _____

AND...CATCH!

Directions:

1. Place one hand (*not* the hand you write with) just over the edge of a desk with your thumb about two inches away from your fingers.

2. Have your partner hold the 30-centimeter end of a ruler so that the ruler's opposite end hangs just between your thumb and fingers.

3. Without warning, your partner gently lets the ruler fall, and you catch it as quickly as you can. Under your name and "First Try," record the centimeter measurement just above your finger or thumb.

4. Repeat Steps 1–3 nine times. Then switch places with your partner and repeat. After you've both caught the ruler ten times, find your median measurements.

5. Now you each get a second try! Repeat Steps 1–4, recording your results under the columns marked "Second Try."

Reaction Times

Trial Number	Partner 1 _____		Partner 2 _____	
	First Try	**Second Try**	**First Try**	**Second Try**
1				
2				
3				
4				
5				
6				
7				
8				
9				
10				
Median				

On your own paper, answer each question.

A. Did you catch the ruler quicker on the second tries than on the first tries? What can you conclude about your response times?

B. Did your partner catch the ruler quicker on the second tries than on the first tries? What can you conclude about your partner's response times?

C. Can you draw a conclusion about everyone's response times in this experiment? Why or why not?

D. Describe the path of the neurons receiving and sending messages in this experiment.

4 Experiments for Inquiring Minds!

1 Hold It Steady!

Materials: open paper clip, table knife, desk surface

Directions:

1. Hold the knife parallel to the tabletop.
2. Don't brace your arm or let your elbow touch the table.
3. Balance the paper clip on the blade of the knife.
4. Hold the knife still with the paper clip barely touching the table.
5. Try to hold your arm perfectly still.

What happens? Describe it. Why do you think this happens?

2 In a Pinch

Materials: pinch clothespin, clock with a second hand, paper

Directions:

1. Make a chart that looks like the one shown.
2. Hold the clothespin between your thumb and index finger.
3. See how many times you can open and close the clothespin in 30 seconds. Be sure to open the clothespin completely each time.
4. Record your data in the chart. Then repeat two more times.

	First Try	Second Try	Third Try
Clothespin pinches			

What happens? Describe it. Why do you think this happens?

3 One, Two, Curl

Materials: clock with a second hand, desk surface, paper

Directions:

1. Make a chart that looks like the one shown.
2. Lay your arm on a desktop with the palm of your hand up.
3. See how many times you can make a fist in 30 seconds. Be sure to open your hand completely and form a tight fist each time.
4. Record your data in the chart. Then repeat two more times.

	First Try	Second Try	Third Try
Number of fists			

What happens? Describe it. Why do you think this happens?

4 Give Me a Lift

Materials: book, clock with a second hand, paper

Directions:

1. Make a chart that looks like the one shown.
2. Hold the book in your hand. Stand with the book hanging at your side.
3. See how many times you can lift the book shoulder height in 30 seconds. Be sure to keep your arm straight as you lift the book each time.
4. Record your data in the chart. Then repeat two more times.

	First Try	Second Try	Third Try
Book lifts			

What happens? Describe it. Why do you think this happens?

Answers for Inquiring Minds!

1 Hold It Steady!

What happens? The paper clip moves to the end of the knife and falls off, no matter how hard you try to stay still. As you try to keep your arm in the same position, your muscles must make minor adjustments to keep the arm from leaving that spot. Your muscles make up-and-down movements. These small quivers set the paper clip in motion.

2 In a Pinch

What happens? The number of times you were able to complete each activity probably decreased with each repetition. Muscles in the body can tire quickly when you put them to work. This tiring of muscles is called fatigue. If muscles seem to get fatigued too quickly, it may mean that they are not getting enough exercise.

Muscles in the hand are called *tendons* because they are strong, slender cords. In each hand, you have 20 tendons that are arranged so your hand and fingers can move precisely.

3 One, Two, Curl

What happens? The number of times you were able to complete each activity probably decreased with each repetition. Muscles in the body can tire quickly when you put them to work. This tiring of muscles is called *fatigue*. If muscles seem to get fatigued too quickly, it may mean that they are not getting enough exercise.

You use muscles on the palm side of your forearm to close your fingers. You use muscles on the back side of your forearm to open your fingers.

4 Give Me a Lift

What happens? The number of times you were able to complete each activity probably decreased with each repetition. Muscles in the body can tire quickly when you put them to work. This tiring of muscles is called *fatigue*. If muscles seem to get fatigued too quickly, it may mean that they are not getting enough exercise.

You have 35 strong muscles that move each hand. Fifteen of those muscles are in each forearm.

Note to the teacher: Use with "Inquiring Minds" on page 185.

Social Studies

• State Heraldry

State symbols, research (W.4.7)

For this idea, share with students the paragraph about coats of arms. Then guide each student to research his state and design a unique coat of arms that shows the state symbols and elements of the state flag and state seal. Next, have the child write to describe his coat of arms, explaining the importance of each symbol on a coat of arms—shaped piece of paper. Then post students' work on a display titled "Regal State Reports."

Carol Lawrence, Madera, CA

Coats of arms were used almost like identification cards by European knights in the 1100s. During battles, the knights were hidden behind heavy armor, so they put their coats of arms on their shields. That way their followers could find them. The symbols on a coat of arms identified a person's family. The family used its coat of arms to mark its possessions and important papers. By the 1200s, laws about coats of arms stated that no two families could have the same coat of arms; the design on each one had to be unique.

Custom-Made Map

Map skills

Have each student choose a topic in which he is interested, such as basketball, playing a trumpet, his pet dog, or reading. Next, have the child draw the outline of a state or country in the shape relating to the theme, such as a ball, trumpet, dog bone, or book. Then have the student label the region with a fun name related to the topic, add a compass rose, and create a map key and scale similar to the ones shown. After that, read aloud the directions shown and have each student add the features to his map. To follow up, have each student write five questions about his map, exchange papers with a partner, and answer his partner's questions.

1. Draw a highway or road that travels north and south on your map. Name and label it. Then draw a highway or road that travels east and west on your map. Name and label it.
2. Draw a mountain range in the northern area of your map. Name and label it.
3. Draw a lake in the southwest corner of your map. Then draw three rivers. Make one river flow into the lake on your map. Name and label the lake and rivers.
4. Draw a state or national park in the center of your map. Name and label it.
5. Add four cities if your region is a state or four states if your region is a country in the western side of your map. Name and label each one.
6. Add six cities or states in the eastern side of your map. Name and label each one. Make one city the capital.

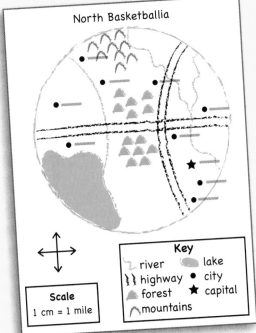

North Basketballia

Key
river — lake
highway • city
forest ★ capital
mountains

Scale
1 cm = 1 mile

Name _____

Date _____

Canine Country Coordinates

Use the map to complete the charts.

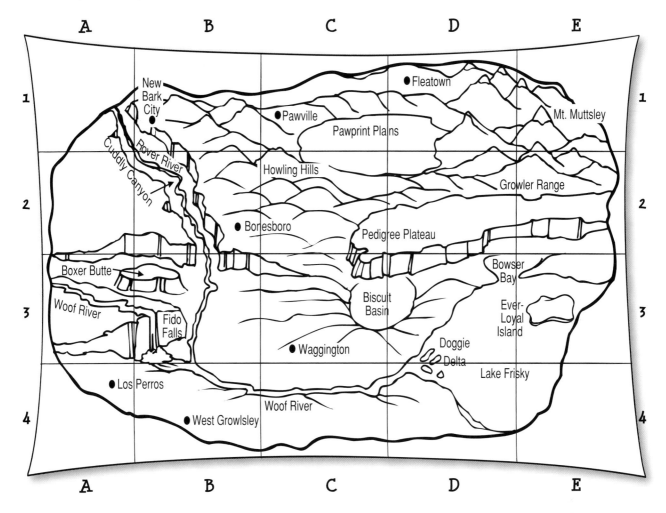

City	Location
1. New Bark City	B1
2. Bonesboro	
3.	D1
4. West Growlsley	
5.	A4
6. Waggington	

Point of Interest	Location
7. Boxer Butte	A3, B3
8. Biscuit Basin	
9. Cuddly Canyon	
10. Doggie Delta	
11. Fido Falls	
12. the mouth of Woof River	
13. Ever-Loyal Island	
14.	E1
15. Pawprint Plains	
16. Pedigree Plateau	

Bonus: In how many grid squares is Lake Frisky? List them.

With a World View
Conducting short research projects, taking notes (W.4.7, W.5.7)

Encourage multicultural awareness, with a simple project that's easy to repeat. First, have each child staple a construction paper handle to a manila file folder and decorate the folder so that it resembles a suitcase. Next, have each small group of students choose a country, research it, and create a sheet of important and fascinating facts about the country. Then have each group share its research. While the group reports, guide remaining students to take notes. After each report, have each student tuck her notes in her folder and draw a travel sticker on her cover to represent the country. **Vanessa Boyle, Merrimac, MA**

Chapter Recap Mini Book
Summarizing important ideas from a text (RI.4.2, RI.5.2)

Instead of giving your students a test to find out what they learned at the end of a chapter, have them make mini book summaries! Have each student fold a sheet of card stock in half two times and then fold each edge toward the middle as shown. Next, post a checklist, such as the one shown, to guide students' work. Then use the checklist to grade each mini book before adding it to your class library or having each child share her work with a younger student. **Stacey Ogden, New Vision Charter School, Loveland, CO**

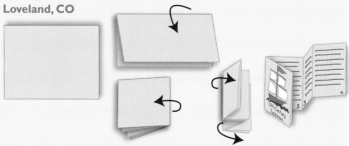

Mini Book Checklist

- [ ] Cover includes a title and illustration that show the chapter's main topic.
- [ ] On pages 1 through 6, summarize the chapter's main ideas. Include supporting details for each main idea.
- [ ] On page 7, list four of the chapter's important terms and each term's definition.
- [ ] Balance words and pictures throughout the mini book.
- [ ] Open your mini book. On the inside, draw a map, diagram, or chart that provides important facts about the chapter topic.

An Alphabetic Challenge
State studies (W.4.7)

For this activity, have each pair of students complete a copy of page 203. Then have each duo check its work against another pair's. Where multiple responses are possible, have students verify each other's entry. Then challenge each small group to use the pages to write a list poem about your state.

tip If students are researching different states, have them use the page to guide their research!

Names _____

Date _____

An Alphabetic Quest

A	B	C	D
The state's average **annual** temperature:	One of the state's largest **businesses** or industries:	The **capital** of the state:	Interesting **data** about the state's population:
E	F	G	H
Source of most of the state's **energy**:	A **festival** held in the state:	One of the state's major **geographic** features:	One of the state's main **historic** sites:
I	J	K	L
An **interstate** that runs through the state:	The state's average **July** temperature:	Distance across the state in **kilometers**:	One of the state's major **lakes**:
M	N	O	P
A well-known **musical** group from the state:	One of the most important **natural resources** in the state:	The state's **official** bird:	A **quality** product made in the state:
Q	R	S	T
A state **park**:	A **river** that runs through the state:	Location where **settlers** in the state first lived:	The state's official **tree**:
U	V	W	X
The state's largest **urban** area:	A type of **vegetation** that grows naturally in the state:	A city on the state's **western** border:	Part of the state most likely to have a **xeriscape** (landscape that doesn't need very much water):
Y	Z		
The state's average **yearly** rainfall:	The **zoo** closest to the state capital:		

©The Mailbox® • TEC44063 • Oct./Nov. 2012

Note to the teacher: Use with "An Alphabetic Challenge" on page 202.

EXPLORING Social Studies

How Sweet It Is!
State maps

For a fun mapping activity, make a double batch of sugar cookie dough and divide the dough evenly among each small group of students. Have each group use its dough to form your state's shape on a cookie sheet and then use toppings such as string licorice, chocolate chips, or fruit rolls to re-create the state's capital, cities, rivers, lakes, and other important features. While students' cookies are baking, have each student draw and describe his group's work. Then have each group display its work for class viewing before divvying up its geographical treat! **Amy Sloan, Millcreek Elementary, Corning, OH**

Important Events in the Lewis and Clark Expedition

Date: **1803** President Jefferson asked Congress to finance an exploration of the west.

Date: **1804** Going up the Missouri River

Date: **1804** Hiring Toussaint Charbonneau and Sacagawea

Date: **1805** Reaching the Great Falls of the Missouri River

Trekking With Lewis and Clark
Westward expansion, summarizing (W.4.7, W.5.7)

To help students explore the Lewis and Clark expedition, post important events from the journey at a center along with copies of the boot pattern from the bottom of this page, access to research materials, and clothespins. Then have each child choose an event and research it. Next, the student summarizes the event on a boot pattern. When she finishes, she clips her boot so it's in order on a class timeline. **Marsha Erskine, Madison, NC**

Boot Pattern
Use with "Trekking With Lewis and Clark" on this page.

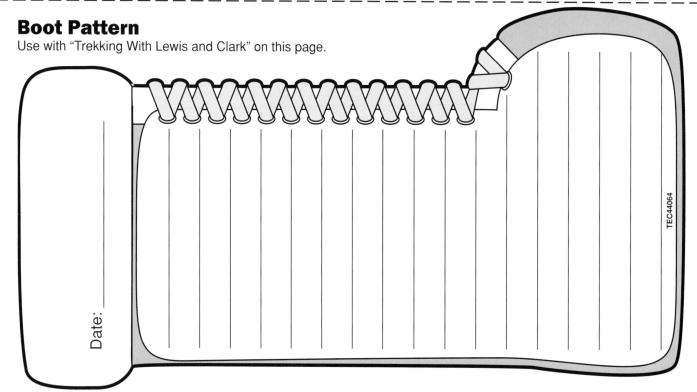

Date: _____

TEC44064

• I-Spy State Reports
State studies (W.4.7, W.5.7)

Here's a hands-on twist for state research projects. To begin, have each student research a state and list ten to 15 important facts about the state. Next, have each child find a small object to represent each fact and make a list of his objects. (If he can't find a suitable object, have him write the fact on both sides of a paper strip.) Then guide each student to follow the directions below to prepare an I Spy state-report bottle. After that, have each pair of students trade bottles and try to find all of each other's objects. **Sarah McBride, Wertheimer Middle, Richmond, TX**

Materials for each student: clear plastic bottle with a lid (16 ounce or one liter), funnel, state-related objects, filler (birdseed, rice, or sand), length of yarn, permanent marker, hole puncher, glue

Steps:
1. Use the marker to write your name on the bottle.
2. Use the funnel (or roll up a scrap of paper) to pour filler in the bottle until the bottle is about one-fourth full.
3. Put half of your objects in the bottle. Pour filler in the bottle until the bottle is one-half full and then put the rest of your objects in the bottle.
4. Pour filler in the bottle until it is about one inch from the bottle's top.
5. Then spread glue inside the bottle cap and put the cap on the bottle. Roll the bottle to mix everything up. Make a final copy of your list, punch a hole in it, and tie it to your bottle with yarn.

• Getting Down to Business
Exploring free enterprise (W.4.3, W.5.3)

For this idea, have each student name a business she'd like to own and then draw and cut out a picture of what it would look like. Next, guide the child to identify her business's potential *resources*. Then guide the student to think about *competition* with other businesses for customers and how that might affect her prices and access to resources. Finally, guide each student to predict what her *profits* might be. After that, have each child summarize her imaginary business's resources, competition, and profits on paper trimmed to match the shape of her drawing. Then post students' work on a board titled "Getting Down to the Business of Studying Free Enterprise." **Vickie Hall, Waverly Elementary, Waverly, WV**

Sarah's Dog-Washing Spot

Chapter Accountability
Comprehending content-area texts (RI.4.2, RI.5.2)

Before a child reads a chapter in a textbook, have him fold a sheet of paper in half to make a booklet and record the chapter title on the front cover. Next, have him create a table of contents inside on the left, listing important topics and their page numbers from the chapter. After he reads, have the child summarize the chapter's main ideas on the right side. Then guide the student to list key words and their definitions on the back cover. Finally, have the child illustrate the chapter's most important event on his booklet's front cover. The booklet lets you know he read the chapter and makes a great study guide when it's time for the test! **Angela Rood, Dyersburg Intermediate, Dyersburg, TN**

EXPLORING Social Studies

Getting Globally Creative
Map skills

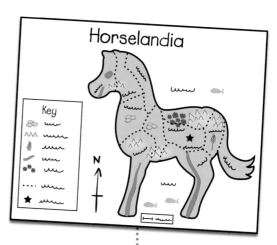

Horselandia

Key

N

Want to assess students' map skills? Have them invent their own countries! Begin by having each student choose a theme, create a country, and name it. Next, have the child design a map of the country, complete with a key, compass rose, and scale. Then have the student add landforms; divide the country into states, provinces, regions, or districts; and label the capital city. After that, have the child add natural resources and industries. Finally, have each student share his work before posting it on a board titled "Putting Our Skills on the Map!"

Jessica Lawler, Abundant Life Academy, Nutley, NJ

 tip **Extend the activity** by having each student invent a currency system, create the country's flag (and explain each symbol's meaning), write the country's national anthem, or invent the country's history (including when it was founded, who founded it, and the main reason it was founded).

Hail to the Chief!
Government, executive branch

Help students understand the president's responsibilities by displaying the list shown. Next, have each small group of students rank the responsibilities according to importance. Then have each group share its ranking, citing at least one reason for each ranking. After that, divide a bulletin board into seven columns labeled with the responsibilities. Then have students find articles about the president, summarizing their articles to share them with the class. After a student shares an article, lead the class to decide which executive responsibility it reflects and then post the article in the matching column.

From One to Another
State studies (RI.4.1; RI.5.3)

Students can learn a lot about their home state by comparing and contrasting it with another state. Have each child choose a state other than yours. Then have him research the state and complete a copy of page 207 to compare the state with his home state.

Chief executive: makes sure all federal laws are enforced, develops federal policies, plans the country's budget, nominates officials such as Supreme Court judges and ambassadors, and appoints other high officials
Commander in chief: serves as commander in chief of the Army, Navy, Air Force, Marines, and Coast Guard
Foreign policy director: speaks for our country in dealing with foreign nations
Legislative leader: makes proposals for new laws and urges Congress to act on them
Party head: leads his or her political party
Popular leader: puts the country and its needs first, ahead of any one state or any one citizen
Chief of state: represents the US government, showing pride in American achievements and traditions

Name _____

Date _____

A STATELY COMPARISON

Choose a state to compare with yours. Then research both states to complete the chart.

Topic	My state:	Another state:
Region, location		
Climate		
Landforms		
Wildlife		
Natural resources		
Agriculture		
Industry		
Interesting sites		

©The Mailbox® • TEC44066 • April/May 2013

Note to the teacher: Use with "From One to Another" on page 206.

What Would You Wish For?

Economics—wants and needs

For this higher-level thinking activity, copy and cut apart the cards on page 209. Next, divide the class into six small groups. Then shuffle the cards, give each group six cards, and have the students in each group imagine they are stranded on an island with only the items on their cards. Challenge the students in each group to study their cards, decide which address wants and which meet needs. After establishing ground rules, have students in each group barter with students in other groups to get the cards that will meet their needs. Follow up with a class discussion.

Fact Finders

Current events

Encourage students to pay attention to world, national, and local events with this simple idea. Choose news stories from three different sections of your newspaper and have each student create a chart like the one shown. Then display each article, read it with students, and guide them to identify the answers to reporters' classic questions. Follow up by having students use their notes to compare and discuss the articles in a group discussion.

	World News	National News	Local News	Headline
Who?				
What?				
When?				
Where?				
Why?				
How?				

Tic Tac Map

Map skills

Here's a simple game that challenges students' longitude and latitude skills. First, display a map with lines of longitude and latitude. Next, divide the class into two groups and challenge each group to name four pairs of coordinates in a line on the map. Then have one team name the coordinates for a point on the map. Using a wipe-off marker, draw an *X* at the point. In turn, the second team names the coordinates for a point that begins its own line or blocks the first team's line. Draw an *O* on the map at the second team's point. Play continues until one team names four coordinate points in a row. **Mary Samson, Rockfish-Hoke Elementary, Raeford, NC**

Forty degrees North, one hundred degrees West.

clean water	books	flashlight	batteries
TEC44067	TEC44067	TEC44067	TEC44067
binoculars	rope	fishing hooks	blanket
TEC44067	TEC44067	TEC44067	TEC44067
sunscreen	matches	first aid kit	Swiss army knife
TEC44067	TEC44067	TEC44067	TEC44067
clean water	books	flashlight	batteries
TEC44067	TEC44067	TEC44067	TEC44067
binoculars	rope	fishing hooks	blanket
TEC44067	TEC44067	TEC44067	TEC44067
sunscreen	matches	first aid kit	Swiss army knife
TEC44067	TEC44067	TEC44067	TEC44067
clean water	books	flashlight	batteries
TEC44067	TEC44067	TEC44067	TEC44067
binoculars	rope	fishing hooks	blanket
TEC44067	TEC44067	TEC44067	TEC44067
sunscreen	matches	first aid kit	Swiss army knife
TEC44067	TEC44067	TEC44067	TEC44067

C
1 Go back 2 spaces.
2 Europe
3 Michigan
4 Texas
5 Rio Grande
6 Denver

D
1 Indian
2 Vermont
3 Columbus
4 Atlantic
5 West Virginia
6 Austin

E
1 Arctic
2 New Jersey
3 St. Lawrence
4 Go back to start.
5 South America
6 Phoenix

F
1 Idaho
2 Richmond
3 North America
4 Alabama
5 Superior
6 Antarctica

G
1 Oklahoma
2 Jackson
3 Pacific
4 Arizona
5 Europe
6 Annapolis

H
1 Cheyenne
2 Africa
3 Little Rock
4 Snake
5 Go back 3 spaces.
6 Tennessee

B
1 Delaware
2 Carson City
3 Pacific
4 Maine
5 Africa
6 Atlanta

I
1 St. Paul
2 Texas
3 Erie
4 Asia
5 Pierre
6 Arkansas

A
1 Asia
2 Virginia
3 Trenton
4 Huron
5 Sacramento
6 Indiana

START

ON THE RIGHT TRACK!

Partner Game

Directions:

1. When it's your turn, roll the die and move your marker.
2. On your space, read the line that matches the number you rolled. If there is a direction, follow it. If there is a name, tell whether it is a state capital, state, country, continent, ocean, lake, or river.
3. Have your partner check the key. If you're correct, leave your marker. If you're incorrect, move back one space.
4. The first player to reach Finish wins.

J
1 Iowa
2 Columbia
3 Nebraska
4 Tahoe
5 Des Moines
6 Florida

FINISH

K
1 Indian
2 Go back to start.
3 Michigan
4 Topeka
5 Tallahassee
6 Denmark

R
1 Santa Fe
2 Europe
3 Missouri
4 Bismarck
5 Libya
6 Portugal

Q
1 New Hampshire
2 Harrisburg
3 Trade places with opponent.
4 Indianapolis
5 New Mexico
6 Honolulu

P
1 Minnesota
2 Salem
3 Antarctica
4 Nashville
5 Wyoming
6 Utah

O
1 Australia
2 Kansas
3 Albany
4 Juneau
5 Move ahead 2 spaces.
6 Helena

N
1 Dover
2 Platte
3 Ohio
4 Olympia
5 Kentucky
6 Raleigh

M
1 South America
2 Hartford
3 Go back 3 spaces.
4 Madison
5 Concord
6 Montana

L
1 Atlantic
2 South Dakota
3 Baton Rouge
4 Trade places with opponent.
5 Georgia
6 Providence

©The Mailbox® • TEC44065 • Feb./Mar. 2013

Answer Key for "On the Right Track!"

I
1 state
2 state capital
3 state
4 lake
5 state capital
6 state

K
1 ocean
2 Go back to start.
3 state
4 state capital
5 state capital
6 country

L
1 ocean
2 state
3 state capital
4 Trade places with opponent.
5 state

M
1 continent
2 state capital
3 Go back 3 spaces.
4 state capital
5 state capital
6 state

N
1 state capital
2 river
3 state
4 state capital
5 state
6 state capital

O
1 continent
2 state
3 state capital
4 state capital
5 Move ahead 2 spaces.

P
1 state
2 state capital
3 continent
4 state capital
5 state
6 state

Q
1 state
2 state capital
3 Trade places with opponent.
4 state capital
5 state
6 state capital

R
1 state capital
2 continent
3 state
4 state capital
5 country
6 country

A
1 continent
2 state
3 state capital
4 lake
5 state capital
6 state

B
1 state
2 state capital
3 ocean
4 state
5 continent
6 state capital

C
1 Go back 2 spaces.
2 continent
3 state
4 state
5 river
6 state capital

D
1 ocean
2 state
3 state capital
4 ocean
5 state
6 state capital

E
1 ocean
2 state
3 river
4 Go back to start.
5 continent
6 state capital

F
1 state
2 state capital
3 continent
4 state
5 lake
6 continent

G
1 state
2 state capital
3 ocean
4 state
5 continent
6 state capital

H
1 state capital
2 continent
3 state capital
4 river
5 Go back 3 spaces.
6 state

Note to the teacher: Each pair of students needs a copy of the page and a die.

Looking Back

1 Prompt

Underline the main topic in each question below. Then jot one or two facts you already know about each topic. Next, circle one question to research.

> If you had been a fugitive slave, would you have returned to be a conductor for the Underground Railroad like Harriet Tubman? Why or why not?

> Which part of the Lewis and Clark expedition do you think was the most dangerous? Describe it.

> Would you rather be George Washington working to establish the United States or Abraham Lincoln working to keep the United States united? Explain.

> If you had been infected with gold fever and gave up everything to join the gold rush, what would your life have been like?

2 Research

What is the main topic you are researching?

What is the time period?

What are some interesting facts about this topic?

What are important events from this topic?

What are important facts?

Sources (Record every source you use.)

©The Mailbox® • TEC44065 • Feb./Mar. 2013 (W.4.7, W.5.7)

3 Plan

Consider your research for this topic and then write your answer to the question you circled.

What's the most powerful fact or event from your research? (It will be good to use in your introduction or your conclusion.)

List facts and events that support your answer. (If you don't have facts and events that support your answer, do a little more research!)

-
-
-
-
-
-
-
-

4 Write

Now that you know all about this topic, write a speech from a historic character's point of view that details your research and explains your answer. Use supporting facts and events from your findings. Then prepare a dramatic presentation to share your research.

©The Mailbox® • TEC44065 • Feb./Mar. 2013 (W.4.10, W.5.10, SL.4.4, SL.5.4)

212 THE MAILBOX **Note to the teacher:** Use with "Looking Back" on page 211.

Social Studies Activity Cards

Cut out a copy of the cards to use as center or free-time activities.

The President's Cabinet

US government

Find and list the names of the current cabinet members. (Try using a current almanac.)

Vice President		
Attorney General	Secretary of Agriculture	Secretary of Commerce
Secretary of Defense	Secretary of Education	Secretary of Energy
Secretary of Health and Human Services	Secretary of Homeland Security	Secretary of Housing and Urban Development
Secretary of the Interior	Secretary of Labor	Secretary of State
Secretary of Transportation	Secretary of the Treasury	Secretary of Veterans Affairs

TEC44065 (W.4.7–8, W.5.7–8)

Take a Spin!

Research, history

Choose a country and take notes that answer each question below. Then use your notes to create a trifold brochure about the country's history.

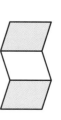

- Which **three** events in this country's past were the most important in its history?

- Why was each event so important?

TEC44065 (W.4.7–8, W.5.7–8)

IN THE SPOTLIGHT

Research, geography

Choose a country and research it to answer each question below. Then make a word search of the answers.

1. In which hemisphere is it located?
2. What is its size compared to the size of the United States?
3. What features or countries form its boundaries?
4. What are four or more of its different landforms?
5. What are five or more of its natural resources?
6. What bodies of water are most important to the country?

TEC44065 (W.4.7, W.5.7)

Project Discovery

Map skills

Use a map with latitude and longitude lines to find each country, body of water, city, or feature. Then write questions about ten of them. Write each answer in parentheses. (See examples.)

Between which two latitudes does **most** of the United States lie? *(30°N and 50°N)*

What is the southernmost sea that touches the continent of North America? *(Caribbean Sea)*

What is the approximate latitude of Mexico's capital? *(about 20°N)*

Canada	Gulf of California
Mexico	Great Lakes
Cuba	Mississippi River
Haiti	Rio Grande River
Dominican Republic	St. Lawrence River
Jamaica	Panama Canal
Arctic Ocean	Washington, DC
Gulf of Mexico	Ottawa, Canada

TEC44065 (5.G.A.2)

4 First-Class Ideas for Current Events

Whether your students read local newspapers, national newspapers, magazines, or other media, check out these tips for helping them connect with and report on current events!

1 Categorically Concerned

At the beginning of the week, assign each small group of students one of the categories shown. Have the group read articles from that category during the week. Then, on Friday, have each group present a summary of the week's events. (SL.4.4, SL.5.4)

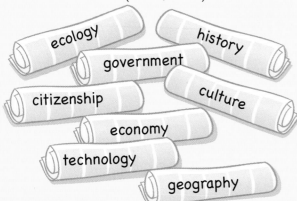

ecology
history
government
citizenship
culture
economy
technology
geography

2 Color My World

Display a political world map that has not been colored. Then challenge your students to find news articles about different countries. Each time a student shares a current-event report about a different country, have him color the country on the map. Then award the child five bonus points or a small reward. Students love filling in the map. They make personal connections with the countries, and the display sparks many current-event discussions!

tip → As an alternative, display a political map of the country and challenge students to find news about every state. Or display a political map of your state and challenge students to find news about every county!

4 Share and Share Alike

Provide a menu of report options, such as those shown. Have each pair of students read an article and choose an option for reporting on it. Then have the partners share their work. (W.4.7)

> Summarize the article, making sure to describe the five Ws: What happened? Where did it happen? Why did it happen? Who was involved? When did it happen?

> Illustrate the article with three or more pictures. Then write a caption for each illustration.

> Write five questions about the article. Then answer each question.

> Write a short play about what happened in the article.

> Write a letter to the editor about the article. Share your opinion about the news and support your opinion with details from the article.

3 Newshounds

Encourage students to be alert to the news around them with this fun challenge! Just before lunch or near the end of the day Friday, set a timer for two minutes and challenge each student to list the most countries, events, environmental issues, court rulings, or people (not including celebrities) that were in the news that week. Then, as time allows, have students share, compare, and discuss their lists.

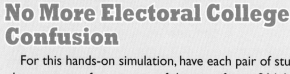

In Pursuit of the Presidency
Activities for Exploring the Presidential Election

Just Right for the Job

What does it take to be a leader? To help students examine this question, post five leadership traits, such as those shown. Next, guide each small group of students to discuss the traits and decide why they would be good qualities for someone who wants to be president. Then have each group brainstorm five more presidential qualities and discuss each one. Finally, have the group rank all ten of the characteristics from most to least important. Then lead a class discussion in which each group shares its ideas and rankings. (SL.4.1, SL.5.1)

persistent   honest

confident

fair

determined

No More Electoral College Confusion

For this hands-on simulation, have each pair of students choose a state from a copy of the top of page 216. Next, give each pair of students a penny and have the duo decide which candidate will be represented by "heads" and which candidate will be represented by "tails." Then have the partners simulate a popular vote by flipping the coin 30 times and tallying each result as a vote. When they finish, have the students determine which candidate received at least 51 percent of the popular votes and, thereby the electoral votes for that state. Then draw a chart, similar to the one shown, on the board and have each pair record its results. While students wait for final results, have them respond to the questions on the page.

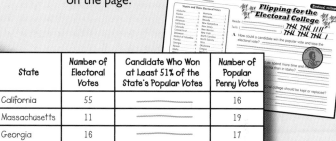

State	Number of Electoral Votes	Candidate Who Won at Least 51% of the State's Popular Votes	Number of Popular Penny Votes
California	55	————	16
Massachusetts	11	————	19
Georgia	16	————	17
New Jersey	14	————	20

It's All About Qualifying!

Inspire students to set presidential goals with this quick activity! First, have each student complete a copy of the bottom half of page 216 as guided. Next, explain that there are only three constitutional requirements to be the president of the United States and challenge each child to star the three phrases that are actual conditions. After students make their guesses, read the excerpt from the Constitution aloud and have each student revise her guess. Then have each student respond to the journal prompt by writing about what she thinks of these conditions for the most important job in the country.

"No Person except a natural born Citizen, or a Citizen of the United States, at the time of the Adoption of this Constitution shall be eligible to the Office of President; neither shall any Person be eligible to that Office who shall not have attained to the Age of thirty five Years, and been fourteen Years a Resident within the United States."

Name _____

Date _____

Flipping for the Electoral College

States and Their Electoral Votes

Alabama	9	Montana	3
Alaska	3	Nebraska	5
Arizona	11	Nevada	6
Arkansas	6	New Hampshire	4
California	55	New Jersey	14
Colorado	9	New Mexico	5
Connecticut	7	New York	29
Delaware	3	North Carolina	15
District of Columbia	3	North Dakota	3
Florida	29	Ohio	18
Georgia	16	Oklahoma	7
Hawaii	4	Oregon	7
Idaho	4	Pennsylvania	20
Illinois	20	Rhode Island	4
Indiana	11	South Carolina	9
Iowa	6	South Dakota	3
Kansas	6	Tennessee	11
Kentucky	8	Texas	38
Louisiana	8	Utah	6
Maine	4	Vermont	3
Maryland	10	Virginia	13
Massachusetts	11	Washington	12
Michigan	16	West Virginia	5
Minnesota	10	Wisconsin	10
Mississippi	6	Wyoming	3
Missouri	10		

Heads: (_____) _____

Tails: (_____) _____

A. How could a candidate win the popular vote and lose the electoral vote? _____
_____
_____

B. Why would a candidate spend more time and money campaigning in California than in Idaho? _____
_____
_____

C. Do you think the electoral college should be kept or replaced? Explain. _____
_____
_____

©The Mailbox® · TEC44063 · Oct./Nov. 2012

Name _____

Date _____

To Be President

Check each phrase you think is a requirement for becoming president of the United States.

A person who wants to become president should...

1. ☐ have a driver's license
2. ☐ be a millionaire
3. ☐ be married
4. ☐ be a natural-born citizen
5. ☐ never have been arrested
6. ☐ be a lawyer
7. ☐ have served in one branch of the armed forces
8. ☐ have passed a physical and be in good health
9. ☐ have at least one college degree
10. ☐ be at least 35 years old
11. ☐ be a registered voter
12. ☐ have been a senator, congressperson, or governor
13. ☐ have a social security number
14. ☐ know how to read
15. ☐ own a house and land in the United States
16. ☐ have lived in the United States for 14 years
17. ☐ have worked for at least 10 years
18. ☐ know every amendment to the Constitution

What do you think? Are the constitutional requirements for being president rigorous enough? What requirements would you put in place?

©The Mailbox® · TEC44063 · Oct./Nov. 2012

Note to the teacher: Use "Flipping for the Electoral College" with "No More Electoral College Confusion" on page 215.
Use "To Be President" with "It's All About Qualifying!" on page 215.

The Colonial Experience

3 ideas for giving students a peek into colonial life!

1 A Colonial Market

For this simulation, review with students that, instead of using money, colonists bartered, or traded, goods with each other. Next, give each student several sheets of construction paper and have the child create construction paper goods such as those shown. Then have students take turns displaying goods on their desks and walking around bartering. Follow up with a class discussion of the pros and cons of a bartering system. adapted from an idea by Becky Fuentes, Highland Elementary, Lake Stevens, WA

Colonial Goods

yarn
cloth
cheese
poultry
eggs
vegetables
candles
cloth
soap

18th Century Greetings

Good day.

A good morning to you, friend (or sir or madam).

A good day to you, friend (or sir or madam).

men's greeting: How do you do, friend (or sir or madam)? I'm right heartily glad to see you.

women's greeting: How do you do, friend (or sir or madam)? I am glad to see you.

2 You Don't Say!

For colonial flavor, address students and have them address each other with 18th century greetings, such as those shown. Then, at the end of each class or at the end of the day, try a colonial farewell.

18th Century Farewells

By your leave.

With your permission.

Adieu.

Good day to you.

3 Colonial Penmanship

Give students an idea of what writing was like during colonial times. In advance, soak the tips of a class supply of four-inch or longer craft feathers in soapy water for at least five minutes. Then guide each student to follow the directions shown to make a quill pen. Next, provide small containers of craft paint or ink and copies of the hornbook primer on page 218. Then have each child practice copying the primer using his quill and scrap paper. For a fun follow-up, post a strip of white paper titled "Your John Hancock, Please" and have each student sign his name using his quill pen.

How to Make and Use a Quill Pen

Materials for one pen: presoaked craft feather, scissors, pushpin, paint or ink, felt scrap

Steps:

1. Trim off one inch of the bottom feathers on the quill.
2. Cut off the end of the quill stalk at an angle, creating a *nib*, or point.
3. Use the pushpin to carefully clean out the inside of the stalk at the end.
4. Cut a small slit in the nib to control the ink or paint flow.
5. Dip the nib in the paint. If necessary, gently blot the excess ink or paint from the nib on a piece of felt. You're ready to write.
6. Hold the pen at a slant to write; then experiment with different angles and pressures. When the pen runs dry, dip it in the paint again. If the nib wears down, simply repeat Steps 2–4 to cut a new one.

a b c d e f g h i j k l m
n o p q r s t u v w x y z
A B C D E F G H I J K L M
N O P Q R S T U V W X Y Z

"Liberty, when it begins to take root, is a plant of rapid growth."

George Washington

"Early to bed and early to rise

Makes a man healthy, wealthy, and wise."

Benjamin Franklin

"United we stand, divided we fall."

Patrick Henry

"If men were angels, no government would be necessary."

James Madison

TEC44064

SEASONAL

Colorful Introductions

Back-to-school

Here's a sweet and simple icebreaker for the first day of school! Give each student a small disposable cup and a snack-size bag of Skittles or M&M's candies. Direct each student to put three different-colored pieces of candy in his cup. Then post a chart like the one shown. In turn, ask each student to share about himself using the chart and the colors of the candies in his cup. Don't forget to save a bag of candy for yourself; even older kids love learning about their new teacher! **Rebecca Juneau, Highland Elementary, Lake Stevens, WA**

Code	
yellow =	Share about the best part of your summer.
green =	Share about something you wish you had done this summer.
red =	Share three things that you love to do.
orange =	Share two facts about your family.
purple or blue =	Share a question you have about this school year.

Four by Four

Back-to-school

Start off a new year with a fun getting-to-know-you activity that helps students quickly learn a little about their new classmates. Give each student a copy of the grid on page 222. Allow students to circulate around the room to search for classmates who match the grid statements. When a student finds a match, he has that child sign the appropriate box on his grid. To increase interaction, stipulate that students may only sign each classmate's grid once. When time is up, have students return to their seats and share as a class or in small groups what they discovered about their new classmates. **Karen Aita, Northampton County Public Schools, Machipongo, VA**

Pseudo Students

Open house

Need a different idea for this year's open house? Instruct each student to bring in an old long-sleeved shirt. (Pick up a few extras at a local thrift shop.) Before students leave school on the day of open house, each child places her shirt on the back of her chair and tapes its sleeves to the top of her desk. Then she traces both of her hands on paper, cuts out the tracings, and tapes one hand in each sleeve cuff. Next, the student creates a tagboard head that resembles her and attaches it to her shirt's neckline. Finally, the student places books and papers on her desk to make it seem like her stand-in is hard at work. Parents are sure to flip over this unique project that doubles as a great open house conversation starter! **David Reitz, Glenwood Elementary, Virginia Beach, VA**

Career Close-up
Labor Day (SL.4.5, SL.5.5)

Use the September focus on our nation's workers to help your students learn about careers. Have each student interview a relative about his or her job, using the chart shown to direct his questions. (Ask a few staff members to step in as interviewees if needed.) After he has conducted his interview, the student creates a poster about his person's career to share with the class. This project is a great lead-in to a discussion about setting goals and forming good work habits.
Ruth Albert, Whispering Pines Elementary, Boca Raton, FL

 tip Display students' posters in your room. Then have each student put a sticky note labeled with his name on each poster that highlights a career that interests him.

Include the following in your poster:
- Name of the career
- Name of the person you interviewed
- Length of time the person has done the job
- Responsibilities of the job
- Training needed
- Special clothing or equipment
- Hours of the job
- Likes and dislikes about the job
- Photos and/or illustrations

Birthday History
Back-to-school (SL.4.4, SL.5.4)

Put a new spin on class birthdays with an activity that provides practice giving short presentations. At the beginning of the year, share with students websites that list significant events that happened on "this day in history." Several days before his birthday, each student searches the websites and selects an event that occurred on his big day. Then he prepares a short, creative presentation about the event. The student might pretend to be a reporter, speak as a witness to the event, or share his information via a poster or display. On the student's birthday, he gives his presentation to the class. What about students with summer birthdays? Let them share their birthday histories on their half-birthdays!
Connie Carver, St. Charles School, Parma, OH

"Grand-Dandy" Descriptions
National Grandparents Day (SL.4.5, SL.5.5)

Celebrate National Grandparents Day (the first Sunday after Labor Day) with a descriptive writing activity that delivers grand learning benefits! First, ask each student to write the name of a grandparent or other older relative or friend at the top of her paper. With students, brainstorm qualities or actions that grandparents display, listing students' responses on the board. Next, have each student copy five to seven of her favorite qualities from the board and add descriptive details using a dictionary or thesaurus. Once her list is complete, the student writes her descriptions as a poem in the center of a sheet of sturdy paper. She completes her project by adding drawings and magazine clippings around the poem. Then each student shares her mini poster with the class before she delivers it to her lucky grandparent.

 Check out the reproducible on **Constitution Day and Citizenship Day** on page 240.

Four by Four
Getting-to-Know-You Grid

You'll need to "yak" with your classmates to complete this grid!

I have read at least one Diary of a Wimpy Kid book.	I do not like to eat vegetables.	I am an only child.	I have lived in another state.
I was born in another country.	I have more than one pet at home.	Science is my favorite subject.	I can play a musical instrument.
I like to draw.	My favorite color is green.	I was named after someone.	I am ticklish.
I once won something.	Summer is my favorite season.	I like my handwriting.	My favorite ice cream flavor is not chocolate.

SKILLS FOR THE SEASON

● Uncanny Categories
Classifying according to physical properties

For this hands-on center, provide different types of creepy toy bugs and copies of the top of page 224 for each pair of students. At the center, guide a pair of students to follow the directions shown to sort the toys into two groups and then divide each group into two more groups according to the toys' attributes. Then have the partners record their results and explain their sorting process. **Dana St. Pierre, Edna Louise Spear Elementary, Port Jefferson, NY**

Directions:
1. Name an attribute that all the toys have. Write the attribute in box A.
2. Divide the toys into two groups according to an attribute one group has and one group doesn't have. Record the classifications in boxes B and C.
3. Divide the toys from the B group into two groups according to an attribute one group has and one group doesn't have. Record the classifications in boxes D and E.
4. Divide the toys from the C group into two groups according to an attribute one group has and one group doesn't have. Record the classifications in boxes F and G.

● Football Math Mania
Stem-and-leaf plots, data analysis (6.SP.B.5c)

Here's a math idea that works with a favorite fall activity—football! On Monday, provide access to the results of the professional football games from the week before. Next, have each student record the points earned by the winning team in each game on a copy of the bottom half of page 224 and then arrange the points in order. Have the child make a stem-and-leaf plot and identify the range, median, mode, and mean of the winning teams' points to practice analyzing real data! **Allysa Vasko, J. D. Parker Elementary, Stuart, FL**

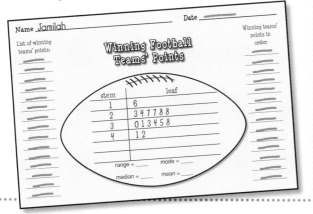

● Lyrical Entanglements
Writing a quatrain

Take the first line from the childhood song "The Itsy-Bitsy Spider" and challenge each student to write a quatrain about where else the spider might have gone. To publish her work, have the child cut out a felt spider body and glue wiggly eyes on it. Next, have her cut two pipe cleaners into eight legs and glue them on each side of the body. Then have the student draw a web on a small paper plate and glue the spider on the plate. Finally, have the child write the final version of her poem on an index card and tie it to the plate as shown. **Crissie Stephens, Kelly Edwards Elementary, Williston, SC**

The itsy-bitsy spider climbs up
the closet door.
Along comes my mother and knocks
it to the floor.
The frightened little spider speeds
quickly out of sight
And decides it's safer to come out
just at night.

Name _____

Date _____

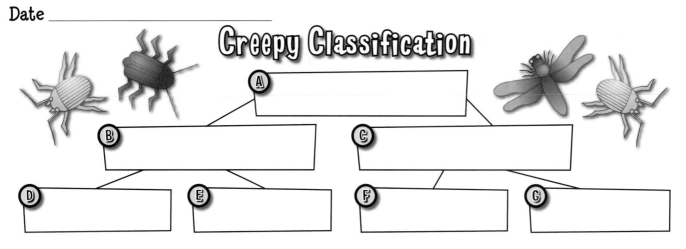

Creepy Classification

How did you decide which attributes to use? _____

_____

_____

_____

_____

©The Mailbox® • TEC44063 • Oct./Nov. 2012

Name _____   Date _____

List of winning
teams' points:

_____

_____

_____

_____

_____

_____

_____

_____

_____

_____

_____

_____

Winning Football
Teams' Points

stem	leaf

range = _____   mode = _____

median = _____   mean = _____

Winning teams'
points in order:

_____

_____

_____

_____

_____

_____

_____

_____

_____

_____

_____

_____

©The Mailbox® • TEC44063 • Oct./Nov. 2012

Note to the teacher: Use "Creepy Classification" with "Uncanny Categories" on page 223. Use "Winning Football Teams' Points" with "Football Math Mania" on page 223.

• A Wintry Illusion
Exploring scientific phenomena, persistence of vision

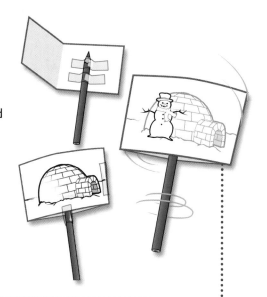

For this idea, give each student a copy of the snowman and igloo card from the top of page 227. Then guide the child to fold and tape the card to a full-length colored pencil as shown. Next, have the child watch the card as he spins the pencil, making the card flip back and forth. After a few minutes, have each child record a description of what he sees. *(As the paper spins, the images seem to blend into one, making the snowman appear to be near the igloo.)* Then have students repeat the exercise and discuss with them the reasons behind the illusion. *(Due to persistence of vision, we see an image for about $\frac{1}{10}$ of a second after we look at it. So the images of the snowman and the igloo blend together.)* For a fun extension, challenge students to make their own unique cards that demonstrate the phenomena.

Shannon Shuey, Sanlee Middle School, Sanford, NC

Dreidel Challenge
Problem solving, evaluating progress, changing course

With this simple-to-set-up game, students practice plenty of mathematical reasoning! Copy the bottom half of page 227 for each pair of students. Then explain that each child takes a turn shading one or two dreidels on the page. Have each student use a different-colored marker to play. The winner is the player who shades the last dreidel.

tip → Slide a copy of the page in a plastic page protector, have students use wipe-off markers, and play over and over!

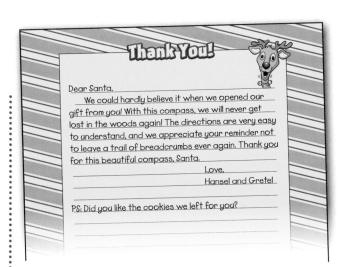

Thank You!
Dear Santa,
　　We could hardly believe it when we opened our gift from you! With this compass, we will never get lost in the woods again! The directions are very easy to understand, and we appreciate your reminder not to leave a trail of breadcrumbs ever again. Thank you for this beautiful compass, Santa.
　　　　　　　　　　Love,
　　　　　　　　　　Hansel and Gretel

PS: Did you like the cookies we left for you?

Fantastic Gratitude •
Writing thank-you notes (W.4.3, W.5.3)

Put a fairy-tale twist on this seasonal task! Have each student choose a fairy tale character and imagine what Santa Claus might give the character for Christmas. Then guide the child to write a note from the character, thanking Santa for the perfect gift. As time allows, have each student read his note aloud.

Linda Marshall, Poquoson Elementary, Poquoson, VA

Guess My Gift
Using descriptive details (W.4.3, W.5.3)

Here's a writing activity based on the fact that, at this time of year, many students are thinking about presents they want, think they're getting, or already got. Begin by having each child draw a 3-D box on a sheet of paper and decorate it so it resembles a wrapped present. Next, have the student write a paragraph describing the ultimate present without naming it. Then have the child glue her paragraph onto the center of her paper and make a gift tag with her name on one side and the name of her gift on the other. Display students' projects on a board titled "Guess the Gift—It's All in the Details!" In students' free time, have them read each other's descriptions, guess what the gifts are, and flip the tags to check their guesses. *Cheryl Ochsner, Warner Elementary, Warner, SD*

If I found this gift on Christmas morning, I would be flabbergasted. To begin with, it would be in a very big box because it is a large item. It is actually almost as tall as I am. I hope my parents would have already assembled it and pumped air into its two tires. Its metal frame would be a shiny, metallic blue.

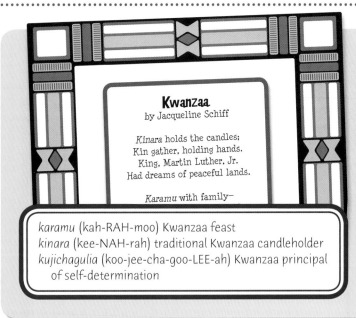

Kwanzaa
by Jacqueline Schiff

*Kinara holds the candles;
Kin gather, holding hands.
King, Martin Luther, Jr.
Had dreams of peaceful lands.*

Karamu with family—

karamu (kah-RAH-moo) Kwanzaa feast
kinara (kee-NAH-rah) traditional Kwanzaa candleholder
kujichagulia (koo-jee-cha-goo-LEE-ah) Kwanzaa principal of self-determination

A Lyrical Observation
Kwanzaa

Commemorate Kwanzaa by displaying the poem on page 228. Then guide students to read the poem aloud, using the pronunciation guide to help. After reading the poem several times, have each child illustrate the line or stanza of the poem he feels best describes the holiday. Post students' work along with the poem. **Jacqueline Schiff, Moline, IL**

In Martin's Footsteps
Martin Luther King Day

In the week before Martin Luther King Day, have each child research Martin Luther King Jr. and choose a quote from one of his speeches that most impresses her. Next, have the student trace one of her feet on construction paper and cut out the shape. Then have the child record her quote on her cutout. On Martin Luther King Day, have each student tape her quote to the floor outside your classroom, so that those who walk by your room can walk in Martin Luther King Jr.'s steps. *adapted from an idea by Colleen Dabney, Williamsburg, VA*

"I have a dream that my four little children will one day live in a nation where they will not be judged by the color of their skin but by the content of their character."

Martin Luther King Jr.

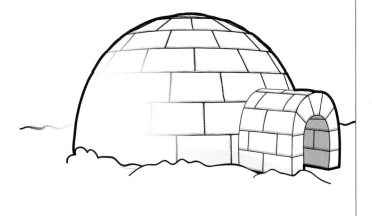

TEC44064

©The Mailbox® • TEC44064 • Dec./Jan. 2012–13

Note to the teacher: Use with "Dreidel Challenge" on page 225.

Name

Date

Hanukkah

Problem solving, evaluating progress, changing course

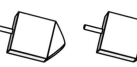

DREIDEL CHALLENGE

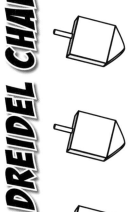

Kwanzaa
by Jacqueline Schiff

Kinara holds the candles;
Kin gather, holding hands.
King, Martin Luther, Jr.
Had dreams of peaceful lands.

Karamu with family—
A feast for young and old.
Kale, a green that's eaten,
Anansi stories told.

Kujichagulia—
A principle of pride.
I'll write my own life story.
I'll be what I decide.

In Kiswahili greetings
And in songs of praise,
We hear the best of Kwanzaa—
All seven precious days.

karamu (kah-RAH-moo) Kwanzaa feast
kinara (kee-NAH-rah) traditional Kwanzaa candleholder
kujichagulia (koo-jee-cha-goo-LEE-ah) Kwanzaa principle of self-determination

©The Mailbox® • TEC44064 • Dec./Jan. 2012–13

Note to the teacher: Use with "A Lyrical Observation" on page 226.

At First Light
Black History Month (February) (W.4.3, W.5.3)

Help students relate to slaves who escaped through the Underground Railroad by reading stories such as *Trouble Don't Last* by Shelley Pearsall, *F Is for Freedom* by Roni Schotter, or *The House of Dies Drear* by Virginia Hamilton. Next, have each child imagine she is a slave who has just escaped. Then post the questions shown and guide each student to plan and write a narrative from the slave's point of view. To publish her work, have the child follow a copy of the directions from the top of page 231 and post her work on a display titled "Shedding a Narrative Light on the Underground Railroad."

Who are you, and where did you live while you were a slave?
How old are you?
What kind of work did you do for your master or mistress?
How did he or she treat you?
What were your living conditions like?
How did you find out about the Underground Railroad?
How did you make your first contact?
What was your journey like?
What was your closest call? How did you escape it?
What other dangers or obstacles did you encounter?
How and where did your journey end?

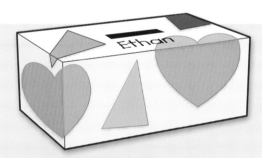

Decoration Suggestions

- two congruent hearts
- scalene triangle
- isosceles triangle
- equilateral triangle
- name written using only line segments
- circle with a diameter of 8 centimeters
- asymmetrical heart
- cube with a symmetrical heart inside

Double Duty
Perimeter, area, volume (4.MD.A.3, 5.MD.C.5b)

For this idea, have each student bring in a box for Valentine's Day cards. Before students exchange valentines, have each child draw a diagram of his box, label each vertex, measure the prism's sides, and record the measurements on his diagram. Next, have the student find and record the perimeter of each face. Then have him find the area of each face. After that, guide the child to find the prism's volume. Finally, have each student decorate his box with mathematic elements, such as those shown, and then save his box for Valentine's Day festivities! **Vicky Ryan, Weller Elementary, Centerville, OH**

Wall of Honor
Research, summarizing (W.4.10, W.5.10, RI.4.2, RI.5.2)

Commemorate National Women's History Month (March) with an honorable hall display. First, have each student choose and research a notable woman she admires. Next, challenge the child to write a three-sentence summary that captures the most important information about the woman. Have each child draw a statue of the woman and then write the summary on a pedestal. Post students' work in the hall with the title "A Salute to Notable Women."

Eleanor Roosevelt was a famous speaker and humanitarian. She stood up for human rights, civil rights, and women's rights. By the way, she was also President Franklin D. Roosevelt's wife.

Pizza "Pi" Day
Exploring circle attributes, circumference

Celebrate Pi Day (March 14) with an exploration that guides students to discover the relationship between a circle's circumference and its diameter. To begin, have each pair of students use a length of string and a metric ruler to follow the directions on a copy of page 232. Then hold a class discussion, guiding students to draw conclusions about their quotients and recognize that pi is approximately equal to 3.14. **developed from a suggestion by Karen Jansen, High Mount School, Swansea, IL**

tip → For a fun follow-up, make tortilla pizzas! For each one, spread a tablespoon of spaghetti sauce and some grated mozzarella or cheddar cheese on a tortilla. Broil or microwave it to melt the cheese, cut it into slices using sanitized scissors, and eat it!

Recipe for Practice
Problem solving, adding mixed numbers (5.NF.A.1)

Here's a St. Patrick's Day nod to mixed number computation! To begin, display a copy of "Top o' the Mornin' Soda Bread" from the bottom half of page 231. Next, pose the questions shown and guide students to use the recipe to answer them. Then send a copy of the recipe home with each student and encourage him to make a loaf with his family. Or surprise students by making a batch or two of the bread in advance for an authentic and nonpinching celebration! **Amy J. Ryan, Kingston Intermediate School, Kingston, MA**

Top o' the Mornin' Queries

1. If you add together the sugar, salt, and baking soda, how many teaspoons of ingredients would you have? (*5¼ teaspoons*) Convert to the greatest measurement possible. (*1 tablespoon, 2¼ teaspoons*)

2. You've decided to make three loaves of the bread for your St. Patrick's Day party. According to the recipe, how many teaspoons of sugar will you need altogether? (*7½ teaspoons*)

3. If you bake each loaf separately, how long will it take to bake the three loaves? (*2 hours to 2¼ hours*)

4. Your friends ate all the bread at the party, so you're going to make a small loaf just for yourself. Rewrite the list of ingredients so that it is for only half the recipe. (*2 cups all-purpose flour, 1¼ teaspoons sugar, ¾ teaspoon salt, ⅝ teaspoon baking soda, ¾ cup buttermilk*)

LANTERN DIRECTIONS

Materials for each student: 9" x 12" sheets of black and yellow construction paper, scissors, glue, ruler, pencil

Steps:

1. Measure the black paper and cut it into the sections shown.

2. Glue the two half-inch black strips to the yellow paper to create four equal-size panes as shown. Trim the excess from the horizontal strip.

3. Glue the large black triangle to the yellow paper as shown. Snip off the tips of the triangle's vertices. Then glue the $\frac{3}{4}$" black strip to the bottom of the lantern and trim the excess.

4. Cut a ring from the scrap paper. Glue it to the top of the lantern as shown.

5. Write the final copy of your narrative in the panes of your lantern. Use the flip side of the lantern if you need more space.

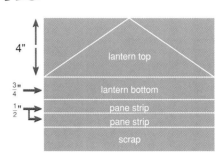

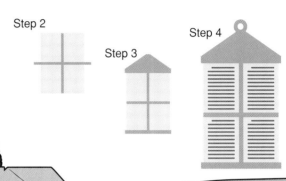

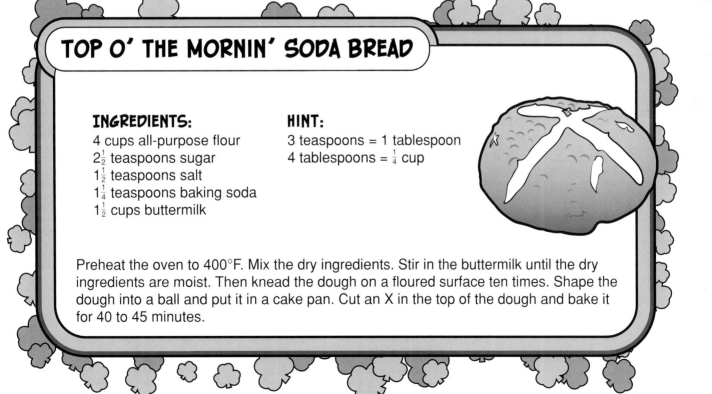

TOP O' THE MORNIN' SODA BREAD

INGREDIENTS:
4 cups all-purpose flour
$2\frac{1}{2}$ teaspoons sugar
$1\frac{1}{2}$ teaspoons salt
$1\frac{1}{4}$ teaspoons baking soda
$1\frac{1}{2}$ cups buttermilk

HINT:
3 teaspoons = 1 tablespoon
4 tablespoons = $\frac{1}{4}$ cup

Preheat the oven to 400°F. Mix the dry ingredients. Stir in the buttermilk until the dry ingredients are moist. Then knead the dough on a floured surface ten times. Shape the dough into a ball and put it in a cake pan. Cut an X in the top of the dough and bake it for 40 to 45 minutes.

Note to the teacher: Use "Lantern Directions" with "At First Light" on page 229. Use "Top o' the Mornin' Soda Bread" with "Recipe for Practice" on page 230.

Name _____

Date _____

Pizza "Pi"

Directions:

1. Use string to measure the circumference of, or distance around, each pizza. Using a ruler, measure the string to the nearest tenth of a centimeter. Record the measurement in the chart.
2. Use a ruler to measure the distance across, or the diameter of, each pizza. Record the measurement in the chart.
3. Divide the circumference by the diameter. Record the quotient to the hundredths place in the table.

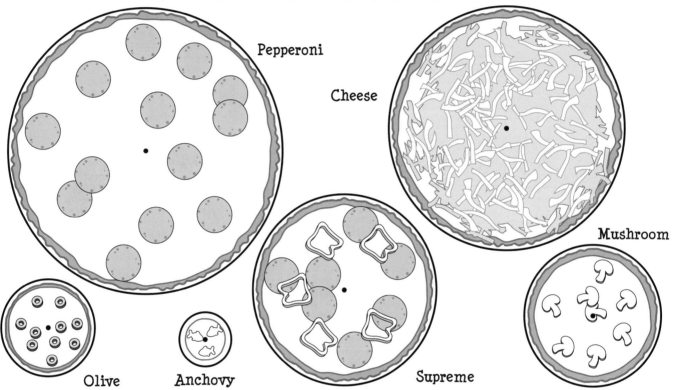

Pepperoni

Cheese

Mushroom

Olive   Anchovy   Supreme

Pizza	Circumference	Diameter	Quotient
Anchovy			
Cheese			
Mushroom			
Olive			
Pepperoni			
Supreme			

©The Mailbox® • TEC44065 • Feb./Mar. 2013 • Key p. 311

Note to the teacher: Use with "Pizza 'Pi' Day" on page 230.

SKILLS FOR THE SEASON

"Eggs-tra" Practice
Review activities

Put a splash of color in your spring reviews with these clever ideas for using plastic eggs!

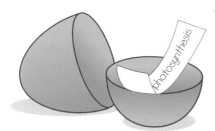

- Keep **vocabulary terms** fresh in students' minds by writing them on paper strips. Then put one strip in each plastic egg and keep a basket of eggs handy. When you have a few minutes, have a student volunteer take an egg, open it, and silently act out the word inside for the class. Let the child who guesses the word take an egg and act out the next word as time allows. (L.4.6; L.5.6) **Rachel Harrar, Key Elementary, Washington, DC**

- Scramble the letters of each **spelling** word on a separate paper strip and put two or three strips in each plastic egg. A student takes an egg, opens it, unscrambles each word, returns the strips, and then takes another egg as time allows. **To extend the challenge**, give the child an egg timer too and encourage her to spell all the words before time runs out! (L.4.2.d; L.5.2.e) **Jennifer Otter, Oak Ridge, NC**

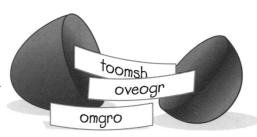

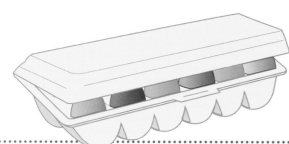

- Write standards-based **math problems** on paper strips and put each strip in a plastic egg. (Or cut apart a copy of a worksheet.) Next, put the eggs in a clean egg carton labeled with the standard. Then keep the cartons in a handy stack for instant reviews students will be eager to take a crack at! (4.OA.A.1) **Annmarie Andersen, Gretchen Reeder Elementary, Omaha, NE**

May Flowers
Decimal notation for fractions (4.NF.C.6)

Have each pair of students cut apart the cards and answer key from a copy of page 234. Next, have one player shuffle the cards, deal half of the cards to himself and half to his partner. Then the partners take turns asking each other for decimal or fraction cards that match the cards in their hands. Each time a player gets a matching pair, he sets it aside. When all the cards have been played, the player with more pairs wins. **For students who struggle** with the skill, provide tenths and hundredths grids and have each child shade tenths or hundredths to match each card.

Flower Cards and Answer Key

Use with "May Flowers" on page 233.

$\frac{2}{10}$ TEC44066	$\frac{20}{100}$ TEC44066	0.2 TEC44066	0.20 TEC44066	0.02 TEC44066
$\frac{2}{100}$ TEC44066	$\frac{4}{100}$ TEC44066	0.04 TEC44066	$\frac{4}{10}$ TEC44066	0.4 TEC44066
$\frac{5}{100}$ TEC44066	0.05 TEC44066	$\frac{5}{10}$ TEC44066	0.5 TEC44066	$\frac{50}{100}$ TEC44066
0.50 TEC44066	$\frac{6}{100}$ TEC44066	0.06 TEC44066	$\frac{6}{10}$ TEC44066	0.6 TEC44066
$\frac{60}{100}$ TEC44066	0.60 TEC44066	0.08 TEC44066	$\frac{8}{100}$ TEC44066	$\frac{8}{10}$ TEC44066
0.8 TEC44066	0.80 TEC44066	$\frac{80}{100}$ TEC44066	0.07 TEC44066	$\frac{7}{100}$ TEC44066

> The most important thing I've learned this year is that when you divide a whole number by a fraction, you get a bigger number.

The Most Important Thing
End of the year

Here's a touching tribute for the last week of school. Have each student copy and complete the following statement: "The most important thing I've learned this year is…" Then, after checking with your office staff, have several students share their statements during the school's morning or afternoon announcements. Keep a copy of students' statements for yourself too. They make great additions to your portfolio, and for a great open house bulletin board next year, just copy several students' statements with their names on sentence strips and add them to a display titled "Learning Is the Most Important Thing!"

It's a Wrap!
Problem solving (4.MD.A.2)

Taking down your bulletin boards can send a signal to your students that school is already out and lead to challenging behaviors. To avoid that, head to your local discount store and buy a package of cheap but cheerful wrapping paper for each bulletin board. Then challenge each small group of students to cover one board using only a package of wrapping paper. When the group finishes, have the students add the title "We're Wrapping Up a Great Year!" Problem solved!

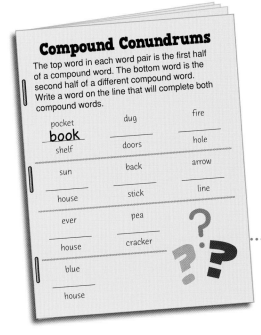

Compound Conundrums

The top word in each word pair is the first half of a compound word. The bottom word is the second half of a different compound word. Write a word on the line that will complete both compound words.

pocket	dug	fire
book	_____	_____
shelf	doors	hole
sun	back	arrow
_____	_____	_____
house	stick	line
ever	pea	
_____	_____	
house	cracker	
blue		
_____		
house		

A Word to the Wise
Building vocabulary (L.4.4; L.5.4)

Looking for a meaningful activity to keep students engaged even though you've collected their textbooks and summer's just around the corner? Try this! Have each student cut apart the boxes on a copy of page 236 and staple them together to make a booklet. Then have him complete the activities on the pages in whatever order he chooses, building his vocabulary as he goes! Don't need an activity to keep students engaged? Have students make the booklets and take them home to forestall summer boredom!

Booklet Pages
Use with "A Word to the Wise" on page 235.

Compound Conundrums

The top word in each word pair is the first half of a compound word. The bottom word is the second half of a different compound word. Write a word on the line that will complete both compound words.

pocket	dug	fire
book	_____	_____
shelf	doors	hole

sun	back	arrow
_____	_____	_____
house	stick	line

ever	pea	
_____	_____	
house	cracker	

blue	stop	
_____	_____	
house	dog	

"Zat's" All, Folks!

Add the letter *z* to each word and then rearrange the letters to spell a new word.

1. bale _____
2. bear _____
3. coy _____
4. doe _____
5. done _____
6. eon _____
7. hay _____
8. heal _____
9. lay _____
10. moo _____
11. nay _____
12. ore _____
13. piper _____
14. race _____
15. rage _____
16. ripe _____
17. same _____
18. their _____

In Other Words

This letter contains some archaic (old fashioned and outdated) words. Underline each one. Then write a word you think it might mean. Write the letter. Does it make sense? Keep trying different words until the letter makes sense.

My dear poplolly,

You little murfled breedbate! I was very carked when I heard that your parents were sending you to the jungle to study woolly malshaves. What fadoodle! Don't you realize that you'll have to live in a grass cosh and that you won't be able to eat your favorite belly-timber?

Plus your crinets and flesh-spades will grow terribly long! Why, I'd give all the chinkers in the world to talk you out of this crazy trip!

Please be hoful. I will simply cry my wink-a-peeps out if something terrible happens to you!

Thigging you not to go,

Aunt Clara

Answer Keys

"Compound Conundrums"
pocketbook, bookshelf
dugout, outdoors
fireman, manhole
sunlight, lighthouse
backyard, yardstick
arrowhead, headline
evergreen, greenhouse
peanut, nutcracker
bluebird, birdhouse
stopwatch, watchdog

"'Zat's' All, Folks!"
1. blaze
2. zebra
3. cozy
4. doze
5. dozen or zoned
6. zone
7. hazy
8. hazel
9. lazy
10. zoom
11. zany
12. zero
13. zipper
14. craze
15. graze
16. prize
17. mazes
18. zither

"In Other Words"
My dear poplolly, **special loved one**
You little murfled breedbate! **freckled mischief maker** I was very carked **annoyed** when I heard that your parents were sending you to the jungle to study woolly malshaves. **caterpillars** What fadoodle! **nonsense** Don't you realize that you'll have to live in a grass cosh **hut** and that you won't be able to eat your favorite belly-timber? **food**
Plus your crinets **hair** and flesh-spades **fingernails** will grow terribly long! Why, I'd give all the chinkers **money** in the world to talk you out of this crazy trip!
Please be hoful **careful**. I will simply cry my wink-a-peeps **eyes** out if something terrible happens to you!
Thigging **begging** you not to go.

©The Mailbox® • TEC44067 • June/July 2013

Ready to Go!

Name _____

Date _____

Circle the misspelled word in each sentence. Then write it correctly in the puzzle.

1. I allways pack my bag the night before school starts.
2. I don't want to forget somthing at home.
3. Are school supply list was pretty long.
4. I'm exsited about using calculators in math class.
5. My teacher will probly ask us about our summer vacation.
6. I finaly get to see who else is in my class!
7. It's fun to wear new close and shoes to school.
8. How many peopel can ride the school bus at one time?
9. The principal thaught everyone looked happy.
10. My frends liked the color of my new backpack.
11. We have a diffrent class schedule than last year.
12. I could hardly wait to see my friends at scool.
13. The teacher gave everyone a daily planner.
14. There mite be a new student in our class tomorrow.
15. I had better get going befor I'm late!

What did one calculator say to the other calculator?

To find out, write the circled letters from the puzzle from the top down on the lines below.

_ _ _ _ _ _ _ _ _ _ _ _ _ _ _ _ _ !

Bonus: Explain your strategy for spotting misspelled words.

©The Mailbox® • TEC44062 • Aug./Sept. 2012 • Key p. 311 • (L.4.2d, L.5.2e)

Name _____

Date _____

Back to the Books

In each row, cross out the number in standard form, word form, or expanded form that doesn't match. Then write the correct form on the line.

	Standard Form	Word Form	Expanded Form	
A.	50,483	fifty thousand, four hundred eighty-three	5,000 + 400 + 80 + 3	50,000 + 400 + 80 + 3
B.	6,192	sixty thousand, one hundred ninety-two	6,000 + 100 + 90 + 2	
C.	5,760	five hundred seventy-six	500 + 70 + 6	
D.	957	nine thousand, five hundred seven	900 + 50 + 7	
E.	11,380	eleven thousand, three hundred eighty	1,000 + 100 + 300 + 80	
F.	7,923	seven thousand, two hundred ninety-three	7,000 + 200 + 90 + 3	
G.	1,649	one thousand, six hundred forty-nine	1,000 + 600 + 90 + 4	
H.	96,074	ninety-six thousand, seven hundred four	90,000 + 6,000 + 70 + 4	
I.	22,282	twenty-two thousand, one hundred eighty-two	20,000 + 2,000 + 100 + 80 + 2	
J.	8,673	eight thousand, six hundred seventy-three	80,000 + 600 + 70 + 3	
K.	3,038	three hundred thirty-eight	3,000 + 30 + 8	
L.	39,907	thirty thousand, nine hundred seven	30,000 + 9,000 + 900 + 7	
M.	8,743	eighty-seven thousand, four hundred thirty	80,000 + 7,000 + 400 + 30	
N.	58,201	five thousand, eight hundred twenty-one	5,000 + 800 + 20 + 1	
O.	384	three hundred eighteen four	300 + 80 + 4	

Bonus: Choose five numbers from above. Write each number in a more detailed expanded form as shown. 70,262 = 7 x 10,000 + 2 x 100 + 6 x 10 + 2 x 1

©The Mailbox® • TEC44062 • Aug./Sept. 2012 • Key p. 311 • (4.NBT.A.2)

A Latin Legacy

Add or subtract. Simplify each sum or difference.

M $\dfrac{1}{3} + \dfrac{2}{3} =$

B $\dfrac{2}{8} + \dfrac{3}{8} =$

E $\dfrac{5}{6} - \dfrac{4}{6} =$

A $\dfrac{1}{5} + \dfrac{3}{5} =$

I $\dfrac{11}{10} - \dfrac{5}{10} =$

L $\dfrac{8}{12} + \dfrac{2}{12} =$

C $\dfrac{9}{12} - \dfrac{2}{12} =$

H $\dfrac{2}{4} + \dfrac{1}{4} =$

N $\dfrac{6}{8} - \dfrac{3}{8} =$

P $\begin{array}{r} \frac{3}{5} \\ -\ \frac{1}{5} \\ \hline \end{array}$

T $\begin{array}{r} \frac{15}{100} \\ -\ \frac{5}{100} \\ \hline \end{array}$

R $\begin{array}{r} \frac{7}{10} \\ +\ \frac{2}{10} \\ \hline \end{array}$

X $\begin{array}{r} \frac{7}{12} \\ -\ \frac{3}{12} \\ \hline \end{array}$

O $\begin{array}{r} \frac{2}{6} \\ +\ \frac{1}{6} \\ \hline \end{array}$

S $\begin{array}{r} \frac{1}{3} \\ +\ \frac{1}{3} \\ \hline \end{array}$

U $\begin{array}{r} \frac{8}{10} \\ -\ \frac{6}{10} \\ \hline \end{array}$

To reveal the missing regions in the paragraph below, write each letter on its matching numbered line or lines.

National Hispanic Heritage Month is observed from September 15 to October 15. The observation was started in 1968 as Hispanic Heritage Week. During this month, we celebrate the histories, cultures, and contributions of people from

Bonus: List all the possible pairs of fractions that equal the sum of $\frac{11}{12}$.

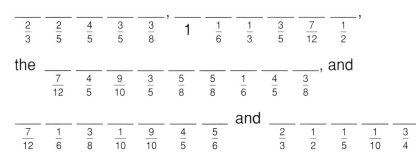

$\dfrac{2}{3}$ $\dfrac{2}{5}$ $\dfrac{4}{5}$ $\dfrac{3}{5}$ $\dfrac{3}{8}$ 1 $\dfrac{1}{6}$ $\dfrac{1}{3}$ $\dfrac{3}{5}$ $\dfrac{7}{12}$ $\dfrac{1}{2}$,

the ___ ___ ___ ___ ___ ___ ___ , and
$\dfrac{7}{12}$ $\dfrac{4}{5}$ $\dfrac{9}{10}$ $\dfrac{3}{5}$ $\dfrac{5}{8}$ $\dfrac{5}{8}$ $\dfrac{1}{6}$ $\dfrac{4}{5}$ $\dfrac{3}{8}$

___ ___ ___ ___ ___ ___ ___ and ___ ___ ___ ___ ___ ___ ___ ___ ___ ___ .
$\dfrac{7}{12}$ $\dfrac{1}{6}$ $\dfrac{3}{8}$ $\dfrac{1}{10}$ $\dfrac{9}{10}$ $\dfrac{4}{5}$ $\dfrac{5}{6}$ $\dfrac{2}{3}$ $\dfrac{1}{2}$ $\dfrac{1}{5}$ $\dfrac{1}{10}$ $\dfrac{3}{4}$ $\dfrac{4}{5}$ 1 $\dfrac{1}{6}$ $\dfrac{9}{10}$ $\dfrac{3}{5}$ $\dfrac{7}{12}$ $\dfrac{4}{5}$

A Bill of Rights

In each statement, circle the cause-and-effect signal word or words.
Then cross out the word or words on the feather quill.
In each item, underline the key words of the cause and draw a box
   around the key words of each effect.

1. When the Constitution was written, some states would not approve it as it was. So the first ten amendments were written.

2. Because people wanted to be heard without being punished, the first amendment gave people the right to speak or write freely.

3. Citizens can keep guns in their homes since the second amendment gave people the right to bear arms.

4. The third amendment states that people do not have to take soldiers into their homes. This was written as a result of the British forcing colonists to house British soldiers.

5. The fourth amendment said the government could not search a person's home without legal permission so that people would feel safe in their homes.

6. Because of the fifth amendment, a person is protected from having to be a witness against himself in a trial.

7. Since the sixth amendment gave each citizen the right to a fair trial, a person could prove his innocence in court.

8. The Constitution's authors wrote the seventh amendment, giving people the right to fair civil trials, due to the fact that the authors were committed to having fair trials.

9. The eighth amendment banned cruel and unusual punishment so that prisoners would be treated humanely.

10. The Constitution listed citizens' rights. Consequently, some people worried it might seem that they had no other rights.

11. The purpose of the Constitution and Bill of Rights was to protect citizens' rights, even ones they didn't describe. So the authors wrote the ninth amendment, saying the Constitution did not deny other rights.

12. State governments wanted to preserve their rights to make decisions about matters in their own states. As a result, the tenth amendment was written, reserving some powers for the states.

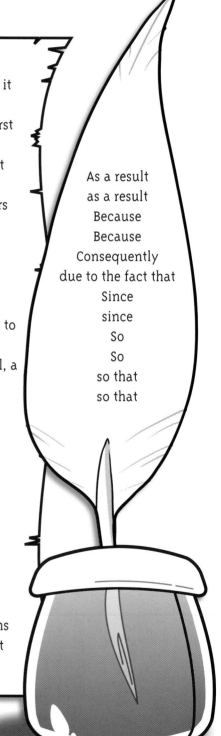

As a result
as a result
Because
Because
Consequently
due to the fact that
Since
since
So
So
so that
so that

Bonus: Think about three rules in your school. List each rule and then write about whose rights each rule was most likely written to protect.

©The Mailbox® • TEC44062 • Aug./Sept. 2012 • Key p. 311 • (R1.4.5)

Puzzled About the Preamble?

The Preamble is a 52-word sentence that introduces the Constitution. This very long sentence explains the purpose for writing the Constitution. Read the Preamble. Then follow the directions below.

"We the people of the United States, in order to form a more perfect **Union**, establish **justice**, insure **domestic tranquility**, provide for the **common defense**, promote the **general welfare**, and **secure** the blessings of liberty to ourselves and our **posterity** do **ordain** and **establish** this Constitution for the United States of America."

Huh?

Find the meaning of each word below in a dictionary. Use the context of the Preamble to pick the best definition for each word. Write the definitions on the lines.

1. Union: _____

2. justice: _____

3. domestic: _____

4. tranquility: _____

5. common: _____

6. defense: _____

7. general: _____

8. welfare: _____

9. secure: _____

10. posterity: _____

11. ordain: _____

12. establish: _____

Now it's your turn to update the Preamble! Use the definitions above to help you write a modern version of the Preamble on your own paper.

Bonus: We celebrate birthdays with cake, cards, and gifts. What would be an appropriate way to celebrate Constitution Day and Citizenship Day (September 17)?

End Zone Mischief

In each number below, circle the digit in the thousandths place.
Then round the number to the nearest hundredths place.

A. 17.96(8)5

17.97

B. 7.0791

C. 41.5146

D. 7.5217

E. 5.50721

F. 26.6306

G. 0.84541

H. 64.3283

I. 9.28794

J. 12.6391

K. 3.9042

L. 34.12316

M. 86.7146

N. 5.8875

O. 0.2239

P. 5.30146

Q. 13.7587

R. 69.2563

S. 9.08462

T. 0.41328

Bonus: Choose ten numbers and round each one to the nearest whole number.

©The Mailbox® · TEC44063 · Oct./Nov. 2012 · Key p. 311 · (5.NBT.A.4)

Name _____

Date _____

Adding and subtracting multidigit whole numbers

LOTS O' LOOT

Add or subtract.
Then write each sum or difference in the puzzle.

ACROSS

B.   481,850
      − 479,456

C.   161,914
      + 425,394

F.   135,262
      − 32,335

G.   985,753
      − 919,397

J. 849,092 − 456,613 =

M. 627,527 − 285,765 =

N. 591,780 − 581,829 =

O. 823,815 + 83,689 =

DOWN

A.   314,657
      − 249,189

B.   210,858
      + 71,835

D.   623,926
      + 148,217

E.   452,651
      + 317,926

H. 526,392 + 146,452 =

I. 347,036 + 236,143 =

K. 704,178 − 461,241 =

L. 948,439 + 39,705 =

BONUS: Write and then solve two new subtraction and two new addition problems using your sums and differences above as subtrahends, minuends, and addends.

©The Mailbox® • TEC44063 • Oct./Nov. 2012 • Key p. 311 • (4.NBT.B.4)

A Day for Honor

Decide whether each statement is a fact or the author's opinion. Then shade the star in the matching column.

	Fact	Opinion
1. World War I, also known as The Great War, officially ended June 28, 1919.	R	B
2. World War I, which lasted four years, was the worst war ever fought.	I	T
3. In 1919, President Woodrow Wilson declared November 11 Armistice Day.	S	W
4. *Armistice* is a truce, or an agreement, between warring groups to stop fighting.	W	C
5. President Wilson was one of the best presidents in United States history.	H	N
6. At first, Armistice Day was meant to celebrate victory and honor those who had died in World War I.	G	T
7. Those who had served in the war were very brave and ought to have been honored.	A	W
8. In 1938, Armistice Day was made a legal holiday and was set aside as a day to honor veterans.	E	S
9. Then people wanted to recognize veterans who fought in World War II and Korea too.	I	Y
10. On June 1, 1954, November 11 became Veterans Day—a day to honor the American veterans of all wars.	P	D
11. Veterans Day is the most important holiday that is celebrated in November.	L	O
12. Then, on October 8, 1954, thanks to a presidential order, a committee was formed to organize a national Veterans Day observation.	E	N
13. It took a long time, but veterans are finally the well-deserved focus of the November holiday.	E	H
14. On Veterans Day, veterans are honored for being patriotic, loving their country, and making sacrifices for the common good.	D	R
15. Everyone should organize, march in, or watch a parade on Veterans Day.	M	D

Which president issued the proclamation that changed Armistice Day to Veterans Day?

To find out, write each shaded letter on its matching numbered line or lines.

___ ___ ___ ___ ___ ___ ___ ___ ___   ___ ___ ___ ___ ___ ___   ___.   ___ ___ ___ ___ ___ ___ ___ ___ ___ ___
10 1 12 3 9 15 8 5 2   14 4 9 6 13 2   14   8 9 3 12 5 13 11 7 8 1

Bonus: Rewrite three of the opinion statements above so they are not opinions.

ODE TO AN ANNUAL DINNER

Ode to a Glass of Milk

Oh, milk, ice-cold glass of milk,
You chill my tongue with every drink.
You make me smile and Leave a mustache on my lip.
I love you so, ice-cold glass of milk.

Write words and phrases that describe the qualities about Thanksgiving dinner that make it different from every other meal.

Write words and phrases that describe what you like best about Thanksgiving dinner.

How do you feel about Thanksgiving dinner overall?

Why do you feel this way?

How do these best parts of Thanksgiving dinner make you feel?

Why do they make you feel this way?

- Use the organizer to plan a poem that pays tribute to Thanksgiving dinner.

- Using the words and phrases from your completed organizer, write ten or more statements about Thanksgiving dinner.

- Next, read the sample "Ode to a Glass of Milk." Then revise your statements or lines as guided below to write your ode.

★ Add extra feeling to boring lines.

★ Choose the best line for your opening.

★ Choose the line that tells how you feel for your closing.

★ Rearrange the rest of your lines so they sound great when you read them out loud.

©The Mailbox® • TEC44063 • Oct./Nov. 2012 • (W.4.3–5, 10)

Note to the teacher: Have each child use a copy of the organizer to write an ode to Thanksgiving dinner.

Name

Date

All in the Family

Circle the idiom in each sentence. Then write the letter of the matching meaning.

A. help him
B. free of responsibilities and duties
C. wrote a short letter
D. so busy she didn't have time for anything else
E. exactly the right time
F. made me hungry
G. knows what's going on even if she can't see it
H. go to bed
I. stayed up working late
J. took the part of the mean person
K. very happy
L. lot of fun
M. nearly silent
N. laughing very hard
O. all of something
P. saying something that wasn't true

1. If you ask me, my grandmother has eyes in the back of her head.

2. Grandma dropped everyone a line, inviting us to dinner the first evening of Hanukkah.

3. She was on cloud nine when she found out the whole family could come.

4. Grandma had her hands full getting everything ready to feed 28 people.

5. I think she ended up burning the midnight oil the night before the big dinner.

6. Aunt Gloria arrived at 6:00 on the dot with her famous latkes.

7. My cousin had us all in stitches when he showed up dressed as a latke.

8. Grandpa asked my little sister to lend him a hand lighting the *shamash*.

9. Uncle Don brought his state-of-the-art camera to record the whole shebang.

10. My brother said he knew all about the camera, and I told him he was full of beans.

11. When Grandma called us to dinner, everything looked so good it made my mouth water.

12. Once we started eating, it was so quiet you could hear a pin drop.

13. After dinner, my mom played the heavy and made us kids do the dishes.

14. Then we were footloose and fancy-free, so we found a dreidel and started to play.

15. When Uncle Don showed his video of the evening, we had a barrel of fun.

16. It was a great night, but we were all ready to hit the hay!

Bonus: Make a list of five or more idioms that your family and you use. Then tell what each one means.

©The Mailbox® • TEC44064 • Dec./Jan. 2012–13 • Key p. 311 • (L.4.5b, L.5.5b)

Synonyms, antonyms

Name _____

Date _____

PRESENTS GALORE!

Shade the bow of each present that contains a pair of antonyms.

If a present contains two synonyms, write an antonym for the pair on the tree.

BONUS: Write a synonym for one word in each present with a shaded bow.

1. bend / straighten

2. evacuate / vacate

3. departure / arrival

4. transparent / opaque

5. rich / affluent

6. happiness / bliss

7. cease / terminate

8. bravery / cowardice

9. empty / vacant

10. close / distant

11. agree / concur

12. genuine / certified

13. simple / difficult

14. honorable / unethical

15. huge / immense

16. courteous / rude

17. juvenile / adolescent

18. mix / combine

19. permanent / temporary

20. scarce / plentiful

A Symbolic Celebration

Follow the directions.

		Mazao (crops)	Kikombe cha Umoja (unity cup)	Kinara (candleholder)
1.	Name one angle in each circle that measures 45°.	∠XQR		
2.	Name one angle in each circle that measures 90°.			
3.	Name one angle in each circle that measures 180°.			
4.	Name one angle in each circle that measures 30°.			
5.	Name one angle in each circle that measures 120°.			
6.	Name one angle in each circle that measures 60°.			
7.	Name one angle in each circle that is a reflex angle.			

8. Name four angles on the circle Q that equal 360°.

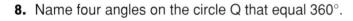

9. Name four angles on the Unity cup's circle that equal 360°.

10. Name four angles on the candleholder's circle that equal 360°.

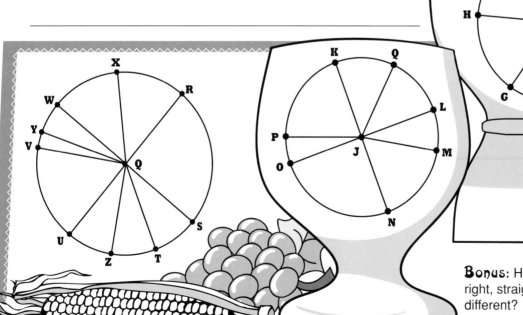

Bonus: How are acute, obtuse, right, straight, and reflex angles different?

©The Mailbox® • TEC44064 • Dec./Jan. 2012–13 • Key p. 311 (4.MD.C.5a)

Name _____

Date _____

A Man of Words

Multiply. Write each product in lowest terms.
Then cross out each box with a matching fraction. The words you do not cross out will spell out an important quote from Dr. Martin Luther King Jr.

1 $\dfrac{4}{5} \times \dfrac{5}{12} =$

2 $\dfrac{11}{12} \times \dfrac{1}{3} =$

3 $\dfrac{1}{4} \times \dfrac{7}{100} =$

4 $\dfrac{5}{6} \times \dfrac{1}{8} =$

5 $\dfrac{7}{12} \times \dfrac{1}{2} =$

6 $\dfrac{23}{100} \times \dfrac{2}{3} =$

7 $\dfrac{3}{4} \times \dfrac{9}{10} =$

8 $\dfrac{17}{100} \times \dfrac{3}{5} =$

9 $\dfrac{2}{3} \times \dfrac{3}{10} =$

10 $\dfrac{5}{6} \times \dfrac{19}{100} =$

11 $\dfrac{7}{8} \times \dfrac{4}{5} =$

12 $\dfrac{1}{2} \times \dfrac{3}{100} =$

13 $\dfrac{5}{12} \times \dfrac{2}{5} =$

14 $\dfrac{9}{10} \times \dfrac{1}{3} =$

15 $\dfrac{5}{8} \times \dfrac{1}{4} =$

16 $\dfrac{3}{10} \times \dfrac{3}{8} =$

Bonus: Choose three fractions that you did not cross out. Multiply the fractions by each other. Write the product in lowest terms.

$\frac{7}{10}$ Freedom	$\frac{11}{36}$ Unity	$\frac{3}{8}$ Peace	$\frac{7}{8}$ is	$\frac{9}{80}$ come	$\frac{22}{45}$ not	$\frac{27}{40}$ only	$\frac{3}{8}$ merely	$\frac{1}{5}$ some
$\frac{5}{6}$ a	$\frac{4}{35}$ distant	$\frac{1}{3}$ planning	$\frac{3}{16}$ goal	$\frac{2}{27}$ we	$\frac{7}{24}$ to	$\frac{1}{6}$ succeed,	$\frac{8}{9}$ seek,	$\frac{3}{200}$ and...
$\frac{3}{80}$ but...	$\frac{7}{400}$ when	$\frac{8}{15}$ it	$\frac{5}{32}$ we	$\frac{6}{11}$ is a	$\frac{4}{21}$ means	$\frac{4}{7}$ by	$\frac{23}{150}$ truth	$\frac{6}{11}$ which
$\frac{51}{500}$ good	$\frac{22}{45}$ we	$\frac{10}{60}$ arrive	$\frac{19}{120}$ overcome	$\frac{9}{10}$ at	$\frac{5}{48}$ win	$\frac{4}{10}$ that	$\frac{3}{10}$ freedom.	$\frac{3}{6}$ goal.

A Secret Life

Write <, >, or = to compare each set of measurements.

1 mile = 1,760 yards
1 mile = 5,280 feet
1 yard = 3 feet
1 mile ≈ 1.6 kilometers (km)
1 km = 1,000 meters (m)

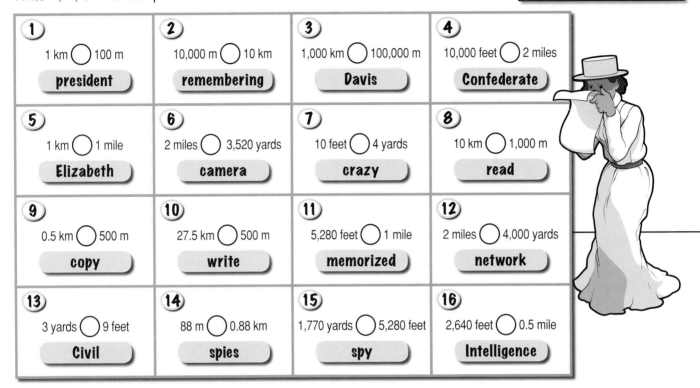

1 1 km ◯ 100 m
president

2 10,000 m ◯ 10 km
remembering

3 1,000 km ◯ 100,000 m
Davis

4 10,000 feet ◯ 2 miles
Confederate

5 1 km ◯ 1 mile
Elizabeth

6 2 miles ◯ 3,520 yards
camera

7 10 feet ◯ 4 yards
crazy

8 10 km ◯ 1,000 m
read

9 0.5 km ◯ 500 m
copy

10 27.5 km ◯ 500 m
write

11 5,280 feet ◯ 1 mile
memorized

12 2 miles ◯ 4,000 yards
network

13 3 yards ◯ 9 feet
Civil

14 88 m ◯ 0.88 km
spies

15 1,770 yards ◯ 5,280 feet
spy

16 2,640 feet ◯ 0.5 mile
Intelligence

Mary Elizabeth Bowser (1839—unknown) was born a slave in Richmond, Virginia. When her owner died, his wife and his daughter gave Mary her freedom. Then his daughter, Elizabeth, sent Mary to school in Philadelphia. Mary was an excellent student. After she graduated, Mary moved back to Richmond and stayed in contact with Elizabeth. When the Civil War started, Mary and Elizabeth both supported the Union in a surprising way.

To read the rest of Mary's story, write each word from above in order in the section with the matching symbol.

< To make sure the people in Richmond, the _____ capital, left her alone, _____ acted as though she was _____ . While her neighbors were calling her Crazy Bet, Elizabeth was really running a _____ of Union _____ . Mary started helping Elizabeth by acting like she was an illiterate servant named Ellen Bond.

> As Ellen Bond, Mary went to work in the house of the Confederate _____ , Jefferson _____ . No one thought Ellen could _____ or _____ , which helped her in her work as a _____ . At the time, servants were expected to work so that no one even noticed them. Since Ellen was not watched closely, she heard conversations and read key documents that were left on Davis's desk.

= Mary had an amazing talent for _____ what she read. (She didn't have a _____ or access to a _____ machine!) So Mary _____ the information she read so she could pass it on. In 1995, more than 100 years after the _____ War, Mary Bowser was named to the Military _____ Corps Hall of Fame for her work during the Civil War.

©The Mailbox® • TEC44065 • Feb./Mar. 2013 • Key p. 312 (5.MD.A.1)

Name

Date

LOVE IS IN THE AIR

Use editing marks to add quotation marks and commas where they are needed. If no punctuation marks need to be added, shade the heart.

HINT Use quotation marks around the speaker's exact words.

HINT Use a comma to separate the action or the speaker from the speaker's words.

1. (A) Leo says, "I love my job. I work one day a year, Valentine's Day, spreading love—lovebug style!

2. (E) Lola says, This is my first Valentine's Day. I could sure use some pointers!

3. (K) "That's a good one—pointers!" Leo says, "Okay, let's give that guy over there a little nip."

4. (N) Mo shouts, rubs his neck, and looks at Mia, the girl next to him. Then he cries "I think I'm in love!

5. (W) Then Lola stings Mia, but Max catches her eye instead of Mo. So she says, "Max is the one for me!"

6. (P) Leo next strikes Milton, who declares, "Mabel, I think I'm in love with you!"

7. (O) "Excuse me?" Mabel asks, just as Lola stings her left pinkie.

8. (V) Mabel hops up because of the sting and spots Mort. Then she calls Will you be my cuddle bug?"

9. (T) Leo buzzes over and stings Mort on the ear. Mort shouts "What's going on?

10. (L) Suddenly, Maya catches Mort's attention. He forgets the sting and boldly calls Maya, be mine!"

11. (D) Before Maya can respond, Lola stings her, and she exclaims, "I think Merv is my Prince Charming!"

12. (I) Just then, Leo stings Merv, who grabs some flowers, hands them to Millie, and says These are just for you.

13. (Y) Millie starts to smile, but Lola stings her, causing her to notice Mo and then mumble Mo is the one for me!

14. (Z) Lola buzzes around the park and tells Leo, "I think we stung everyone! Is that all we're supposed to do?"

15. (C) "Yep! Our work here is done," Leo tells Lola. "Let's take off!"

BONUS Write two more lines of dialogue between lovebugs Leo and Lola. Use correct punctuation.

On Valentine's Day, what does one lovebug give another?

To find out, write the unshaded letters on the matching numbered line or lines.

" __ __ __ __ __ __   __ __ __ __ "!
  1 8 1 10 2 4   9 12 4 13

©The Mailbox® · TEC44065 · Feb./Mar. 2013 · Key p. 312 (L.4.2b)

A Mind for Math

Complete both input-output tables. Next, plot each coordinate pair on the grid. Then use a ruler to connect the points and use the grid to answer the questions below.

When I was in school, math was my best subject.

Line 1

x	y = 2x	Ordered Pair (x, y)
0	0	(0, 0)
1		
2		
3		
4		
5		
6		

Line 2

x	y = 3x	Ordered Pair (x, y)
0	0	(0, 0)
1		
2		
3		
4		
5		
6		

y-axis

O

P

x-axis

Use the grid to answer the questions.

1. How are the two lines similar? Explain. _____

_____

2. How are the two lines different? Explain. _____

_____

3. If you extend line 1, will it intersect point O or point P? How do you know? _____

_____

4. If you extend line 2, will it intersect point O or point P? How do you know? _____

_____

Bonus: Graph the equation y = 4x, using 0, 1, 2, and 3 for x. How is the line similar to Lines 1 and 2? How is it different?

©The Mailbox® • TEC44065 • Feb./Mar. 2013 • Key p. 312 (5.G.A.1–2)

Women With Influence

Read each pair of sentences about a woman who helped shape United States history. Then combine the sentences using an appositive phrase.

> An appositive is a noun phrase next to a noun or pronoun. It is set off by commas and modifies (explains or identifies) the noun or pronoun.
>
> Abigail Adams was President John Adams' wife. She wrote a letter urging him to "remember the ladies" in the laws of the new nation.
>
> **Abigail Adams, <u>President John Adams' wife</u>, wrote a letter urging him to "remember the ladies" in the laws of the new nation.**

1. Helen Keller was a crusader for the civil rights of blind and disabled citizens. Helen Keller lost her sight and hearing when she was a year and a half. _____

    _____

2. Maria Mitchell was an astronomer who discovered a new comet in 1847. Mitchell became the first female member of the American Academy of Arts and Sciences in 1848. _____

    _____

3. Harriet Tubman was a famous conductor of the Underground Railroad. She helped 300 slaves escape before the Civil War. _____

    _____

4. Margaret Bourke-White was a daring news photographer. Once, Ms. White took a picture of some geese by dangling from a helicopter by a cable. _____

    _____

5. Marian Anderson was one of America's finest concert singers. In 1955, she was the first African American soloist to sing with the Metropolitan Opera in New York City. _____

    _____

6. Elizabeth Cochrane Seaman was a newspaper reporter who went by the pen name Nellie Bly. Ms. Seaman wrote a report on the cruel treatment patients received inside a mental hospital that led to key reforms. _____

    _____

7. Grace Murray Hopper developed the first computer programming language someone besides a scientist could use and understand. She was a rear admiral in the Navy. _____

    _____

8. Shirley Chisholm represented New York in the US House of Representatives from 1969 to 1983. She was the first African American woman to serve in Congress. _____

    _____

Bonus: Write three sentences about a woman or women you admire. Use an appositive in each sentence.

Vocabulary in Bloom

So many flowers—so little time!

I. Use the chart to decide what each word means. Then write your definition on the lines.

tele- *(distant)* + graph *(write)* = telegraph: a message or something written and sent far away

Word Part	Meaning
-ant, -ent	one who
com-, con-, co-	with, together
dis-, dif-, di-	apart
equ-	equal
graph	write
-ion	act or condition of
-ity, -ty, -y	state of, character of
-logy	study of
-ous	full of
pon, pos, pose, posit	to place
port	to carry
re-	again, back
tele-	distant
trans-	across, beyond, through
un-, uni-	one
ver, vers, vert	to turn

1. trans + port = transport: _____ _____

2. equ + ity = equity: _____ _____

3. di + vert = divert: _____ _____

4. posit + ion = position: _____ _____

5. re + vers = reverse: _____ _____

6. uni + ty = unity: _____ _____

II. Each word below contains a prefix, root, and/or suffix from the chart. Circle the word part or parts in each word. Then find the matching definition and write the letter on the line.

_____ **7.** occup(ant)

_____ **8.** mythology

_____ **9.** villainous

_____ **10.** conversion

_____ **11.** filmography

_____ **12.** transportation

_____ **13.** disadvantage

_____ **14.** component

_____ **15.** equitable

A. act of changing from one thing to another

B. state of not having an advantage

C. study or collection of myths

D. one who lives in a place or occupies it

E. state of dealing fairly with all concerned

F. having a wicked character like that of a villain

G. list of movies on a particular topic

H. act of moving people or things from one place to another

I. important part of something

Bonus: Make a list of five or more words not on this page that include word parts from the chart.

©The Mailbox® • TEC44066 • April/May 2013 • Key p. 312 • (RF.4.3a; RF.5.3a)

The Three Rs

Solve. Show your work.

Reduce—make the problem simpler!
Reuse—use a strategy that works!
Recycle—go back and check your work!

M $(3 \times 6) + 4 \times 4 - 14 =$	**T** $72 - (14 - 7) \times 5 + 6 =$	**E** $16,170 \div 42 =$
L $237.25 \times 87 =$	**R** $7\frac{3}{4} - 5\frac{3}{12} =$	**D** $\frac{3}{5} + \frac{1}{3} + \frac{1}{6} =$
Y $\frac{7}{8} \times \frac{3}{5} =$	**A** Find the volume. 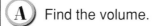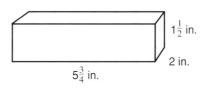 $5\frac{3}{4}$ in. $1\frac{1}{2}$ in. 2 in.	**I** Find the volume. 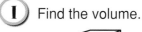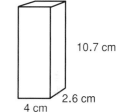 10.7 cm 2.6 cm 4 cm
N Add 3.842, 2.168, 0.71, 4.95, and 7.636. Then round the sum to the nearest hundredth.	**K** The distance from Thimbleton to Needlepoint through Scissor Springs is 1,275 miles. If the distance from Thimbleton to Scissor Springs is 839 miles, how far is Scissor Springs from Needlepoint?	**S** The girls in Lana's troop set a goal to sell 1,000 boxes of cookies this year. There are 13 girls in the troop. At least how many boxes of cookies should each girl sell to reach their goal?

Have you heard the joke about the skunk on Earth Day?
To answer the riddle, write each letter on the matching numbered line or lines.

____ ____ V____ ____ ____   ____ ____ ____ ____ ____ ; ____ ____ ____
19.31 385   385 $2\frac{1}{2}$ 20 111.28 19.31 $1\frac{1}{10}$ 111.28 43

____ ____ ____ ____ ____ ____   ____ ____ ____ ____ ____ ____ !
$2\frac{1}{2}$ 385 $17\frac{1}{4}$ 20,640.75 20,640.75 $\frac{21}{40}$ 77   43 111.28 19.31 436 77

Bonus: The first Earth Day was celebrated in April 1970. How many months ago did the first celebration take place? Write an equation for the problem. Solve it.

May Day! Mayday!

Each paragraph needs more details.
Using your own words, paraphrase the facts and details below each paragraph
   and add them where they make the most sense.
Then rewrite each paragraph on another sheet of paper.

May Day

English people once set aside the first day of May for spring

celebrations. After a long, dreary winter, this spring holiday was

their favorite. They decorated with flowers, and they put up special

poles. People would dance around the pole holding ribbons. Villagers sang spring carols.

For medieval villagers, May Day was the best way to welcome spring.

- English villagers loved May Day during medieval times which lasted from 400 until about 1400.

- To celebrate, people decorated their homes and churches with wildflowers and green branches.

- Villagers sang carols about spring. The people they sang to would give the carolers gifts.

- In each village, a May tree, or maypole, was set up with ribbons streaming from the top.

- Dancers held onto the maypole's ribbons, weaving them around the pole. After the dance, the maypole was covered in bright colors.

Mayday!

The storm took Captain Tidewater and her crew by surprise. Captain Tidewater struggled with

the steering wheel. Waves kept hitting the ship. The ship was in trouble. The captain reached for

the radio and said, "Mayday, Mayday, Mayday! This is The Big Clipper!

Mayday." Everyone was relieved when they heard an answering call.

Captain Tidewater and The Big Clipper crew would be okay.

- The thunderstorm seemed to come out of nowhere.

- The storm brought strong winds and large rolling waves.

- In a sudden storm, the captain stays calm and takes control of the situation.

- When waves hit the side of a ship, they can cause the ship's load to shift. This can cause the ship to list, or lean to one side.

- Mayday is an internationally recognized call for emergency help at sea. To make the emergency call, say "Mayday" three times in a slow and clear voice.

Jessica's Journal

In each paragraph, find four places where the tense shifts but should not. Circle the incorrect verb or verb phrase. Then write the correct verb or verb phrase in order on a line to the right.

Dear Journal,

It is almost the end of another school year. This year is my final year of elementary school. Next year, I would be attending middle school. I will not be in the same class all day, seeing the same faces. I have been switching classes, and there will be different students in my classes. Because kids from my school and two other elementary schools went to the same middle school, there will be kids at school I have never met before. I will meet new people and make new friends. I hope I will have made a lot of new friends.

When I think about changing classes and opening my locker, my stomach will be feeling nervous. I worried about getting lost between classes and not being able to open my locker. What if the work is too hard or the teachers did not like me? When our class visits the middle school, I am going to smile at all the middle school teachers. I wanted each one of them to get a good impression of me right from the start.

Now that school was almost over, it is time for the end-of-the-year activities. Our class will be going on a field trip to an outdoor education camp. We will learn how to identify edible plants and how to survive if we got lost in the woods. After that, we will have competed with the fourth graders for bragging rights in the school field day. Each one of us will compete in three different competitions. I could hardly have waited.

More later...

Me—Jessica

1. _____

2. _____

3. _____

4. _____

5. _____

6. _____

7. _____

8. _____

9. _____

10. _____

11. _____

12. _____

Bonus: Write a journal entry about the last week of school. Make sure you don't have any incorrect shifts in verb tenses.

Name _____

Date _____

Desk Duty

A. Circle the letter that describes each object's transformation.

	Reflection	Rotation	Translation
1.	S	O	C
2.	I	Y	K
3.	R	G	L
4.	M	A	I
5.	A	L	C
6.	S	B	L
7.	F	T	D
8.	M	O	D
9.	K	C	O
10.	H	W	E
11.	U	N	D
12.	P	H	B

When you turn a figure around a point, you **rotate** it.
When you slide a figure, you **translate** it.
When you flip a figure over a line, you make its **reflection**.

Which school has no beginning and no end?

To answer the riddle, write each circled letter on the matching numbered line.

___ ___ ___ ___ ___
4   2   11 7   3   10

___ ___ ___ ___ ___ !
6   9   12 1   8   5

Bonus: How would 90°, 180°, and 270° rotations of a figure be different? Explain. Use diagrams to help.

B. In each box, draw the figure's transformation as guided.

13. Draw a **reflection**.

14. Draw a **translation**.

15. Draw a **rotation**.

16. Draw a **reflection**.

©The Mailbox® • TEC44067 • June/July 2013 • Key p. 312

Name ____________________

Date ____________________

Summer

Decimal fractions and decimal equivalents

Jumping In With Both Feet!

Solve.
Then write the letter next to the matching decimal.

	A. $\frac{1}{10} + \frac{3}{100} =$	**B.** $\frac{70}{100} + \frac{7}{100} =$	**C.** $\frac{6}{10} + \frac{1}{100} =$
D. $\frac{90}{100} + \frac{2}{100} =$	**E.** $\frac{8}{10} + \frac{4}{100} =$	**F.** $\frac{40}{100} + \frac{5}{100} =$	**G.** $\frac{3}{10} + \frac{8}{100} =$
H. $\frac{0}{10} + \frac{5}{100} =$	**I.** $\frac{10}{100} + \frac{5}{100} =$	**J.** $\frac{50}{100} + \frac{5}{100} =$	**K.** $\frac{1}{10} + \frac{4}{100} =$
L. $\frac{4}{100} + \frac{4}{100} =$	**M.** $\frac{2}{10} + \frac{5}{100} =$	**N.** $\frac{1}{100} + \frac{6}{100} =$	**O.** $\frac{40}{100} + \frac{9}{100} =$

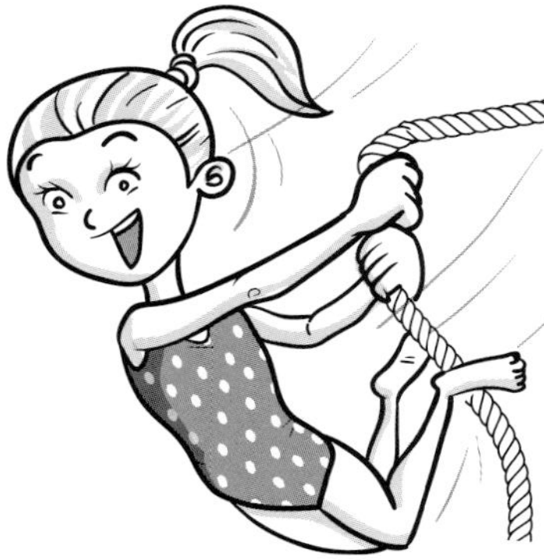

- ◯ 0.77
- ◯ 0.08
- ◯ 0.84
- ◯ 0.15
- ◯ 0.38
- ◯ 0.61
- ◯ 0.14
- ◯ 0.55
- ◯ 0.13
- ◯ 0.25
- ◯ 0.49
- ◯ 0.07
- ◯ 0.92
- ◯ 0.05
- ◯ 0.45

Add.

P. $\frac{6}{10} + \frac{1}{100} =$ ______

Q. $\frac{7}{10} + \frac{3}{100} =$ ______

R. $\frac{2}{100} + \frac{9}{10} =$ ______

S. $\frac{16}{100} + \frac{8}{10} =$ ______

T. $\frac{3}{10} + \frac{16}{100} =$ ______

U. $\frac{47}{100} + \frac{2}{10} =$ ______

Bonus: Write the decimal equivalent for sums P through U.

Name _____

Date _____

SOME SUMMER!

PART 1

Tell whether each statement is a complete sentence, a sentence fragment, or a run-on sentence. Then cross off the matching term on the car.

1. If it's mine. _____

2. My friends are coming soon we're having a sleepover.

   _____

3. We might watch a movie tonight, or we might play games. _____

4. They're here! _____

5. Have you seen my phone I can't find it! _____

6. Sure, in your bag. _____

7. Dad can't cook he ordered pizza. _____

8. When the pizza gets here! _____

9. We can ride bikes for 20 minutes or so. _____

10. I forgot my helmet do you have an extra one? _____

11. Yes, over in that corner, on the shelf. _____

12. I appreciate it. _____

13. No problem! _____

14. I think I saw the pizza delivery car let's head home. _____

15. It's going to be a great summer! _____

PIZZA

complete   fragment   run-on
complete   fragment   run-on
complete   fragment   run-on
complete   fragment   run-on
complete   fragment
           fragment

PART 2

Choose two statements from above that are sentence fragments and two that are run-on sentences. Write each statement's number in a circle and then rewrite the statement so it is a complete sentence.

BONUS: How did you decide whether Statement 8 was a complete sentence, a sentence fragment, or a run-on sentence? Explain.

◯ _____

◯ _____

◯ _____

◯ _____

©The Mailbox® • TEC44067 • June/July 2013 • Key p. 312 • (L.4.1f; L.5.1)

1 A Special Note

To help ease students' first-day jitters, cut out a paper circle for every two students in your class and then cut each one into two unique pieces. Also write a note that welcomes each student to your class, guides her to bring the half circle with her on the first day of school, and outlines one or two fun activities you have planned. Then tuck the note and half circle into an envelope. On the back of the envelope, write the note shown. About two weeks before school starts, send a prepared envelope to each student. After you greet your students on the first day, have each child meet another one by finding the classmate with the matching half circle.

DO NOT OPEN UNTIL YOU WAKE UP ON THE FIRST DAY OF SCHOOL!

2 Meet and Greet Jigsaw

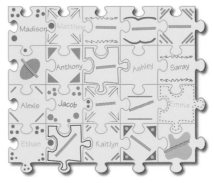

Before the first day, divide a long piece of bulletin board paper into puzzle pieces (one piece per student). Write a student's name on each piece and then cut the puzzle apart. On the first day of school, have each child decorate his puzzle piece. Then have students work together to assemble the puzzle on the classroom floor. Tape the finished puzzle together and hang it on the wall for a quick and colorful display titled "Working Together From Day One."

5 IDEAS FOR A FAB FIRST DAY

3 A Name Game

For this simple game, students sit in a circle; one student stands in the center and is it. The student who is it points to another student, says "Zip!" or "Zap!" and then starts counting to ten. If he said "zip," the other student must name the child to her left. If he said "zap," the student must name the child to her right. If she fails to name the appropriate student before the student who is it counts to ten, she changes places with him.

4 Take a Walk!

The first day of school can be a long one! Break up the day by taking students for a walk around the school. As you walk, challenge students to find an object beginning with each letter of the alphabet. The walk is a great opportunity to chat with students and the challenge will give you a peek at students' problem-solving and social skills.

5 Anchors Aweigh!

Looking for a simple and fun back-to-school theme? Give your room a nautical flair! Program cutout copies of the ship pattern below with students' names. Then post the ships on your door with the title shown. Use copies of the ship pattern to make desk and coat hook tags too. Then label your back-to-school information with the heading "Welcome aboard!" Schedule activities with seafaring themes throughout the day and, if students' energy starts to flag, hand out—what else—Life Savers candies.

- Have each student write a message to you about the upcoming year, roll it up, and slip it into a clean bottle. (Use one big bottle for all students' letters, so they'll be easy for you to retrieve.)

- Make flash cards on cutout copies of a ship pattern or program ship cutouts with more challenging problems sure to keep your early finishers busy.

- Start reading aloud *Island of the Blue Dolphins* by Scott O'Dell.

- Review the water cycle with a quick demonstration and have students diagram it.

- Divide students into crews. Have each crew pick a location on a world map and have the students write an SOS message to describe their location. Then redistribute SOS messages and have each crew locate another one.

Ship and Captain Patterns
Use with "Anchors Aweigh!" on this page.

TEC44062

TEC44062

You're Invited!

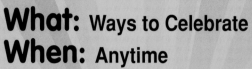

What: Ways to Celebrate
When: Anytime
Where: Your classroom

Theme Days

Replace holiday parties with related theme days. For example, honor Mad Scientist Day on Halloween. Treat students to fun experiments, have them imagine and write about life as mad scientists, and then make science-related snacks and fruit punch concoctions. Or replace Valentine's Day with Merry Manners Day—a day that includes learning rules of etiquette, practicing those skills at an in-class dining experience, and writing a silly advice book. *Gail Tanner, Columbus Academy, Gahanna, OH*

Tunes and Talk

With this idea, students boogie their way to better grades! Use students' pre-assessment scores to determine a goal for each child. Then, after each student completes the post-assessment, award her a point or a certain number of points for progress toward her goal, tallying students' points. When the class total reaches a predetermined number, turn on the music and celebrate with 15 to 30 minutes of tunes, talk, and a little boogie on the side! *Kendra McCall, Charlotte, NC*

Make Mine Motivational

Students earn this celebration. First, post a 5 x 5 grid labeled as shown. Also program 25 paper strips with the grid's coordinates. When students meet a class goal, have a child draw a strip and mark an X in the matching space on the grid. When all the sections have been marked, celebrate with a popcorn, pop music, and soda pop party. Recognize mini benchmarks (five spaces in a row or column) with smaller rewards, such as a night without homework or ten minutes playing students' favorite whole-class game. *Clare Cavanaugh, Orchard Park, NY*

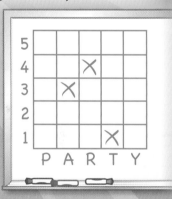

Tips for Any Celebration

Set up each party activity as a station. Provide directions and ask a parent volunteer to supervise the activity. This makes the celebration easier to manage, and students get to enjoy a variety of activities. *Jennie Stever, Apache Elementary, Albuquerque, NM*

Put student desks into groups (tables) and cover each table with bulletin board paper (tablecloths). While students wait for activities or food, invite them to draw on their tablecloths or write notes to a tablemate. Managing students will be easier, and cleanup will be a breeze! *Laurie Huggins, Arlington Elementary, Arlington, TN*

Invite the other classes at your grade level to join in your fun. It will help develop the grade-level community by allowing students to mingle, you can set up different activities for the students in the different classrooms, and you can get help from other teachers! *Camy Ng, Coquitlam River Elementary, Port Coquitlam, British Columbia, Canada*

MARK YOUR

CALENDAR

Whether it's gearing up for testing, winding down after testing, or just celebrating the wonder of your school community, use any or all of these easy-to-adapt ideas for a fun-filled school spirit week.

We Can Make a Difference Day

Start the week off by encouraging students to think of others. Challenge each student to bring in one canned good for a local food bank. Then award certificates to each class that participates. **As an alternative,** designate a school charity and then have each class participate in a penny drive.

Stuffed Animal Day

Invite everyone at school (including the principal) to bring in a favorite stuffed animal. Make student copies of page 265 or plan learning activities, such as writing and solving math problems based on the toy guests or studying the real-life counterparts of the stuffed animals.

Cool Characters Day

On this day, have students transform themselves into their favorite story characters. For fun, designate lunch as a time that students not only dress so they resemble their characters but also talk and act like them. At the end of the day, have a schoolwide parade.

Too Tacky Day

Mismatched clothes, crazy colors, out-of-date apparel—encourage it all on this day! Have individual classes vote for the student with the most colorful combo, craziest vintage wear, best use of school colors, etc. Post the names of each class's winners, with photographs, in a hallway for everyone to enjoy.

Swap and Trade Day

To wrap up the week, have each student bring in a white elephant article to trade. Establish ground rules for trading; then let the fun begin. Students may trade among their classmates, with students at their grade level, or with the entire school. These silly items are sure to become cherished mementos of the week!

Name _____

Date _____

Not Just Kids' Stuff

Choose ___ or more activities.
Complete each activity on another sheet of paper.
When you finish an activity, color its number.

1 Imagine there is a contest to pick a new school mascot. Write a letter that will convince your classmates to vote for your stuffed animal to be the new school mascot.

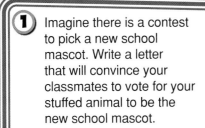

2 Create a timeline of your stuffed animal's existence. Include ten or more important events, such as when it became yours.

3 Imagine your stuffed animal comes to life. What do you think it would do first? Write a story about its adventure.

4 Make a Venn diagram that compares your stuffed animal with its real-life counterpart.

Alphie   Lion

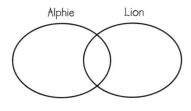

STUFFED ANIMAL DAY!

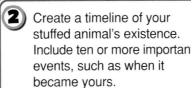

5 Determine your stuffed animal's vital statistics and then use them to create its own identification card. Measure its

- total length
- arm length
- leg length
- girth (distance around its middle)
- head circumference

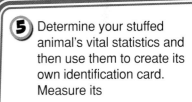

6 Write and solve four word problems based on the stuffed animals in your class. Write one problem for each function: addition, subtraction, multiplication, and division.

7 What do you think will become of your stuffed animal in ten years? Describe where it will be, what it will look like, and how you will feel about it.

8 Research your stuffed animal's real-life counterpart. Answer the question below and cite three or more facts that support your opinion.

If your stuffed animal were a real animal, would it be a good pet?

Note to the teacher: Use with "Stuffed Animal Day" on page 264. Program a copy of this page with the number of activities students should complete; then make student copies.

Crazy 'bout QUILTS

A Cozy Collection of Cross-Curricular Activities

Getting the Point

Identifying the main idea and explaining how it is supported by key details

For this idea, have each student cut out an action picture from a magazine and give her a copy of the main quilt block pattern from page 267. Next, have her record the picture's source information in corner sections of the quilt block and tell whether the picture was from an article or advertisement. Then, in boxes around the center, the child describes the picture's main idea, citing key details that support her statement. After that, the student cuts out the most important part of the picture so it will cover the quilt block's center square. The child embellishes the corners with scraps from her picture, glues the pieces in place, and adds her work to a display titled "Piecing Together Main Ideas."

Carla Terrian, Comanche Intermediate Center, Dodge City, KS

In this picture of a woman playing with her dog.

Patches of the American Revolution

American history

Nathanael Greene was one of the most important military leaders of the Revolutionary War.

Here's a great idea for wrapping up your American Revolution studies! Have each student choose an important revolutionary figure, event, or place. Next, have the child describe his topic, summarize its importance, illustrate it, cut it out, and mount it on a clearly titled red, white, or blue construction paper square. Then display students' work in a repeating pattern with the title "A Revolutionary Patchwork."

Marjie Vertrees, North Harrison Elementary, Ramsey, IN

Focused on Facts

Conducting short research projects (W.4.7, W.5.7)

Have each student choose a current topic of study or a topic in which she is interested. Have the child research the topic and then illustrate it in the center of a copy of a quilt block pattern from page 267. Next, have the student record an important fact about the topic in each small corner section of the quilt block. Then have her summarize her research in the remaining sections around the center. To display students' work, arrange the cutout blocks on a board titled "A Crazy Quilt of Facts."

A Different Angle

Classifying shapes by properties of their lines and angles (4.G.A.2)

Want students to practice describing shapes by their properties? Try this! Display an enlarged copy of a quilt block pattern from page 267 and number a different shape in each section. Then guide students to classify each shape according to whether it has parallel lines, perpendicular lines, acute angles, obtuse angles, or right angles.

Morgan horses

tip Copy page 267 in different colors and then arrange students' work in an eye-catching pattern.

Quilt Block Patterns

Use with "Getting the Point," "A Different Angle," and "Focused on Facts" on page 266.

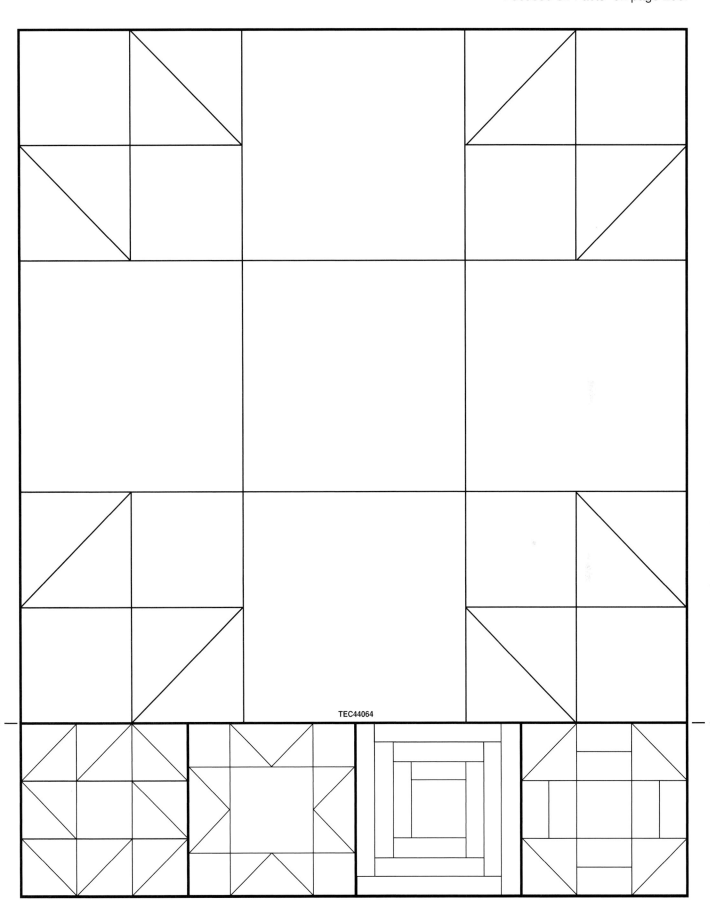

TEC44064

GET THEIR BEST ON THE TEST

5 Easy Ways to Inspire Your Students

1 Have each student bring a small rock to class. Next, provide permanent markers or bright paints and paintbrushes. Then have each child decorate her rock with a favorite symbol, animal, or design. When it's testing time, have each student place her rock on or in her desk as a reminder that she can "rock" the test.

Colleen Dabney, Williamsburg, VA

2 For this idea, have each child create an imaginary app that includes a tip, rule, or mnemonic device on which he counts. Next, have the child label and decorate a paper square with a symbol for his app and the tip. Then glue students' squares onto bulletin board paper made so it resembles a smartphone or tablet and label the display "Testing: We've Got the 'App-titude'!"

Laura Coleman, Pembroke Pines FSU Campus Charter Elementary, Pembroke Pines, FL

3 To prepare for testing time limits, place an old, nonworking clock where all students can see it. When you make an assignment, give a time limit and have students determine the stop time. Adjust the clock to reflect the end time. Encourage students to compare the current time with the stop time while they work. As students have more practice budgeting their time, they'll become more confident in what they can accomplish within various time limits.

4 Decorate a bulletin board with a fun title related to the upcoming test, such as "Ready, Set, Rock the Test!" Then attach several pens to the display and invite parents, teachers, and other staff members to fill the board with encouraging messages and test-taking tips.

5 Before testing, post motivating statements, such as the one shown, and encourage students to brainstorm others. Then have each child choose a statement and use it to create a motivational mini poster. Before students arrive on the first day of testing, put a poster on each child's desk for a positive greeting. **As an alternative,** have students label and decorate paper cutouts to make buttons, badges, or ribbons for classmates to wear.

Colleen Dabney

I KNOW YOU BROUGHT YOUR "A" GAME!

Thanks for the Memories

Looking for just the right way to celebrate the end of the year? Start here!

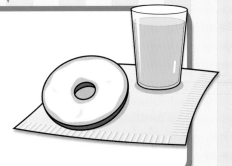

Top of the Morning!

Host an end-of-the-year awards breakfast! Reserve your school cafeteria or another meeting place before the start of a selected school day. Next, contact a few parents to provide coffee, juice, doughnuts, bagels, and paper goods. Then award special student awards or plan the breakfast to coincide with the school's award program. The breakfast takes little preparation and provides a great ending to a successful year!

Home Run Publishing Party!

Celebrate the writing successes of the past year with a baseball-themed publishing party! Divide the program into nine innings. During each inning, have a small group of students share their writing. Then have everyone move around and participate in vocabulary-stretching activities during the seventh inning. In the ninth inning, wrap up the program with a choral reading of "Casey at the Bat" by Ernest Lawrence Thayer and follow up with stadium-style refreshments!

Sweet but Not Sweet

The end of the year can bring mixed emotions. Help students discuss their emotions—excitement about summer vacation, sadness about leaving school and friends, or anxieties about a new year. Then guide each child to write about how she feels. Give students lemonade, lemon drops, or sweet-and-sour gummy candies to snack on while they work. **For a fun follow up**, explain what an *oxymoron* is *(a combination of two words that have nothing to do with each other or even have opposite meanings)*. Display examples—such as *awfully nice*, *dull roar*, *jumbo shrimp*, *same difference*, or *almost totally*—and then challenge students to create a list of oxymoronic terms about summer.

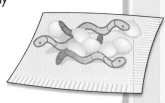

Games Galore!

Play learning games! Get out a timer and an assortment of games students have played throughout the year. Then draw names and set the timer. Have each pair of students play until the timer rings. Then have each twosome rotate to another game. Periodically take a snack break and rearrange student partners for a fun session that takes students down memory and remembering lane!

Top Five!

Celebrate your students' growth with this fun project! Post the suggestions shown and have each child choose one. Next, guide each child to list five items to complete her list, writing the list in reverse order, so that number five is listed first and number one is listed last. Once each child has completed her list, set aside time for her to share it one item at a time, starting with number five and counting down to number one. What a fun way to count down the best parts of the year!

List suggestions:
- Five Facts I Learned This Year
- Five Fun Topics We Studied This Year
- Five Things I'd Tell a Student Who's Going to Be in My Teacher's Class Next Year
- Five Math Problems I Couldn't Have Solved Last Year but Can Solve Now
- Five Things I'll Never Forget About
- Five Fascinating People I Learned About This Year
- Five of My Favorite Characters From Stories and Books We Read This Year
- Five Things I'm Really Glad I Did This Year

Moving On

Help students who are going to middle school in the next school year celebrate their legacies with this moving display. After discussing students' changing roles throughout elementary school, read the poem shown. Then guide each student to write about what he hopes to be remembered for at this school and the elementary lessons that will help him succeed in middle school and beyond. Next, have each child create a life-size profile of himself walking. After that, have the student staple the final copy of his work inside construction paper cut so it resembles a bag or backpack and glue it to his profile. Then display students' creations along a wall titled "Moving On." *Jackie V. Batkins, Seven Pines Elementary, Sandston, VA*

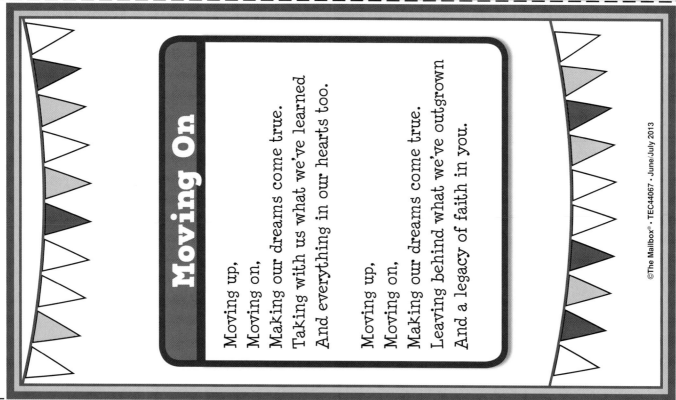

Moving On

Moving up,
Moving on,
Making our dreams come true.
Taking with us what we've learned
And everything in our hearts too.

Moving up,
Moving on,
Making our dreams come true.
Leaving behind what we've outgrown
And a legacy of faith in you.

©The Mailbox® • TEC44067 • June/July 2013

Note to the teacher: Use with "Moving On" on this page.

Top-Notch Tips for Packing up Your Classroom

FIRST BOX

Label a box "1" on every side. Then, as you pack your room, leave the box open for things you use up to the last minute, such as your stapler, scissors, markers, pens, and sticky notes. When it's time to get ready for the new school year, that will be the first box you open, and it will have all the tools you need to get started! **Nikki McDorman, Fort Worth, TX**

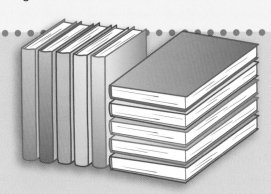

IT ALL ADDS UP

Make it easier to count textbooks with a little help from your students! As students turn in their textbooks, have them stack their books in alternating groups of five books. Then you can easily count the books by fives, even if you're across the room! **Suzanne Whitehurst, Lake Magdalene Elementary, Tampa, FL**

THE LITTLE THINGS...

Instead of tossing little items from around your room into the nooks and crannies of this box or that crate, try this! Use heavy tape to attach small bags or manila envelopes to the inside of your closet doors. Then fill the bags with bulletin board letters, dice, overhead manipulatives, balloons, pipe cleaners, or other small items. They'll be right at your fingertips, and you won't have to wonder which box you dropped them into. If you use manila envelopes, be sure to label each one for quick reference! **Gaylin Black, Westside Elementary, Angleon, TX**

OPEN HOUSE FILE

Don't toss those class awards, pictures of class activities, or notes from and about this year's students! Keep them in a file labeled "Open House." Then, when you're preparing for next year's open house, pull out the file and post its contents to give your new students' parents a glimpse of the fun and learning yet to come. **Colleen Dabney, Williamsburg, VA**

AT THE READY

Pack a handy checklist in your first box to make sure that, when you come back to school in the fall, you'll start out organized and ready to roll! **Cyndi Smith, Fairview Elementary, Carthage, MO**

See the checklist on page 272!

MORE THAN ONE PLACE

Does filing overwhelm you because some pages belong in too many categories? Try this! Store the materials for a specific topic or unit in a labeled file folder. Then tuck a sheet of paper in each folder titled "See Also." On this page, list other files in which you have tucked ideas that relate to this theme, including magazines with additional material on the topic and relevant websites. **Donna Charles, Southport Elementary, Indianapolis, IN**

LAUNCHING A NEW SCHOOL YEAR!

Back to School or Bust

- ☐ arts-and-crafts materials
- ☐ bulletin boards
- ☐ _____
- ☐ _____
- ☐ classroom equipment
  - ☐ computers
  - ☐ television
  - ☐ projector
  - ☐ telephone
  - ☐ _____
  - ☐ _____
- ☐ classroom furniture
- ☐ classroom library
- ☐ textbooks
- ☐ reference resources (dictionaries, thesauruses, encyclopedias)
- ☐ class list
- ☐ class helper chart
- ☐ class rules
- ☐ class website
- ☐ parent letter_____
- ☐ _____
- ☐ daily schedule
- ☐ seating chart
- ☐ birthday chart
- ☐ weekly lunch menu
- ☐ breakfast menu
- ☐ _____
- ☐ _____

- ☐ first day
  - ☐ lesson plans
  - ☐ getting-acquainted games, activities
  - ☐ class routines
  - ☐ forms parents need to sign and return
  - ☐ _____
  - ☐ _____
  - ☐ _____
- ☐ first week
  - ☐ lesson plans
  - ☐ homework
  - ☐ reading assessment
  - ☐ math assessment
  - ☐ _____
  - ☐ _____
  - ☐ _____
- ☐ students' supply checklist
- ☐ students' special needs or health requests
- ☐ teacher assistant/volunteer tasks
  - ☐ _____
  - ☐ _____
  - ☐ _____

Note to the teacher: Use with "At the Ready" on page 271.

DISPLAYS THAT DO MORE THAN DECORATE

DISPLAYS
That Do More Than Decorate

For a fun back-to-school display, write each student's name on a construction paper bowling ball cutout. Then decorate your classroom door with copies of the pin from the bottom of page 275 and the bowling balls. **Donna DeRosa, Good Shepherd Academy, Nutley, NJ**

To make this classroom helper board, enlarge the smartphone on page 281. Then write each student's name on a speech bubble shape and post one next to each job. Keep the rest of the speech bubbles nearby for easy rotating at the beginning of each week. **Paige Brizek, Mt. Nittany Middle School, State College, PA**

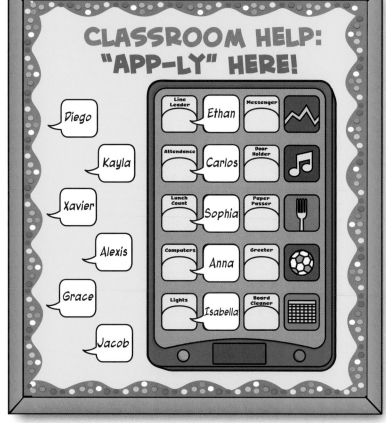

A Wall of TRANSITIONAL WORDS

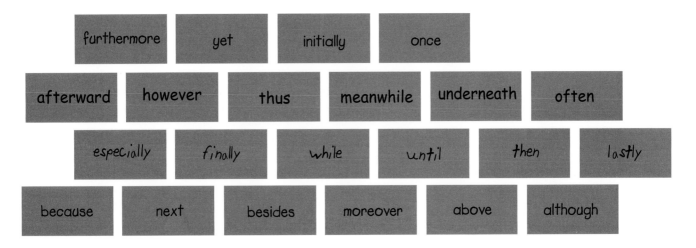

furthermore	yet	initially	once		
afterward	however	thus	meanwhile	underneath	often
especially	finally	while	until	then	lastly
because	next	besides	moreover	above	although

Help students remember to use transitional words with this sturdy display. Have each pair of students cut a sheet of red construction paper into six 3" x 6" bricks and then skim a how-to book or other informational text, looking for transitional words. The partners record each word they find on a brick and then add it to the display to build a reference wall one brick at a time. (W.4.3c, W.5.3c)

Bowling Pin Pattern
Use with "Fifth Grade Is Right Up Our Alley!" on page 274.

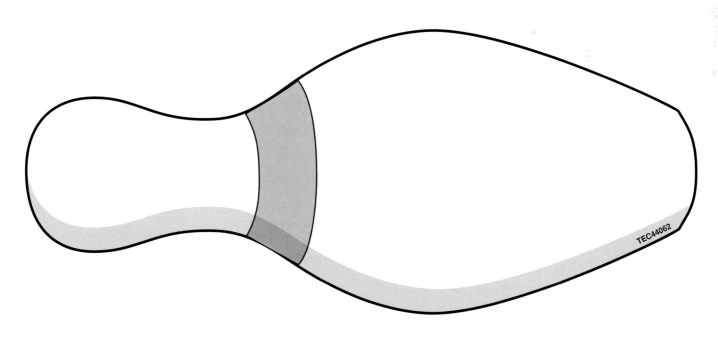

TEC44062

DISPLAYS That Do More Than Decorate

Keep your early finishers engaged with this display. Enlarge the cap pattern from page 282. Then make copies of the feather patterns on the page and program each one with a different task, such as those shown. Post the cap and feathers on a display handy for all your early finishers. **Colleen Dabney, Williamsburg, VA**

For this tempting student work display, put up a plastic tablecloth for the background. Then have each student make a personalized paper pizza (pattern on page 283) and post it on the board. Have the child choose a sample of her best work, explain her choice on a pizza topping shape, and staple her work along with the explanation on top of her pizza. Regularly rotate students' samples. *Fantastico*! **Julia Alarie, Williston, VT**

DISPLAYS That Do More Than Decorate

Inve$t in Your VOCABULARY!

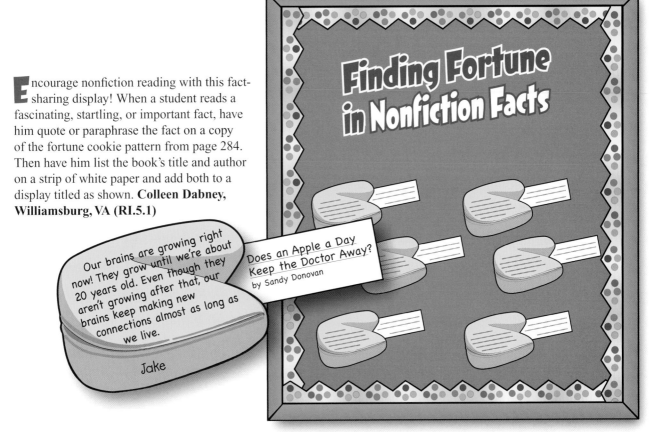

Bring value to students' vocabulary skills! Have each child personalize a copy of the piggy bank pattern from the top of page 284; then staple her bank to the display so it forms a pocket. Have the student record and define new vocabulary terms on copies of the currency pattern from page 284. Next, have the student put the bills in her bank, withdrawing them during free time or at your request to review alone or with a partner. **adapted from an idea by Earnie Wade, Wetumpka Intermediate, Wetumpka, AL (L.4.4, L.5.4)**

Encourage nonfiction reading with this fact-sharing display! When a student reads a fascinating, startling, or important fact, have him quote or paraphrase the fact on a copy of the fortune cookie pattern from page 284. Then have him list the book's title and author on a strip of white paper and add both to a display titled as shown. **Colleen Dabney, Williamsburg, VA (RI.5.1)**

Finding Fortune in Nonfiction Facts

Our brains are growing right now! They grow until we're about 20 years old. Even though they aren't growing after that, our brains keep making new connections almost as long as we live.

Jake

Does an Apple a Day Keep the Doctor Away?
by Sandy Donovan

For this good-work display, have each student draw and color a winter scene on a copy of the snow globe pattern at the bottom of this page. Then direct each student to choose an example of her work that shows growth or her best efforts. Post the child's snow globe and work on a board decorated as shown. **adapted from an idea by Nancy Cline, Shepherdstown Elementary, Shepherdstown, WV**

tip → For a fun extension, have each child predict the date of the new year's first snow day or storm. Then have the student record her prediction on her snow globe.

Snow Globe Pattern

Use with "A Wonderland of Great Work!" on this page.

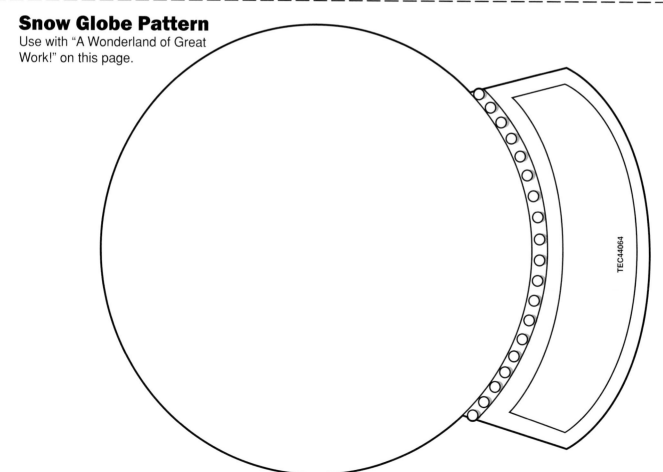

TEC44064

DISPLAYS That Do More Than Decorate

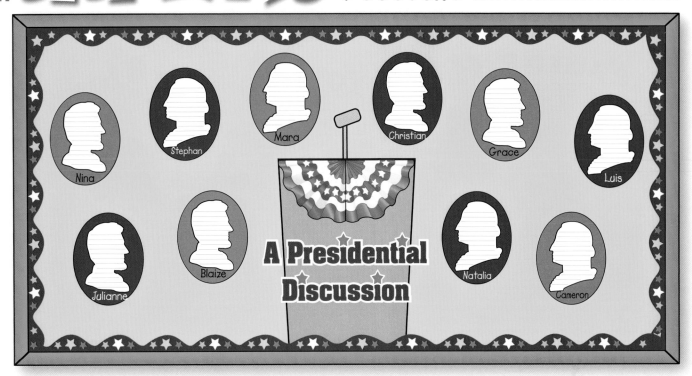

For a Presidents' Day display, have each student respond to the prompt "Being president of the United States would be…" Next, have the child write her response on an enlarged copy of a president pattern from page 285. Then post students' work on a board decorated as shown. **Tzivia Blumenfeld, Mkor Boruch Elementary, Passaic, NJ (W.4.3, W.5.3)**

For this good-work display, have each student choose a sample of his best work. Direct him to label a copy of the pot of gold pattern from page 285 with the reason he chose his sample. Then have the student cut out and color the pot of gold, attach it to his paper, and post his work on a board decorated as shown.

DISPLAYS That Do More Than Decorate

Reading Helps Your Mind Bloom!

For this double-duty display, have students record the titles of their favorite poems, articles, stories, and books on colorful one-inch paper strips, making sure they use the correct punctuation. Then have the students staple the strips and construction paper scraps to a display titled as shown, creating flowers that share their reading recommendations! *Punctuating titles (L.5.2d)* **adapted from an idea by Denise Wilson, Russellville Elementary, Russellville, AL**

We're HOOKED on Mnemonic Clues!

Please Excuse My Dear Aunt Sally

HOMES

Dad, Mom, Sister, Brother

ROY G. BIV

Never Eat Soggy Waffles

Here's a fun way to remind students of catchy phrases for hard-to-remember facts and processes! Program copies of the fish patterns on page 286 with the phrases and then add them to a board decorated as shown. **Colleen Dabney, Williamsburg, VA**

Feather and Cap Patterns

Use with "Finished? Feathers for Your Thinking Cap" on page 276.

TEC44063

TEC44063

TEC44063

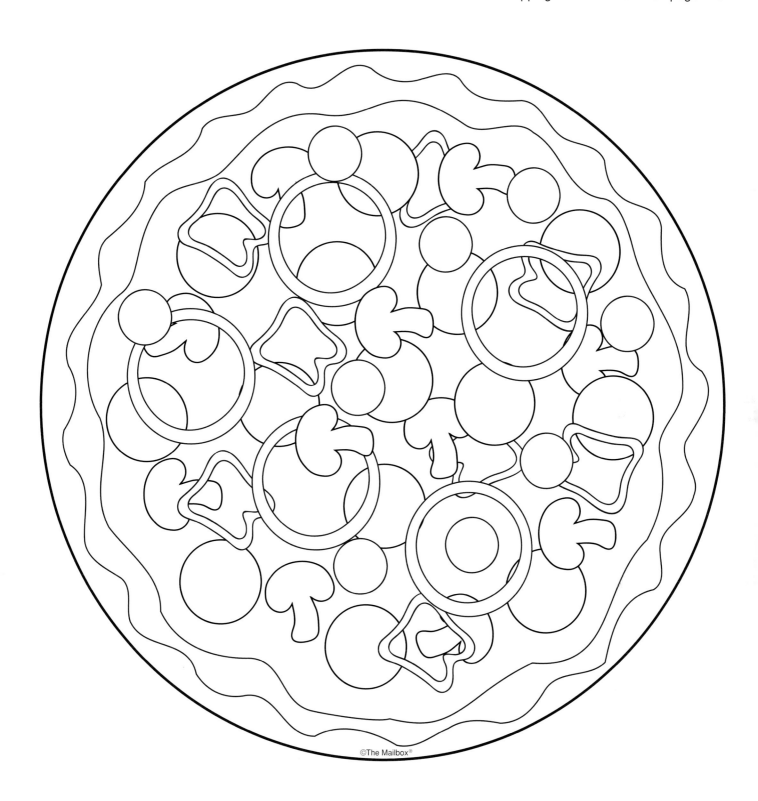

©The Mailbox®

Piggy Bank and Dollar Bill Patterns

Use with "Invest in Your Vocabulary!" on page 277.

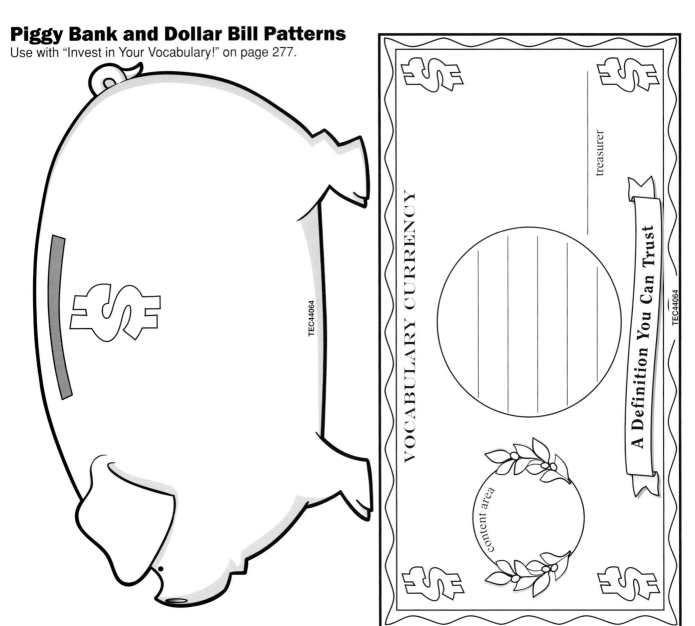

VOCABULARY CURRENCY

treasurer

content area

A Definition You Can Trust

TEC44064

Fortune Cookie Pattern

Use with "Finding Fortune in Nonfiction Facts" on page 277.

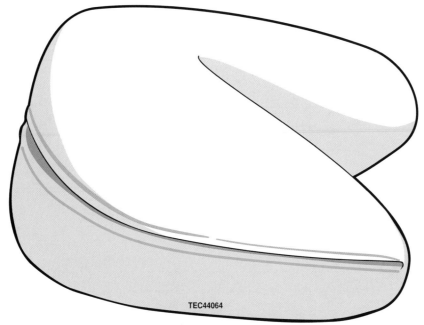

TEC44064

President Patterns

Use with "A Presidential Discussion" on page 279.

TEC44065

TEC44065

Pot of Gold Pattern

Use with "Good as Gold" on page 279.

TEC44065

Fish Patterns

Use with "We're Hooked on Mnemonic Clues!" on page 280.

TEC44066

TEC44066

PROBLEM SOLVED!

Problem Solved!

How do you establish *class rules*?

Your Solutions to Classroom Challenges

On the first day of school, I teach my students that the **3 Rs**—responsibility, respect, and readiness—rule our way of working in the classroom. Then I have students define the terms and brainstorm ways they should and shouldn't act. I praise my students' behaviors, and, most of all, I try to be responsible, respectful, and ready every day.

Lidia Cisneros, Horace Mann Elementary, San Jose, CA

At the start of the year, I have my students sit in groups of four and create lists of agreements they think would help our class run smoothly. Then each group presents its list to the class. The class picks the group's most important agreement, and we add it to the official **Class Agreements chart**. (Students know I have the final say, but I make sure one idea from each group makes it to the chart.) Then I have each student sign the bottom of the chart (somewhat like the Constitution).

Renee Silliman, Spring Shadows Elementary, Houston, TX

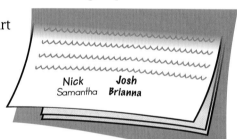

I introduce each rule one at a time. After introducing a rule, I ask a student volunteer to **role-play** a situation involving the rule with me. In the role-play, I break the rule. Next, I have the volunteer and the rest of my students write about the situation and my actions. Then I have them describe the classroom and real-world consequences. After I've introduced all the rules, we have a class discussion to answer any questions.

Karen Kanter, Franklin Middle School, Somerset, NJ

After introducing the class rules, I set up a quick reward for following them! I draw a banner across the top of my board. On the banner, I draw a blank line for each letter of the sentence "We choose to be our best!" Then, whenever I see a student, a group of students, or the class conscientiously following a class rule, I add a letter to the sentence. As soon as we finish the sentence, we celebrate with ten minutes of extra recess or a homework-free night!

Terri Schonhoff, St. Charles School, Bloomington, IN

"Every student knows that he or she is to behave. They are just waiting for the discipline plan to be revealed so that they know the limits of the classroom."
—Harry and Rosemary Wong

It's your turn! Share your ideas.
themailbox.com/submitideas

Problem Solved!

How do you assess *kids who don't test well*?

Your Solutions to Classroom Challenges

For **students who have trouble with written responses**, I read each question aloud to the student and have him give his response orally. Then I jot notes about his answer on a copy of the test and use the information to find his total score. As the year progresses and his confidence grows, I read fewer questions aloud and have him write more of his answers.

Amy Payne, Clara J. Peck Elementary, Greensboro, NC

I put sets of ten test items in learning centers and on independent practice sheets to get more information about **students who have test anxiety**. I number each set and, after a child completes it, record her results on an index card labeled with the matching skill. After a child takes a test, I refer to the card to compare her results with how she responded in less stressful circumstances.

Ann E. Fisher, Toledo, OH

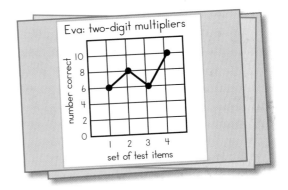

Eva: two-digit multipliers

Researchers conducting a study on the effects of high-stakes testing, predicted that as many as ten million elementary and secondary students in the United States perform poorer on tests than they should because of test anxiety and weak test-taking strategies.

To **make vocabulary tests less intimidating**, I divide the words and definitions into groups of five words rather than ten or more at a time. This means a student can focus on just a few concepts instead of trying to remember all the definitions at once.

Lavone Novotny, Liberty Elementary, Caledonia, OH

I **give students an extra boost of confidence** by using bold print to signal key words in directions. This helps each student focus on the task, and it helps her make sure she completes all the steps.

Lavone Novotny

Chapter 4 Test
1. The sun provides energy to Earth. **Give an example** of one living thing that uses the sun's energy and **explain** what would happen without it.

_____

_____

_____

It's your turn! Share your ideas.
Go to themailbox.com/mailboxideas

Problem Solved!

Your Solutions to Classroom Challenges

Even older students come to class wanting to share stories about their families, friends, and the latest happenings, especially at this time of year. To avoid the delays these stories can cause, I set aside a **bulletin board for our class news** and keep paper titled "Ms. Boynton's Class News" nearby. Then, if a student gets off topic, I point out that his story would be a great event to post on our class news board. Students use free time to write their stories and post them on the board. During transitions I have student volunteers read their news aloud!

Charlene Boynton, Paige Elementary, Schenectady, NY

How do you keep students engaged *during the week or days before a school holiday?*

We do a **readers' theater** production! I choose a script that fits the holiday and grabs my students' interest. During the week, students keep busy practicing their parts (all the while improving their reading fluency skills). Then we wrap up the week with a performance for another class!

Cristin Sayers, Robison Elementary, Erie, PA

tip Can't find the perfect readers' theater script? Have students create their own using picture books or novel chapters that contain plenty of dialogue!

I help students **set behavior and performance goals for the week**. Then I give each child a sticky note and have her draw a T chart on it labeled "Stick With It" and "Stuck With It." Anytime the student recognizes a challenging situation, she draws a tally in the "Stick With It" column. If she successfully avoids the pitfall, she draws a tally in the "Stuck With It" column. During the week, we review each student's progress, celebrating the successes and making plans for the next pitfalls.

I will make sure I finish my work instead of talking to my neighbors.	
Stick With It	Stuck With It
III	II

Kim Minafo, Apex, NC

To make sure my students don't check out yet, I stock up on healthy snacks and then designate certain classes as **Work-and-Eat sessions**. Before one of these surprise sessions, I write "Work and Eat" on the board. Then I give each student who meaningfully participates a snack to eat while we work. (I don't hand out a snack unless the student is really involved!) Participation climbs dramatically!

Felicia Collier, Saluda Trail Middle, Rock Hill, SC

Even though winter break doesn't cause brain drain like summer vacation does, the National Urban Alliance recommends giving students a fun project to work on during winter vacation. Children who engage their brains every day during breaks from school tend to return more interested in what they're studying than those who don't.

It's your turn! Share your ideas.
Go to themailbox.com/mailboxideas

Problem Solved!

How do you get school *off to an effective start* each day?

Your Solutions to Classroom Challenges

 I keep pocket folders labeled with the days of the week stapled to the bulletin board closest to my classroom door. At the beginning of the week, I stock each folder with work for each day. Then, each morning, students walk into the room, grab the papers they need, and quietly start working as soon as the bell rings. *Sheri Switzer, Northridge Middle School, Crawfordsville, IN*

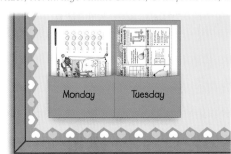

 I greet each student individually every morning. As each child walks in the room, I look her in the eye and say, "Good morning." Then I shake her hand, pat her on the back, or give her a quick hug or a meaningful nod. *Laurie Currence, Oak Woods School, Granbury, TX*

"Focus is the process of directing one's attention to a specific issue for an extended period of time, and is addressed in much of the literature as attention. Teachers can provide guidelines to students to help them control and increase their attention…."
R. J. Marzano

 Once I establish my morning routine so that my students know I expect them to come in and get right to work, I add daily themes.

- **Math Monday:** I put math review problems on the board and have students solve the problems in their math journals.
- **Tell-All Tuesday:** I ask students to write all they know about a topic we've recently studied or to share their background knowledge on an upcoming topic.
- **Wordy Wednesday:** I list everyday words and challenge students to find ten or more synonyms and/or antonyms for each word.
- **Thinking Thursday:** I write a quotation on the board. Then students write what they think it means and why they think that.
- **Free Friday:** I include short writing prompts, coloring pages, math flash cards, vocabulary crossword puzzles, and other self-checking pages.

Becky Fuentes, Highland Elementary, Lake Stevens, WA

 Before my students arrive each day, I start playing a CD of soft music and dim the lights. As each child enters, he moves his nametag to show his lunch choice for the day and that he is present. Next, the student responds to a posted journal prompt and begins working on a daily math sheet. Within ten minutes of the school bell, I turn off the music and turn on the lights. Then I greet my students, lead them in the Pledge of Allegiance, and move into the first lesson of the day.

Shirley Kohls, Wilson Elementary, Beaver Dam, WI

It's your turn! Share your ideas.
themailbox.com/submitideas

Problem Solved!

How do you *manage transitions?*

Your Solutions to Classroom Challenges

I **use review questions my students write** to make sure we don't waste time standing in line. During every unit we study, I have my students write questions and answers about the topic on index cards. I double-check the cards for accuracy and then slip them into a pocket chart labeled with each subject. Then, if my students are lined up and ready to go, but we have to wait, I draw a card and read a question. I award a class point for every correct answer, keeping a running tally toward a whole-class reward.

Kathryn Davenport, Partin Elementary, Oviedo, FL

If you lose ten minutes a day to transitions from one activity to another, that's 29 hours of lost instructional time in one school year! (Ten lost minutes a day times 174 school days equals 1,740 minutes or 29 hours.)

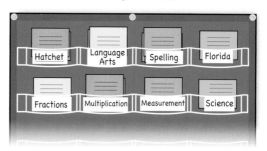

When it's time to transition between subjects or classes, I announce which materials students will need and **set a time limit**. If every student is not prepared and quiet when the time is up, I start my "Waste Timer" and count each extra second. I record the wasted seconds on the board throughout the day and add them up at the end of the day when we discuss the impact of wasted time. Then we start each new day with the goal of beating yesterday's wasted time!

Jessica Lawler, Abundant Life Academy, Nutley, NJ

Waste Timer

17 seconds

When one of my students is causing a ruckus during a transition, I **remind myself that discipline is one of the things I teach** my students. Then, using the same tone and mind-set I would use to correct a spelling or grammar error, I avoid a power struggle by calmly and quietly talking to the child and reminding him how to behave in this situation.

Julia Alarie, Williston, VT

To **keep my students engaged as they transition** from one activity to the next, I ask a question, pose a brain teaser, or quote a thought-provoking statement with a connection to something we're studying. Next, I give students one minute to clean up their areas or prepare for the next activity. By the end of the minute, I expect each child to be ready and to have an answer to the question or teaser or a reaction to the quote.

Jennifer Deluca, Julius West Middle School, Rockville, MD

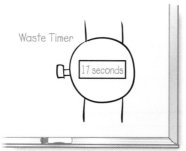

What are three possible causes for the following effect? Jed put his bread in the toaster, but it did not get toasted.

It's your turn! Share your ideas.
themailbox.com/submitideas

OUR READERS WRITE

Our Readers WRITE...
(and EMAIL and BLOG and TWEET and POST)

"I have been teaching for 26 years and *The Mailbox* has been a part of my classroom for most of those years!*—Debbie Fodrie via Facebook*

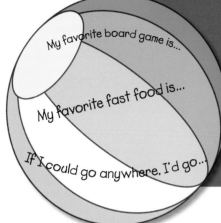

My favorite board game is...

My favorite fast food is...

If I could go anywhere, I'd go...

Beach Ball Ice Breaker

To **get to know my new students**, I write 20 different sentence starters on an inflatable beach ball. Then, during the first day of school, I toss the ball to a student. I ask her to complete a starter near her right thumb and toss the ball back to me. I complete one of the sentence starters and toss the ball to another student. We play until every student has a chance to share something. I also use the beach ball later in the year anytime a new student joins our class! *Jennifer Piechocki, St. Pius X School, Southgate, MI*

The "Write" Tools

At the beginning of the school year, I bring in a **writing toolbox**. I talk about the items inside and then put the toolbox on display as a handy reminder. As I work with student writers, it's easy to target specific writing skills by cueing students to think about a certain writing tool—corny, but effective! *Donna Spannagel, Cumberland Middle School, Toledo, IL*

Writing Toolbox

- A variety of pens and pencils—Having a pen or pencil that is comfortable to write with is like having sports equipment that is just right for you.
- A telephone receiver—Identify the audience of every paper you write and focus on that audience as you write.
- A shower hook—Remember to hook your audience by asking a question, beginning with a quote, telling a joke, or starting with an interjection.
- A box of crayons—Always add color and descriptive details to your writing.
- A compass—Are you staying on track?
- A mirror—Reflect on your writing. Does it say what you wanted it to say?

MAKING IT COUNT

One of my biggest challenges as a math teacher was convincing my students to **check the reasonableness** of their answers. Then I tried asking students to think about a problem as if it involved money—their own money. Suddenly, the answer mattered, and the students were more interested in taking the extra step to review their answers. *Amy Dalley, Naalehu Elementary, Naalehu, HI*

Sixteen hundred divided by four equals forty? If you divided sixteen hundred dollars among four friends, would you be satisfied with a forty dollar share?

The **MAILBOX** BLOG

"Opening *The Mailbox* magazine and books is like Christmas for me. I can always count on finding fresh twists for teaching traditional concepts."*—Marcia Snarski Wuest via Facebook*

Nothing to Sneeze At

For the **first book report** of the school year, I have each student describe her book's story elements on construction paper pieces cut to fit the sides of a tissue box. Then I have the child glue each piece to a new, unopened tissue box (one of the many students have brought in). I grade students' reports on separate forms and stack the boxes on our class shelves. They look great, and when it's time to put out a fresh tissue box, I take one from the shelf and have the student whose work is on the box share her report before putting the box out for general use. (This is one project we toss instead of sending home.) *Patricia Twohey, Smithfield, RI*

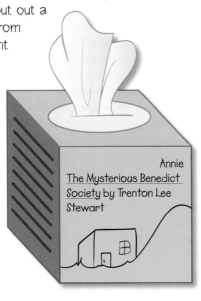

Annie
The Mysterious Benedict Society by Trenton Lee Stewart

ON THE FIRST...

I love to share celebrations with my students, so I came up with **monthly mini holidays** that are not based on religious events. My students and I celebrate the first school day of every month. For each celebration, we have a healthy snack and I give them small trinkets that I incorporate into lessons throughout the day. For example, on the first school day of last September, I gave each student a small container of clay. (I found them at a local discount store for less than a dollar each!) Students used the clay to make models of main characters and to squeeze while they wrote. Then we had an afternoon snack of dried apples, and students took the clay home for spelling practice. *Wendy Whitney-Scherer, Wyalusing Academy, Prairie du Chien, WI*

Four-Fold Strategy

To help my students be organized **problem solvers**, I have them fold their paper into four columns. After a child reads a problem, he circles key facts and terms, such as numbers and clue words. Next, the student records each circled item in the first column on his paper and rereads the problem. In the second column, the child writes the problem's question. In the third column, the student works the problem, finding the answer. Then, in the fourth column, he explains how he got his answer. *Abigail Green, McIntire Munson Elementary, Zanesville, OH*

38 each	If each box contains 26 treats. how many treats does he have in all?	38 × 26 ————— 228 + 760 ————— 988	I multiplied the number of treats in each box by the number of boxes.
26 in all			

Bowser's favorite doggie treats are on sale. Bowser buys (38) small boxes. If (each) box contains (26) treats, how many treats does he have (in all)?

Our Readers WRITE...
(and EMAIL and BLOG and TWEET and POST)

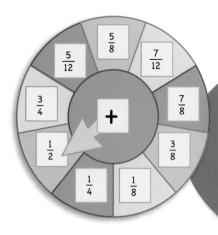

Wheel of Fractions
(4.NF.B.3a, 5.NF.A.1)

To give my students practice adding and subtracting fractions, I reuse my Uno game spinner. Depending on the practice a small group of students needs, I write fractions with like denominators or unlike denominators on small sticky notes and stick them over the sections on the spinner. Next, I put a sticky note in the center of the spinner so the group knows which operation to perform. Then the students take turns spinning, recording fractions, and adding or subtracting them. *Beth Vos, St. Stephen the Martyr School, Omaha, NE*

MEANINGFUL MELODY

Before my students start reading, I sing a catchy tune that reminds them to think while they read. *Barclay Marcell, Chicago, IL*

Reading Strategy Song
(sung to the tune of "If You're Happy and You Know It")

If you want to get the meaning
When you read,
If you want to get the meaning
When you read,

Ask questions and find answers
And check your background
knowledge.
'Cause you need to get the meaning
When you read!

The MAILBOX BLOG

We use a bulletin board in the main hallway of our school to display photos of staff members reading in various places. As the year progresses, the kids bring in pictures of themselves reading and we add them to the board. We see people reading in other countries, in their homes, and with their children or pets!—*Anne Robinett via The Mailbox® Blog*

"I don't know what I'd do without *The Mailbox®* magazines! I love the easy, practical, and relevant activities in each magazine. My students always love the activities, and the magazine saves me a ton of time!"—*Danielle Hudson via Facebook*

Games Galore!

My students know that, when there is indoor recess, a review game is in order! I keep handy a list of easily adaptable games that my students love to play. When the recess bell rings, I randomly list six of the games and have a student roll a die. Then we play the game that matches the number she rolls, and everybody wins! *Laura Johnson, South Decatur Elementary, Greensburg, IN*

1. Tic-tac-toe: Divide the class into teams and ask a review question before each turn.
2. Charades: Students act out scenes from historic events, novels, lives of important people, and even scientific processes.
3. Around the World
4. The class's favorite board game: Divide the class into teams and ask a review question before each turn.
5. Buzz, or Sparkle
6. Battleship Spelling

Our Readers WRITE...

SOMETHING TO PONDER

At the beginning of each week, I post a quote. My students copy the quote in their journals and then write about what it means to them and how it might apply to them. Throughout the week, we discuss the quote and students share their thoughts. Then, on Friday, I have each student revisit the quote and paraphrase it in his own words. *Amy Stokes, Lebanon Road Elementary, Charlotte, NC (W.4.10, W.5.10)*

> "Reading is to the mind what exercise is to the body."
> Joseph Addison

I love using *The Mailbox®* ideas and activities as a curriculum supplement. Many of the activities are great for creating portable centers. I put the activities in resealable plastic bags, baskets, or recycled shoeboxes so students can complete the activities anywhere!—*Charisse Audra Collier via Facebook*

Career-Minded

I want more of my students to pursue science careers, so I have them research occupations such as engineers, environmentalists, and veterinarians. Once each student chooses an occupation to study, I give him a form to guide his research. (To make sure a variety of careers are researched, I let only two students research the same specific field.) Next, each child uses his research to create a poster that will persuade fellow students to consider his field. Then students share their work in an afternoon version of a career night! *Beverly Tatum, York West End Junior High, York, AL (W.4.7, W.5.7)*

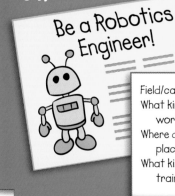

Be a Robotics Engineer!

Field/career:
What kind of tasks does a person working in this field do?
Where does this kind of work take place?
What kind of education and/or training is required?

Geometric Gestures

To help my students understand lines and angles, I challenge them to create arm movements that represent lines, line segments, rays, points, intersecting lines, and angles. After they practice their movements, we use them in a game of Simon Says. It's a great transition activity, reason to get students out of their seats, and quick assessment of students' understanding of concepts! *Tiffany Kimball, Esperanza Elementary, Farmington, NM (4.G.A.1)*

Line segment!

The MAILBOX BLOG

I think the key to working with parents is building relationships. I try to have a social gathering once a month so that parents can get to know each other and their children's friends.—*Karri Nachtigal via The Mailbox® Blog*

Our Readers WRITE...
(and EMAIL and BLOG and TWEET and POST)

Judge a Book

Wondering what to do with extra book club flyers? I use them to give students practice **identifying an author's purpose**. I have each student fold a large sheet of construction paper into fourths and then unfold it and label each section with a different author's purpose. Next, each child reads through the flyer's summaries, cutting out examples for each type of author's purpose and gluing them to her paper. It's a resourceful and fun review! *Amy Stokes, Lebanon Road Elementary, Charlotte, NC*

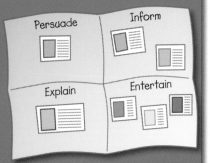

Persuade | Inform
Explain | Entertain

The **MAILBOX** BLOG

SHAPING UP (4.G.A.1–3)

I use clay for a hands-on **geometry assessment** that my students love! To check geometry concepts, I give each child a bit of clay and ask her to mold it into specific forms or shapes. As each student molds the clay, I walk around the room, taking notes about which child needs to review which concept. I can give quick corrections or follow up later with students in small groups. *Lynn Schramel, Rochester City School #1, Rochester, NY*

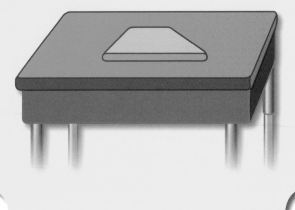

Show me a quadrilateral with two acute angles, two obtuse angles, and two parallel sides.

A Great Act

To help students **build inferring skills**, I challenge them to name words in games of charades. I list emotion terms, character traits, or vocabulary words on paper strips. Then I have a student volunteer take a strip and silently act out the word for the class. If a class member names a synonym for the word, the acting student draws the letter *S* in the air to indicate a synonym has been named and students refine their guesses. When the term is correctly named, we discuss the clues that led to the guess. This is a great introduction to a reading lesson, as students are already reading between the lines! *Kimberly Richman, The Learning Zone, Des Moines, IA*

disappointed | eager | selfish | polite | courageous

Our Readers WRITE...

DISCUSSION STARTER

Reading aloud to my students is a great way to generate discussions on topics we're currently studying. Several mornings a week, I choose two or three picture books that address a particular theme, topic, or genre. I display the books on a whiteboard ledge. As my students arrive, each child places a tally mark above the book he wants to hear. Then I read the book with the most votes as a lead-in to a conversation in which students are already invested. *Teresa Vilfer-Synder, Fredericktown, OH*

The MAILBOX BLOG

Praiseworthy Email

My best tip for working with parents is to send them a quick email about something specific their child said or did in class. The biggest hit is to send a photo of their child working on something.—*Jill Exe, Harold Kaveolook School, Kaktovik, AK, via The Mailbox® Blog*

The MAILBOX BLOG

"I love *The Mailbox* magazines. I have kept them over the years and have quite a collection! The magazines are jam-packed full of great stuff!—*Mary McGowan via The Mailbox® Blog*

Get Down With Division (4.NBT.B.6)

When we start a division lesson, we warm up with this **long-division cheer.** I also teach my students to do a quiet version without cheering and snapping their fingers so they can remember the steps while they work independently. *Sharon Moder, North Dearborn Elementary, Guilford, IN*

Divide!	*Extend both arms straight out on each side.*
Multiply!	*Cross arms in front of body in the form of an X.*
Subtract!	*Uncross arms and place them on top of each other parallel to the floor.*
Check!	*Snap fingers on both hands.*
Bring down!	*Bend elbows with fists pointing toward ceiling. Pump arms.*

Fair Game

Different types of questions make this **football review game** a success for all my students. To begin, I draw a football field on the board, divide the class into two teams, and place a game marker for each team in one end zone. In turn, a student chooses a question by its yardage: 5 yards (true or false), 10 yards (multiple choice), 15 yards (fill in the blank), 20 yards (give a definition), or 25 yards (open-ended question). If the student is correct, she moves her team's marker ahead the matching number of yards. Once a team reaches the opposite end zone, it earns six points. We play until I run out of questions or we run out of time. The team with more points is the winning team, but this game scores with all my students! *Laura Johnson, South Decatur Elementary, Greensburg, IN*

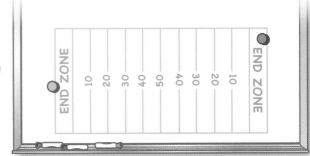

Our Readers WRITE...
(and EMAIL and BLOG and TWEET and POST)

A "Re-marker-able" Review

To review any skill or topic, I use an activity that has become a class favorite! After dividing the class into groups, I ask each group to write three review questions or problems on index cards. When groups are finished, I collect the cards, give each child a dry-erase marker and a tissue, and have students clear their desks. Then I project one of the questions on the board. Each student writes the answer directly on his desktop with the marker. After I quickly glance at students' answers, they wipe their desks clean to get ready for the next question. **Alice Derrick, Eastside Elementary, Clinton, MS**

What is the verb phrase?

My dog has eaten all of his food.

has eaten

 "I love all the resources from *The Mailbox*® magazines!"—*Sandra Freeland via Facebook*

Magic Number

For a quick mental math drill I can use all year long, I tape a number line from 0 to 9 on each child's desk. Then I give my students clues toward finding a "magic number," such as "My number is not one of the digits in the difference of 100 minus 50 minus 20 minus 6." My students calculate the answer in their heads. *(24)* Then each child uses a dry-erase marker to mark off the two digits in the answer *(2 and 4)* on her number line. I continue with more clues until the magic number is revealed. *Heather Finn, Grant Line Elementary, New Albany, IN*

PAPER-SAVING STUDY GUIDE

When I use PowerPoint presentation software to present information to my students, I make a one- or two-page condensed copy of the slides for each student. I tell him to cut out each slide, leaving a two-centimeter border on the left of each one. Then I have the student staple or glue the slides together, in order, to make a minibooklet study guide. **Karen Slattery, Dunrankin Drive Public School, Mississauga, Ontario, Canada**

Rocks and Minerals

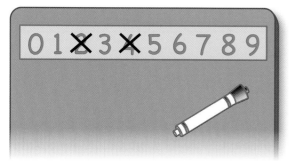

Gavin
The Perfect Hideaway

MAP MYSTERIES
(W.4.3, W.5.3, RL.4.1, RL.5.1)

I use directory maps from sites such as shopping malls, museums, and amusement parks to reinforce inferring, map, and writing skills. I laminate an assortment of maps and place them at my writing center. I have a student take a map and choose a secret location on it. Next, he writes a story about his day at the site, including clues about the secret spot. Then his classmates read the story and use the map to identify the mystery location. **Rebecca Juneau, Highland Elementary, Lake Stevens, WA**

Field Trip Finds

Before a field trip, I go online and research the facility we will visit to create a challenging scavenger hunt for my students. I select ten obvious and ten hard-to-find items that I want students to find. On the day of the trip, I give each pair of students a copy of the scavenger list. I direct students to quietly mark off each item they notice and record its location. When we return to the classroom, students tell where the items on the list were located. **Terry Healy, Marlatt Elementary, Manhattan, KS**

Scavenger Hunt
Science Museum

- ☐ largest dinosaur leg bone
- ☐ trilobite
- ☐ saber-toothed tiger
- ☐ woolly mammoth
- ☐ prehistoric fossil

The MAILBOX BLOG

An Evening Read-Aloud

To emphasize the importance of reading at home, we hold a family reading night at our school. Each teacher picks a story to read aloud, and families can come dressed in their pajamas. We keep the evening organized and on schedule by having each family join a group. To start, each group goes to its first scheduled reader. After a set amount of time, a bell rings and each group moves to the next reader, rotating around the school, hearing one great story after another. Throughout the evening, our parent-teacher organization serves milk and cookies. It's an unforgettable evening for everyone!—**Cheryl Ener via The Mailbox® Blog**

Don't Let the Pigeon Drive the Bus!

words and pictures by mo willems

Our Readers WRITE...
(and EMAIL and BLOG and TWEET and POST)

All Systems Go

To maximize my technology center, I keep a spreadsheet of programs or apps that I want my students to use. I set up the spreadsheet so there is a column for the name of each program or app, device or equipment with the program, skill being reinforced or practiced, and difficulty levels. I post the spreadsheet at the center where it's handy for my students and me! *Brenda Armstrong, Ann Whitney Elementary, Hamilton, TX*

Ms. Armstrong's Tech Center			
Program/App	Device/Equipment	Skill	Levels

The MAILBOX BLOG

A Musical Cue

I use a music box to get my students to line up quickly. I wind the box on Monday morning. Then, each time my students line up, I let the music play, stopping it as soon as my students are in line and ready to move out the door. At the end of the day on Friday, I play the music box. If there is any music left, I reward the class with extra recess time the next week. *Jody Erickson via The Mailbox® Blog*

f **I have been a subscriber for 15 years.**—*Andrea Liebowitz via Facebook*

In Touch With Learning

For a fun springtime review, I bring out sweetened powdered drink mix. I pour a bit of the mix onto a paper plate for each child. Then I pose a question and have each student write her answer with her finger in the powdered mix. I quickly check students' answers before having them gently tap their plates to level the powder; then I can ask the next question. What a fun way to practice spelling, math facts, and more! *Debra Frost, Austintown Middle School, Youngstown, OH*

PART OF A PAIR

I put students' fraction skills to work when I want to randomly pair students! I write pairs of equivalent fractions on lids from plastic water bottles, making sure I have one lid for each student. (If you have an odd number of students, add an extra unlabeled lid.) Then I put the lids in a container. When students need a partner, I have each child take a lid from the container. Then, on my signal, each child finds the classmate whose lid has the equivalent fraction. If a child gets the unlabeled lid, I let him join a pair of his choice. *Heidi Gross, Avoca Central School, Avoca, NY*

$$\frac{9}{24}$$

$$\frac{3}{8}$$

Initial Rounds

Here's a review game students love to play. I put a set of plastic letters in a bag and divide the class into two teams. Next, I have each student write her initials at the top of her paper. Then I ask a question and draw a letter from the bag as students record their answers. After I announce the answer, I reveal the letter. Each student with a matching initial and the correct answer earns a point for her team. I quickly tally points on the board, return the letter to the bag, and ask another question. The team with more points wins! *Laura Mihalenko, Harry S. Truman Elementary, Parlin, NJ*

L. A. B.
photosynthesis
chlorophyll
solar energy

> Find a word that came from another language on page 540.

On the Hunt

When we have a few minutes to spare, I sneak in vocabulary-building fun with this dictionary challenge. I have each child grab a dictionary. Then I name a page number and a clue, such as "Find the longest word on page 80." I have the first student who finds the matching word write it on the board, and we all explore its definition. Then I announce another clue and send students on the hunt again! *Isobel Livingstone, Rahway, NJ*

BRIGHT IDEA

My classroom windows double as writing surfaces! I've had my students use washable window markers when they brainstorm, explore vocabulary, compare and contrast characters, and more. We have even used three windows in a row to create a Venn diagram. When they are writing on the windows, my students are engaged and cleanup is a snap! *Rachel Hillenbrand, J. A. Caywood Elementary, Edgewood, KY*

f I love *The Mailbox*® magazine.—*Linda Matsumoto via Facebook*

Division Ditty

To help my students better remember the steps involved in long division, I made up this song. *Marsha Joyner, Davis Elementary, Marietta, GA*

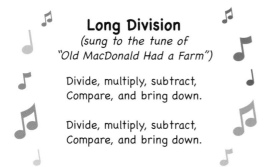

Long Division
(sung to the tune of "Old MacDonald Had a Farm")

Divide, multiply, subtract,
Compare, and bring down.

Divide, multiply, subtract,
Compare, and bring down.

The MAILBOX BLOG

I have my students work on our class overhead projector as one of my language centers. I just put worksheets on skills my students need to practice along with fine-tip markers at the overhead. What looked like a worksheet suddenly becomes an engaging center! *Jill Exe via The Mailbox Blog*

Our Readers WRITE...
(and EMAIL and BLOG and TWEET and POST)

The Sky's the Limit

I take advantage of warm temperatures to challenge my students' circle knowledge. First, I gather several Frisbee flying discs and use masking tape to demonstrate different circle terms. Then I lead students outside and have them scatter within a given space. Next, I throw a disc to a student, have him name the term shown on the disc and then throw it back to me. I throw a different disc to another student, alternating discs until each child has had a turn. **Heidi Gross, Avoca Central School, Avoca, NY**

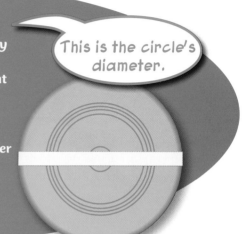

This is the circle's diameter.

Bound Together

To tuck in one more community-building activity at the end of the year, I read aloud *Wilfrid Gordon McDonald Partridge* by Mem Fox. Then I use the story to lead a discussion about different kinds of memories. Next, I guide each child to write about a memory from this school year. After each student edits her work, I copy her final pages. Then I make a book of all the memories for each child. Before we depart as classmates, I set aside time for each student to share her memory. It's a beautiful way to end the year! (W.4.3; W.5.3) *Rachelle Neuman, Torah Academy for Girls, Far Rockaway, NY*

The MAILBOX BLOG

Game Central

I use magazine holders to hold my math games and centers. To keep track of the skills covered by the games, I label the outside of each holder with the game title and the standard or skill it addresses. So, when it's time for me to grab a math game or center, they are all organized and ready to go! **Ashley Cahill, Olympic View Elementary, Lacey, WA**

f "Thanks for such great books—each with lots of wonderful ideas and suggestions... I love *The Mailbox*! I've been a subscriber for many years!"—*Ellen Cleary Bennett via Facebook*

CRAFTING GOOD DIRECTIONS

To help my students understand the importance of using specific details when writing explanatory pieces, I give each pair of students a set of craft materials. (Foam project kits from craft stores are inexpensive timesavers.) Each student assembles the craft and then compares his product with those from the rest of the class. Next, we discuss the projects' differences and the importance of having specific directions to complete a task. Then I have each student write directions that tell how she completed the craft, step-by-step. (W.4.2; W.5.2) **Diana Boykin, DeZavala Elementary, Midland, TX**

First, I

EVERY WORD COUNTS

One way I encourage students to write concise summaries is to charge them fees for the words they use. I tell students that a summary should include all the key information from a reading without wasting any words. After a student writes a summary, I have him calculate the cost of his words by multiplying the total number of words by the factor of the day. Then he jots the total on his paper and circles it. When I grade each summary, I make sure the student included the key information, and then I decide whether the summary was a bargain or overpriced! *(RL.4.2; RL.5.3; RI.4.2; RI.5.2) Pitiya Le Huu, Charlottesville, VA*

68 words x 7 cents = 476 cents (\$4.76)

Bargain!

"Thanks to *The Mailbox* for all you do to help us in our classrooms. When we can't find what we need, you have it!"—*Dolores Davis via Facebook*

The MAILBOX BLOG

Spot-On System

I use index cards and sticky dots to organize differentiated centers or stations in my classroom. I have an index card labeled for each student. I put yellow stickers on the cards of students who work with me to check homework. I put red dots on students' cards if I will have them complete related practice or enrichment with a partner. I use blue dots for students who work independently on an extension activity, and I stick green dots on the cards of students who are ready for an assessment. Those stick-on dots make it easy to organize student workstations, so I can meet the needs of all my learners. *Gail Picking, Oakdale Middle School, Ijamsville, MD*

Ava

Noah

Rhyming Rule

My students love this reminder for rounding numbers! First, a student underlines the digit in the place to which he is rounding. Then he looks at the digit to the immediate right. If the digit is greater than four, the child says, "Five and above, give the underlined digit a shove." He increases the underlined digit by one and adds zeros to the right until he matches the number of places in the number. If the digit is four or less, he knows to leave the digit alone and then add the zeros. *Michelle Sims, Courthouse Road Elementary, Spotsylvania, VA*

Five and above,
Give the underlined digit a shove.
Round to the nearest ten thousand:
135,987 rounds to 140,000.

Answer Keys

Page 33

1. !	9. **X**
2. **X**	10. !
3. **X**	11. →
4. !	12. **X**
5. →	13. you're
6. **X**	14. probably
7. !	15. always
8. →	16. Having

Bonus: Sentences will vary.

Page 36

1. moose	9. fishermen
2. geese	10. thieves
3. species	11. themselves
4. loaves	12. hippopotamuses, or hippopotami
5. leaves	
6. teeth	13. mice
7. people	14. wolves
8. fish, or fishes	15. deer

Bonus: bases, crises, diagnoses, emphases, hypotheses

Page 38

1. Jack London; January 12, 1876
2. December, turquoise or zircon; January, garnet
3. Janus had two faces: one that looked into the past and one that looked into the future.
4. *decem*, ten
5. Ben Franklin, January 17, 1706; Ethan Allen, January 10, 1738; Benedict Arnold, January 17, 1741
6. Texas; state flower, bluebonnet; state bird, northern mockingbird
7. January 30, 1882; He was elected four times.
8. June 21, 1788; Delaware
9. John Hancock; January 23, 1737
10. Barton carried supplies to soldiers and nursed wounded men on the battlefields.
11. near Kitty Hawk, North Carolina; 12 seconds
12. December 5, 1955; one year, 16 days

Page 40

1. C	7. I
2. D	8. I
3. E	9. O
4. G	10. O
5. G	11. S
6. H	12. T

It needs GOOD "ICE-SIGHT"!

Bonus: Analogies will vary.

Page 41

1. accurate, 2
2. inaccurate, 3 and 4
3. accurate, 6
4. accurate, 7
5. inaccurate, 8
6. accurate, 9
7. inaccurate, 11
8. inaccurate, 12
9. accurate, 13 and 14
10. accurate, 15
11. inaccurate, 17, 18, and 19
12. accurate, 14, 15, 16, and 19

Bonus: Answers will vary.

Page 42

1. Both, and	5. either, or
2. Not only, but also	6. neither, nor
3. both, and	7. either, or
4. whether, or	8. whether, or

Possible answers include the following:
9. I will either meet my friends at the mall or play soccer.
10. I will finish both my science project and my history report.
11. Not only will I take my dog for a walk, but I will also build a tree house.
12. I am not sure whether I will go skateboarding or visit my cousins.

Bonus: Answers will vary.

Page 43

1. road	10. all right
2. really	11. Our
3. course	12. They're
4. than	13. piece
5. may	14. you're
6. choose	15. It's
7. pour	16. feat
8. whole	17. passed
9. dessert	18. well

Page 44

1. cycle	9. dedicate
2. appear	10. kind
3. believe	11. taste
4. history	12. hope
5. love	13. add
6. comfort	14. exist
7. circle	15. move
8. govern	16. music

Bonus: countertop; Answers will vary.

Page 45

1. geese	9. scarves
2. shelves	10. heroes
3. children	11. fish or fishes
4. wolves	12. elves
5. trout or trouts	13. pianos
6. tomatoes	14. ox or oxen
7. leaves	15. roofs
8. thieves	16. teeth

Bonus: fathers-in-law, mothers-in-law, sisters-in-law

Page 46

1. 3-bedroom apartment
2. no; Pets are not allowed.
3. possibly; The seller is accepting the best offer.
4. yes; No experience is necessary.
5. Mention the ad.
6. no; Washing machines are not on sale.
7. Main and 5th streets
8. no; The ad lists an address instead of a store's name.
9. helmet or pants
10. yes; He has roofing experience.

Bonus: Answers will vary.

Page 47

Bonus: Answers will vary.

Page 48

1. I; each spring, we welcome flutters of monarch butterflies⊙
2. U, that
3. R, which
4. O; my brother and I met an entomologist⊙
5. Y, whom
6. E; she wants to help save monarch butterfly populations⊙
7. A; she explained one way we could help⊙
8. L, that
9. H; then the entomologist taught us how to spot a monarch egg⊙
10. M; so we planted milkweed in our yard⊙
11. S, that
12. F; we checked on the egg every day⊙
13. C, that
14. T, which
15. B, that
16. N; it finally emerged as a beautiful orange-and-black butterfly⊙

BUTTERFLIES IN YOUR STOMACH!

Bonus: Answers will vary.

Page 49

1. inventory	7. pneumonia
2. reluctant	8. paramount
3. barricade	9. mishandle
4. machinery	10. blueprint
5. recipient	11. insurance
6. alternate	12. whimsical

With a "tuba" toothpaste!

Bonus: attribute

Page 50

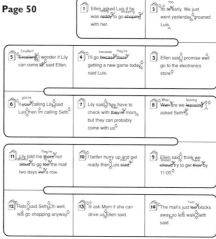

Bonus:
1. Ellen asked, "Luis, are you ready to go shopping with me?"
11. Lily said, "We're not allowed to go to the mall two days in a row."

Page 51

Answers for 1–3, 5, 7, and 8 will vary.

4.

Present Tense Form		Irregular Past Tense Form	
begin	rise	began	rose
bring	shake	brought	shook
do	swim	did	swam
drink	tear	drank	tore
fly	weave	flew	wove

6. Sentences will vary. Verb forms include the following: was talking, am talking, will be talking; was hiking, am hiking, will be hiking; was painting, am painting, will be painting; was gathering, am gathering, will be gathering.
9. Sentences will vary. Verb forms include the following: had dug, have dug, will have dug; had caught, have caught, will have caught; had hidden, have hidden, will have hidden; had known, have known, will have known.

Page 55
1. foot, boot, bolt, boll; fall, ball, balk, back
2. Possible answers include knight, night; knew, new; knead, need; knot, not; knit, nit; and knob, nob.
3. A. dragon wagon
   B. best guest
   C. shoe glue
   D. silly lily
   E. smart heart
4. Answers will vary.
5. multitude
6. A. High five!
   B. Get more bang for your buck.
   C. As good as new!
   D. Reach for the stars!
7. robin, owl, duck, hawk, seagull, falcon, goose, dove, wren, eagle
8. Answers will vary but could include the following: ticker, ticket, tickle, tickles, tickled, tickler, ticking, ticklish, ticks, ticktack, and ticktock.

Page 56
1. Van Buren; Obama; Tyler, Taylor, Taft, or Truman; Eisenhower
2. Answers will vary.
3. able, acre, airs, ally, also, aqua, area, army, auto, away, axle
4. A. PEACH
   B. GRAPE
   C. LIME
   D. ORANGE
   E. APRICOT
5. Answers will vary.
6. A. colors
   B. vegetables
   C. types of winds
   D. quilted covers for beds
   E. species of lizards
7. A. winning spinning
   B. last blast
   C. cold mold
   D. wet pet
   E. deep sleep
8. One Way, No Passing Zone, Do Not Enter, Do Not Pass, Pass With Care

Page 57
Answers for 2, 3, 5, 6, and 8 will vary.
1. A. hand, arm, leg
   B. joke, trick, riddle
   C. sofa, chair, bed
4.

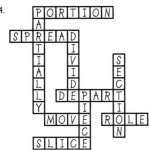

7. A. room
   B. eggshells
   C. water
   D. can
   E. dumps
   F. board
   G. line

Page 58
1. 1. banana split
   2. long underwear
   3. square meal
   4. last but not least
   5. sign on the dotted line
2. s and a
3. 1. symmetry
   2. perpendicularity
   3. hexagons
   4. pentagon
   5. triangular prism
4. 1. food preparation terms
   2. mixtures
   3. ways of cooking
   4. types of bread
   5. types of dessert
5. A. red, blue
   B. peach, pear
   C. Spain, China
   D. Taft, Tyler
   E. Texas, Maine, Minnesota, Montana
6. 1. Lincoln
   2. Raleigh
   3. Columbus
   4. Madison
   5. Jackson
7. 1. spoonbill
   2. pitchfork
   3. forklift
   4. pocketknife
   5. jackknife
   6. spoon-feed
8. 1. ice-skate
   2. snowman
   3. frost
   4. blizzard
   5. mittens

Page 59
1. A. Thomas Jefferson
   B. Mark Twain
   C. Harry Truman
   D. Martin Luther King
   E. Al Gore
2. A, B, and F are important. C, D, and E are unimportant.
3. tulip, lilac; Boise; bed, table; tell, let, bet, belt, lit
4. math: intersect, probability, range, surface, equation, integer; reading: moral, selection, theme, metaphor, summarize, simile
5. threw, aloud, eight, chilly, rays or raze, hole, would, soar, haul, grate
6. red, tan; shoe, dress, vest; category; clothing
7. Answers will vary.
8.
r	e	u	s	e
w	a	s	t	e
t	r	e	e	s
s	t	e	e	l
h	u	m	u	s

Page 60
1. The Cat in the Hat, The Miraculous Journey of Edward Tulane, A Wrinkle in Time, Hop on Pop, Where the Sidewalk Ends, Cloudy With a Chance of Meatballs, From the Mixed-Up Files of Mrs. Basil E. Frankweiler; The words are prepositions.
2. cane, chain, crane, rain, rein, sane, Cain, Shane
3. A. Buckle up.
   B. Just between you and me…
   C. reading between the lines
   D. a raise in pay
4. A. antonyms   B. synonyms   C. synonyms   D. antonyms
   E. synonyms   F. synonyms   G. synonyms   H. antonyms
5. A. knits, stink: bad smell
   B. desserts, stressed: worried
   C. golf, flog: to whip or beat
   D. stew, wets: covers something with liquid
6.
```
        R H I N E
      N I L E
        V O L G A
    M A C K E N Z I E
  M I S S O U R I
    T H A M E S
```
7, 8. Answers will vary.

Page 61
"Time for a Tune-Up"
chronological, chronic, synchronize, chronicle
hydrant, dehydrated, hydraulics, hydroplane
dictator, contradict, dictate, predict
spectator, inspection, prospect, spectacular

Explanations will vary.

"Tackling Word Analysis"
Possible words include the following: incredible, incredibly, inscribe, inscriber, inscription, instruct, instructor, instruction, inject, injectable, injector, injection, prescribe, prescriber, prescription, disrupt, disrupter, disruption, conscribe, conscript, conscription, construct, constructor, constructable, construction, report, reportable, reporter, reject, rejection, interrupt, interrupter, interruption, interject, interjection, credible, credibly

Definitions will vary.

Page 62
"On the Plus Side"
1. (scent) odor
2. (skinny) slim
3. (curious) nosy
4. cheap, (inexpensive)
5. (young) childish
6. (easygoing) lazy
7. sloppy, (casual)
8. (challenging) difficult
9. (debate) argue
10. impatient, (eager)

"On Track"
Paragraphs will vary. Incomplete sentences are the following:

At least, my dad's favorite activity!
Walking trails and state parks too.
Snowshoe 12 miles?
Stopping often to look, rest, and have snacks.
Not a bear's tracks or a mountain lion's.
The tracks of a cross-country skier.
So instead of slogging along 12 miles.

"By George!"
Margaret plants roses in her garden, and she plants pansies and snapdragons.
Frederick may ride his pony this afternoon, or he may go fishing.
Phillip loves to play cricket, so he watches every cricket match he can.
Gertrude got up at 4:00 AM, for she wanted to watch the sunrise.
Elizabeth missed her friends, so she invited them to a tea party.
For dinner, Reggie wants fish and chips, but Margaret prefers vegetable soup.

Page 63
"Far Out"
1. decrease, reduce, descend
2. sequence, succession, continuation
3. support, foundation, base
4. measure, survey, assess
5. enlarge, increase, extend

"A Messy Room!"
Answers will vary.
1. B   5. H
2. C, D   6. I
3. G   7. E
4. F   8. A

"Make No Mistake"
1. verb   6. verb
2. noun   7. noun
3. verb   8. noun
4. verb   9. verb
5. noun   10. noun

"From the Heart"
1. Madison and Alex wanted to help the animals at the local shelter.
2. The students would raise money by having a yard sale.
3. "Thank you very much!" Madison told each person who bought an item.
4. When one man heard what the students were doing, he gave them a hundred dollar bill.
5. Alex said, "The money will help the dogs, cats, and birds at the shelter."
6. A story about the students was printed in the Springfield newspaper.
7. A news reporter asked, "Why did you decide to do this project?"
8. "We want to help the animals find good homes," Alex answered.
9. The students' picture was put on the front page of the Springfield Times.
10. The article was titled "From the Heart."

Round	Player A	Player B	GCF
I	1, 2, 3, 4, 6, 12	1, 2, 4, 8, 16	4
2	1, 2, 3, 6, 9, 18	1, 2, 4, 5, 10, 20	2
3	1, 2, 4, 5, 8, 10, 20, 40	1, 2, 3, 5, 6, 10, 15, 30	10
4	1, 2, 4, 8, 16, 32, 64	1, 2, 3, 6, 7, 14, 21, 42	2
5	1, 2, 3, 4, 6, 8, 12, 24	1, 2, 4, 7, 8, 14, 28, 56	8
6	1, 2, 5, 7, 10, 14, 35, 70	1, 3, 5, 7, 15, 21, 35, 105	35

Page 115

3,300.3 = 3,000 + 300 + 0.3 = 3 thousand, 3 hundred and 3 tenths = three thousand, three hundred and three tenths

3,300.03 = 3,000 + 300 + 0.03 = 3 thousand, 3 hundred and 3 hundredths = three thousand, three hundred and three hundredths

3,300.003 = 3,000 + 300 + 0.003 = 3 thousand, 300 and 3 thousandths = three thousand, three hundred and three thousandths

30,300.3 = 30,000 + 300 + 0.3 = 30 thousand, 3 hundred and 3 tenths = thirty thousand, three hundred and three tenths

30,300.03 = 30,000 + 300 + 0.03 = 30 thousand, 3 hundred and 3 hundredths = thirty thousand, three hundred and three hundredths

30,300.003 = 30,000 + 300 + 0.003 = 30 thousand, 3 hundred and 3 thousandths = thirty thousand, three hundred and three thousandths

Page 118

1. 10
2. 12
3. 11
4. 15
5. 8
6. 16
7. 4
8. 6

Page 121

Die Roll	1	2	3
11, 13, 15, 17	19	21	23
48, 41, 34, 27	20	13	6
1, 4, 9, 16	25	36	49
729, 243, 81, 27	9	3	1
72, 63, 54, 45	36	27	18
2, 3, 5, 8	13	21	34

Die Roll	4	5	6

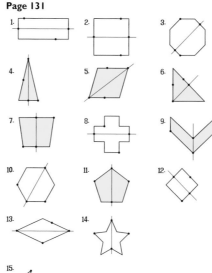

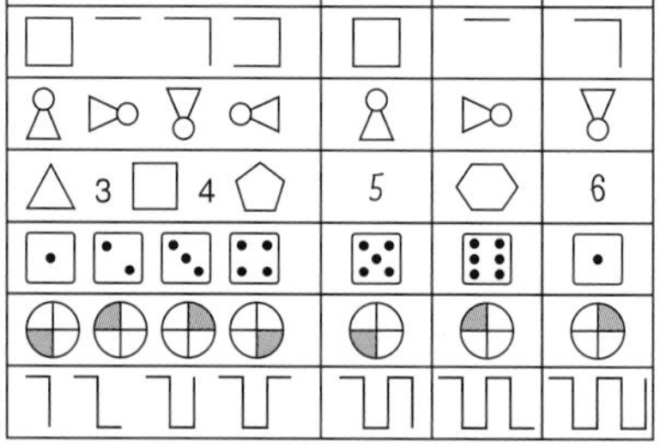

Page 123

Burrow A
1. 134 R2
2. 242
3. 126 R2
4. 165
5. 158 R4
6. 112 R6
7. 121
8. 120 R1
9. 133
10. 209
11. 110 R3
12. 231

Burrow B
1. 248 R2
2. 115
3. 373
4. 168
5. 114 R3
6. 176 R1
7. 233 R2
8. 248 R1
9. 130 R2
10. 102
11. 107 R1
12. 152

Page 130

A. 680
B. 504
C. 759
D. 3,127
E. 2,232
F. 1,548
G. 2,204
H. 3,276
I. 3,366
J. 6,438
K. 4,484
L. 945
M. 6,305
N. 5,236
O. 1,638
P. 4,266
Q. 1,534
R. 3,528
S. 3,016
T. 1,944
U. 4,750
V. 2,430
W. 5,141
X. 2,625
Y. 3,363
Z. 6,864
AA. 3,312
BB. 2,790
CC. 1,922
DD. 4,232

Page 131

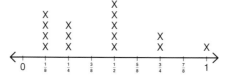

Bonus: See colored figures above.

Page 132

A. 180 in.^{3}
E. 5,400 cm^3
H. 216 in.^{3}
I. 1,000 in.^{3}
J. 400 in.^{3}
K. 5,544 cm^3
N. 192 in.^{3}
O. 3,120 cm^3
R. 210 in.^{3}
T. 3,500 cm^3

Bonus: 12 inches; Explanations will vary.

"Wooden Shoe" <u>LIKE TO HEAR ANOTHER JOKE?</u>

Page 133

```
                         X
                         X
        X           X    X
        X      X    X    X         X
        X      X    X    X    X     X
  ←—————┼——┼——┼——┼——┼——┼——┼——————→
  0     1/8 1/4 3/8 1/2 5/8 3/4 7/8  1
```

1. ½ yard; 1 yard
2. ¾ yard
3. the ½-yard strings; They would be 2½ yards.
4. 2¼ yards
5. 4 lengths
6. ¼ yard
7. 2 yards
8. 1¾ yards

Bonus: 3 yards

Page 134

A. 1,092; Estimate: 40 × 30 = 1,200
B. 1,012; Estimate: 50 × 20 = 1,000
C. 1,599; Estimate: 40 × 40 = 1,600
D. 4,941; Estimate: 80 × 60 = 4,800
E. 737; Estimate: 10 × 70 = 700
F. 660; Estimate: 60 × 10 = 600
G. 3,822; Estimate: 80 × 50 = 4,000
H. 1,892; Estimate: 90 × 20 = 1,800
I. 5,100; Estimate: 70 × 80 = 5,600
J. 3,813; Estimate: 90 × 40 = 3,600
K. 792; Estimate: 20 × 40 = 800
L. 4,558; Estimate: 50 × 90 = 4,500
M. 2,736; Estimate: 70 × 40 = 2,800
N. 2,720; Estimate: 90 × 30 = 2,700

Bonus: Explanations will vary.

Page 135

A. 1⅝
B. 1
C. ¾
D. 1⅙
E. 2¹¹⁄₁₂
F. 1⁵⁄₁₀
G. ⅖
H. 2¼
I. 2⅜
J. ³⁄₆
K. ⁹⁄₁₀
L. ⁷⁄₁₂

Bonus: Answers will vary.

Page 136

1. 3 feet
2. 3 feet
3. 5½ feet
4. 4½ feet
5. 2½ feet
6. 5½ feet
7. 4 feet
8. 7½ feet
9. 2 feet
10. 3½ feet
11. 5½ feet
12. 6½ feet

Bonus: Answers will vary.

Page 137

A. ¹⁄₃₂
B. 32
C. ¹⁄₁₈
D. ¹⁄₉₀
E. 48
F. 54
G. ¹⁄₂₁
H. 21
I. 100
J. ¹⁄₁₀
K. 55
L. ¹⁄₂₇
1. 20 ÷ ⅕ = 100
2. ⅕ ÷ 20 = ¹⁄₁₀₀
3. unit fraction
4. whole number

Bonus: 5, ⅕

Page 138

1. no; The liquid measures 1.8 liters. Mia needs 0.2 more liters to fill the container.
2. 9,000 grams to the right side
3. 3 kilometers
4. $5.00
5. 4 lengths of ribbon
6. 16 patties; 80 grams of ground beef is left.
7. 2.05 grams
8. 4.35 kilograms
9. 2 meters
10. no; the quartz rock that is 52 millimeters will not fit because 52 millimeters equals 5.2 centimeters.

Bonus: Answers will vary.

Page 139

1. six hours
2. 2:00 PM
3. 11:30 AM
4. 3:00 PM
5. 1:45 PM
6. "How to Find Babysitting Jobs," "Recognizing Safety Hazards," and "How to Handle a Tantrum"
7. one hour and 45 minutes
8. "How to Find Babysitting Jobs," "Recognizing Safety Hazards," "How to Handle a Tantrum," "How to Feed a Toddler," "Naptime"

Bonus: Answers will vary.

Page 140

1. polygon
2. sides
3. acute
4. parallel
5. triangle
6. pentagon
7. equal
8. angle
9. four
10. right
11. hexagon
12. one
13. obtuse
14. perpendicular

<u>Neither one is any good without a point!</u>

Bonus: square, rectangle, right triangle

Page 141

O. $\frac{7}{12}$	R. $1\frac{3}{20}$
N. $\frac{1}{24}$	I. $\frac{29}{30}$
M. $\frac{13}{20}$	F. $1\frac{11}{24}$
E. $1\frac{2}{15}$	A. $\frac{7}{24}$
S. $\frac{19}{40}$	Y. $\frac{1}{6}$
H. $\frac{1}{30}$	D. $1\frac{1}{5}$

HIS HORSE IS NAMED FRIDAY!

Bonus: Answers will vary.

Page 142

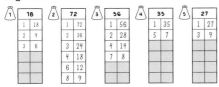

1	18		2	72		3	56		4	35		5	27
1	18		1	72		1	56		1	35		1	27
2	9		2	36		2	28		5	7		3	9
3	6		3	24		4	14						
			4	18		7	8						
			6	12									
			8	9									

6	48					7	12
1	48					1	12
2	24					2	6
3	16					3	4
4	12						
6	8						

8	81		9	24		10	60		11	32		12	96
1	81		1	24		1	60		1	32		1	96
3	27		2	12		2	30		2	16		2	48
9	9		3	8		3	20		4	8		3	32
			4	6		4	15					4	24
						5	12					6	16
						6	10					8	12

Bonus: Answers will vary.

Page 143
1. N; 11, 13
2. R; 8, 15
3. F; 174, 175
4. A; 90, 88
5. Y; 6, 9
6. T; 4,120; 4,112
7. S; 6, 12
8. O; 3¾, 7¾
9. H; 40, 48
10. E; 20½, 41
11. X; 60, 120
12. I; 36, 43

THEY SIT NEXT TO THEIR FANS!

Bonus: B

Page 144
Stories and models will vary.
1. $\frac{1}{25}$ of the fish food
2. 20 times
3. $\frac{1}{16}$
4. 25
5. $\frac{1}{18}$
6. $\frac{1}{12}$
7. 21
8. 24

Bonus: Answers will vary.

Page 145
1. a. 24 inches
   b. 504 inches²
2. a. 315 inches²
   b. 72 inches
   c. 235 inches²
   d. 550 inches²
3. a. 24 inches
   b. 78 inches
   c. 720 inches²
4. a. 24 inches
   b. 192 inches²
   c. 384 inches²

Bonus: 192 tiles

Page 146
1. decimal
2. factor
3. partition
4. tenth
5. benchmark fractions
6. equivalent
7. fraction
8. mixed number
9. denominator
10. thousandth
11. compare
12. operation
13. multiple
14. hundredth
15. equivalent fractions
16. decompose
17. numerator
18. unit fraction

IT HAD AN "OX-IDENT"!

Bonus: Answers will vary.

Page 147
Answers for 5 and 7 will vary.
1. A. 5 x 3 = 15
   B. 8 x 3 = 24
   C. 12 x 3 = 36
   D. 11 x 3 = 33
2. GCF — Number Pair
   10 — 35 and 63
   8 — 16 and 28
   4 — 20 and 30
   7 — 36 and 54
   9 — 32 and 72
3. 30, 42, 60; 36, 60, 66; 24, 42, 72
4. A. 1, 2, 4, 8, 16
   B. 1, 3, 9, 27
   C. 1, 2, 3, 5, 6, 10, 15, 30
   D. 1, 2, 7, 14
6.

Number of Factors	Number	Factors
2	17	1, 17
3	25	1, 5, 25
4	27	1, 3, 9, 27
5	81	1, 3, 9, 27, 81
6	18	1, 2, 3, 6, 9, 18

8. A. The number 10 has six (four) factors.
   B. Two (Six) is the greatest common factor of 12 and 30.
   C. The number 25 has more (fewer) factors than the number 18.
   D. The numbers 24 and 30 have six (four) of the same factors.
9. A. 9, 84 1
   B. 18, 46 5
   C. 54, 63 3
   D. 72, 108 8

Page 148
Answers for 3 and 5 will vary.
1.

Mystery Factor	Multiples
3	12, 21, 45
5	15, 30, 55
7	14, 49, 63
11	22, 77, 99

Multiples added will vary.
2.

Multiple of 5 / Multiple of 3 / Multiple of 2: 25, 15, 9, 10, 30, 6, 4

Multiples added will vary.
4. A. 40   B. 12   C. 42   D. 24
6. LCM of 3, 4, and 5 is 60.
7. A. 70   B. 28   C. 54   D. 41
8.

Factor Pair	LCM
3, 4	12
3, 8	24
2, 9	18
5, 6	30
8, 7	56
8, 9	72

9. A. 105   B. 36   C. 40   D. 140

Page 149
1. A. 20 cubes for one layer, 4 layers, 80 cubes
   B. 18 cubes for one layer, 4 layers, 72 cubes
   C. 10 cubes for one layer, 4 layers, 40 cubes
2. A. 864 cubes   B. 108 cubes   C. 13½ cubes
3. 3 cubes tall, 8 cubes tall
4, 5. Answers will vary.
6. A. 70 ft.³   B. 27 ft.³   C. 198 ft.³
7. A. 378 in.³   B. 208 in.³   C. 132 in.³
8. A. 76 cm³   B. 600 cm³
9. v = 144 in.³

Page 150
Answers for 1, 4, 5, 7, and 9 will vary.
2. four
3. Figures A and C
6. A. 5   B. 6   C. 7   D. 4
8. A regular polygon, or a polygon with equal sides and angles, has the same number of sides as lines of symmetry.

Page 151
Level A
1. 2016, 2020, 2024, 2028, 2032, 2036, 2040, 2044, 2048, 2052; Ages will vary.
2. Answers will vary.
3. 625 miles
4. no; There is enough room for only the letters and one football cutout. The banner is 102 inches long and the letters and spaces are 97 inches long.
5. ¼
6. 2,400 tiles; Drawings will vary.
Level B
1. less than 750; The total student population is 725.
2. yes; 24 x 25 = 600
3. $\frac{405}{5} = 81$
4. 10:35 AM
5. no; Lena's shape could only be a quadrilateral.
6. A. 457.4
   B. 19.0
   C. 4.4
   D. 10.8

Page 152
Level A
1. no
2. $21.95
3. nine times
4. six ways: Emma, Kyle, Mason; Emma, Mason, Kyle; Kyle, Mason, Emma; Kyle, Emma, Mason; Mason, Emma, Kyle; Mason, Kyle, Emma
5. yes; There are four prime numbers between 10 and 20 and only two between 20 and 30.
6. 96, 192, 384, 768; Each number doubles.
Level B
1. ten minutes
2. $3.50
3. (4 + 6) x 8 = 80; 96 + (4 x 8) = 128
4. Answers will vary.
5. 2 liters
6. $\frac{9}{16}$

Page 153
Level A
1. Ian
2. 21 ounces
3. 1 feet and 5$\frac{7}{10}$ inches
4. octagon, 8 lines of symmetry
5. 18; Lyle added before multiplying.
6. 24: 1, 2, 3, 4, 6, 8, 12, 24; 48: 1, 2, 3, 4, 6, 8, 12, 16, 24, 48. 48 has more factors.
Level B
1. 18.94, 19.05, 19.28, 19.35, 19.5
2. no; There are 28¼ hours until they leave.
3. Jen's lunchbox volume = 126.75 in.³, Jake's lunchbox volume = 121.5 in.³
4. quadrilaterals with parallel and perpendicular lines: square, rectangle; quadrilaterals with congruent sides: square, rhombus
5. 8 + (12 ÷ 4) x 2 = 14
6. (48 ÷ 8) x 9 = 54 or 9 x (48 ÷ 8) = 54

Page 154
Level A
1. Answers will vary
2. A. 3⅝   B. 5$\frac{10}{16}$ C. 7⅞
3.
4. no
5. 108 bulbs
6. 83°, 83°, and 114° or 14°, 14°, and 152°
Level B
1. 240 students donated books to the community library, and 160 students donated books to a local charity; 80 students donated books to children in other communities
2. The area of the teachers' lounge is four times the area of Ms. Reddy's office.
3. A. 5 + (10 x 9) − 6 = 89
   B. (12 ÷ 6) x (11 + 9) = 40
4. 2:05 PM
5. 0.5, half of the stick, or six meters
6. 12th floor

Page 155
Level A
1. Tammy's friends
2. $\frac{3}{4}$, $\frac{7}{10}$, $\frac{4}{7}$, and $\frac{8}{15}$
3. 11:40 AM
4. A. 2 right angles, 1 acute angle, and 1 obtuse angle
   B. 2 right angles, 1 acute angle, and 2 obtuse angles
5. 84
6. A. 3,800
   B. 500
   C. 203,600
   D. 91,000

Level B
1. 48 games
2. Michaela, 3 ounces
3. 1,280 cm^3; Answers will vary.
4.

$y = x + 3$	
x	y
6	9
4	7
3	6
2	5

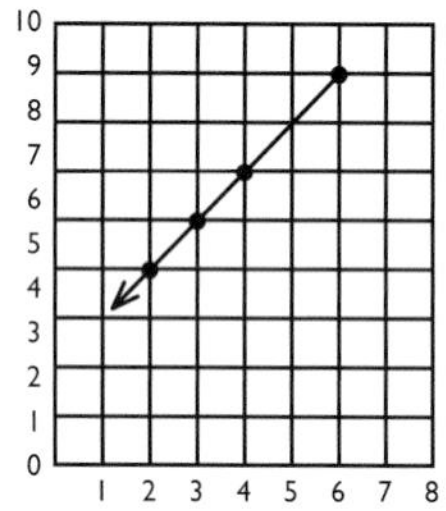

5. no; Not all parallelograms have four right angles.
6. $85.00

Page 156
Level A
1. A. $\frac{7}{100}$
   B. $\frac{25}{1,000}$
   C. $\frac{9}{10}$
2. 419 ÷ 7 and 2,212 ÷ 9
3. C
4. ∠DBE = 54°, ∠ABC = 80°
5. fifth, odd; sixth, even; seventh, odd
6. more than 54 years

Level B
1. 9,766 miles
2. no
3. 15 inches, or 1 foot 3 inches
4. B and C
5. 8 and 9
6. $329

Page 157
1. 214; Problems will vary.
2. 5 and 41 belong to Set A; The sum of each number's digits is five.
   9, 18, and 27 belong to Set B; The numbers are multiples of three.
3.
```
     342
11)3,762
  - 33
     46
   - 44
      22
    - 22
       0
```
4. $22\frac{1}{2}$ inches
5. squares
6. A. The earliest date for Labor Day is September 1.
   B. The latest possible Labor Day date is September 7.
   C. Since Labor Day is September 3 this year, it will be September 2 next year.
   D. Labor Day will be on September 7 in 2015.
7. 12 letters; A, I, M, I, H, I, A, T, i, o, I, i
8. largest value = $0.65, smallest value = $0.17

Page 158
1. Thanksgiving Day and Christmas
2. square, rectangle, parallelogram, rhombus
3. no, no
4. Luke
5. A and D
6. 3,024; Factors will vary.
7. Answers will vary.
8. 13

Page 159
1. Carol's Comics
2. 351
3. A.  B.  C.  D. 
4. A. true B. false C. false D. true
5. Answers will vary. One possible equation is [(5 ÷ 5) x (5 ÷ 5)] + 5 = 6
6. six factors; 3, 6, 12, 24, 48, 96
7. 2.183 or 1.842
8. 22 faces in figure A; 42 faces in figure B; 64 faces in all

Page 160
1. hamburger, fries, and milk shake or hamburger, hot dog, and cola
2. $85.00
3. D, n = 27
4. (l x w) – (a x b) = units²
5. Answers will vary.
6. A. 2,017
   B. 8,062
   C. 428
   D. 1,234
   E. 315
   F. 5,678; E C D A F B
7. 90°, right; 27°, acute; 180°, straight; 149°, obtuse
8. A. 84 B. 39 C. 52

Page 161
1. A. 5, multiples of 7
   B. 25, multiples of 3
   C. 14, multiples of 8
   D. 46, multiples of 6
2. 9 x 1 + 2 = 11
   9 x 12 + 3 = 111
   9 x 123 + 4 = 1,111
   9 x 1,234 + 5 = 11,111
   9 x 12,345,678 + 9 = 111,111,111

The number of the digit one in each answer is the same as the number being added in the equation.

3. A. $\frac{1}{3}$ B. $\frac{1}{5}$ C. $\frac{5}{15}$
4. A. isosceles triangle
   B. scalene triangle
   C. equilateral triangle
5. A. 216 B. 96 C. 0
6. A. 56,000
   B. 560,000
   C. 5,600,000
   D. 56,000,000
7. The numbers represent the letters' positions in the alphabet; P = 16, F = 6, N = 14
8. A. 3 = angles in a triangle
   B. 4 = right angles in a square
   C. 90 = degrees in a right angle
   D. 5 = sides in pentagon

Page 162
1.

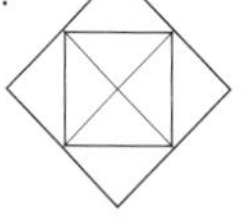

2. 1,002 is not a multiple of 5. $\frac{3}{4}$ is not equivalent to $\frac{5}{8}$. $\frac{35}{10}$ is not equivalent to 0.35.
3. HAPPY SUMMER!
4. 52,328; 20
   3,675; 21
   769; 22
   46,058; 23
   13,398; 24
   203,596; 25
   The second number is the sum of the digits in the first number. Each sum is one greater than the preceding sum.
5. A. 531 B. 98,541 C. $76.53 D. 8,654.3
   The answers are all multiples of three, have digits in descending order, and are odd numbers.
6. 90th day, March 31; 150th day, May 30; 220th day, August 8
7. number times itself, or squared, + 1
8. 28

Page 163
"'Grid-dled!'"
Solutions will vary. One possible solution is

2	6	8	4
8	4	2	6
4	8	6	2
6	2	4	8

"A Work in Progress"

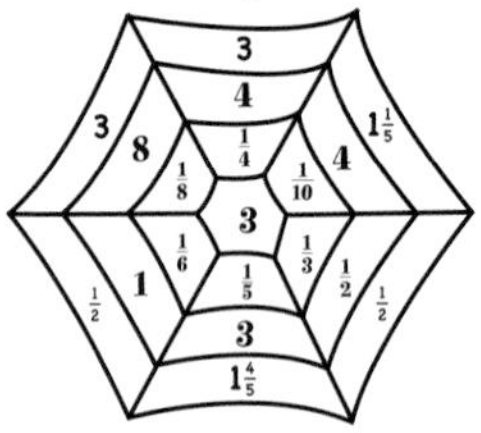

3 + $1\frac{1}{5}$ + $\frac{1}{2}$ + $1\frac{4}{5}$ + $\frac{1}{2}$ + 3 = 10

"Apple Pie Order"

1.02	2.13	3.12	4.04	5.19
1.07	2.21	3.17	4.07	5.21
1.09	2.31	3.21	4.21	5.36
1.28	2.72	3.22	4.23	5.45
1.69	2.90	3.28	4.29	5.61
1.93	2.92	3.34	4.39	5.72
2.03	2.99	3.39	4.76	5.92

Page 164
"Too Many Snacks"
18 possible combinations

Cookie	Drink	Candy
chocolate chip	milk	candy cane
chocolate chip	milk	lollipop
chocolate chip	hot chocolate	candy cane
chocolate chip	hot chocolate	lollipop
chocolate chip	eggnog	candy cane
chocolate chip	eggnog	lollipop
sugar	milk	candy cane
sugar	milk	lollipop
sugar	hot chocolate	candy cane
sugar	hot chocolate	lollipop
sugar	eggnog	candy cane
sugar	eggnog	lollipop
gingerbread	milk	candy cane
gingerbread	milk	lollipop
gingerbread	hot chocolate	candy cane
gingerbread	hot chocolate	lollipop
gingerbread	eggnog	candy cane
gingerbread	eggnog	lollipop

"At the Meet"
Heat 1: 12.51, 12.53, 12.56, 12.58, 13.36, 13.45; Grace had the fastest time.
Heat 2: 12.48, 12.49, 12.98, 13.01, 13.26, 13.36; Jacob had the fastest time.
Heat 3: 12.50, 12.51, 12.53, 13.04, 13.17, 13.27; James had the fastest time.
Jacob had the fastest time overall.

"Missing Links"
1, 3, 6, 10, <u>15</u>, 21, <u>28</u>, <u>36</u>, 45, <u>55</u>, 66, 78, <u>91</u>, <u>105</u>, 120, <u>136</u>, <u>153</u>, 171, <u>190</u>, <u>210</u>
The rule is add the next consecutive number to each number, beginning with 2.
The resulting pattern is two even numbers followed by two odd numbers.

Page 165
"Something's Fishy"
630 ÷ 7 = 90; 560 ÷ 7 = 80; 210 ÷ 7 = 30; 490 ÷ 7 = 70; 420 ÷ 7 = 60; 840 ÷ 7 = 120; 350 ÷ 7 = 50; 280 ÷ 7 = 40

"Polly Want a Cracker?"
1. A, C, D, E
2. A, I, J
3. five
4. two
5. A, C, J

"That's 'Sum' Difference!"
1. $4\frac{1}{2} - 3\frac{4}{8}$
2. $5\frac{3}{4} + 3\frac{4}{8}$ or $5\frac{3}{4} + 4\frac{1}{2}$
3. $4\frac{1}{2} - 3\frac{1}{9}$, $4\frac{1}{2} - 2\frac{5}{6}$, $3\frac{1}{9} - 1\frac{2}{5}$, or $5\frac{3}{4} - 4\frac{1}{2}$
4. $4\frac{1}{2} + 1\frac{2}{5}$ or $2\frac{5}{6} + 3\frac{1}{9}$
5. $3\frac{4}{8} - 2\frac{5}{6}$ or $3\frac{1}{9} - 2\frac{5}{6}$
6. $3\frac{4}{8} + 2\frac{5}{6}$ or $3\frac{4}{8} + 3\frac{1}{9}$

Page 166
1. $39
2. 13 hours
3. 1,225 leaves
4. 70 times
5. 54 pounds
6. 250 hours, or ten days and ten hours
7. 12 apps
8. 14 screens

Page 168
1. 2,616 centimeters
2. more, $390
3. $15,102
4. 45 pounds; 1,125 pounds
5. 5,950 gallons
6. 1,120 pounds; 910 pounds
7. 10,053 pounds
8. Iona; $20,725

Page 170
1. $7/12$ of the players
2. $7/40$ of Monday's practice
3. $2/15$ of the team
4. $23/60$ of the time
5. $4/15$ of the players
6. $1/10$ of her speech
7. $17/24$ of the players
8. $3/10$ of their games

Page 172
1. 120 centimeters tall, 80 centimeters wide
2. 140 centimeters
3. 5.1 meters
4. 1.36 meters
5. 3,796 centimeters
6. 583.64 meters
7. 6,080.7 centimeters
8. 79.6928 centimeters

Page 174
1. $31.05
2. 36.04 gallons
3. 6.3 ounces
4. 115.66 miles
5. $5.35
6. 1 hour 40.38 minutes, or 100.38 minutes
7. $12.89
8. $42.78

Page 175
1. $22,035
2. 85 fruits
3. 413 miles
4. 207,648 bites
5. 51 weeks, 4 days
6. 3,264 supersensitive hairs
7. 4,068 bingo bango bugs
8. one year

Page 180
1. four sides
2. right angles
3. vertical lines of symmetry
4. five sides
5. equal-length sides
6. at least one pair of parallel sides

Bonus: All quadrilaterals have four sides and four vertices. Rhombuses are quadrilaterals, so rhombuses have <u>four sides and four vertices</u>.

Page 194
"Which Is Heavier: Saltwater or Freshwater?"
The blue saltwater will sink to the bottom of the lower jar because it is heavier than the tap water. The lighter tap water will move up over the saltwater as the saltwater sinks.

"Fun With a Wet Nickel"
Students should see drops of water adhering to the surface of the nickel and forming a dome. The number of droplets will vary but should range from at least 50 to 70 drops. *(The water forms a dome over the surface of the nickel because of the special nature of water. Water molecules have a strong attraction for one another. These molecules are attracted in all directions. The water dropped on the surface of the nickel has no water molecules above it. Therefore, it is attracted downward by the water molecules below it. These forces are strong enough to keep the drops on the nickel until the amount of water becomes too much for the surface tension to hold, and the water overflows.)*

Page 201
2. B2
3. Fleatown
4. B4
5. Los Perros
6. C3
7. S3, D3
8. A1, B1, B2
10. D3, D4
11. B3
12. D3, D4
13. E3
14. Mt. Muttsley
15. C1, D1, C2, D2
16. C2, C3, D2, D3, E2

Bonus: four; D3, E3, D4, E4

Page 232
Anchovy	4.7 cm	1.5 cm	3.13
Cheese	20.4 cm	6.5 cm	3.14
Mushroom	11.9 cm	3.8 cm	3.13
Olive	8.2 cm	2.6 cm	3.15
Pepperoni	23.6 cm	7.5 cm	3.15
Supreme	16 cm	5.1 cm	3.14

Page 237
1. always
2. something
3. our
4. excited
5. probably
6. finally
7. clothes
8. people
9. thought
10. friends
11. different
12. school
13. everyone
14. might
15. before

YOU CAN COUNT ON ME!
Bonus: Answers will vary.

Page 238
A. 50,000 + 400 + 80 + 3
B. six thousand, one hundred ninety-two
C. 576
D. nine hundred fifty-seven
E. 10,000 + 1,000 + 300 + 8
F. 7,293
G. 1,000 + 600 + 40 + 9
H. ninety-six thousand, seventy-four
I. 22,182
J. 8,000 + 600 + 70 + 3
K. three thousand, thirty-eight
L. thirty-nine thousand, nine hundred seven
M. 87,430
N. 5,821
O. three hundred eighty-four

Bonus: Answers will vary.

Page 239
M. 1	I. $3/5$	N. $3/8$	X. $1/3$
B. $5/8$	L. $5/6$	P. $2/5$	O. $1/2$
E. $1/6$	C. $7/12$	T. $7/10$	S. $2/3$
A. $4/5$	H. $3/4$	R. $9/10$	U. $1/5$

During this month, we celebrate the histories, cultures, and contributions of people from <u>SPAIN</u>, <u>MEXICO</u>, the <u>CARIBBEAN</u>, and <u>CENTRAL</u> and <u>SOUTH AMERICA</u>.

Bonus: Possible answers include $10/12 + 1/12$, $9/12 + 2/12$, $8/12 + 3/12$, $7/12 + 4/12$, and $5/12 + 6/12$.

Page 240
1. When the Constitution was written, some states would not approve it as it was. So the first ten amendments were written.
2. Because people wanted to be heard without being punished, the first amendment gave people the right to speak or write freely.
3. Citizens can keep guns in their homes since the second amendment gave people the right to bear arms.
4. The third amendment states that people do not have to take soldiers into their homes. This was as a result of the British forcing colonists to house British soldiers.
5. The fourth amendment said the government could not search a person's home without legal permission so that people would feel safe in their homes.
6. Because of the fifth amendment, a person is protected from having to be a witness against himself in a trial.
7. Since the sixth amendment gave each citizen the right to a fair trial, a person could prove his innocence in court.
8. The Constitution's authors wrote the seventh amendment, giving people the right to fair civil trials, due to the fact that the authors were committed to having fair trials.
9. The eighth amendment banned cruel and unusual punishment so that prisoners would be treated humanely.
10. The Constitution listed citizens' rights. Consequently, some people worried it might seem that they had no other rights.
11. The purpose of the Constitution and Bill of Rights was to protect citizens' rights, even ones they didn't describe. So the authors wrote the ninth amendment saying the Constitution did not deny other rights.
12. State governments wanted to preserve their rights to make decisions about matters in their own states. As a result, the tenth amendment was written, reserving some powers for the states.

Bonus: Answers will vary.

Page 242
A. 17.96<u>85</u>; 17.97
B. 7.07<u>91</u>; 7.08
C. 41.51<u>46</u>; 41.51
D. 7.52<u>17</u>; 7.52
E. 5.50<u>721</u>; 5.51
F. 26.63<u>06</u>; 26.63
G. 0.84<u>541</u>; 0.85
H. 64.32<u>83</u>; 64.33
I. 9.28<u>794</u>; 9.29
J. 12.63<u>91</u>; 12.64
K. 3.90<u>42</u>; 3.90
L. 34.12<u>316</u>; 34.12
M. 86.71<u>46</u>; 86.71
N. 5.88<u>75</u>; 5.89
O. 0.22<u>39</u>; 0.22
P. 5.30<u>46</u>; 5.30
Q. 13.75<u>87</u>; 13.76
R. 69.25<u>63</u>; 69.26
S. 9.08<u>462</u>; 9.08
T. 0.41<u>328</u>; 0.41

Bonus: Answers will vary.

Page 243
B. 2,394
C. 587,308
F. 102,927
G. 66,356
J. 392,479
M. 341,762
N. 9,951
O. 907,504
A. 65,468
B. 282,693
D. 772,143
E. 770,577
H. 672,844
I. 583,179
K. 242,937
L. 988,144

Bonus: Problems will vary.

Page 244
1. R
2. T
3. S
4. W
5. N
6. G
7. W
8. E
9. I
10. P
11. O
12. E
13. H
14. D
15. D

PRESIDENT DWIGHT D. EISENHOWER

Bonus: Answers will vary.

Page 246
1. G, has eyes in the back of her head
2. C, dropped everyone a line
3. K, on cloud nine
4. D, had her hands full
5. I, burning the midnight oil
6. E, on the dot
7. N, had us all in stitches
8. A, lend him a hand
9. O, the whole shebang
10. P, full of beans
11. F, made my mouth water
12. M, so quiet you could hear a pin drop
13. J, played the heavy
14. B, footloose and fancy-free
15. L, barrel of fun
16. H, hit the hay

Bonus: Answers will vary.

Page 247
Presents 1, 3, 4, 8, 10, 13, 14, 16, 19, and 20 should be shaded.
Antonyms for 2, 5, 6, 7, 9, 11, 12, 15, 17, and 18 will vary.

Bonus: Answers will vary.

Answers for 1–6 will vary but should include one of the following:

	Mazao (crops)	Kikombe cha Umoja (unity cup)	Kinara (candleholder)
1.	∠WQX, ∠XQR	∠KJQ, ∠QJL	∠IAB, ∠IAH
2.	∠UQW, ∠WQR, ∠RQS, ∠UQS, ∠VQZ	∠OJN, ∠OJK, ∠KJL, ∠LJN	∠HAF, ∠FAD, ∠BAD, ∠HAB
3.	∠UQR, ∠SQW	∠KJN, ∠OJL	∠HAD, ∠FAB
4.	∠ZQT, ∠TQS, ∠VQW, ∠ZQU	∠LJM	∠GAF, ∠CAD, ∠FAE
5.	∠ZQW, ∠TQR, ∠TQV	∠KJM	∠EAH, ∠FAC, ∠DAG
6.	∠ZQS, ∠VQU, ∠UQT	∠NJM	∠EAD, ∠BAC, ∠HAG, ∠GAE

7–10. Answers will vary.

Bonus: Acute angles measure less than 90°, and right angles measure exactly 90°. Obtuse angles measure greater than 90° but less than 180°, and straight angles measure exactly 180°. Reflex angles measure greater than 180° but less than 360°.

Page 249

1. $\frac{1}{3}$ 5. $\frac{7}{24}$ 9. $\frac{1}{5}$ 13. $\frac{1}{6}$
2. $\frac{11}{36}$ 6. $\frac{23}{150}$ 10. $\frac{19}{120}$ 14. $\frac{3}{10}$
3. $\frac{7}{400}$ 7. $\frac{27}{40}$ 11. $\frac{7}{10}$ 15. $\frac{5}{32}$
4. $\frac{5}{48}$ 8. $\frac{51}{500}$ 12. $\frac{3}{200}$ 16. $\frac{9}{80}$

Peace is not merely a distant goal we seek, but…it is a means by which we arrive at that goal.

Bonus: Answers will vary.

Page 250

1. >   5. <   9. =   13. =
2. =   6. =   10. >   14. <
3. >   7. <   11. =   15. >
4. <   8. >   12. <   16. >

To make sure the people in Richmond, the Confederate capital, left her alone, Elizabeth acted as though she was crazy. While her neighbors were calling her Crazy Bet, Elizabeth was really running a network of Union spies. Mary started helping Elizabeth by acting like she was an illiterate servant named Ellen Bond.

As Ellen Bond, Mary went to work in the house of the Confederate president, Jefferson Davis. No one thought Ellen could read or write, which helped her in her work as a spy. At the time, servants were expected to work so that no one even noticed them. Since Ellen was not watched closely, she heard conversations and read key documents that were left on Davis's desk.

Mary had an amazing talent for remembering what she read. (She didn't have a camera or access to a copy machine!) So Mary memorized the information she read so she could pass it on. In 1995, more than 100 years after the Civil War, Mary Bowser was named to the Military Intelligence Corps Hall of Fame for her work during the Civil War.

Page 251

Hearts on sentences 3, 5–7, 11, 14, and 15 should be shaded.
1. Leo says, ♥I love my job. I work one day a year, Valentine's Day, spreading love—lovebug style!♥
2. Lola says, ♥This is my first Valentine's Day. I could sure use some pointers!♥
4. Mo shouts, rubs his neck, and looks at Mia, the girl next to him. Then he cries, "I think I'm in love!♥
8. Mabel hops up because of the sting and spots Mort. Then she calls, ♥Will you be my cuddle bug?"
9. Leo buzzes over and stings Mort on the ear. Mort shouts, "What's going on?♥
10. Suddenly, Maya catches Mort's attention. He forgets the sting and boldly calls, ♥Maya, be mine!"
12. Just then, Leo stings Merv, who grabs some flowers, hands them to Millie, and says, ♥These are just for you.♥
13. Millie starts to smile, but Lola stings her, causing her to notice Mo and then mumble, ♥Mo is the one for me!♥

A "VALENTINY"

Bonus: Answers will vary.

Page 252

Line 1		
x	y = 2x	Ordered Pair
0	0	(0, 0)
1	2	(1, 2)
2	4	(2, 4)
3	6	(3, 6)
4	8	(4, 8)
5	10	(5, 10)
6	12	(6, 12)

Line 2		
x	y = 3x	Ordered Pair
0	0	(0, 0)
1	3	(1, 3)
2	6	(2, 6)
3	9	(3, 9)
4	12	(4, 12)
5	15	(5, 15)
6	18	(6, 18)

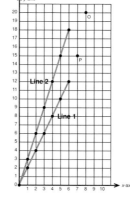

1, 2. Answers will vary.
3. no; Answers will vary.
4. no; Answers will vary.

Bonus: A line connecting coordinates (0, 0), (1, 4), (2, 8), and (3, 12) should be added to the grid. Answers will vary.

Page 253

1. Helen Keller, a crusader for the civil rights of the blind and disabled, lost her sight and hearing when she was a year and a half.
2. Maria Mitchell, an astronomer who discovered a new comet in 1847, became the first female member of the American Academy of Arts and Sciences in 1848.
3. Harriet Tubman, a famous conductor of the Underground Railroad, helped 300 slaves escape before the Civil War.
4. Margaret Bourke-White, a daring news photographer, once took a picture of some geese by dangling from a helicopter by a cable.
5. In 1955, Marian Anderson, one of America's finest concert singers, was the first African American soloist to sing with the Metropolitan Opera in New York City.
6. Elizabeth Cochrane Seaman, a newspaper reporter who went by the pen name Nellie Bly, wrote a report on the cruel treatment patients received inside a mental hospital that led to key reforms.
7. Grace Murray Hopper, a rear admiral in the Navy, developed the first computer programming language someone besides a scientist could use and understand.
8. Shirley Chisholm, the first African American woman to serve in Congress, represented New York in the US House of Representatives from 1969 to 1983.

Bonus: Answers will vary.

Page 254

1. carry across
2. state of being equal
3. to turn apart
4. act of placing something
5. to turn back
6. state of being one
7. occup(ant), D
8. mytho(logy), C
9. villain(ous), F
10. (con)(ver)sion, A
11. filmo(graph)(y), G
12. (trans)(port)at(ion), H
13. (dis)advantage, B
14. (com)(pon)ent), I
15. (equi)table, E

Bonus: Answers will vary.

Page 255

M. 20   Y. $\frac{21}{40}$
T. 43   A. $17\frac{1}{4}$ in.³
E. 385   I. 111.28 cm³
L. 20,640.75   N. 19.306 rounded to 19.31
R. $2\frac{1}{2}$ K. 436 miles
D. $1\frac{1}{10}$ S. 77 boxes

NEVER MIND; IT REALLY STINKS!

Bonus: $n = (2013 - 1970) \cdot 12$, $n = 516$ months

Page 257

Dear Journal,
   It is almost the end of another school year. This year is my final year of elementary school. Next year, I (would) be attending middle school. I will not be in the same class all day, seeing the same faces. I (have been) switching classes, and there will be different students in my classes. Because kids from my school and two other elementary schools (went) to the same middle school, there will be kids at school I have never met before. I will meet new people and make new friends. I hope I will (have made) a lot of new friends.
   When I think about changing classes and opening my locker, my stomach (will be feeling) nervous. I (worried) about getting lost between classes and not being able to open my locker. What if the work is too hard or the teachers (did) not like me? When our class visits the middle school, I am going to smile at all the middle school teachers. I (wanted) each one of them to get a good impression of me right from the start.
   Now that school (was) almost over, it is time for the end-of-the-year activities. Our class will be going on a field trip to an outdoor education camp. We will learn how to identify edible plants and how to survive if we (got) lost in the woods. After that, we (will have competed) with the fourth graders for bragging rights in the school field day. Each one of us will compete in three different competitions. I (could) hardly (have waited).

                    More later…
                    Me—Jessica

1. will   7. do
2. will be   8. want
3. go   9. is
4. make   10. get
5. feels   11. will compete
6. worry   12. can wait

Bonus: Answers will vary.

Page 258

1. O   10. E
2. I   11. D
3. L   12. H
4. M   13. [triangles]
5. L
6. S   14. [marks]
7. D
8. O   15. [shapes]
9. C   16. [eyes]

MIDDLE SCHOOL!

Bonus: The greater the degree a figure is rotated, the farther around an imaginary circle the figure will move. Diagrams will vary.

Page 259

A. $\frac{13}{100}$ B. 0.77   P. $\frac{61}{100}$
B. $\frac{77}{100}$ L. 0.08   Q. $\frac{73}{100}$
C. $\frac{61}{100}$ E. 0.84   R. $\frac{92}{100}$
D. $\frac{92}{100}$ I. 0.15   S. $\frac{96}{100}$
E. $\frac{84}{100}$ G. 0.38   T. $\frac{46}{100}$
F. $\frac{45}{100}$ C. 0.61   U. $\frac{67}{100}$
G. $\frac{38}{100}$ K. 0.14
H. $\frac{5}{100}$ J. 0.55
I. $\frac{15}{100}$ A. 0.13
J. $\frac{55}{100}$ M. 0.25
K. $\frac{14}{100}$ O. 0.49
L. $\frac{8}{100}$ N. 0.07
M. $\frac{25}{100}$ D. 0.92
N. $\frac{7}{100}$ H. 0.05
O. $\frac{49}{100}$ F. 0.45

Bonus: 0.61, 0.73, 0.92, 0.96, 0.46, 0.67

Page 260

1. fragment   6. fragment   11. fragment
2. run-on   7. run-on   12. complete
3. complete   8. fragment   13. fragment
4. complete   9. complete   14. run-on
5. run-on   10. run-on   15. complete

Answers for Part 2 will vary.

Bonus: Answers will vary.

INDEX